# ARCHETYPES IN ARCHITECTURE

Thomas Thiis-Evensen

# ARCHETYPES IN ARCHITECTURE

NORWEGIAN UNIVERSITY PRESS

Norwegian University Press (Universitetsforlaget AS), 0608 Oslo 6
Distributed world-wide excluding Scandinavia by
Oxford University Press, Walton Street, Oxford OX2 6DP

London   New York   Toronto
Delhi   Bombay   Calcutta   Madras   Karachi
Kuala Lumpur   Singapore   Hong Kong   Tokyo
Nairobi   Dar es Salaam   Cape Town
Melbourne   Auckland
and associated companies in
Beirut   Berlin   Ibadan   Mexico City   Nicosia

© Universitetsforlaget AS 1987

Translated by Ruth Waaler (The Floor, The Wall, The Roof) and
Scott Campbell
Cover design by the author

Published with a grant from the Norwegian Research Council for
Science and the Humanities

ISBN 82-00-07700-4 (paper)
ISBN 82-00-07874-4 (cloth, USA only)

British Library Cataloguing in Publication Data
Thiis-Evensen, Thomas
Archetypes in architecture.
1. Architectural design
I. Title
721'.01    NA2750

Typeset by ComputerText A.S, Oslo
Paste-up: BK Grafiske, Oslo
Printed in Norway
by Lie & Co, Oslo

# CONTENTS

# PREFACE

As regards the question of architectural experience, post-war education in architecture seems to be characterized by a contrast between two extremes. The first is the belief in rational technology and the expressiveness that is inherent in prefabrication and standardization. The second is the belief in a subjective creativity which manifests itself in an 'anti-pedagogy' with its attending individualities. The former has led to a disturbingly schematic architecture which has to a great extent dominated new housing; the latter has led to a subjectivity that is especially typical of many 'expressive' monumental constructions, and just as disturbing.

These two extremes, however, represent a well-known dilemma found in both architects' and users' relationship to architecture. On the one hand, we have the need for something stable and universal — a basis for prediction and recognition — and, on the other, the need for personal and emotional identification.

The question raised in this book is whether or not it is possible to establish a theory based not on technology alone but on the entire phenomenon of architecture itself. Such a study is quite relevant in relationship to the contemporary architectural debate concerning postmodernism and its use of, among other things, metaphors and historical motifs as experiential elements. This debate is the result of a tradition that began as early as the 1960s. Two books are central to this development: *Intentions in Architecture* by Chr. Norberg-Schulz (1963) and *Complexity and Contradiction in Architecture* by R. Venturi (1966). The former provided an important contribution to the understanding of architecture as a psychological phenomenon, the latter established a theory of concepts and categories pertaining to architectural form.

### THE GRAMMAR

The following study attempts to continue this tradition, which is concerned with the subject of form and its expression. We will try to classify a set of particular archetypes which can contribute to an understanding of the universality of architectural expression. This will be done by constructing a grammar comprising the most basic elements of architecture, which are the *floor*, the *wall*, and the *roof*. This system of archetypes on which variations are composed will be illustrated by examples from architectural history.

## THE EFFECTS OF THE GRAMMAR

The archetypes can be discussed from various points of view. The present work is limited to the question of how the archetypes affect us psychologically. We will show that these effects are dependent both on the conditions which have dictated an architectural form and on those associations which are the beholder's. An architectural form can in this way be determined by technical, economic and functional as well by stylistic prerequisites. Similarly, associations can be contingent upon personal and social as well as upon cultural circumstances.

In relation to this, the book will concern itself with the constant phenomena on which these prerequisites are based. In terms of architecture, it is a question of the relationship between *inside* and *outside* and the role of archetypes in such a context. This relationship is described as a dynamic dialogue between exterior and interior spaces and represents a problem that will always exist no matter what the project, time or place. Additionally, we will concentrate on the commonalities in our architectural experiences. We wish to show that these things are based on our physical experiences, and that we transfer them to what we see. This means that the archetypes elicit specific meanings, thus influencing one's experience of the relationship between inside and outside.

## THE PURPOSE OF THE BOOK

The book has a design-oriented goal. With a more precise knowledge of the archetypes and their variations, it is possible to replace the schematic architecture of recent years without necessarily falling back on and copying motifs from the past. In addition, a more reliable basis for the emotional content of architecture can replace the generally subjective 'feelings' about the qualities of buildings.

The archetypes cannot cover all the combinations that give architecture meaning. Consequently, this work is not a recipe for right and wrong. Moreover, its intent is to point out the *possibilities* which lie at the roots of architecture, and which in the hands of a creative practitioner, can give the art of building a more humane countenance.

## ACKNOWLEDGEMENTS

The author hereby expresses his gratitude to three institutions for their professional and economic assistance: first and foremost his place of employment, the Oslo School of Architecture, secondly the Norwegian Research Council for Science and the Humanities for underwriting the translation. He is particularly grateful for the Henrik Steffen Stipendium from the Christian Albrect University in Kiel, Germany, autumn 1978/spring 1979.

This made possible a sabbatical year for studies at The German Institute in Rome. The book was first published in Norway in 1982. The same year the author received the degree of *Doctor Philosophiae* at the University of Oslo for the work of which this book is a concentrated version, both regarding the text and especially the footnotes.

Special thanks go to three individual researchers who, each in his own way, have meant a great deal for the author's understanding of architecture: firstly Professor Dr. Techn. Christian Norberg-Schulz, with whom the author has had the pleasure of working closely for many years. With his humanistic outlook on architecture, Norberg-Schulz has provided an invaluable contribution to architectural debate in Norway and the rest of the world. Secondly Professor Dr. Philos. Hans Peter L'Orange († 1983), who as leader of The Norwegian Institute in Rome provided vital inspiration for the author's interest in classical architecture. Finally Associate Prof. Jan Georg Digerud for many beneficial discussions about modern architecture. It is natural also to thank the students of architecture whom the author has met during his 14 years as a teacher. Each in his or her own way has provided an expanded understanding of the breadth of the subject and has, with a free critical approach and an open inquisitiveness, been a source of continual inspiration.

Thomas Thiis-Evensen
Oslo
September, 1985

1. Building (from C. Sandburg, *The Family of Man*).

INTRODUCTION

2. Architecture as experience (photo by P.-E. Knutsen).

## ARCHETYPE, EXISTENTIAL EXPRESSION, AND SHARED EXPERIENCE

Typically, first impressions of a building take the form of purely qualitative evaluations. Buildings and rooms are spontaneously characterized as 'intimate', 'monumental', 'dull', 'depressing', 'spartan', etc. (Fig. 2). As a rule, it is difficult to describe one's reaction. The assertion is simply made that different buildings elicit different responses. One gets an immediate sense of the whole which 'overwhelms', 'establishes a mood', and which concerns the architectural expression or atmosphere. One need not be acquainted with the building's functions, their meaning, or the distribution of rooms in order to react. In this way, an overall impression of the spirit of the building, which need not correspond to the building's function, can be quickly apprehended.

Artists have similarly come to the conclusion through their works that specific forms can establish certain moods:

> A narrative picture will move the feelings of the beholders when the men painted therein manifest clearly their own emotions. It is a law of our nature... that we weep with the weeping, laugh with the laughing, and grieve with those who grieve.[1] (Fig. 3).

The same is true for architects who have consciously attempted to establish completely specific correlations between space and experience. According to Etienne-Louis Boullée, the most essential aspect of buildings is that 'the images they offer our senses should arouse sentiments analogous to the use which these buildings are dedicated'.[2] Indeed, this is the main task of the architect, according to Geoffrey Scott, because 'he designs his space as a work of art; that is, he attempts through its means to excite a certain mood in those who enter it'.[3] Similarly, Le Corbusier saw moods as the essence of architecture: 'By the use of raw materials and *starting from* conditions more or less utilitarian, you have established relationships which have aroused my emotions. This is Architecture'.[4] In that sense, architecture is directed toward feelings:

> Architecture is a thing of art, a phenomenon of the emotions, lying outside questions of construction and beyond them. The purpose of construction is to make things hold together; of architecture to move us.[5] (Fig. 4).

Such conditions within architecture prompt the practising architect to ask: How can one *plan* specific architectural effects?

The first condition for such planning is that the architect must be acquainted with the expressive characteristics of form before he starts designing. Another condition is that one is able to choose those forms which are appropriate to the intended expression.

The immediate objection may arise that an architect does not select forms; he creates them for each situation depending on the function. The credo of functionalism — *form follows function* — which implies that a form

15

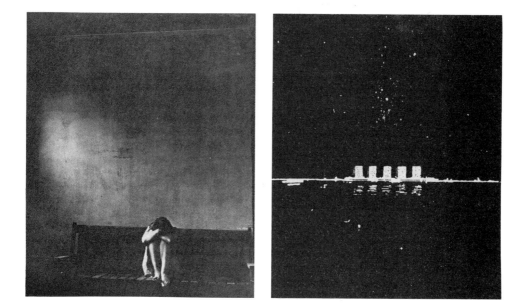

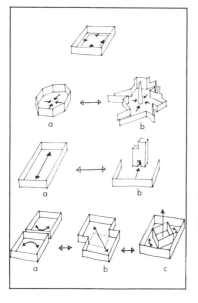

3. Sorrow (photo by H. Cooke).

4. The poetry of the skyscraper (sketch by Le Corbusier from Sestoft, *Arkitektur, idé og sammenheng*).

5. The square archetypes based on Zucker (from top to bottom): the closed square, the nuclear square, the dominated square and the grouped square. In addition, there is the amorphous square (not shown).

is developed in direct response to individual functional conditions, is also well known.

More recent architectural theory has, however, pointed out that such axioms are no longer unconditionally valid. It has gradually been perceived that creativity is primarily related to the way in which certain *basic* forms are combined and varied.

## ARCHETYPES AND THEIR CLASSIFICATIONS

These basic forms can be referred to as the *archetypes* of architecture. The original Greek meaning of the word archetype is 'first form', or 'original model' as it exists as a basis for all later variations and combinations.[6]

In other words, behind the plurality of the many forms in history lies a simple set of archetypes which we can call the grammar of architecture. These archetypes may be understood as images which can be identified in relation to both architectural form, function and technology.

The term archetype, which was originally employed within psychology by C.G. Jung, was first used systematically within architectural theory by Paul Zucker in his book *Town and Square* from 1959. On the basis of a description of five square archetypes, he uses specific examples to show how history chooses that form which is appropriate and how these typologies, owing to dissimilar functional characteristics, vary from antiquity up to the present day (Fig. 5). The theory of archetypes was further developed in the 1960s, with Aldo Rossi's book *The Architecture of the City* from 1966 representing an important step forward. During the 1970's, the theory of archetypes has increasingly been utilized as a basis for architectural practice, through the work of, among others, Michael Graves, Rob and Leon Krier and Mario Botta (Fig. 6).

As far as being acquainted with the expressive potential of form is concerned, a theory of archetypes must have three goals: the first is to *classify* the archetypes in a concentrated overview, the second is to attempt to *describe* them in order to point out the potential expression which exists within them. The third goal has to do with the following question: Will the expression be at all perceived by the user, and does not the experience of architecture vary from person to person? The aim of this goal must then be to show that there is a *common language* of form which we can immediately understand, regardless of individual or culture.

Not until these three conditions are met can we begin to choose forms, because we then become aware of their potentialities to the greatest possible extent.

In the following, consideration will be limited to those archetypes which constitute the elements of spatial *delimitation:* the floor, the walls, and the roof. This does not mean that the spatial volume itself is disregarded, such

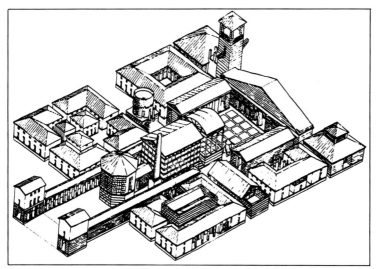

6. Volumetric archetypes (project for a school by Leon Krier).

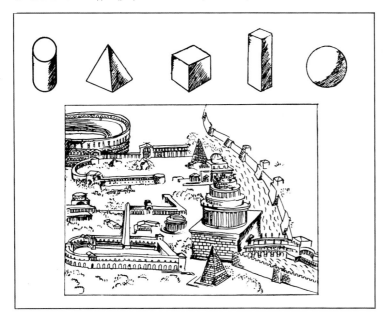

7. Volumetric archetypes volumes (from Le Corbusier, *Towards a New Architecture*).

as the cube, the sphere, the cylinder, the cone, etc. (Figs. 7, 8, 9). Volume and delimitation are mutually dependent, in that the design of the spatial boundaries will be able either to strengthen or to weaken the spatial form. The prioritization is based more on the desire to study *building* as a specific phenomenon, which means the study of the construction of the elements of the roof, walls and floor.

In terms of form, the floor element, the wall element, and the roof element can be divided into categories which at the same time represent four levels of scale within the construction of the delimiting elements. The first is concerned with the elements' *major forms.* The second has to do with the *construction system,* which shows whether or not the main forms are massive or skeletal. The third concerns itself with the *surface treatment* of the major forms, and the fourth has to do with the *openings* in the major forms.

On each of these levels (major form, construction system, surface treatment, and openings), clearly defined archetypes exist which represent general solution to problems of form that remain the same regardless of time, place or function. Respectively, they are referred to as themes and motifs. The themes are related to the functions of the elements, or rather to what they 'do', as with a floor, for example, which directs, delimits and supports. The motifs suggest how the elements do their job, which means the specific interpretations within each of the themes. As an example, the delimiting theme of a floor is interpreted in principle by a limited group of motifs, such as lowering, raising, frame, central patterns, surface patterns.

## MOTION, WEIGHT, AND SUBSTANCE AS THE BASIS OF EXISTENTIAL EXPRESSION

An archetype's expression can be found in an exact description of what they *are* or as suggested above, what they 'do', and how they do it. As stated, such a description also creates a basis for the division of classifications into themes and motifs.

But do not roofs, walls, and floors 'do' completely different things, in that a roof spans above, a floor covers the ground below, and a wall encloses around? These functions cannot be seen as different, in that they represent dissimilar ways of accomplishing fundamentally similar ends. This architectural commonality is that the delimiting elements separate interior space from exterior space. The exterior space that is bounded by the roof exists over us (the sky), the walls adjoin the exterior space that is around us (the landscape, people), and the floor defines the exterior space that is beneath us (the ground) (Fig. 10).

In other words, the elements of the roof, wall and floor all do the same thing — they balance the forces of *inside* and *outside.* The battle between these forces is an existential prerequisite for mankind. Without shelter, in

10. Man surrounded by nature's roof, walls and floor (photo by W. Eugene Smith).

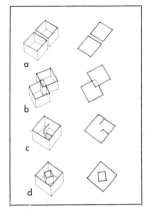

8. Archetypical relationships: a) addition, b) penetration, c) division and d) 'space in a space'.

9. Archetypical modes of organization: centrality, axiality and network (from Norberg-Schulz, *Existence, Space & Architecture*).

the broadest sense, man cannot live upon this earth. In this context, these delimiting elements embody a fundamental meaning and thereby a fundamental expressive potential, in that we *evaluate* them in relation to their principal role of protecting an interior space from an exterior space. This expressive potential lies in how the roof, walls, and floor relate to the surroundings. In other words, the expression of the delimitation is visualized in the span between *opening* and *closure*. Each work of architecture must find its place somewhere between complete closure and complete openness (Figs. 11, 12).

How then can a roof be open and closed? The roof bounds the exterior space of the sky and is in balance with this space in the curve of the dome, climbs up towards it in the point of the gable roof, and closes against it in the low flat roof.

How then can a wall be open or closed? A wall bounds the exterior space with its landscapes and people. If it stands firmly on the ground, as in the stone masses of a fortress wall, it remains closed. If it rises up towards the sky as in the lines and towers of a Gothic cathedral, it opens both upward and outward. And if a wall is permeated by similar window openings, as in the walls of a Renaissance palace, interior and exterior space are in balance.

How then can a floor be open or closed? A floor bounds the exterior space of the ground, the space of the earth beneath us. A massive stone floor closes the space. It is the ground itself that rises up and exerts pressure, while a shining mirror floor opens up the space downward, and the surface layer of a wooden floor strikes a balance between the life of the interior and the substance of the earthly space.

From this description, we see that there are three qualitative concepts which are essential to the description of how the three delimiting elements close or open between inside and outside. These concepts are *motion, weight,* and *substance.* They are necessarily utilized in any architectural description which attempts to suggest a building's reality. Motion describes the dynamic nature of the elements, whether they expand, contract or are in balance. Weight describes the heaviness of the elements and is related to gravity. It describes whether they stand, fall, weigh down or lighten up. Substance is related to the materiality of the elements, whether they are soft, hard, coarse, fine, warm or cold.

These qualities can be described as the *existential expressions* of architecture. Existential expressions are characteristics of a form which are at the base of symbolic meanings with their stylistic and regional variations. As an example, the existential expression of the Gothic style is its verticality and lightness. All of its other cultural characteristics such as symbols and regional articulations are governed by this general quality. The opposite

11. The wall is lightweight and encourages contact between inside and outside. The original cube seems to be dissolved frames, columns and stairs which immediately encourage penetration in, over, under, through and betwenn (M. Graves, Benacerraf House, Princeton 1969).

12. The wall is heavy and discourages contact between inside and outside. The volume is precise and geometric, the stripes give the form a restive weightiness while the incisions emphasize the thickness of the mass (M. Botta, Casa Unifamiliare, Switzerland 1975—76).

quality is typical of Greek temples, in which massiveness and heaviness are the primary characteristics. On the other hand, one Gothic building can seem heavier than another, albeit relative to the general quality of the style. Similarly, the Parthenon seems 'lighter' than the Temple of Hera at Paestum, but here within the realm of massivity (Figs. 13, 14).

In the same way, motion, weight, and substance also suggest the expressive foundation for the archetypes found within the categories of roof, wall, and floor. On each level, both in terms of major forms, construction systems, surface treatments and openings, the archetypes can be described and thereby associated with a specific expressiveness based on these concepts. For what is it that the roof, the floor and the wall do? As a motion, the roof rises or falls (Fig. 15). The walls stand up or sink, the floor spreads out, climbs or descends (Fig. 16). In this way, weight is also implied. That which rises is light, that which falls is heavy. And if the roof is bright and soft as a sail, it is open. If it is dark and of stone, it is closed (Figs. 17, 18). If the openings in a wall are tall and narrow, they ascend, if they are short and wide, they sink. A soft and fine floor is warm and open, but if it is hard and coarse, it closes and is heavy.

In summary, it can be stated that the existential expression in an architectural form can be characterized by a description 'von Gegenstand her'. That means a description of what an architectural form 'does', in terms of motion, weight, and substance seen in relation to the function or meaning the form is to have.

## MOTION, WEIGHT AND SUBSTANCE AS THE BASIS OF SHARED EXPERIENCE

We have asserted that it is important for an architect to be acquainted with the nature of the archetypes in order to be able to plan the effects of architecture more securely. We have also asserted that the existential expressions of architectural forms can be described by what motion, weight and substance those forms have.

But how can we be sure that the forms are experienced as we wish them to be? Besides the competence of the architect, the user's *attitude* is essential to the architectural experience. Is not the effectiveness of the expression dependent on each individual's attitude and background (age, sex, group, culture)?

These conditions represent our most *conscious* relationship to how our surroundings are experienced. The communicative aspect of architecture is dependent on a number of changing experiential levels. We can group them in two major categories, both related to conventions and based on recognition: *private* experiences and *social* experiences. Private experiences are connected to our personal experiences and individualities

13. The verticality and lightness of the Gothic style (St. Chapelle, Paris, 12th century).

14. The massiveness and heaviness of the Greek style (Propylaea, Athens, 4th century).

15. The space rises. This is due to the fact that the space 'helps' the perspective by stepping inward as it rises and due to the fact that the columns are arranged densely as joined lines, and finally due to the fact that the space opens at the top toward the light (T. Watanabe, Nakauchi House, Nara 1975).

16. The stair leads upwards. We 'are' on top by gazing at the form (Astronomic Observatory in Delfi, 1724).

(such as comprehensive abilities!). We may like a piece of furniture that others consider ugly because it was owned by and reminds us of someone we were once close to. The social experience is related to common cultural associations — certain cultural agreements are necessary if the meaning of form is to be comprehended. In this manner, yellow is the colour of mourning in India, while black serves the same purpose in the West.

This part of the teachings of expressionism, which deals with architectural elements as symbols, has surely been given more attention than any other areas of study within architectural theory. Postmodernism is to a great extent based on such culturally specific associations. Charles Jenck's book, *The Language of Postmodern Architecture* from 1977 is an example of such a theory. It is characteristic of both the private and social levels of experience to view architectural forms as *symbolic expressions*. This means that the forms are primarily seen as signs of an *external* reality.

The intention of this book is to study a third level of experience alongside the private and social levels. This level, which is to a great extent independent of cultural determinants, can be termed the *universal* level. These shared experiences are difficult to put one's finger on because they belong to our spontaneous and unconscious reactions to architecture. They are defined by our reactions to the inherent structure of architectural forms, independent of their symbolic associations.

Shared experiences, like symbolic meanings, are based on recognition, but this time with reference to our *bodily experiences* (Figs. 19, 20). Such experiences are common to all people and are gained through confrontations with the phenomena which surround us. These things are givens, such as gravity and the forces of nature. Experiences with these phenomena can be described in terms of motion, weight and substance. As acting individuals, we move in relation to a dynamic reference which is defined by gravity and which therefore represents a vast range of characteristics for us: we lie, we sit, we stand, we run, we bend and twist. Day and night provide experiences differentiated by light and dark. Tactile experiences teach us about the differences between soft and hard, coarse and fine, wet and dry. These experiences form a complex net of references which are the basis for our reactions when we move in relationship to objects in space. These movements are described vis-à-vis physical relationships to the things around us. We walk on something, we ascend something, descend something, walk along something, through something, between something, under something, etc. But the *manner* in which we do these things is not immaterial, in that the experience differs if what we walk on is steep or slack, broad or narrow — if what is above us is low and heavy or high and light — is what we walk alongside of is soft or hard, coarse or shiny.

In other words, the existential expression of an architectural form, which

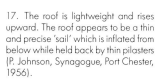

17. The roof is lightweight and rises upward. The roof appears to be a thin and precise 'sail' which is inflated from below while held back by thin pilasters (P. Johnson, Synagogue, Port Chester, 1956).

19. Man in motion (photo by G. Mili).

18. The roof is heavy and presses downward. This is due to the relatively modest ceiling height, the 'unstable' columns ad the rusticated, half-ruined treatment of materials (A. Goudi, Crypt church in Barcelona, 1908–15).

20. Man and substance (photo by W. Bullock).

is based on the form's motion, weight and substance, is recognized on the basis of our common experiences with natural phenomena. In the same way as symbolic meanings in architecture, existential expressions form images to which we react. This means that we 'use' our surroundings psychologically prior to using them physically. This is stated also by architectural theorists such as H. Wöllflin:

> . . .we interpret the whole outside world according to the expressive system with which we have become familiar from our own bodies. That which we have experienced in ourselves as the expression of severe strictness, taut self-discipline or uncontrolled heavy relaxation, we transfer to all other bodies (Fig. 22)[7].

If we see a door on the opposite side of a room, we 'go' through it in our minds before we do so in reality. It acts as a sign of its use as a door because of our indoctrination through past experiences. However, the actual experience of passing through the doorway is dependent on whether it is high or low, wide or narrow, whether it is part of a solid wall or exists as an element in a skeletal wall system, etc.

In the same way, we 'sit' in a chair before we actually do so physically, and we sit comfortably in a soft chair, uncomfortably in a hard chair, relaxed in a lounge chair and formally in a straight-back chair (Fig. 21). And a table gathers individuals hierarchically if it is long and narrow, intimately if it is round.

Additionally, we wish to 'be' what a volume does. Therefore, we walk swiftly in a corridor and slowly and ceremoniously in a broad space. We 'are' in the end of a deep room and in the centre of a round room, and at the top if a staircase is rising and at the bottom if it is falling.

We also wish to be what the delimiting elements do somewhere between the assault of the phenomena of nature and the resistance of the enclosing elements, where the feeling of security or insecurity is decided by the degree to which the interior space is threatened or victorious. An interior space is like a pulsating membrane that surrounds us, soon contracting and threatening as a prison cell. 'In the innermost part of my house I live in peace while the enemy burrows his way from one direction slowly and quietly towards me',[8] or soon expanding and optimistic as in Paxton's Crystal Palace (1851),[9] or soon heavy, balancing on a tight-rope as a log cabin's obstinancy in the face of a winter storm (Figs. 23, 24). It is because we 'participate' in these things that we are uplifted under an elevated dome and borne down upon under the nearness of a cellar vault. We bear the load of the roof with the walls, and with them we protect in order to survive in the world: 'With its thickness and its strength, it protects man against destruction'.[10]

At all scales, security is the driving force, while shared experiences pro-

21. Lounge chair by M. Breuer, 1936 (from Watson, *History of Furniture*).

22. The surroundings enhanced as unconscious 'opportunities' (From Gehl, *Livet mellom husene*).

vide points of existential reference. The existential expression then is linked to the characteristics of a space which we immediately recognize independently of cultural determinants.

Of course, this does not mean that the existential expression cannot be influenced by symbolic meanings and attitudes. Nevertheless, the existential expression is always there as the very reference for the symbolic meanings. If we stand at the base of a steep stair, the existential expression is the *resistance* itself which lies in the steepness. We know what lies ahead as we mount the stair, thus accepting its invitation. However, the sensation of resistance varies with the goal at the top. Ascending to the gallows and ascending to a victory stand are two completely different things. In the former instance, the resistance could be experienced as reluctance, in the latter as a challenge to be overcome. In the same way, sick people and healthy people will have the same experiential reference, but will *respond* differently in the same situation. For a wheel-chair user, a narrow door is seen as a special hindrance. As a healthy individual, he will experience the door as an opening, but for the wheel-chair user, it will be an opening that cannot be penetrated. What the surroundings do and what we can do in them are not experienced completely differently from individual to individual, rather they exist as different possibilities within the same 'offer'.

In summary, we can state that the existential expression has a fundamental effect on our architectural experiences, not as a quality separate from the symbolic meaning, but as an integrated part thereof. In other words, the study of the expression of form in terms of motion, weight and substance links the art of building to universal qualities and manifests itself as a phenomenon in relationship to existing cultural and personal associations.

23.   The open and expanding interior (Crystal Palace by J. Paxton, London 1851, From Hersey,   *High Victorian Gothic*).

24.  The closed and secure interior (Norwegian log house from Bru, Bugge/Norberg-Schulz, *Stav og Laft*).

25.  The floor as experience (photo by P.-N. Nilsson, Sandburg, *The Family of Man*).

THE FLOOR

# WHAT THE FLOOR DOES

The floor has three main functions in relation to our actions (Fig. 25). It *directs* us from one place to another, it *delimits* a space from its surroundings, and it *supports* us by providing a firm footing.

Therefore, these tasks, i.e. what the floor 'does', are prerequisities that make it possible for us to consider the floor as a phenomenon. This means, furthermore, that the floor defines an interior space affected by an exterior space which is both *around* and *beneath* the floor. Directing and delimiting may be done by both walls and roof. Thus, what is most important for the expression of the floor is its vertical relation to the space beneath — the natural ground. The question therefore, is: what are our shared experiences with nature's floor and how do these experiences determine our impression of the floor in architectural terms?

In the following we shall describe these experiences with the natural floor through its qualities of motion, weight, and substance. Then, on the basis of these qualities, we shall explore the expressive potentialities of the built floor. These potentialities will then be related to the archetypes in floor architecture.

# NATURE'S FLOOR

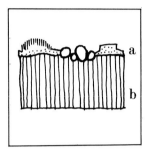

26. The parts of nature's floor: the surface and the mass.

Nature's own floor, *the ground,* is experienced as a combination of two parts, a surface and beneath it a mass. These two parts have essentially different functions in existential space (Fig. 26).

The *surface* is the actual plane on which we walk. It is what meets our feet and makes it possible for us to walk back and forth. This surface, which may be of grass, sand, snow or stone, varies from place to place. In the desert it is sand that dominates, in the north it is snow, along the coast rolling stones prevail, and in the forest, moss and grass (Fig. 27). Seen in this way it is the surface which illustrates that part of the ground which guides our movements and expresses regional variations.

In contrast, the *mass* below the surface has a far more permanent meaning. As a phenomenon it is a tangible reality consisting of stone, earth, fire and water (Fig. 28). But, as an existential reality it has meaning because it is *firm* and solid. This firmness is a precondition for our existence on earth, imbedded within us as a fundamental background for our entire feeling of security.[1]

Although the mass is permanent due to its firmness, it is not necessarily uniform. It affects our movements by being flat or by rising or sinking (Fig. 29). Considered in this light, the mass can sink and 'we fall', it can rise and thereby 'hinder' us, or it can be level, giving us 'freedom' of action.

Indeed, the expressive qualities of the mass are determined by a combination of three factors: its *expression of weight,* which is firmness, its *expression of motion,* which varies between rising and sinking, and its *expression of substance,* which is the earth's own material phenomenon.

## INTERPLAY IN NATURE'S FLOOR

The expressive potentialities in nature's floor are derived through the interplay of surface and mass.

Seen in this way, the same surface may have an essentially different impact depending upon whether the underlying mass rises, sinks or is level. To wade through a deep layer of snow can be two quite different experiences depending upon whether the ground beneath is level or uneven.

28. The mass of nature's floor: stone, earth and cave (photo *Aftenposten*).

27. The surface of nature's floor: the forest floor (photo by R. Jucker).

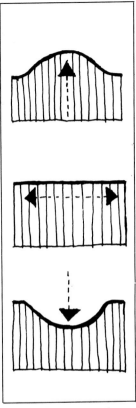

29. The three motions of mass: rising, planar and falling.

If it rises, movement is more difficult, the ascent becomes an added hindrance to our progress, and we must exert ourselves to continue. If it descends, we become in a way captives of the decline itself.

Similarly, various surfaces may affect our movements even if the ground otherwise has the same form. Thus, a stony surface will seem heavy and more a part of the ground itself, whereas grass is lighter and is perceived as a light covering 'carpet'.

In this way we see that the expression of nature's floor is determined by whether the surface appears to be *independent of, dependent upon,* or *part of* the underlying mass (Fig. 30 a-f). These qualities may be characterized by prepositions which are used in describing how the surface affects us in relation to the ground beneath.

If our actions are *upon* the ground, we have a basic feeling of having a safe and firm foothold, the ground and we are as one (Fig. 30a). The very essence of the ground as something which supports, something which is permanent and unchanging, determines the impression.

If our actions take place *below* the ground, we become dependent on its characteristics, we are in the clutch of the ground. We are faced with primordial forces, the ground's own phenomena. To be beneath the ground means that we have left the near and familiar which is above ground to enter into a lower region unknown and confining. The way in which the surface leads us down into the ground is, however, decisive for our impressions (Fig. 30 b-c). If the surface cracks and breaks open, we 'fall'. The sensation of falling, of plunging through empty space is fraught with fear and danger. If, on the other hand, the earth sinks as in a trough, the ground follows along and we feel we are being 'guided' down.

We are also dependent upon the ground if it rises *up* in front of us because then our progress is made more difficult. The determining factor in this case is the way in which the ground rises (Fig. 30 d-e). If the surface breaks away from the ground and rises sharply, the top level will be isolated and limited. But, if the surface is undulating, it gives the impression of being pushed upwards as if by some underlying pressure just as when a wave swells and rises. In both cases we are confronted by a counter-force in the ground itself, one which causes us to pause before continuing to move on.

If the level of our actions is *above* the mass, our spontaneous reaction is one of independence (Fig. 30 f). We are in control of the ground and liberated from the depths beneath. In this case a feeling of superiority may be the result. The scale of variations within this shared experience depends upon equally specific situations. Of course, floating in an aeroplane over Mont Blanc, and standing on a single step plateau, are experiential extremes, but they derive from the same situation: in both cases we are above

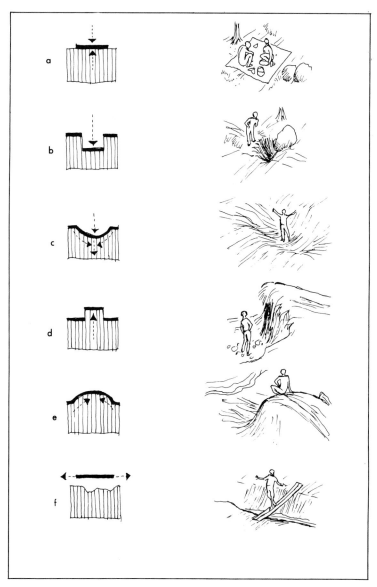

30 a-f  The expression of nature's floor: the relationship between the surface and the mass: a) the surface *upon* the mass, b,c) *below* the mass, d,e) *up out of* the mass and f) *above* the mass.

and independent of what is below.

At this point we must consider the built floor in relation to these various expressions in nature's floor.

Considering what the floor 'does' we find three themes in floor architecture: the *directing,* the *delimiting,* and the *supporting* floor themes. As will be shown, the supporting theme, which is the manifestation of the natural floor's own characteristics, affects the expression of both the directing and the delimiting theme.

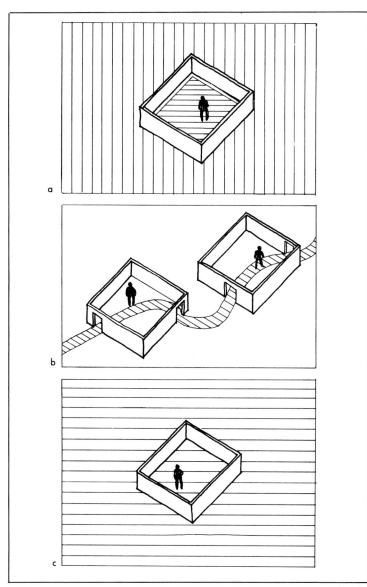

31 a-c  The directional floor theme: a)*within* the space and *outside* of the space, respectively b) as a path, and c) as a surface.

# THE DIRECTIONAL THEME

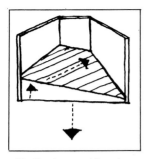

32. The directional floor theme and the conflict between the form of the space, the form of the floor and the floor pattern.

34. The directional floor theme and a floor pattern that emphasizes the form of the room (St. Peter's, reconstruction from L'Orange/Thiis-Evensen, *Oldtidens bygningsverden*).

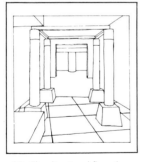

35. The directional floor theme and a floor pattern that provides a contrast to the form of the space (Sunar Showroom by M. Graves, from *A.D. 5/6, 1980*).

The directional theme concerns the way in which the form of the floor emphasizes certain motions, connecting one place to another.

This occurs mainly in three ways (Fig. 31 a-c). In the first, the floor acts within surrounding wall's; it leads from one side of the space to another. In the other two, the floor leads out öf the space, either as a 'path' through a series of spaces or as only a delimited part of a larger area which continues outside.

These motions may be generated either by the floor's *surface*, by its *form*, or by *paths* which cross the space. Each of them may act alone or in combination. A space, therefore, may simultaneously have a floor in which the form slopes in one direction, the surface pattern runs in another while the form of the space itself indicates a third direction (Fig. 32).

## THE SURFACE

A typical surface pattern is the one created by the boards in a wooden floor. These indicate directions which either cross or parallel the main direction of the space. The setting of stones in a stone floor may do the same (Fig. 33). In old St. Peter's (333) the reconstruction shows that the pattern of the paving stones accentuates the spatial form of the basilica (Fig. 34). In the narrow, directional aisles the paving stones are rectangular and 'active' while in the broad and calmer nave they are quadratic and static. In Michael Grave's Sunar showroom (1979) the reverse is the case. Here, the floor tiles run diagonally to the space (Fig. 35).

## THE FORM

Examples of floor motion are found when an entire surface slopes, undulates or shifts levels through the use of steps and landings.

The first may be illustrated in the architecture of Sigurd Lewerentz, in which important places and zones are emphasized by lowered or raised parts which shift into a billowing mass otherwise unrelated to the spatial form (Fig. 36).

In Lund & Slaatto's St. Hallvard Church, Oslo (1966), the entire floor rises

33. The directional floor theme and the surface (photo by J. Haug).

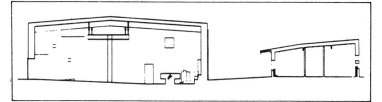

36. The directional floor theme and the form (section through 'Klippan' by A. Lewerentz, from Uhlig,'*Klippan', lewerentz kirke*.

37. The directional floor theme and the path (19th century living room, Nordic Museum, Stockholm, Sweden).

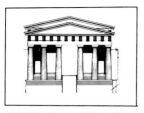

38. The directional floor theme and the ramp which penetrates the floor (the Propylaea on the Acropolis of Athens, from Coulton, *Greek Architects at Work*).

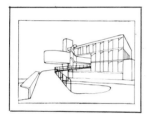

39. The directional floor theme and the ramp which runs over the floor (Carpenter Center, after Giedion, *Space, Time and Architecture*).

evenly towards the altar at one end of the space. The space itself, however, is cylindrical, with the result that the directional rising and the centralized delimitation are in sharp contrast and thus accentuate each other.

## THE PATH

A path is created in a floor when an independent pattern emerges as a figure against the background of the rest of the floor.

In Scandinavian farmhouses such paths are indicated by strips of woven rag rugs laid freely *on* the floor, connecting entrances and exits (Fig. 37). In medieval mosaic floors, similar runners were formed in stone. In St. Miniato in Florence (thirteenth century) such a stone path leads straight from the entrance to the altar baldachin at the other end of the nave (Fig. 84). But, it does not merely act as a connection between the entrance and the goal. It also emphasizes the small baldachin in relation to the rest of the large overfilled and restless space.

The path, however, may also be sunk *into* the floor as seen in front of the Propylaea on Athen's Acropolis (431 B.C.). Now the path takes the form of a ramp cutting through the rising levels of the steep cliff (Fig. 38).

The path may also run *above* the floor like a free-standing 'bridge' as found in Le Corbusier's Carpenter Center (1963), where the entrance ramp continues right on through the building connecting several spaces simultaneously (Fig. 39). The path may also emerge in the form of stairs either rising up from the floor or leading down to it as found in typical entrance motifs throughout architectural history.

41. The delimiting floor theme ('Tempietto' by A. Palladio, from Cevese, *Palladio*).

# THE DELIMITING THEME

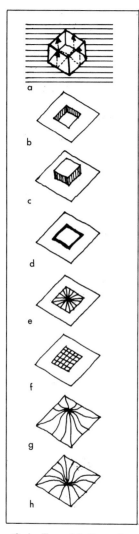

40a-h. The delimiting floor theme: a) continuous floor/wall, b) sinking, c) raising, d) framed, e) centralized, f) equal directional, g, h) undulating floor, (Transitional directional theme/delimiting theme).

Thus, we see that the directional floor concerns the quality of our *forward* movements. With varying motifs it may invite us to go up or down, straight ahead or in curves, to walk quickly or slowly.

The delimiting floor, on the other hand, indicates the way in which the floor may create a stationary situation by keeping us either in a centralized position or containing us within a boundary. This separation from the surroundings is brought about in two ways.

In one, the floor is *connected to* the surrounding walls in such a way that the volume is totally enclosed and cut off from its surroundings (Fig. 40 a). One example of this is found in the plain floor of Functionalism which without any apparent transition merges with the white walls around the space. The ideal was the stereometric volume, clearly defined as a self-contained world of its own. Other examples of the same are found when the floor is linked with a corresponding wall pattern. In Andrea Palladio's circular 'Tempietto' in Maser (1580) the columns around the space are carried on into the floor mosaic as double lines coverging at the central point of the floor (Fig. 41).

The other way to mark a specific floor zone is to *separate* a smaller area from a larger (Fig. 40 b-f). In this way, the separeted part of the floor emerges as a clearly defined figure against a larger neutral background. Most important is the separation itself. This may be achieved either by sinking the floor into the ground so that the surrounding edges form a three-dimensional border or by raising it to a higher level as a separating platform (Fig. 40 b-c). Alternatively, the separated part may be on the same level as the rest of the floor but have its borders marked by an accented edge or by the use of colours and materials which differ from the surrounding surface (Fig. 40 d-f). These delimited floor areas may show equal directional tendencies to all sides or be centralized so that one is drawn into the area and not out of it.

If the borders are not clearly marked, transitional forms are generated which fall somewhere between typical directional and typical delimiting floors. The undulating surface provides just such an example. It differs from

42. Transition directional theme/delimiting theme (Piazza D'Italia by Ch. Moore, from *A.D.* 5/6, 1980).

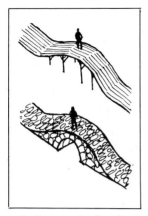

43. The supportive floor theme: wooden bridge and stone bridge.

the norm by the fact that it both rises and sinks while the continuity of its curves ties it together (Fig. 40 g-h). The same applies to a centralized surface pattern which may be read not only inwards towards the centre but also outwards towards the surroundings. An example of this is Charles Moore's Piazza d'Italia, New Orleans (1979), in which the ring patterns seem to spread out from the centre to 'touch' the neighbouring buildings (Fig. 42)

## THE SUPPORTING THEME

We have seen from the above that both the directional and delimiting themes deal primarily with the floor's horizontal characteristics, that is, its relation to the surrounding exterior.

The supporting theme, on the other hand, deals first and foremost with the vertical nature of the floor, that is, its relationship to the ground below. First of all this relationship describes the floor's position, whether it lies above the ground, on the ground or below the ground. It concerns, as well, the questions as to whether the floor is soft or hard, loose or solid, lightweight or heavy.

The supporting theme concerns primarily the floor's expression of weight and substance, whereas the directional and delimiting themes concern first and foremost motion expression. From this we see that support expression applies equally to the delimiting and to the directional floor. Every floor, no matter what type, may seem heavy or light, be sunk into the ground or hover above ir, be soft or hard. There is, therefore, a great difference in the way we perceive its borders if the same floor is at one moment sunk into the ground and at the next raised above it. Similarly, the 'speed' of the motion in a wooden bridge arching above the ground is completely different from that of the same bridge built of stone and lodged heavily on the ground (Fig. 43).

This means that the expression found in every floor, and this includes the interior space which it defines, depends upon the relationship of the floor with the 'exterior space' below. Seen in this light, the floor is a constructed ground surface, one in which various means are used to interpret our motion relationship to the earth on which we walk.

In the following, therefore, we shall examine the supporting theme in particular and point out what importance weight and substance have for the expressive nature of a floor. This means that in relation to the main task of the floor, which is to 'carry us', we shall find the universal expressions of strength found in the archetypes. With references to specific examples we shall point out the importance this has for the way we experience the inside-outside relation, including both that which surrounds the floor and that which is beneath it.

46. Wooden floor as detached layer (photo by R. Jucker).

47. Stone floor as attached layer (photo by R. Jucker).

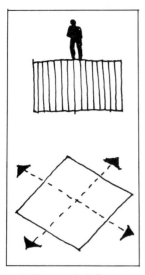

44. The attached floor: one with the ground.

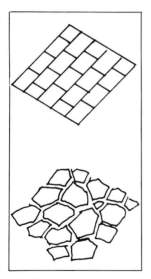

45. The geometricized and rusticated surfaces.

Architectural history reveals that the supporting theme may be divided into six basic motifs. The first is the floor that rests firmly on the ground, which we shall call (1) *the attached floor*. Floors that are sunk into the ground and are physically beneath the ground's surface we shall call (2) *the sunken floor* but will use the term (3) *the open floor* if the decline is merely optical. Floors that rise from below we shall call (4) *the rising floor*, whereas floors that are independent of the ground may be called respectively (5) *the detached floor* if they lie above the ground and (6) *the directional floor* if they guide us along the ground.

## THE ATTACHED FLOOR

The attached floor emphasizes our conception of the ground as something firm and immovable and conveys the feeling of a solid footing. In this it is similar in character to the ground; the two are of the same massivity (Fig. 44). This necessitates two main requirements in the form of the floor. First of all the floor surface must seem heavy, in other words, it must rest solidly either on or below the ground surface.

Secondly, the floor should resemble the ground. In principle this means that the more geometric and prepared the floor surface is, the more it stands out as a constructed level separated from the ground beneath (Fig. 45).

### ATTACHMENT AND MATERIAL

We can already see that the material used in the floor's construction affects its degree of attachment to the ground. It follows that there is a great difference between a wooden floor and a stone floor. A wooden floor will always maintain the character of a detached layer above the ground (Fig. 46). There are many reasons for such an effect.

One is that the wooden floor is alive when we walk on it. It gives slightly if the span is great, it creaks and groans if the joints are tight, and it stretches and is 'warm' beneath our feet. It is independent and light, it 'yields' and thus, in essence, differs greatly from the compact ground. Stone, on the other hand, is a part of the ground itself. The stone floor is related to the mass on which we walk (Fig. 47). Stone is the substance of mountains, and the mountain 'rises' from beneath to break through the earth's crust. Moss, grass and earth give a cloak-like covering to the stone, while the stone itself is always something beneath and 'inside'[2]. Our interference with stone amounts to no more than surface scratches. Whereas the soil allows what is beneath to escape and grow, the very substance of stone is locked in and 'dead'.[3]

48. Attached stone (Katasura garden, from Alex, Japanese Architecture).

49. Attached stone (Daitokuji) Temple garden, from Alex, *Japanese Architecture.*

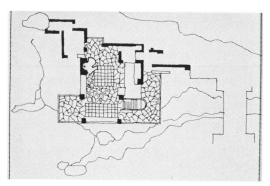

50. Stone floor and fireplace (plan of Falling Water after Kaufmann/Raeburn, *Frank Lloyd Wright, Writings and Buildings*).

51. Stone floor, chimney and house (Falling Water by F.Ll. Wright, from Norwich (ed.), *Verdensarkitekturen*).

The stone floor corresponds to the main aspects that we found typical of the expression of the attached floor.

Stone is solid and dependable; it does not give way but bears us up, we are safe. At the same time it reflects the permanency in nature itself. As a result we understand that the more clearly a stone floor reproduces the rustic and original character of natural stone, the stronger becomes the emphasis on its connection with nature's own floor.

Traditional Japanese gardens illustrate these two aspects. A characteristic feature of this architectural landscaping is seen in rounded stones which are deeply imbedded in the very crust of the earth. These are meant to express the ground's elements of security. Set closely together they 'stiffen' the ground, and in rows they pilot us safely through the changing landscape of lakes, swamps and hilly terrain. The houses, too, rest on them. In Japan, to set a house on the ground means to balance the foundation posts on small 'mountains' (Fig. 48).[4]

This impression of firm attachment is further sublimated in sacred temple gardens (Fig. 49). 'Haphazard' groups of dark stones crop up from the meticulously raked sand surface. The stripes of the raking pattern follow the contours of the stone as expanding rings. The stones appear as 'islands' of safety in a changing landscape, in which the sand, representing life's mutability, encloses the mountain's primeval forces.

## ATTACHMENT AND THE RELATIONSHIP BETWEEN INSIDE AND OUTSIDE

What importance, then, does the firmly anchored floor have in the inside-outside relationship?

In architecture we can distinguish between the use of two types which individually correspond to the two aspects of the expression. In some cases the element of security is emphasized, and here the floor marks a centre, a firmly anchored interior. At other times the emphasis is on the similarity between inside and outside, thus eliminating the difference between the interior floor and nature's floor.

We shall examine one example within each group. The firmly anchored centre will be illustrated by a description of Frank Lloyd Wright's Falling Water, Penn., USA (1936). The connecting, integrated plan will be shown in the floor of the Gothic cathedral.

## FALLING WATER AND THE SECURE INTERIOR

In Wright's Falling Water the central point in the interior is dictated by the top of the cliff on which the house lies. The cliff juts up from the floor as the foundation for the fireplace which is the focus of the composition (Fig. 50). The visible bedrock is important psychologically in an otherwise bold and

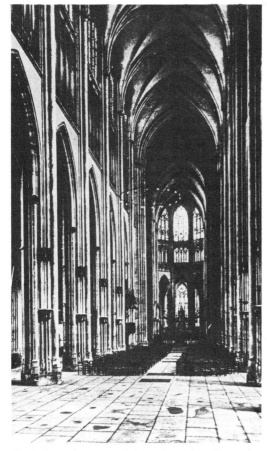

53. Gothicism and nature's floor.

52. Gothic architecture and the enchored floor (Rouen, from Frankl, *Gothic Architecture*).

54

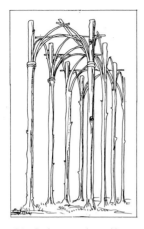

54. Gothicism and trees (the origin of Gothic architecture by J. Hall, after Rykwert, *On Adam's House in Paradise*).

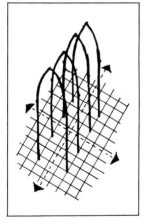

55. Gothicism's open space.

'perilous' architecture. This peril lies in the wild and steep, craggy surroundings above which the house 'hovers' (Fig. 51). The cantilevered balconies projecting in all directions demonstrate a supreme will to survive in the face of the depths beneath. This corresponds completely with Wright's architectural ideas in which the act of building is 'life itself taking form', and where it is precisely the horizontal plane that expresses the principle of life itself: 'the human line of tenure on this earth'.[5] But, to be on this earth involves not only 'tenure'. In addition to spreading out 'by native character to environment', a house should also be 'married to the ground'.[6] In other words, the bedrock, fireplace and chimney are the inside that makes expansion to the outside psychologically possible.

## THE GOTHIC CATHEDRAL AND INTEGRATION OF INSIDE AND OUTSIDE

In most early Gothic cathedrals of the twelfth and thirteenth centuries, the stairs leading into the church are shallow and have few steps (cf. entrance steps to the cathedrals in Strasbourg, Rouen and Wells). This was clearly intentional since the church was considered a body growing directly from the earth without a separating foundation level.

Exceptions are to be found, especially in Italy. In both Orvieto and Siena the cathedrals are raised on staircase bases with rich marble incrustation. This conception of the building as an independent entity in relation to its surroundings was due to classical traditions which never quite lost their hold in Italy.[7] The Gothic tradition, however, emerged north of the Alps as an independent phenomenon and was only indirectly influenced by classical forerunners. This tradition was based on the principle of *dynamic growth* in contrast to the restful balance found in Antiquity.

With this principle in mind the firmly anchored character of the Gothic church floor should be understood. The floors were often composed or closely laid paving stones, both large and small (Fig. 52). The floor unfolded in a continuous 'patchwork', usually without regard to individual spaces such as the nave, aisles and chapels.[8] The impression was one of a heavy undifferentiated surface without accented directionalities, which could, in principle, be freely extended.

Compared to the rest of the architecture it is remarkable how 'little' has been done with the floor. In both French and German as well as English cathedrals, it is as though the weight of Romanesque tradition has been retained in the floor surface, whereas walls, columns, and roofs have dissolved into a network of richly worked and highly detailed forms. The dissolving layer effects, the clustered columns, and enormous glass wall areas of the entire space bear witness to an *open* architecture built 'in spite of stone'.

57. The Farnsworth House and expansion (by Mies van der Rohe, photo by S. Campbell).

58. Villa Savoye and isolation (by Le Corbusier, from Ch. Jencks, *Le Corbusier and the Tragic View of Architecture*).

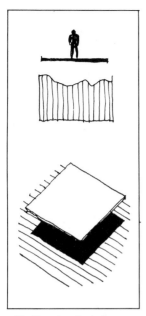

56. The detached floor: independent of the ground.

Two circumstances may explain these characteristics. One is a matter of form. The light, transparent walls seem to 'need' the heavy floor, which, with its composite surface, acts as a firm base for the entire ascending play of lines.

The other explanation must be sought in the symbolism of the church. The Gothic expression is frequently related to nature and interpreted as a stylized forest in which the columns are tree trunks with the ribs representing branches and foliage (Figs. 53, 54).[9] In this light, the floor's firmly fixed character takes on a deeper meaning. The floor is the *ground,* the natural forest floor from which the trees spring forth. Such an interpretation is also valid when the overall character of the space is considered. With its light, translucent qualities the space of a Gothic cathedral opens outwards. Inside and outside are united. The floor strenghtens this concept by uniting the nave and aisles while continuing yet further out to nature's floor itself (Fig. 55).[10]

In this way, the stone floor plays its part in joining town and landscape to the interior of the church, a spatial manifestation of the symbolic unity between 'God and the world'.

## THE DETACHED FLOOR

We have seen how an attached floor rests heavily *upon* the ground. Its surface is as one with the ground beneath.

In walking on a detached floor one finds oneself on a level divorced from the ground. The floor level may either be raised physically above the ground or lie lightly on the ground (Fig. 56).

As examples of the first we shall examine two houses on stilts, one by Ludwig Mies van der Rohe, the other by Le Corbusier. For the second type we shall consider the carpeted floor.

### FARNSWORTH HOUSE AND VILLA SAVOYE

Mies' Farnsworth House (1946) is *detached* from the ground both literally and formally (Fig. 57). The precise and narrow rectangular form of the floor frees the building and gives it an air of dynamic motion. 'Mies' home was a very American sort of statement, dynamic cantilevered almost in motion'.[11] The house is 'on its way', about to be torn loose from its location, an aspect that is underlined by both the flat roof and the construction itself, which presses the floor between the columns and gives it a unique extensiveness. This dynamic expansion is further emphasized by the panoramic view of the landscape through the glass walls. Nature becomes an abstract phenomenon in the distance, not concrete and near but in a way a thing 'in the future'. The Farnsworth House, therefore, is cited as an expo-

59. The physical protection of the grass carpet
(photo by E. Haas).

60. The 'concealment' of the sand carpet (Sahara Desert, photo by Th. Höpker, from Mack,
*Expedition*).

nent of 'the modern way of life', in which the detached floor perhaps most clearly symbolizes the modern dynamic and optimistic hope for the future.

Le Corbusier's Villa Savoye (1931) is an elevated place. In this house, Mies' place-less independence is replaced by a clearly contained interior borne high above the ground on metre-high columns (piloti) (Fig. 58). Le Corbusier did not intend the interior to expand outwards over the ground as did Mies, on the contrary, it was the ground which was to run freely beneath and in spite of the building.[12] He strove, therefore, to find a contrast between the open landscape and a cubic and precise exterior in which the floor plane was contained within the walls. The interior was conceived as a composite and rich world strictly disciplined by the planes of the square. 'Its severe, almost square exterior surrounds an intricate interior configuration glimpsed through openings and from protrusions above'.[13]

Villa Savoye demonstrates the span between freedom and order which is so typical of Le Corbusier's architecture. The desire for freedom lies in the open plan of the interior and the uninterrupted stretches of the landscape, while the desire for order is expressed in the exterior's geometric form, which with its precisely defined surface constitutes an excluding boundary. The columns cause the volume to float without indicating any particular direction. This is also shown by the entrance, a ramp placed in the centre of the house. This diagonal element extends right through the house and up to the roof terrace and thereby accents the interior's independence of the horizontality of the landscape (Fig. 59). It is first upon reaching the roof terrace that curved walls indicate the unlimited freedom of which one is a part when surveying the surrounding landscape.

## THE CARPETED FLOOR

The examples above illustrated the detached floor as a raised horizontal plane. The carpet, on the other hand, is a plane in contact with the floor. The immediate reaction to a carpet, nevertheless, is to a separate detached layer which covers another floor underneath. There are, primarily, two things which account for this impression. One is the quality of the carpet as something movable and the other, as something tactile.

A carpet is something we can remove. It has a non-permanent association as something which covers, something intended to protect either those who walk on it or the floor beneath it. In addition, the carpet is soft, it may be rolled up and put away, whereas the floor 'remains'. Also, the carpet yields beneath our feet and is compliant when we walk on it. It is friendly and sheltering because it both gives and receives.

62. A stone carpet (Roman floor mosaic from Villa d'Italia near Seville, drawn by Koch, from *Kunsthåndverk* 2/3, 1981).

61. The symbolic protection of the flower carpet (Corpus Christi festival in Genzano, painting by J.B. Thomas from Rudofsky, *Streets for People*).

## NATURE'S CARPET

In nature it is especially grass, moss and sand which share the carpet's characteristics (Fig. 60).

Grass and moss protect. When we feel like sitting on the ground, we know that soft grass will cushion and protect us from what is underneath. The ground, which is of earth and stone, can be hard and damp, and grass, which covers it, makes it more 'friendly'.

This is found in certain religious ceremonies. In the annual wreath-laying at the Maria Column in Rome, roses and other flowers are spread to protect the feet of the Pope. Likewise, the entire main street is softened by strewn flowers when the Host and the Wine are borne through Italian villages (Fig. 61).

The architectural carpet repeats and interprets the characteristics of nature's carpet.

## THE SOFT CARPET

An example of both the carpet's importance as something warming and its use in defining a particular place is found in the western use of carpeting to emphasize the difference between inside and outside.

The reason for this is the different life style in the 'cold' part of the world, where winter's cold lends meaning primarily to the carpet's 'warming' character. A typically Nordic situation will illustrate this. We are filled with an immediate feeling of security when faced by a crackling fireplace with a thick wool rug in front of it — we are really *inside*. It is the fire that warms us physically, but it is the rug that invites us to settle down and conveys a psychological feeling of welcome and warm well-being. In northern countries, therefore, the carpeted floor is synonymous with a cosy, intimate interior.

The entire floor may be carpeted from wall to wall as frequently found in modern office landscaping. In this way, these large spaces are given a more contained atmosphere. The very texture of the carpet plays a role in gathering people together. Intimacy and cosiness are always connected with *nearness*. In addition, noise within the space is reduced. Resonance opens a space, whereas muffled sounds close it and draw it inwards.

An example of this gathering aspect is Mies van der Rohe's use of carpets in both the Barcelona Pavilion (1929) and the Exhibition Building in Berlin (1931). In both places one finds large shining floor surfaces interspersed with carpeted areas. The carpets are not placed haphazardly but always where one sits, eats or converses. In this way the carpets create small enclosures, 'spaces within a space', exactly suited to more intimate groups.

65.  A transparent floor elicits a spontaneous feeling of insecurity and danger (photo by W. Vandivert).

64.  View from the Eiffel Tower (from Giedion, *Space, Time and Architecture*).

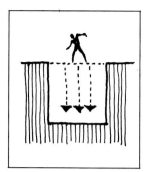

63. The open floor: glass floor.

## THE STONE CARPET

Many floor areas which do not have the carpet's soft qualities may, nevertheless, have the carpet's zone-defining effect. The prerequisite for this is a textural treatment of the floor which conveys the character of a homogeneous and continuous surface.

The richly patterned surfaces of the mosaic floor have often been called built carpets. 'The mosaic floors of St. Mark's are, indeed, nothing more than costly carpets of coloured stone', writes Sven Rasmussen (Fig. 62).[14] The Crusaders' contact with the Near East and its rich carpet tradition, was one factor in the revival of the polychrome floor in the Middle Ages. The Cosmati brothers' long architectural traditions in medieval Italy were important in the revival of the floor's role as a place defining element. To enter a church with a mosaic floor was to experience a complete change of character between inside and outside space — a distinct contrast between the natural tuff stone floor of the outdoors and the abstract value of the interior floor.

## THE OPEN FLOOR

In contrast to both the attached and the detached floor, the quality of the *open floor* is purely visual. This means that the opening effect in such floors is optical only and is brought about by the use of specific materials and patterns in the floor plane. These may be summarized in four archetypes, each of which lends special depth effects to the floor: (1) *transparency,* (2) *mirroring,* (3) *reflection,* (4) *layering*.

### THE TRANSPARENT FLOOR

A floor of transparent glass constitutes the very essence of what we mean by a floor that opens downwards. It is seldom used in architecture and the reason is obvious. Apart from the lack of tensile strength in glass and resulting structural limitations, the glass floor is insecure from a psychological point of view as well. To walk over a void is like walking on nothing (Fig. 63). It gives the same sensation of dizziness and falling as that which we feel on top of a mountain or high tower. The depth has a magnetic effect — it 'sucks' us downward — a phenomenon indicating that depth, just as all other types of space, is a potential sphere of activity which we 'try out' by 'falling'. The transparent floor conveys, therefore, a spontaneous feeling of *insecurity and danger* (Fig. 64).

This feeling of insecurity remains despite knowledge and reason. Although we know that the floor will hold technically, it is only after considerable experience with it that the feeling of insecurity lessens. The sensation of falling is fundamental and also applies to animals, as demonstrated by

68. The reflective floor expands the space downward (Bohuslän, from *Scanorama*, 1978).

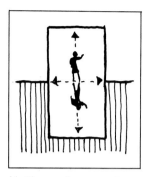

66. The open floor: mirror floor.

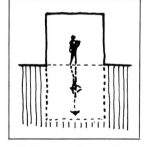

67. The open floor: reflective floor.

experiments. Similar experiments have been carried out with small children. They all avoided crawling onto a glass slab even though they saw precisely the same pattern below as the secure slab on which they sat (Fig. 65).[15]

## THE MIRROR FLOOR

On a transparent floor, whether of glass or grating, one finds oneself between an above and a below which *differ* from one another. Looking down from above one sees things in the depths as something upon which one could fall, just as from a height.

In the mirror floor, what is below is the same as what is above. Ceiling and walls are mirrored in its depths and one finds oneself in an enclosed space, between reality and illusion (Fig. 66). The mirror floor gives no main directional indication to the space — one finds oneself in its centre. But, this centre is not a specific point on the floor, rather it is like the centre of a 'sphere' in which all directions are equal. One's feet and legs constitute the central point, the meeting place between above and below. As a result, the movements of the legs become the shifting centre of a personal space limited both upwards and downwards by the body. On a mirror floor we find ourselves, therefore, in the middle of what is in principle a homogeneous and directionless space.

It is interesting to note that the mirror floor is very frequently used as a dance floor. Not only do the legs initiate the dance but the inherent nature of the dance and music is directionless. 'The dance is independent of any particular direction', says E. Straus.[16]

Many modern discotheques and dance halls exploit this content. A combination of mirrored wall and ceiling areas and flickering, blinking lights creates a total space in which the visitor experiences a feeling of unreality. In contrast to the city outside with its directional and destination-accented network of streets, where noise, people and traffic embody the 'back and forth movement', we comprehend the mirrored space as a detached fairyland in which we ourselves are the affected and ecstatic central point.

## THE REFLECTING FLOOR

The reflecting floor is an 'indistinct' mirror floor.

This means simply that below is not a copy of above. In the reflecting floor the opening effect is determined by the floor's material, structure and colour. By mirroring the walls and ceiling, the floor is given a shifting depth character depending upon whether the surface is of wood or stone, whether it is patterned or is white or black.[17]

Most important, nevertheless, is the reflection itself — its qualities convey the effect. The reflection creates a belowness, one which shifts be-

69. The reflective floor expands the space downward (Seiryoden in Kyoto from Alex, *Japanese Architecture*).

70. The reflective floor expands the floor downward (Sunroom by Jan & Jon from Byggekunst 6/1978).

tween light and dark in that objects, ceiling and walls are transformed and converted into diffuse forms as they are reflected downwards (Figs. 67, 68).

This characteristic has a counter effect on objects above the floor. Objects are optically detached and freed from the floor on which they stand. They seem to stand only on their own shadows. The objects do not appear to stand on a ground equally substantial or stronger than the objects themselves. On the contrary, the floor seems to be non-supporting and thereby increases the detached air of the objects. Our illustration shows the throne dais *(morja)* in Seiryoden in Kyoto, where the dais seems to hover in the middle of a space bounded above by the four surrounding columns and below by their reflection in the floor (Fig. 69).[18]

## REFLECTION AND THE RELATION BETWEEN INSIDE AND OUTSIDE

We realize that in the relation between inside and outside the reflecting floor is important because it 'enlarges' a space.

The space is enlarged not only downwards in optical depth but also outwards because solid boundaries appear to be lighter, more distant and have greater mobility. Typical in this context is the Renaissance and Baroque periods' feeling for highly polished reflecting floors. The Renaissance skeletal wall system appeared lighter, and the curving forms of the Baroque were given even greater life and movement. In modern architecture the reflecting floor plays a similar role. In Jan & Jon's 16 square metre garden room in an Oslo suburban house (1978), the polished floor is essential for an understanding of the space as a whole (Fig. 70).[19] This small interior reaches out in all directions to a larger, ever-shifting environment; up into the ceiling's illusionistic mirror surfaces, out into the landscape through large expanses of fenestration and down into the shimmering depth of the polished stone floor.

The freedom, expansion and movement which the gleaming floor lends to objects applies also to ourselves. Like the objects we too seem to be 'lighter'. The reflecting floor is without the rootless character of the mirrored floor. Its downward opening is mysterious and merely intimated. It reflects objects in a lively interchange of light and shadow and not in exact and comprehensible forms. Brilliance, motion and expansion are the reflecting floor's contribution to interior space. These same words also describe the qualities of a *party* as Rilke interprets them in his poem evoking the mood of a ballroom:

> The flames of the fire burn high and brightly, voices buzz, the tinkle of glass and brightness become one and finally from this even rhythm springs the dance.[20]

73. The layered effect brought about by motion (from Police Headquarters in Oslo, photo by R. Jucker).

75. The layered effect brought about by lines: stone runner (St. Miniato, from Saalman, *Medieval Architecture*).

74. The layered effect brought about by lines (from Oslo City Hall, photo by R. Jucker).

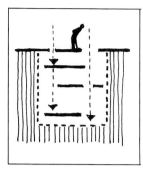

71. The open floor: The layered floor.

# THE LAYERED FLOOR

We have seen that the reflecting floor can also be interpreted as a floor in layers. The shiny surface is seen as a coating on top of the floor plane itself and can be compared to wet asphalt. A layered floor, in this sense, is a floor plane in which the form, material and pattern convey a stratified effect, layer upon layer (Fig. 71). The depth effect and the atmosphere it creates is governed by what each layer 'has to say' as to how it supports us and not the least of all, how the interrelating effectual strength of these layers determines the whole. Thus, a black surface may contribute to an opening effect in a shiny floor, whereas a white surface may weaken this effect.

To understand the layered floor's depth effect it is essential to distinguish between figure and background on the floor plane. In principle, this means that a figure seen against a larger surface may seem to lie beneath it as part of a lower level, as though seen through a hole.

In the following we will emphasize five archetypes within the layered floor. These are carried out with the help of *motion, framework, surface, texture* and *image* (Fig. 72, a-e).

## MOTION AND THE LAYER EFFECT

The first variant is based on the difference in *motion* between the levels (Figs. 72a, 73, 74). We have already noted that the directional floor is actually a layered floor. Whether a path or ramp is imbedded in the floor as a pattern or physically stretches over it like a bridge are degrees within the same expression. Both are directional elements which appear as figures upon a more static ground.

The mosaic floor of St. Miniato, Florence (thirteenth century), is again a good example (Fig. 75) (see p. 45). Like the runner carpet, this path of stone is a guiding route from the entrance right up to the baldachin over the altar immediately beneath the level of the choir. Path and destination comprise one dynamic unit and become a self-contained 'place' detached from the more directionless surrounding floor pattern.

This path in the floor is vital for the meaning of the interior. The architectural treatment otherwise seems like a series of additions, a restless chain of contrasting links, making the space difficult to understand. The central path, on the other hand, is unambiguous and leads straight to an important place in the church. It is both in form and content a secure place to be — one follows it instinctively in order not to 'fall off'.

## SKELETON AND THE LAYER EFFECT

In another variant, the upper layer has a *skeletal* character. These grids seem to be made of beams and convey a sense of security as if safe to walk on because of the 'openings' in between.

76. The layered effect brought about by a skeleton and surface: lines and checkerboard pattern (Medici Chapel by Michelangelo, from Hitchcock (ed.), *World Architecture*).
77. The layered effect brought about by lines and stars (Bygdø Allé 28 B in Oslo, photo by R. Jucker).
79. The depth effect brought about by surfaces (Cube floor in Amritsar, photo by R. Jucker).
80. The layered effect brought about by surfaces (piazza floor by de Giorgio, from Giedion, *Space, Time and Architecture*).

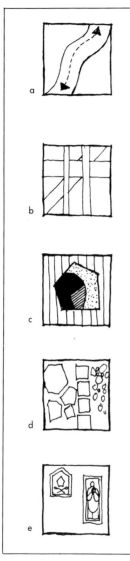

72a-e. The layered floor effect is brought about by: (a) motion, (b) skeleton, (c) surface, (d) texture, and (e) image.

In Michelangelo's Medici Chapel, Florence (1519), the stripes in the floor join the wall pilasters (Fig. 76). The result is an inner space defined by skeletal elements within an outer space of smoothly plastered surfaces. In the floor, this same deeper space is defined by a black and white checkerboard layer. The checks run diagonally in an independent system *beneath* the skeleton. The alternating black and white 'holes' add to the depth effect. Visually the checkerboard is not a strictly solid level but, as we move about within the space, the floor appears to have an alternating upper and lower level.

The dimensions of the floor skeleton are decisive in giving the floor a secure load-bearing effect (Fig. 77). If the 'beams' are very thin, they seem more like 'cracks' and, instead of being safe to walk on, become openings, and the parts that were previously holes now become the firm surface. This phenomenon may be observed in childrens' hopping games on pavements and stone footpaths. They jump from stone to stone and the one to step on a crack is the loser (Fig. 78).

## SURFACE AND THE LAYER EFFECT

This leads us to the next archetype in which planes 'lie' one upon the other and are seen through 'holes' and 'openings' (Fig. 72 c).

The difference in depth which occurs between dark and light areas on a surface is frequently used to obtain a layer effect (Fig. 79). An example is the Renaissance architect Francesco di Giorgio's project for an ideal city square (ca. 1475–1500, Fig. 80). The large pale-coloured checkerboard is interpreted as the upper supporting level. This top layer is the actual floor lying on top of a dark 'depth', which is perceived through openings in between. Here on these pale-coloured paths people walk securely, and it is these which are a continuation of the broad stair flights and on which the heavy triumphal columns stand. The central fountain, too, has its place on a light area. Like an island in a dark well the black fountain draws the water up from the depths below.

## TEXTURE AND THE LAYER EFFECT

A fourth archetype in the relation between above and below in a floor plane is the use of different combinations of coarse and fine *textures* (Fig. 72d).

An interpretation of this is shown in our illustration of the Katsura Gardens in Japan (1636) (Fig. 81). The deepest layer is understood as the coarsest and the 'roughest' zone, while the levels as they rise become increasingly geometric and delicate.[21] The topmost plane consists of a footpath made of square-cut paving stones. Pale in colour and casually combined, they seem to 'float' over the dark background. The next level is created by a gut-

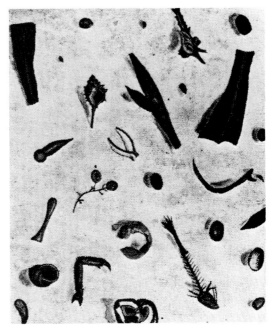

82. The layered effect brought about by images ('The Unswept Floor', Roman floor mosaic, from *Sfinx* I, 1977).

81. The layered effect brought about by textures (Katsura, from Alex, *Japanese Architecture*).

78. The hopping game from square to square.

ter of natural cobblestones imbedded in the lowest level, which is the soil itself. These graduated depths must, at the same time, be seen as a part of a greater whole. One is really not completely at the bottom until one reaches the water level to which the path leads, nor quite at the top before one enters the house with its geometric carpet pattern. This conception of the floor's span from top to bottom, from water and ground at the lowest level to the ordered geometry of the house at the highest level, is at the same time an interpretation of the difference between outside and inside. The *outside* bears the stamp of primeval nature, the *inside* is the seat of humanity and greatest perfection, a place 'in which the spirit alone prevails'.[22]

## IMAGES AND THE LAYER EFFECT

Our final archetype deals with the floor that is decorated with abstract or naturalistic representations of objects, people, animals and flowers (Fig. 72e).

This type of floor is found particularly in Roman Antiquity and was usually composed of mosaic or incrustation. The depth effect in such floors depended on the naturalism and plasticity of the figures represented. In this sense, the Republic's polychrome floors, such as the Alexander mosaic from Pompeii, with its perspective and plasticity, had a greater depth effect than the late-Roman linear patterned monochromes.

Our illustration shows a Roman mosaic floor with all kinds of leftover food strewn about on a white background (Fig. 82). The pale colour of the background 'detaches' the objects; it makes them light and independent. This, combined with the sharply outlined shadow, gives them great plasticity in themselves, enhancing the illusion that they are lying both above and on the floor.

The effect conveyed by a floor with images is determined by two conditions. The first is the significance of the portrayals as *things.* The feeling of possibility 'stumbling' on the objects makes us instinctively try to avoid them, to go around them. This means that the lowest plane, the one beneath and between the objects, becomes our actual level of movement. Our first reaction to the food-strewn floor, therefore, is to fetch a broom!

To this physical reaction, however, must be added the meaning of what the images *represent.* The cross in front of the entrance to many Byzantine churches was not meant to be trodden on. Intuitively, that was felt to be a sacrilege. Similarly, human portrayals are associated with something which 'hurts' to step on. To put one's foot directly on the face of a human portrayal is most uncomfortable. A physical conflict arises between reality and illusion, between the form and the image.

All four motifs within the theme of *the open floor,* which we have exa-

84. The sunken floor: Cave in the amphitheatre (from L'Orange/Thiis-Evensen, *Oldtidens Bygningsverden*).

85. The sunken floor (City Hall piazza in Siena, from Favole, *Piazza d'Italia*).

83. The sunken floor.

mined, have one thing in common. They interpret depth effects on a horizontal plane. The depth effect is purely optical, the downward motion visual and not real. The *transparent floor* and *mirror floor* as well as the *reflecting floor* and *layer floor,* each convey its own specific character depending on the degree of depth and effects. They are all, nevertheless, marked by the same fundamental tension inherent in the relation between the need to have firm ground beneath one's feet and the fear of falling — between nature's primeval forces and the human will to survive.

# THE SUNKEN FLOOR

The sunken floor differs basically from the open floor.

The open floor is physically solid and on the same plane, and downward movement is purely optical. Its effect is in the conflict between a familiar pattern of possible motion and the possibility of falling, which, in principle, is threatening.

In the sunken floor, motion downwards is a physical reality (Fig. 83). In other words, forward and downward motion are one and the same. One ventures into the ground from an upper level. When one is faced with such a sunken floor, a basic reaction occurs, a mental state dictated by two types of previous experience: One involves motion conceptions governed by gravity, the other involves the encounter with underground phenomena.

## GRAVITY AND THE RISING/SINKING ASPECT

When faced with a downward slanting floor, one feels a spontaneous sensation of accelerating *speed*. In contrast to the rising floor, which restrains movement, the downward sloping floor exerts its own additional pull to that which the natural force of gravity exerts on our normal movements (Fig. 84). We transfer this to the floor in front of us. As opposed to the case of the level floor we do not feel 'free' to choose our way. Here it is the ground itself which takes over — in both an upward and downward slope. The result, however, is exactly the opposite — to be up at the top is to be independent, whereas to be down at the bottom is confining. Objects at the bottom of a sunken area, therefore, assume two contrasting values. In one way they seem to be heavy and sinking, rather like a well-cushioned landing of a falling object. In another way they seem to rise *up from* the bottom, to free themselves in the way we feel instinctively that we must do in order not to be imprisoned down there.

In the City Hall piazza in Siena, the rising/sinking effect is a 'built' one, in that the motion is given a plastic response in the form of the building mass at the bottom of the piazza (Figs. 85, 86).

The piazza lies in a natural depression in the valley with residential

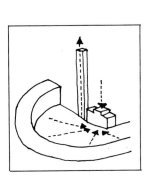

86. City Hall piazza in Siena and the interaction between sinking and rising.

75

87. La Tourette and the differentiated floor (by Le Corbusier, from Basquin, *Eveux*).

houses on the south forming an approximate semicircular boundary between town and square. From this ridge the piazza sinks down to its lowest point immediately in front of the City Hall building facing it. Here lies the piazza's drainage canal, which is connected to gutters forming a fan pattern running up towards the houses.

The City Hall building is massive and heavy. With its breadth and solidity it creates a firmly anchored and heavy block which seems to press down the floor of the piazza. The clock tower on the left, on the other hand, rises dynamically above this sunken volume. With its impressive height, and slender lines, the tower is a manifestation of defiance and upward striving, which in combination with the City Hall's downward press defines the timeless and universal content of Siena's piazza.

## GROUND SPACE PHENOMENA

In introducing the sunken floor, we mentioned that the dynamic aspect must be supplemented by the conception of into *what* we are descending. Architectural history contains many examples showing intuitive understanding that sinking a floor is the same as penetrating the ground itself. In other words, this penetration is interpreted as an encounter with earth's primeval forces, with the rough and natural, with death, water and fire. By tying itself down, the house shows its essential affinity with nature, says G. Bachelard. The house becomes ...'related in a brotherly way to the forces of mountains and water working within the earth'.[24]

In the following we shall look at some typical examples of this encounter.

## RUSTICITY AS A PHENOMENON OF THE GROUND

In our Japanese example we saw that 'down' was interpreted as something elemental and unformed, whereas 'up' was given an abstract and ordered character. In the church at La Tourette, (1959), Le Corbusier has done just this. The floor is built in three levels, each having a different content (Fig. 87).

At the top is the altar platform, the church's most important level, raised by six steps. This floor is the only one in the entire monastery which is black and shiny, a reminder of the spiritual and irrational character of this area. The floor of the nave with its grey, neutral surface, forms the intermediate level. Not only in the nave but in other parts of the building as well, this floor expresses the normal level and is found in ramps, dining-halls and workrooms. Beneath this level we find the chapels of the saints in a deeply sunken space beside the high altar. Here the floor consists of coarse, rugged stone concrete. Combined with intense overhead lighting and the undulating cave-like walls, the architect has led us right down into the ground's own world.

89. The crypt (Lund Cathedral, from Rydbeck, *Lund Domkyrkas Byggnadshistoria*).

90. Vision of the cellar (etching by Piranesi, from Corfiato, *Piranesi Compositions*).

91. The sunken baptistery (St. Michael's Church in Nienburg, from Rappe, *Domus Ecclesiae*).

92. The sunken basin (Fontana de Trevi in Rome).

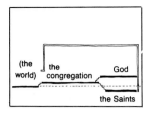

88. The ground's four levels (diagram, section of St. Zeno).

## DEATH AS A PHENOMENON OF THE GROUND

To confront death is also to encounter the earth's interior, the place of the dead. Architecturally this is expressed in the sunken crypt. As early as the seventh century, the crypt, in keeping with increasing sacred relic workship, was gradually becoming more important as a visible part of the church interior. In addition, as a visual element its meaning was expressed by sinking its level in relation to the church nave.

An example of the graduation of levels is St. Zeno in Verona (1070) (Fig. 88). From the church square outside, one moves upwards and in onto the floor level of the nave. This floor ends in a flight of steps leading down to the crypt below the choir. The choir level lies above and is reached by side steps from the aisles. The result is a composition in four different levels, each with a highly differing content. The floor of the square outside belongs to the city, the level of secular life. The floor of the nave is the level for the congregation. Raised above it is the altar level, which in turn is placed immediately above the very lowest level; the place of the martyrs and the dead. Here we encounter an underworld, a crypt, which, like the earth itself is dark, low and cold. Within the crypt we are actually in the earth's inner space; here the coffins and reliquaries stand freely on the floor as if only the sod was removed (Fig. 89). This sinking of the crypt carries with it all the mysterious atmosphere of the cellar as we find it in Giovanni Piranesi's 'Carceri' series (Fig. 90). The sinking of the floor conveys a feeling, as Bachelard says, of being one with the 'cosmic roots' of the house,[25] a confrontation with the nether world which gives the world above its existential meaning.

## WATER AS A PHENOMENON OF THE GROUND

The sunken floor also allows us to encounter water. As in nature itself, the lowest point of the existential level is the water surface — beneath it are the depths, the nether regions. This motif is interpreted in architecture by the sunken pool (Fig. 91).

Fontana di Trevi in Rome, by Nocola Salvi (1762), is in this sense, more than just a fountain (Fig. 92).[26] By being sunk into the ground it becomes primarily an opening to something primitive and elemental. The natural rock formations from which the water trickles forth as if from many sources reveal the very foundations of Rome itself. The rocks rise up from below like a petrified water spring, while the water gushed forth, running down to be tamed in the basin below, framed by the surrounding streets. It is in fact the sunken aspect of the Trevi Fountain which lends to it its content. It is like a slash in Rome's own interior floor revealing nature's forces in an exterior space, both as seen in the tuff landscape *around* the city and as they lie *beneath* the city forming the physical foundations of Rome's architecture.[27]

94. The sunken fireplace (Taliesin West by F.Ll. Wright, after Kaufmann/Raeburn, *Frank Lloyd Wright, Writings and Buildings*).

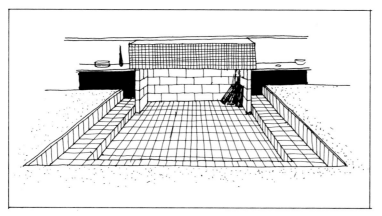

93. The sunken fireplace (fireplace by A. Korsmo, from a photograph).

95. An open fire and the space of light.

## FIRE AS A PHENOMENON OF THE GROUND

Fire too is a part of our conception of the earth's interior (Fig. 93).

Frank Lloyd Wright has frequently interpreted this association. He leads us *down* to the fireplace, where we may warm ourselves. In several of his houses, Taliesin West, Hanna house, and Wingspread, the stone floor around the fireplace is several steps lower than the rest of the floor (Fig. 94).[28]

The background for this is Wright's principle of the house as a part of nature. The house and ground on which it stands should be as one: 'I knew well by now that no house should ever be *on* any hill or *on* anything. It should be *of* the hill, belonging to it, so hill and house could live together each happier for the other.'[29]

What then about fire in this context?

First of all, fire as a phenomenon, conveys an instinctive feeling of being inside. The warmth of a fire is a prerequisite for surviving the cold and frost outside. As a means of preparing food it is also one of life's fundamentals. These basic experiences make fire a symbol. It represents comfort and security, the centre of our innermost being. As a structure too, the fire is the centre of an interior space. The radiating flames of a bonfire at night welcome us as to a cave of light, beckoning us into safety from the devouring darkness around (Fig. 95). In the circle of this light we and those with us gain substance, our identity is established, an identity otherwise hidden by the night.

Secondly, fire as a phenomenon is associated with something which comes from below. In contrast to sunlight, fire is the earth's own light and consequently has a different meaning. The light that falls from above is spiritual, light coming from the side belongs to 'wordly' everyday life, whereas light from below is the earth's alone. That fire belongs to the earth is also factual. The earth itself is a tamed globe of fire which occasionally breaks out in volcanoes. This knowledge, however, is less important than what we actually see in the fire's own structure. Fire rises upwards from below, the flames flicker and grow *up from* the ground.

In Wright's house these qualities are made tangible. They express an inside that is made synonymous with the centre of the house. In all Wright's houses the fireplace and chimney-piece are the central and integrating motif. The fireplace becomes an image of survival which gives him happiness in an open and empty prairie, and he says: 'It refreshed me to see the fire burning deep in the masonry of the house itself'.[30]

By sinking the fireplace the 'inside' is given a cosmic implication. The house is *of* the ground — to dwell is to be firmly rooted. The cave of light which the fire itself outlines becomes, in the form of the fireplace, a place into which we descend as well as enter. The steps, spreading upwards from

81

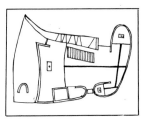

100. Notre Dame and the continuous cross (after Le Corbusier,
*Oeuvre Complète 1910—65*).

98. Notre Dame and the undulating landscape of Belfort
(Notre Dame du Haut by Le Corbusier, from Bolle-Reddat, *Notre
Dame du Haut, Ronchamp*).

99. Notre Dame and the rising floor (from Bolle-Redat, *Notre
Dame du Haut, Ronchamp*).

97. The rising floor.

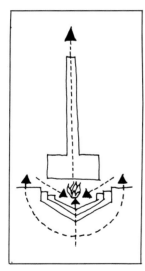

96. Fire, chimney and a sunken area.

the hearth in a rising circle are the visible extension of the radiating flames. Here we can gather *around* and sit while the house, otherwise, glides past and out 'into the open prairie' (Fig. 96).[31]

# THE RISING FLOOR

The rising floor is the flexed muscle of the earth. As we balance our way across it, we sense the power that wells up from *beneath* (Fig. 97).

We shall examine two examples which interpret this expression: Le Corbusier's Notre Dame du Haut (1955) and Michelangelo's Campidoglio (1544).

## UNDULATING GROUND AND NOTRE DAME DU HAUT

The Church of Notre Dame crowns a natural height in a rolling landscape around Belfort (Fig. 98). This mighty panorama along with the climb to the top are the spatial experiences we carry with us when we enter. The form of the floor within reflects the same undulating characteristics. It is already familiar to us. In its soft S-like form, the floor is highest at the entrance, sinks as it approaches the altar and rises again abruptly towards the wall behind (Fig. 99).

On this floor one feels *dependent* upon the ground. One is at the mercy of its changing whims as in a boat on a tossing sea. Whereas the undulating forms outside were perceived as comprising a dynamic part of a free and grandly modelled landscape, the interior floor becomes a concentration of earth's own mighty forces. Like crackle-work on glaze, the flat stones of this undulating floor seem thin and brittle, about to burst open at any moment from the pressure beneath.

Le Corbusier has exploited this atmosphere to accentuate the meaning of the building. The floor, in fact, consists of four low plateaus: the choir level on the east, the chapel levels to the south under the main tower and under the secondary towers to the north as well as a level area for seating along the window wall on the south.

Le Corbusier has interpreted the spiritual levels as tied to each other. A black cross extending the length of the floor joins the altar level and the two chapel levels at each end (fig. 100).[32] In this way, an upper floor level is established — a unified world apart made up of closely linked 'islands' on an undulating lower floor level. That the level area containing the pews, the congregation's only designated place, is *not* similarly connected explains the meaning of the floor-landscape. Man is 'lost' if, in this changing and threatening world, he does not entrust himself to the spiritual and saving dimensions of existence (see p. 323, under Roof).

83

101. Il Campidoglio in Rome (from Portoghesi/Zevi (eds.), *Michelangelo Architetto*).

102. Il Campidoglio as planned by Michelangelo (etching by S. Dupérac, from Portoghesi/Zevi, *Michelangelo Architetto*).

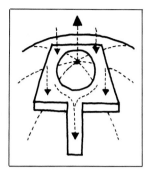

103. Michelangelo's Campidoglio project and the conflict between the piazza floor and the ground.

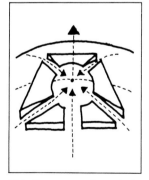

104. The existing Campidoglio and the 'victory' of the ground.

## THE STRUGGLING ASPECT OF THE GROUND AND THE CAMPIDOGLIO

A dramatic example of another variant of the rising floor is Rome's Campidoglio. This urban space, designed by Michelangelo, is situated on one of Rome's most revered heights (Fig. 101).[33]

The form of the floor is the result of a *conflict,* a conflict between the ground beneath, which is the actual rock on which the piazza lies, and the plateau above, which is, in turn, the floor on which the buildings rest. The conflict arises in the way the rock appears to have broken through the surface in the form of a convex oval covered by a stellate pattern, with the equestrian statue of Marcus Aurelius at its centre.

The present form of the piazza interprets this conflict otherwise than Michelangelo's original project as we see it in Dupérac's engraving (1544) (Fig. 102). In it a *struggle* takes place between the rising oval and the floor of the piazza (Fig. 103). In a typical Manneristic way the conflict is between balance and dynamism. The three descending steps to the oval reveal the thickness of the piazza floor and thereby the force needed to break through the surface. The oval is dark and heavy, in keeping with the raw underlying ground of the hill beneath and stands in sharp contrast to the square's light and abstract surface. The star pattern with the emperor's statue at its centre has often been interpreted as a description of the curvature's outward expansion. But, the pattern may also be seen as a net concretely 'restraining' any expansion from beneath. This is held together by the emperor himself, which adds to the motif's ideology in that the emperor is sublimated as the master of nature — man bringing nature under control.

The present execution of the square weakens the balance of this conflict between surface and ground. Several points show that the tension has been relieved and the ground has 'won' by breaking up the entire rising of the piazza. In the first place, all the paving stones of the piazza are in the same grey tone, which reduces the contrast between convex and flat areas. Secondly, the four entrance ramps cut up the horizontal plane into small parts, thereby reducing the floor of the piazza to lesser forecourts adjoining the individual buildings (Fig. 104).[34]

In addition, the main ramp down to the city cuts far into the horizontal plane and thereby serves quite another function than that intended by Michelangelo. In his project this ramp was a branch of the floor of the piazza itself and, as such, the intermediary of a movement from the top downwards. Now it is as if the ground itself has broken free in the form of the ramp's steps and become a part of the bedrock's own rising.

Indeed, Michelangelo's project and the final execution express two different degrees of strength in a conflict between inside and outside, in which the inside is the floor of the square and the outside is the oval. This

105. The street and the goal (project for Pennsylvania Avenue in Washington D.C., from Rudofsky, *Streets for People*).

106. The bridge and the conquest (Perugia, from Rudofsky, *Streets for People*).

is also a conflict between man and nature in that, as C. de Tolnay has maintained, the ground is the earth's cover, which here in the form of the convex oval bursts forth as *'Caput Mundi',* the world's crown.[35]

The architectural history of the Campidoglio is therefore imbued with cosmic ideas of the relationship between local and global. Local is synonymous with Rome, which is the floor of the piazza itself and the buildings around it, whereas the global meaning is expressed in the rising floor representing the Roman Empire.

## THE DIRECTIONAL FLOOR

From what has been said so far it is clear that every floor expresses its own dynamics. In our introduction, apart from the supporting aspect, we divided the floor into two main themes. This was done in order to illustrate the extent to which the *delimiting* floor leaves us at peace within the space or *leads* us forward in a particular direction.

When we now choose, in the following, to treat this directional aspect as a separate motif, it is because certain floor elements are especially designed for the sole purpose of leading us forward. These are the path, the bridge and the stairs.

The *path* is perceived primarily as a means towards a destination and is therefore, in principle, subject to this goal (Fig. 105). On flat ground and with the goal at the end, the path is merely the accentuation of a distant intention. Destination and path become one, which means that the path's space and the goal stand out from the surroundings as a homogeneous space.

On the other hand, the *bridge* and goal together form a composite space. The impressions created by the bridge are linked to our experiences with it. It carries us over an obstacle (Fig. 106). Thus, forward movement towards the goal represents an event in itself not necessarily dictated by the goal. The bridge helps us so that we avoid having to struggle through valley, river or hollow. But, first and foremost, it is the bridge which carries us and prevents our falling into the depths. From the bridge we see this danger on both sides and therefore the bridge becomes the thing we must depend upon and cling to — should it collapse or if we do not follow its course exactly, we are lost.[36] On a bridge we are in a state of tension between insecurity and fear on the one hand (the fall) and total dependency and surrender *(in casu* the bridge), on the other. The bridge assumes value as something independent and active, something strong and victorious which 'occupies' the empty space it spans. Having crossed the bridge, the feeling of having reached the goal comes as a relief from having survived a tense situation. The goal is as if conquered after an effort that the bridge has made for us.

107.  Stairs and the elevated goal (the Royal Palace in Oslo by H.D.F. Linstow).

We have said that the path accents the goal, indeed as a form it is subject to this goal. The bridge, on the other hand 'collects' — it gathers in separate routes and unites them in its own independent and active form.[37]

*Stairs* are the connecting link between below and above. This expression, therefore, depends upon whether the goal to which they lead is up or down, as these two directions *a priori* have very different contents (Fig. 107). A flight of stairs leading upwards guides us to a place of importance. The goal at the top acquires an elevated and 'sacred' quality. In going up, tension and expectation mount with every step. To go up conveys a feeling of reaching something, whereas to go down gives the feeling of leaving something. Descending can evoke a feeling of humility and resignation but may also mean to be filled with 'grace'. One leaves a higher plane as an intermediary of the meaning found there and with the desire to 'share' this experience generously with others. In content, therefore, stairs concentrate a conflict between potential humility and potential exaltation.[38]

In conclusion we may say that on the path, on the bridge, and on stairs, we are influenced towards our destination in different ways. On a path we are guided by the goal, on the bridge we conquer the goal, and on stairs we find the goal either humbling or uplifting.

## STAIRS

In the following we shall limit ourselves to an examination of the expression of the stairs. The meaning of the path's course and of the bridge will only be considered in so far as they affect the form of the stairs. The reason for this is the importance stairs have had throughout architectural history as an intermediary in the relationship between outside and inside, between the house and its environment.

Other limitations are necessary as well. First of all we assume that in all following examples we are standing at the *foot* of the stairs. In addition, we assume that we are about to go from the outside in, which means that the interior space is the goal of the stairs.

The main question is; in what way do the stairs prepare us to ascend and enter?

## THE STAIRS' EXPRESSION OF MOTION

The expression of the stairs is determined by the *motion* impulses it arouses within us (Fig. 108). These are determined by the extent to which the stairs show comparative strength in upward and downward motion. This strength relationship in turn is dependent upon two particular factors. The first is the spontaneous *climbing* impulse which any stairs arouse in the spectator facing them. The other involves the way in which the form in itself can lessen or increase this impulse. Stairs going in the same direction as the spectator

108.  Stairs and motion (Magasin du Bon Marché, from Norwick (ed.), *Verdensarkitekturen*).

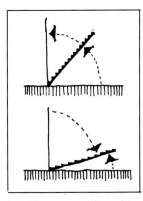

109. The ascent impulse and the angle of the stairs.

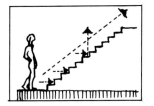

110. The ascent impulse and the steps.

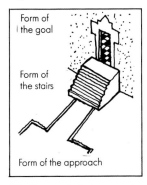

Form of the goal

Form of the stairs

Form of the approach

111. Factors which determine the stair's expression of motion: (1) the form of the approach (the space in front of the stairs), (2) the form of the stairs, and (3) the stairs' goal (entrance and façade).

accent the upward motion impulse, but if they come *towards* the person they counteract this impulse. Both impulses may be experienced in stairs containing both directions which we call a *two-way* flight.

A flight of stairs will always 'invite people to go up', according to Andrea Palladio.[39] This impulse to climb is fundamental and mainly due to two factors.

The first is determined by the expression of the stairs, which is contained in what we have already said about the greater importance of what is at the top than at the bottom. Thus, the top of the stairs is more desirable and alluring than the bottom.

The other factor lies more within the form itself, the basic structure of which is decided by its diagonal form and the form of the steps. A diagonal seems to 'defy' gravity. It always rises in relation to the horizontal but in quite different ways, depending upon its gradient (Fig. 109). If the gradient exceeds 45 degrees, any sinking sensation is overcome and the vertical takes over. If it is less than 45 degrees, the ascent encounters resistance, which increases if the gradient becomes less. Similarly, the steps themselves also visualize a climbing movement (Fig. 110). This is not only because they are sensed as being cut in a way made to fit our feet but also because their plastic expression is both inward and upward.

Whether the expressed motion of the stairs goes in our intended direction, comes towards us, or is two-directional depends upon the overall affiliation of the flight. This means that the impression as a whole is not only dependent upon the form of the stairs themselves but also upon the relationship of the stairs to its surroundings.

Relationship to the environment is determined by the *approach*, which signifies the way in which one gets to the stairs and the *goal*, which in this case is the house façade to which the stairs lead. Both the approach and destination will vary from project to project and accordingly, will have correspondingly varying importance for the stairs' expression (Fig. 111).

In the following, therefore, we shall limit ourselves to examining the body of the stairway as an isolated element. This in turn presupposes that in our descriptions of the basic content of individual variations, the approach and goal will be constants. We shall imagine the stairs as facing an open space below and leading to a flat wall with the same entrance door above.

In a study of architectural stair forms it becomes clear that there are four basic motifs which determine the motion expression: *breadth, slope, attachment,* and *form* (Fig. 112, 1—4).

So, the question is: Is climbing a narrow flight of stairs different from climbing a broad one? What about stairs which are shallow compared to those which are steep or the stair flight firmly attached to the ground compared to one which spans lightly over it? Or, what is the importance of the stairs'

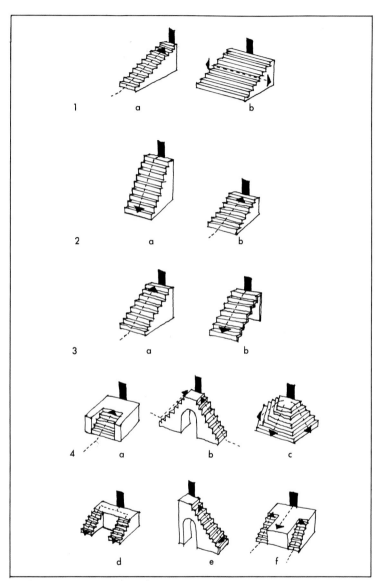

112, 1–4. The stairs' four motifs: (1) breadth: a) narrow, b) wide, (2) slope: a) steep, b) gentle, (3) attachment: a) attached, b) free, (4) form: a) plateau stair, b) frontal stair, c) fan stair, d) divided stair, e) side stair, f) overlapping stair.

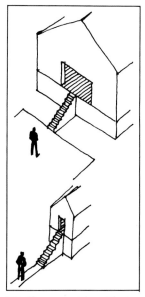

113. The narrow stair and the importance of the scale of the surroundings.

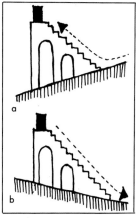

114. The narrow stair and the importance of the inclination of the ground for the motion direction (Diagram of the stair in Giglio Castello).

plastic form, whether it is straight or arched, symmetric or asymmetric?

In the following we shall examine each of these motifs individually. The aim is to show whether the motion expressed by the stairs is coming towards us, going along with us, or doing both, and how this affects the stairs' meaning in the relation between the inside and the outside.

## NARROW STAIRS

First and foremost it is our own physical dimensions which determine whether a flight of stairs is perceived as *narrow*. If it corresponds to our own body width or is at most double that width, it will be considered narrow. The quality is not relative in the sense that it is determined only by visual connection with the surroundings. Stairs which fulfil the above conditions seem narrow whether or not the dimensions of the surroundings otherwise are large or small, even if the impression of 'narrowness' is probably increased in the first case and reduced in the latter (Figs. 112,1a,b, 113).

It follows that a narrow flight of stairs seems intended for the spectator alone or, at most, one other person. It is the visualization of a 'personal space' — it is private. This content is further emphasized in that narrow stairs invite quick movement. The latter quality is to great extent dependent upon the length of the flight and is mainly dictated by two conditions.

The first is visual. A narrow and relatively long flight of stairs accents the line, which in itself concentrates the dynamic principle and reveals a forward movement. The wider and shorter the stairs, the greater will be the effect of its breadth on the motion and thereby a reduction in speed.

The other condition behind this 'speed' effect is determined by past experience. Narrow stairs picture a potential 'struggle' for space with someone approaching from above. If we are actually on the stairs, we feel crowded and the impulse is to hurry up to the top and away from the danger. One 'skips up' a narrow stairway but 'strides' up a broad one. In the first case movement is an individual matter, but in the second case it becomes more solemn and public (see p. 95 f).

## NARROW STAIRS AND THE RELATION
## BETWEEN INSIDE AND OUTSIDE

In its form alone, the narrow stairway implies no directional movement, that is to say, it gives no message as to whether motion is from the outside (from below) or from the inside (from above). This means that the relative strength between inside and outside influencing a narrow flight depends upon how the stairs accord with the surroundings (Figs. 114, 115).

An example of this is Robert Venturi's project for a beach house (1959). There the steps run at right angles to the entrance, climbing straight up from an open beach area in front (Fig. 116). The result is that the *interior* space

115. The narrow stair and motion from below upwards (detail from Giglio Castello).

118. The broad stair and the populated expression (Parthenon, reconstruction by G. Stevens, from Papathanassopoulos, *The Acropolis*).

119. The broad stair and the public expression (St. Maria Maggiore in Rome, façade by C. Rainaldi and others, from Bacon, *The Design of Cities*).

116. The narrow stair and motion from above downwards (project for a beach house by R. Venturi, after Venturi, *Complexity and Contradiction in Architecture*).

seems to open up and emerge. The main reason for this is that the stairs rise directly towards the entrance door, and this creates a visual focus in the overall symmetrical façade.

The symmetry of the house is assured by the roof. This gable roof brings the whole composition together by the way its ridge is both broken and integrated by a dominating chimney. Standing out from the façade immediately beneath the chimney is a small semi-detached vestibule, the link that leads the stairs into the house. The entire house is raised above the ground on narrow stilts.

The outlet itself is formed by the stairs in this composition. From the chimney-accented centre of the house, by way of the vestibule, the interior of the house is led out and down into the sand (Fig. 117). Along with the small vestibule, which is in a way a replica of the house itself, it is as though the entire building 'moves outdoors'. What is private becomes public and is in itself the welcoming agent.

## BROAD STAIRS

The narrow stairway is private, the broad flight has a public character. Broad stairs are described as monumental and considered suitable for public display. 'It is desireable that all parts of the stairs be splendid for there are many who see the stairs but not the rest of the house'.[40]

### BROAD STAIRS AND PUBLIC EXPRESSION

Again it is our physical experience which determines the impression conveyed by the stairs. What is included in the phenomenon 'broad stairs' is, however, more dependent upon a visual relation to the environment than in the case of narrow stairs.[41] Nevertheless, we spontaneously characterize a stairway as broad if it conveys a *stream* of people and not primarily a line of single induviduals as does the narrow stairway. Therein too, lies its content. It is not meant for just one person at a time but for many, the individual being just part of a potential crowd. One feels alone on a broad but empty flight of stairs — a conflict arises between the actual situation and the expression of the stairs as being something potentially filled with people. A broad stairway is generous; it offers space and is inviting (Figs. 118, 119).

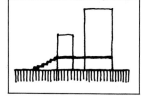

117. Section through Venturi's beach house (after Venturi, *Complexity and Contradiction in Architecture*).

### BROAD STAIRS AND CEREMONIAL EXPRESSION

Movement up a broad flight of stairs is slow. In a broad flight, the breadth is frequently greater than the length. The arresting factor is, therefore, either equal to or stronger than the forward upward motion. Slow forward movement is associated with a measured pace and is thought of in connection with ceremony, which in turn is associated with large and general forms that minimize individual enterprise. The hasty and propelling at-

120. The broad stair and the monumental expression (Crown Hall by Mies van der Rohe, from Hilberseimer, *Mies van der Rohe*).

122. The broad stair and the monumental expression (tax house from Kasuga, from Alex, *Japanese Architecture*).

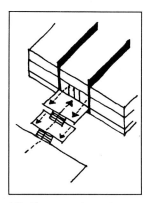

121. The stair in front of Crown Hall and the overlapping between inside and outside.

mosphere of the narrow stairs is replaced by one of reserve and control which assumes an air of solemnity in the ascending movement itself.

## BROAD STAIRS AND MONUMENTAL EXPRESSION

The monumentality of a broad stairway lies, thus, both in its collective quality and in its slow solemnity. We find, therefore, throughout architectural history, that broad stairs have been used to accentuate façades, expecially those of public buildings.

We give one example: the main stairway leading into Mies van der Rohe's Crown Hall, I.I.T. in Chicago (1955) (Fig. 120).

It is formed in such a way that the encounter between the interior space and exterior space is in the stairs themselves. The landing that divides the flight is the same width as the entrance 'space' where the boundaries are set by two powerful roof beams. It is, in fact, the inside space which is led out and down in the form of one great 'step', while movements from outside are conveyed by the smaller flight in the middle (Fig. 121). The entrance itself is through two glass doors, which in turn comprise only half of the stair width. Accordingly, the stairs are wider than 'necessary', and the expression becomes monumental. The broad landing increases this impression — both optically, as the entire stairs seem widened, and also in reality in that the climbing tendency is reduced and 'made solemn'.

We spoke of the dependent relationship between the effect of broad stairs and the environment. A functionally broad stairway may lose its entire monumental expression if it leads up to an over-dimensioned house. The reverse may be true and a small house appear monumental when giving onto a broad flight of steps, even if the stairs functionally do not fulfil the preconditions. An example of the latter is a little Kasuga temple from the Nara period in Japan (Fig. 122). The interior measures only c. 3.5 square metres. It is the stairs which give this 'cottage' such an impressive character.

## STEEP AND SHALLOW STAIRS

In the above we saw that broad and narrow stairs implied only the 'speed' and not the direction of the stair's course.

This is not the case when it concerns the slope of the stairs. The *shallow* flight of steps invites us to ascend (it accords with our intended course), whereas the *steep* flight resists our ascent as if pushing downward (it opposes our intended direction) (Fig. 112, 2a,b).

Extremes in this context are the ladder or the winding stairs in the case of the steep variant and the flat pathway when it comes to the shallow flight.

123. The steep stair as a sacred symbol (stair temple in Tikal, from Robertson, *Pre-Columbian Architecture*).

124. The steep stair as a sacred symbol (La Scala Santa, photo by Natural Colours).

125. The stair up to Aracoeli and Il Campidoglio (early 19th century etching).

## STEEP STAIRS AND SACRED EXPRESSION

Again we find the cause of these expressions in the relation between our physical selves and the force of gravity. Stairs are diagonal and the diagonal signifies a situation of tension midway between vertical and horizontal. 'The diagonal is found as a slanting position between the vertical and the horizontal. Thus it applies as the expressed tension gauge'.[42]

The tension in the stairs varies with the degree of resistance experienced. To climb a steep flight of stairs is physically exhausting; we move against the force of gravity, which presses us downwards. Gravity is personified as an adversary coming at us from above, and it gives our destination at the top an air of inaccessibility. On a really steep flight one is compelled to hurry to the top for fear of falling backwards and down. Steep stairs, therefore, also convey an impression of a struggle for survival. To fall here can mean calamity, whereas to fall on a shallower flight represents less danger.

In this sense, a steep stairway isolates but also makes manifest the house and entrance at the top. The goal is isolated because it is difficult to reach, but at the same time it is in a way emphasized as the 'victor' — in other words, it has occupied the place we ourselves are striving to reach.

These impressions of isolation and strength, of struggle and survival, all combine to make the steep stairway a *sacred* symbol. The steep form is a visualization of the penitential path itself, up to sacred places such as 'the Heavenly stairs' at T'ai San in Shantung or the series of stair flights to the altars atop Mayan stone temples (Fig. 123).[43] This unity of stairs, struggle, and sacredness is concentrated in Rome's Scala Santa (Fig. 124). On their knees, supplicants crawl upward to the crucifix at the top and by this act reveal the very essence of the spirit of the steep stairway.

## SHALLOW STAIRS AND SECULAR EXPRESSION

Shallow stairs are *secular*. With low, widely spaced steps one can 'salire con gravita', says Vincenzo Scamozzi.[44] Widely spaced steps are conducive to a calm and comfortable pace, whereas those in which each tread is relatively narrow to the foot are active and demanding. A broad stairway in which the incline is moderated by widely spaced steps accentuates the slow gliding, ceremonial air of the broad stairs. The shallow, gently sloping stairway is in a way so well arranged that it demands little exertion and is easy and natural. Its content, therefore, signifies the opposite of the steep stairs — struggle is relieved by 'dolcezza'.[45]

## THE ARACOELI AND THE CAMPIDOGLIO STAIRS

It is the slope which creates such a difference of expression in the two stairways up to the Capitoline Hill in Rome (Fig. 125). The flight leading up to

126. The heavy stair. People on their knees (etching from Bergsøe, *Rom under Pius IX*).

127. The stair up to Aracoeli.

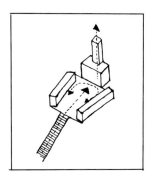

128. The stair up to Il Campidoglio.

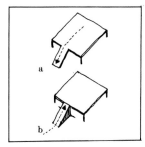

129. The relationship between the interior floor and a stair which is free and a stair which is attached.

St. Maria in Aracoeli (1384) is steep, the other just beside it leading to the Campidoglio is shallow.

In effect, these differences in character are already revealed by the destinations of the stairs. One leads steeply up to the church with its cognomen 'the Heavenly Altar' (Aracoeli), the other ends in the secular centre of Rome.

The Aracoeli stairway is broader than the one up to the Campidoglio. It has, accordingly, a 'slower' tempo than the neighbouring secular stairs. One 'glides' lightly up the Campidoglio stairs; its ramp-like steps are a hardly noticeable variation in the hill itself. This inviting character is also shown in the way the flight follows up the pedestrian's own spatial expansion and from below carves its way right into the plateau of the piazza above (see pp. 85 f).

In sharp contrast, climbing the Aracoeli stairs is a physical self-conquest. Its slow tempo, steep incline, and narrowly indented steps convey a mood of struggle and strength of will. One is subjected to a greater and more powerful dimension than is 'comfortable' in this setting, where the twelve landings that break the course of the stairs into evenly divided sections are scaled to the powerful façade at the top. The landings constitute the stations in a Via Dolorosa sequence which further emphasizes the stairs' meaning. In a stage by stage ascent they reveal the whole *weight* of the movement in contrast to the continuous magnetic flow in the neighbouring ramp (Fig. 126).

At ground level both flights of stairs have the same starting point in the street, Via del Teatro di Marcello. The *goals* at the top, however, are vitally different in form, emphasizing each in its own way, the dissimilar expressive content in the stairs.

Aracoeli's façade rises almost immediately from the lip of the stairs and with its massive brick wall conveys a heavy and closed impression (Fig. 127). It is almost obtrusive in the way it fills the entire space at the top of the stairs. Even the great fluted cornice crowning the building arches out towards the climber. In this sense, the stairs are closely related to the church by being the outlet of this 'thrust' from above. The feeling experienced when coming out of the church confirms this impression. It is as if the congregation is 'emptied' down the stairs. What a contrast this is to standing at the top of the Campidoglio stairs. There one feels the upward movement of those ascending, one 'receives' them.

Nor is the top of the Campidoglio stairs shut off by a solid wall. On the contrary, already at the foot of these stairs one perceives a deep courtyard in front of the tower of the Town Hall at the far end (Fig. 128). The tower serves as the goal of the ascent while the space of the square in front is an invitation to continue moving forwards even after reaching the top. The

130. Barn ramp.

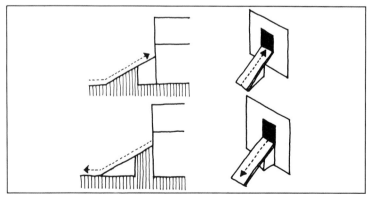

131. The attachment of the barn bridge.

statuary also has the same effect. Both the Dioscuri facing the city on the balustrade and the emperor in the centre suggest a 'place to stop'. In other words, the area is already 'inhabited' and becomes, thereby, a place we too can use — a place which by way of the stairs has encouraged ascent and conquest.

## FIRMLY FIXED AND FREE-STANDING STAIRS

By a firmly *fixed* stairway we mean one in which the whole body rests solidly on the ground in contrast to a *free* stairway, which is released from the ground and stretches over and above it (Fig. 112, 3a, b).

Fixed stairs are like the attached floor and share with it a character of physical unity with the ground which includes the ground's permanent and 'inert' quality (see p. 37). Thus, the stairs may give an impression of the ground itself rising, either by springing up from the ground or by rising with the ground. In any case, these variants are simply nuances of the same basic impression of motion that rises upwards from below and is in principle 'safe' and slow.

This is illustrated by comparing fixed stairs to free-standing stairs. The free stair flight shares the quality of the bridge. It is supreme, active and compels greater speed than the firmly fixed flight. In addition, a free-standing stairway implies another direction than that of its solid counterpart. In principle, it leads from inside to outside. It is as though the interior floor of the house is led down, not as in the case of the solid stairs where the exterior floor is pushed upwards (Fig. 129).

This inside to outside motion in the free-standing stairs is accented in architecture. In Venturi's beach house project, we saw that the entire symmetric disposition of the stairs and house reveal an inside space which unfolds outward (see p. 93 f). The free stairway emphasizes this characteristic. The whole house is raised on stilts; it 'floats' above the ground with the free-standing stair as the only downward contact point. If one imagines the same stair made solid and firmly fixed, the overall impression would be that of an *encounter* between an exterior floor, which, as it rises, leads upwards and a door and interior space which open and empty outwards.

An example of a stairway (actually a ramp) which is both fixed and freestanding is the *barn ramp*.

The lower part is usually built of stone or concrete, the upper part is like a wooden bridge stretching freely over to the entrance (Fig. 130). Speed accelerates gradually on the way up. The climb begins heavily and calmly, gathers momentum as we reach the bridge, where the entire motion tenses and takes off to carry us in a spurt through the barn door. Even the sound is part of this experience. The lower part is the thudding sound of ground,

132. The plateau stair and the Roman temple (Maison Carrée, photo by Fototeca Unione).

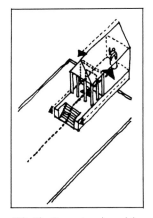

133. The Roman temple and the relationship between inside and outside.

gravel and grass, changing abruptly to a hollow drum-like beat indicating that we have reached the bridge and in doing so have created a spontaneous urge to hurry across and into 'safety'. We may confirm the character of this experience by reversing the process, by freeing the lower part and making the upper part solid (Fig. 131). Now the movement is reversed and accelerates downwards from the solid upper part to the open part below.

## MODELLED STAIRS

In the above paragraphs we have described the importance of breadth, slope, and attachment in the expression of the stairs. The form, however, was the same in all cases. This form is the basic type in all stairs and contains the following qualities: it runs at right angles to the destination, it describes an even diagonal, it is equally broad at top and bottom and has straight steps.

If we assume further that these qualities vary in addition to those already examined, the entire expression of motion will become even more complicated.

Architectural history demonstrates, however, that also when it comes to stair forms there are quite definite archetypes, each of which induces specific ways of ascending. There are six types, which may be grouped according to the motion impulses which they convey. The types that accord with our own directional movement are the *plateau stairs* and *frontal stairs*. The types that resist our advance or seem to come towards us are the *fan stairs* and the *divided stairs*. Two-directional types are the *side stairs* and the *overlapping stairs* (Fig. 112,4a-f).

## PLATEAU STAIRS

Plateau stairs are formed as a solid block into which the stairs are cut (Fig. 112, 4a). The type is well known from classical Antiquity's temple architecture in which the plateau is the raised floor on which the building stands.

The form is a visualization of movement upwards from below. It is as if our own personal space penetrates the block to make way for the ascent.

When one is considering the Roman temple, its form must be understood as a link in a meaningful depiction of overlapping motion between outside and inside (Fig. 132). The Roman temple has been recognized as a directional building. In contrast to the Greek temple, an isolated island within its *temenos,* the Roman temple was meant to be an integrated part of the urban architecture facing the *forum* (Fig. 133). Whereas the Greek temple had a strictly defined interior space, the aim in the Roman temple was to establish contact between inside and outside. Plateau stairs must be seen in this context, one in which they reflect an ascending movement from the lengthy public square up towards the temple.[46] This movement continues

105

134. The front stair up to a Norwegian wooden house (from Brochmann, *Bygget i Norge I*).

136. The fan stair (Chapel in Vitorciano).

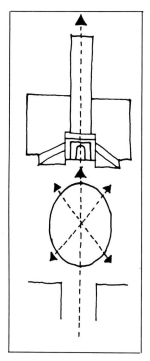

135. Campidoglio: The relationship between the front stair and adjoining space.

at the top as the cella is 'shoved' back to the far end of the platform. Additionally, its deep entrance encourages progress into the space towards the statue at the end.

This inward motion is overlapped by an outward motion found in the column-supported superstructure forming the rest of the temple. In relation to the set-back cella, the gable wall juts forward and, combined with the platform beneath, appears active and prominent. This peculiar quality in Roman temple architecture may have had an ideological meaning. With roots in the Etruscan pattern, the Romans had developed a temple which showed more clearly than did those of the Greeks the interdependence of man and divinity, an interdependence culminating in the deification of the emperor.[47]

## FRONTAL STAIRS

Frontal stairs take the form of a triangle in which two side stair flights lead from opposite directions along the house wall to join in a common landing in front of the entrance (Fig. 112, 4b). It is a typical street stairway adapted to the passing current of movement in the street. It occurs frequently in a monumental version in Norwegian urban wooden architecture (Fig. 134).

This frontal stairway distinctly conveys an impulse to ascend. The reason lies in the triangular form which draws attention to the uppermost point where both flights are joined. The entrance is independent and at a right angle to the stair flights. Clearly, the motion from the entrance plays no part in the form of the stair.

An example of emphasis on the rising qualities of frontal stairs is the double flight in front of Rome's City Hall, facing the Campidoglio. The form was chosen for reasons of space, since a direct flight would have taken up too much of the square. At the same time, however, the frontal stairs convey the impression of an element 'pressed' against the wall by the expanding, rising oval in the floor of the square in front (see p. 85 f) (Fig. 135). In Michelangelo's projected plan from 1544, he intended to introduce a baldachin over the landing at the top. In this way two effects would be achieved. First of all the junction of the two flights would have stood out more clearly. Secondly, the rising quality itself would have been given greater emphasis. The latter is obvious from the way in which the pilaster articulation of the intended baldachin is joined to corresponding pilasters around the niche in the wall beneath. In combination with the main tower immediately above, which also repeats this pattern, an accented vertical effect is achieved. This not only emphasizes the rising quality of the stairs but also repeats the entire ascent to the Campidoglio, the ramp across the square.

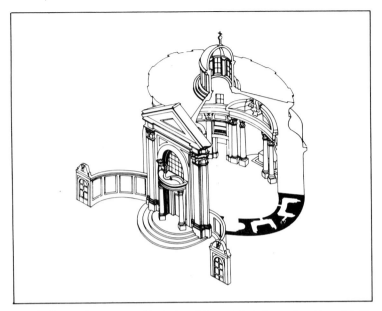

137. The fan stair (axonometric of St. Andrea al Quirinale by L. Bernini, from Norwick (ed.), *Verdensarkitekturen*).

138. The divided stair (Palazzo Farnese in Caprarola by G. Vignola, photo by Anderson).

## FAN STAIRS

The fan stair is formed in the shape of a spreading fan that opens 180 degrees. (Fig. 112, 4c). It occurs sporadically throughout architectural history but perhaps most frequently in high Baroque. Its form is expansive, facing large open spaces and gathering people (Figs. 136, 137).

The form conveys a clearly opposing effect. Its motion is directed dynamically from above as if an interior space is being 'emptied' from the entrance at the top. An accomplished example of the exploitation of the possibilities of fan stairs is the semicircular entrance stairs to St. Andrea al Quirinale by Lorenzo Bernini (1670). The façade is dominated by a huge pediment with a semicircular columned baldachin beneath. This baldachin is directed from inside to outside, as is shown in two ways. In the first place, it appears to be cut out of the wall and 'falls' out of the semicircular window above. At the same time, it is tied to the walls by its powerful cornice, which continues on behind the pilasters and aroünd the oval body of the building.

The stairs repeat the expansiveness of the baldachin's form and appear to spring straight from the entrance beneath. This is the language of the fan stair form, one which is emphasized by the courtyard's concave lines. The courtyard receives, the stairs spring forth, and, by means of this overlapping encounter, inside and outside are tied together.

## DIVIDED STAIRS

As with the frontally attached double stairs described above, the divided stairs are joined together by an upper landing (Fig. 112, 4d). An explicit example is to be found in front of Giacomo Vignola's Palazzo Farnese in Caprarola (1559) (Fig. 138). Here, however, the dominant motion in the flights is reversed as compared to frontally attached stairs. Here both flights seem to expand from the upper level down the one ascending. Two conditions are responsible for this effect. First of all, the form depicts something which is enfolding and receiving. Secondly, the area at the foot of the stairs becomes particularly significant.

We associate spontaneously the two outflung staircases with two 'arms' (see p. 295 the niche motif). This similarity to a meaningful physical gesture affects the preparation to climb the stairs. One seems 'to be grasped' as in a huge embrace.

In addition, Caprarola, with its semicircular stair flights, is a good example of this form's space creating effect *between* the arms. The flights both encircle and flow into a clearly defined oval space, which in itself is a meaningful conclusion to our outward expansion. Vignola has defined this situation by halting forward movement at the accentuated arches placed directly beneath the landing plateau. Our destination, therefore, seems to have been reached already at the lower level and any further movement

141. The divided stair and the fan stair combined (the Paris Opera, main stair by Ch. Garnier, from Dexter (ed.), *The Architecture of the École des Beaux-Arts*).

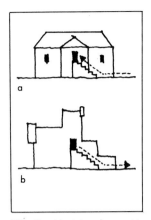

139. The side stair and symmetrical and asymmetrical connections.

upwards is not immediately 'necessary'. This also heightens the descending effect of the stairs. The flights are led downward to fetch us up from a space where we have paused expectantly.

## SIDE STAIRS

Characteristic of the stairs described above is their fundamental symmetry in both form and relation to the entrance. By the side stairway we mean an asymmetric and single flight form (Fig. 112, 4e). The motion expression of the side stairs is, therefore, to a far greater extent than the previous examples, dependent upon its 'setting'.

Essential in deciding the motion effect (whether it accords with or resists our forward motion) is, therefore, whether one of the two levels, top or bottom, is formed after the same asymmetric principle as the stairs (Fig. 139). A single stairway, paralleling the house wall and leading to a door in the centre of a symmetric façade will, in principle, be interpreted as having an ascending movement, in that the exterior is led *up to* an ordered system. In the reverse, the same form placed against an asymmetric façade will have a suppressing effect on this upward motion. The order within the house emerges by way of the asymmetric stairs to 'meet' us.

Typical of the latter is the garden façade of Le Corbusier's Maison Stein in Garches (1927). In contrast to the strict, formal symmetry of the main façade in which the main door's baldachin juts forward almost 'grasping' and drawing the exterior space inside, the freer form of the garden façade with its projecting terrace stairs is an example of an outward expansion of the entire interior space (Fig. 140).[48]

## OVERLAPPING STAIRS

As has been said, the importance of the stairs in expressing the degree of upward or downward motion is also decided by the shape of the steps themselves. In principle, there is no priority of motion either from above or below in stairs with straight steps. Convex steps, however, 'pour' downwards in a flowing mass,[49] whereas concave steps illustrate upward expansion.

We find these three step forms combined in the same flight in the lower part of Charles Garnier's Paris Opera stairs (started in 1862, Fig. 141). The lowest part of the flight, where the stairs are at their broadest, consists of convex steps which moderate upward motion. In the middle part the stair width narrows, the steps straighten and then become concave to assist the upward impulse in the transition to the landing and to further movement on up to each side.

The following example will show how this two-way principle may vary even further both in form and complexity.

140. The side stair and the asymmetrical connection (Villa Stein by Le Corbusier after Le Corbusier, *Oeuvre compléte 1910–65*).

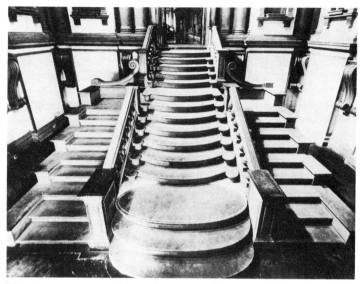

142. An overlapping stair: Biblioteca Laurenziana in Florence (by Michelangelo, from de Tolnay, *Michelangelo*).

The vestibule staircase leading to the *Biblioteca Laurenziana* by Michelangelo (c. 1542) is adapted to two situations. The first is the large library to which it leads and which expands visually outward and down the central flight. The other is our upward movement which is taken care of by the side flights (Fig. 142). The central flight has convex steps and has the same width at the top as the library entrance but widens gradually as it descends. It is as if the inner space pours forth in a great cascade, 'curling' into small waves where it meets the banisters. The centre flight is in a way 'occupied', whereas the side flights with their small steps set into larger ones, by which one penetrates both inwards and upwards, are more inviting to the visitor (see p. 105 f).[50] Slightly more than halfway up, the side flights join the middle flight, but now the opposing aspect of their convexity is overpowered by the increasing view into the library itself.

The volume of the stairs is overdimensioned in relation to the small vestibule. The scale is that of the library and not of the vestibule. This aspect, too, prepares us already beforehand for our encounter with the importance of the interior space.[51]

143 The experiential nature of the wall (photo by R. Crane).

# THE WALL

# WHAT THE WALL DOES

In architecture the main purpose of the wall is to *delimit* a space and to *support* the roof.

Whereas supporting a roof is a particular architectonic and structural problem, delimitation is found not only in landscape forms but also in social behaviour between people. In both cases the wall defines territories, it divides two spaces, each of which has a different content. The built wall shows the actual way in which two diverse areas meet, thus interpreting the *strength relationship* between them. Concerning our main question — the architectural inside-outside relationship — this means the extent to which the wall draws exterior space inside or interior space outside. The wall's architecture, in other words, is a concrete realization of the existential struggle between an 'attacking' exterior and a 'secure' interior and thereby acquires expressive importance (Fig. 143).

What is it in the wall's appearance which conveys a message of the comparative strength of inside and outside space? And, in what way does this strength relationship effect its expression?

116

# THE WALL THEMES

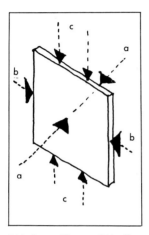

144. External forces which affect the wall: (a) in depth, (b) in breadth and (c) in height.

Strength relationship is understood as the degree of penetration. When we consider a wall that delimits an inside space, it may vary between expressing complete openness, thus inviting us to enter, or complete closure, which rejects us. The background of our reactions to this relationship is again dependent upon the expressions of motion, weight, and substance. In other words, a heavy wall will seem more closed than a light one, a large door stimulates a spontaneous impulse to go through it, whereas the small, low door arrests our movement. Similarly, a 'soft' wooden wall conveys warmth and is inviting as opposed to a rough stone wall which is 'cold' and rejecting.

The expression of penetration is dependent on the relationship between three themes, each of which is a result of the interface between delimited and enveloped space. This interface affects the wall in its *breadth, height,* and *depth*. In other words, the significance of the wall as the mediator between the surrounding spaces lies in the tension between the wall and these surroundings (Fig. 144).

The depth indicates the relation between the spaces *in front of* and *behind* the wall. The height indicates the relation to the spaces *above* and *below,* which are the ground and the roof, and the breadth indicates the relationship to the spaces which meet the corners to the *right* and *left*.

In these encounters with the surroundings, the surface of the wall will achieve completely dissimilar expressions. These expressions vary on a fixed set of archetypes, which are implied by each of the surrounding's three dimensions. In the following, we will briefly examine the themes of breadth and height. Subsequently, we will look in detail at the themes of depth which are directly concerned with the communication between inside and outside.

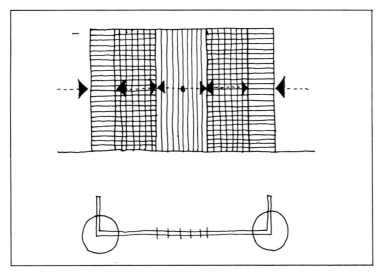

145. The theme of breadth: the vertical tripartition.

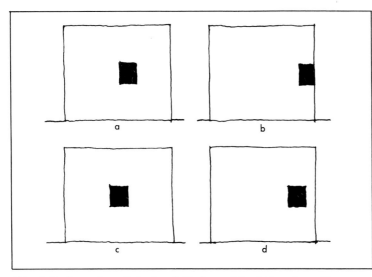

146 a-d. The theme of breadth: the three 'fields of energy', the middle section and the corners: a, b) The window in tension with the fields of energy, c, d) the window in correspondence with the fields of energy.

# THE BREADTH THEME

## THE VERTICAL TRIPARTITION

The *extension* of the wall is linked to the meeting between its own surface and the spaces to the right and left — in other words, the terminations of the wall to each side: its corners. Consequently, the wall's terminations represent separate fields of energy on the surface. These fields decide whether the wall will continue or whether it will stop, and if so, in what way.

But the surface of the wall which is stretched between the corners is also divided into various fields of energy. Our attention to the corners is drawn to each side from a common starting point located centrally on the wall. This means that the effect of the termination in relation to the extension of the wall is read against a central field on the surface where the transitional areas on either side are interpreted as mediators between the corners and the central field (Fig. 145). This phenomenon, which describes a wall's extension as the dynamic relationship between a central field and two peripheral fields, can be called the wall's *vertical tripartition*.

This theme exists as an archetypical reference for the wall's treatment of breadth and can be broken down and strengthened, depending on the desired expression. Every wall surface is comprised by these fields of energy. An example can illustrate this relationship. Windows are located in a straight, white wall (Fig. 146, a-d). In the first example, the window is located just to the side of the centreline of the surface (Fig. 146a). In the other example, the window is located so that its one edge is tangent to one of the corners (Fig. 146b). Both placements involve a tension that can be explained by the fields of energy which attempt to 'press' the windows in other directions. We see that this is correct, if the windows are moved, respectively, to the middle of the surface and a small distance in from the corner (Fig. 146 c and d). Now it is as if the tension is relieved, calm is restored. In the first case, the window corresponds with the centre of the surface; they are no longer at odds. In the second example, the window is moved into the transitional field between the centre and the corner. The corner's field of energy remains in this way untouched and is allowed to exist as an independent element.

### THE EXPRESSION OF THE BREADTH THEME

What is the reason behind our experience of the three energy fields in the surface of the wall?

## SYMMETRY

The theme is by its structure symmetrical. This is a factor that can in itself be the basis for many explanatory models. Symmetry, according to Sven Hesselgren, is an image of fundamental order which we carry with us as a reference for all of our actions.[1] This order emanates from the interface between our body and the force of gravity. We have earlier shown that phenomena such as balance and imbalance play a decisive role in maintaining our existence. We project this over to all of our surroundings, surface not excluded, as a reference for expressions and tensions.

A different and more anthropomorphic explanation takes symmetry to be a sort of image which we recognize from our own bodies. The shoulders terminate and secure our bodily extension, just as the corners of a wall terminate a surface. And the head designates the veritable centrepoint of our bodily structure, at the same time as it is our element of communication, just as the central section of a wall is the central location for the wall's openings between inside and out.

## THE CENTRUM AND CORNERS OF A SPACE

It is likely that these more bodily explanations must be supplemented by a model that is based on man's more general spatial need in relation to what the forms invite us to 'do' (see p. 19 ff) in other words, the relation between our perception of the wall's elementary role as a spatial boundary and our existential need for space and house as something which we can conquer and fathom. The theme of tripartition reflects these needs projected on the delimiting surface of the space. The fact is that the centrum of a space is the place where we experience the essence of the space — the goal of our conquering, while the corners are where the space is given its perceptible form. In other words, the order of the space has a general existential meaning, while the space's form tells us *where* we are and has therefore a more local and concrete meaning. In order to more thoroughly clarify this point, we wish to take a closer look at the centrum and corners of a space one at a time.

## THE CENTRUM OF A SPACE

Man will always seek a place in his surroundings where things achieve their main objective or essence.

What then is the essence of a space? It is its *centrum*. In other words, we first conquer a space when we are inside it. Specifically, this means that we are first in the space when we find ourselves at the midpoint between its corners. This does not necessarily mean its geometric centre. Rather it means that when one finds oneself in the periphery near the space's walls and corners, the space is experienced primarily as another part which lies

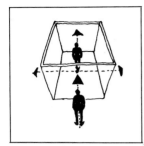

147. The centre of the space: the *goal* for our movements inward and the *starting point* for our movements outward.

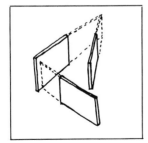

148. The space's corners: free-standing columns act as corners in a space which is defined by invisible walls which span from column to column.

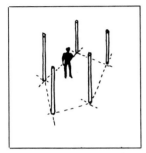

149. The space's corners: free-standing walls are 'extended' thus creating corners which enclose the space.

in front of us, glides past us or comes towards us. It is at the centrum that we command the order of the space, which implies that the egocentric and spatial characteristics of the space converge.

The centrum has an existential dimension, in that the walls — the place where the conflict with the exterior takes place — are approximately equidistant from our person. Confronted with a house or space, an individual will therefore always seek to reach this space by projecting himself into its centrum. At the space's periphery, the space will always remain a 'there' until we at its centrum can perceive it as a 'here'.

But a centrum can also have an opposite role. Specifically, a centrum attains another completely different meaning at the moment it is conquered. After first having been the goal of our spatial perception inward, the centre now becomes the starting point of our expansion outward. At the centrum, the space is our personal space, which we survey and which is the same as our potential space of action."

The centrum of a space is then a place for the space's communication with the surroundings both as a goal for our movement inward and as the starting point for our movement outward (Fig. 147).

## THE CORNERS OF A SPACE

Our relation to a space's centrum has general applicability for all spaces. The conquering of a space's centrum involves the experiencing of a space whether it is based on the point or the line, on repose or motion.

The corners, on the other hand, decide the *form* of the individual spaces. It is the corners or, in other words, the angles between walls which intersect, in addition to how many such corners there are and how large the distance is between them, which dictate whether the space is to enscribe a triangle, a square or rectangle, be polygonal, organic or circular, etc. In this way, the wall which creates the space is a function of the corners. Seen in this light, 'solitary' corners create invisible walls. This is what takes place when we stand in between the masts on a ship or between tree trunks in the forest and sense that we are enclosed as if in a room. We draw invisible boundaries from corner to corner (Fig. 148). But the inverse is also true, in that two wall planes which are located apart from each other are optically extended so that thay meet at the corner and thereby complete the space (Fig. 149).[2]

Thus, corners and walls are mutually dependent on each other for the definition of a space. It is the corners which make the space a figure; it is the corners which tell us *where* we are.

The vertical tripartition, with its various fields of energy, can be explained as a result of the wall's function as a spatial boundary. As a projection of the space in front of or behind the wall, the centre section will be important

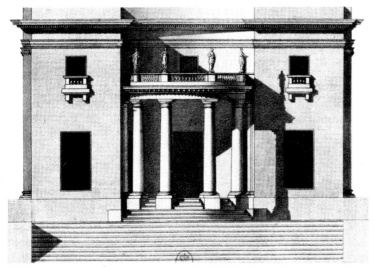

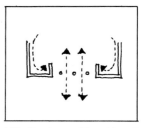

150. The theme of breadth and the relationship between inside and outside: the centre section opens up while the corners close.

151. The theme of breadth and the monumental building (Treasurer's House by Ledoux, after Christ/Schein, *L'Oeuvre et les rêves de Ledoux*).

153. The breadth motif: the largest windows in the centre (facade from Nancy, France).

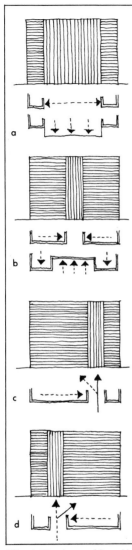

152a-d. The theme of breadth's motifs and their expressions: (a) the breadth motif, (b) the split motif, (c) the right motif, and (d) the left motif.

in terms of accentuating the space's centrum, while the corners on either side have an importance for the delimitation of the space.

Thus, the corner and centre areas have dissimilar meanings. The corners hold the space together. They are the requisite for the space's individuality and 'force of resistance'. The central area, on the other hand, is where the space communicates with its surroundings, i.e. the relationship between inside and outside (Fig. 150).

Thus, the contrast between the corners and the central area as closed and open areas respectively, decides the theme's expression — that which communicates what the wall 'does'. Buildings with façades in which the corners are powerful and the middle section is open, provide then an immediate sense of both *strength* and *publicness*. The corners accentuate and close the interior space, while the centre section mediates and opens a dialogue between interior and exterior spaces. It is therefore common that the theme of breadth is especially emphasized in monumental architecture, such as churches, palaces, city halls and libraries (Fig. 151). These building types have a definite communal role which is expressed by these façades: On the one hand, they are to have open contact with the world, but at the same time, they must stand as a guarantee for the protection and stability of these common values.

## THE MOTIFS OF THE BREADTH THEME

If the theme of breadth is studied further, it can be seen that the tripartition can vary between four fundamentally different motifs. Each motif helps either to accentuate or to weaken the basic meaning of the major expression. We can call these motifs, (a) the *breadth* motif, (b) the *split* motif, (c) the *right* motif, and (d) the *left* motif (Fig. 152 a-d).

In the first two motifs, either the middle section dominates over the corners, or the corners dominate over the middle section. In the two last motifs, the middle section is the same size, but varies between lying to the right and to the left of the surface's centreline.

This means that the expressive nature of the first two motifs is a variation over the theme of opening/closing within the fundamental theme of symmetry, while the expressive nature of the second two motifs is characterized by the dissolution of the theme's symmetry.

### THE BREADTH MOTIF

In the first motif, the middle section dominates (Fig. 152a).

This domination can be accentuated in many ways: The windows in a wall can be larger and greater in number at the centre than at the corners (Fig. 153). The column spacing in a colonnade can be greater at the

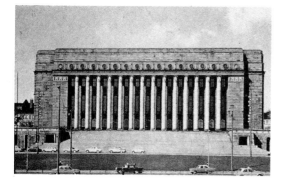

154. The breadth motif: colonnade and corner resolution (Parliament building in Helsinki, Finland by J. S. Sirén).

155. The breadth motif: The projected centre portico (Villa Rotunda by A. Palladio).

156. The split motif: Entry towers (city gate in Lugo).

157. The side motif: Notre Dame du Haut (photo from Bolle-Redat, *Notre Dame du Haut, Ronchamp*).

158. The side motif: villa project from Downing, *The Architecture of Country Houses*).

centre, while they are brought closer together nearer the corners (Figs. 154, 155). A plaster wall can be accentuated with rustication along the edges. Often, the entire middle section is also thrust forward, while the corners are held back (Fig. 155).

This motif emphasizes the public character of a building: the communication between inside and outside is increased. The motif is generous and receptive, the entire building expands outwards either by 'pushing' the corners to the sides, or by springing out in order to meet us.

## THE SPLIT MOTIF

The opposite is true of the split motif. Here, the corners dominate toward the middle, and the open field is pressed together (Fig. 152b).

While the former motif pointed toward openness and expansion, this motif points toward an increasing closure, either by squeezing the middle section together or by pulling it back in relation to the corners.

An example of the first is the city gate into the Spanish city of Lugo (Fig. 156). The powerful, round corner towers, which seem over-dimensioned in relation to the narrow section in the middle, express an almost threatening re-enclosure, which seems to squeeze us together. At other times, the corners can spring forth as protrusions, bay windows or towers in relation to a middle section which lies to the rear. This is the formal language of the castle in which corner towers protrude as active protectors of the castle walls.

## THE SIDE MOTIFS

Common to the next two motifs is that the open middle section is located either to the right or to the left (Figs. 152c, d, 157, 158).

In this way, the corners are also different. The one is strengthend while the other is weakened. Thus, our experience of outside and inside is different from what it is in the symmetrical variant. In the symmetrical façade, we were led into the space's centrum. In the asymmetrical façade, we are led in indirectly. Out of pure impulse, we gravitate toward the strongest corner. Why? Because the strongest most clearly characterizes the interior as a delimited and secure place and thereby makes manifest the intention of our motion inwards. In other words, a localized, subjective centrum is created in relation to this corner, which, in addition to the general midpoint, attracts our attention. An asymmetrical placement between open and closed areas elicits therefore a more private character than does a symmetric placement.

It is obvious that the strength of the accentuated corner, and with it our

159 a-b. The difference between the right and left side: The Sistine Madonna, (a) normal, (b) mirror-image (from Arnheim, *Art and Visual Perception*).

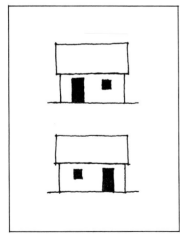

160. The difference between the right and left side: above, 'strongest' to the right, below, balanced.

impression of the interior space itself, varies according to the articulation employed. But in addition, the placement either to the right or to the left of the centre line will, of itself, influence our impression.

We have earlier emphasized the differentiation inherent in the relationship between our right and left sides.[3] Rudolf Arnheim has shown that we project these characteristics onto what we see. That section which corresponds to our right side is immediately understood as being the strongest. An example of this is Heinrich Wöllflin's analysis of the composition of Raphael's Sistine Madonna.[4] He compares the original version with a mirrored image of the painting (Fig. 159 a, b). In the original painting, the composition is balanced in spite of the formal asymmetry which is brought about by the overdimensioning of the papal visage at the lower left. In a mirror image of the painting, the entire composition 'tilts' over to the right. The reason for this is the psychological weighting of the right, to which is added the papal visage.

If we return to the façades, we will see that the movement inward is terminated more 'naturally' if the strongest corner lies to the right rather than to the left (Fig. 160). If it lies to the left, it is as if the visual image is about to re-establish the symmetry, as with the balance in Raphael's painting. It is this differentiation which Kandinsky characterizes by referring to the right side as the direction home *(nach Hause)*, in other words, that which leads to a terminated foundation. On the other hand, the left side is the direction toward the earth *(zur Ferne)* which is the more free, open dimension.[5]

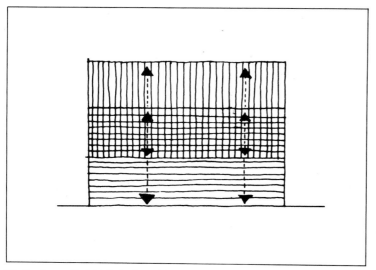

161. The theme of height: the horizontal tripartition.

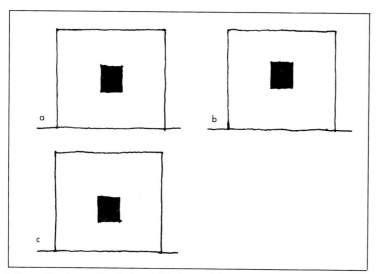

162. a–c. The theme of height: three fields of energy': (a) in tension, (b) rising, (c) sinking.

# THE HEIGHT THEME

## THE HORIZONTAL TRIPARTITION

We have seen that a wall's theme of breadth deals with spaces to either side of a centre. The theme is concerned with the wall's expanse. The *theme of height* reflects the wall's relationship to *up* and *down*. This involves the meeting between the wall and the earth and between the wall and the sky. In architecture, this is the same as the meeting between the floor and the roof (Fig. 161). Again, we can divide the wall into three fields of energy: the upper field belongs to the roof, the lower field belongs to the floor, and the middle field mediates the transition between these two. This theme is referred to by Goethe as architecture's 'three original concepts', specifically, 'the base, the column (including the wall), and the roof'.[6] We shall refer to this as the wall's *horizontal tripartition*.

If we imagine these fields to be of exactly the same size, they would nonetheless express different motion tendencies within the whole. While the upper field tends to seem lighter and to rise *upward,* the lower field tends to seem heavier and to sink *downward.* In the middle field, the tension between these tendencies is interpreted. Thus, it is the middle field which 'decides' whether the wall's character as a whole is to be dominated by the upper or lower field, and whether they are to be linked or separated.

Again, a simple example can illustrate just how an element in the wall can be influenced by these motion tendencies relative to which field they are located. Again we consider a window set in a vertical, white wall.

In the first instance, the window is located in the middle of the wall, in the second, just under the central section, and in the third, just over the central section (Fig. 162 a-c). In the first example, the window is in a sort of ambiguous in-between situation: the upper and lower fields are the same size. In the second instance, the window is about to sink; it is being pulled toward the ground. In the third example, the window is about to free itself from the ground and rise upward.

In addition, we see that the window creates motions in the wall itself, in that the window heightens the meaning of the middle field as the interpretive field of energy. The ambiguity in the first instance is due to the fact that none of the tendencies, either in the upper or lower fields, achieve dominance. In the second instance, the window draws the entire upper field down with itself, it becomes 'heavier', while the lower field is pressed yet more compactly together. An impression is formed that not only the

166. The rising motif in a gable: City Hall in Greifwald, (from Pothorn, *Das Grosse Buch der Baustile*).

*167. The rising motif in a surface (Palazzo Medici by Michelozzo, from Koepf, Baukunst in Fünf Jahrtausenden).*

168. The rising motif as expressed in a plastic form (Main Libary in Vienna by Fischer v. Erlach Jr., from Koepf, *Baukunst in Fünf Jahrtausenden*).

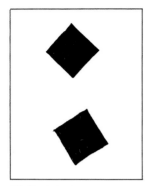

163. The balancing square.

164. The corrected square.

window but the entire wall seems to weigh downward. The opposite takes place in the third example, in which the lower field rises up together with the window, which in turn makes the upper section yet more narrow and thereby 'lighter'.

## THE EXPRESSION OF THE HEIGHT THEME

What is the cause of these experiences, and why are the three fields perceived dissimilarly in terms of their motion tendencies? We have all experienced the difference between up and down — down is the direction of the ground and the earth, up is the direction of the sky and air. The force of gravity teaches us what this implies; up is light and free, down is heavy and bound. Therefore, the wall that links these realities takes on a differentiated life, influenced by which of the two realms it is to meet.

Now, it seems that form can give two opposite motion impressions. The one tends downward, a result of the actual pull towards the earth which gravity exercises. The other tends upward and results as a purely experientially-defined contrast to the pull of gravity. We will attempt to describe these two motion impressions individually.

## GRAVITY AND MOTION FROM ABOVE DOWNWARD

Physically speaking, the ground draws all things to itself. A wall's own weight is greatest toward the bottom and decreases upward. Its role as the bearer of the roof follows the same laws. It leads the weight of the roof downward. Also in terms of foundation, a free-standing wall must be tied into the ground in order to stand.

It is these measurable and empirical laws which explain why the tension in a figure on a surface always refers to a *downward* reality (Fig. 163). This downward reality, the ground on which we walk, is a requisite for our daily reality. A vertical rhombus which is shown alone in a composition seems to balance on a point: the point is the only contact that the form has with the ground — the invisible reference for the entire expression of balance. If the rhombus is positioned at an angle, it immediately seems out of balance: it is about to fall to the ground.

This pull towards the earth also explains why a square has to be made a bit taller than it is wide if it is to appear as an accurate square (Fig. 164).[7] This addition of height is necessary in order to counteract a flattening out of the form which will arise due to the impression of downward force. A form which follows this tendency, for example a horizontally oriented rectangle, will seem bound to the earth and at rest.

## THE EXPERIENCE AND MOTION FROM BELOW UPWARD

Forms which objectively speaking sink towards the earth will in this manner seem to be fighting against this pull by giving us the impression that they do not sink, but rather rise up from the ground (see p. 75 f). The tendency is experientially rather than physically determined. Vernon Lee offers the following description in an analysis of 'the rising of the mountain'.[8]

> What we are transferring…from ourselves to the looked at shape of the mountain, is not merely the thought of the rising which is really being done by us at that moment, but the thought and emotion, the *idea of rising* as such, which had been accumulating in our mind long before we even came into the presence of that particular mountain.[8]

If we return to the wall, we will see the same tendency there. There are especially three conditions which determine such an impression. The first is the wall's function as the support for itself and the roof. The wall lifts both itself and the roof, it holds itself up by rising from the ground in order to carry the roof.

The second condition is related to the fact that the upper section of the wall approaches the sky. The sky, as opposed to the ground which binds, is the infinite space which opens. The sky is for our experience freedom's space, as opposed to the earth to which we are bound by gravity.

The third condition, which defines the expression of ascent, is existentially determined and involves a shared experience which has to do with all of the forms in our surroundings with which we identify ourselves. This is based on experiences which suggest that in order to live, we must defy gravity daily. Gravity will always draw objects and ourselves down, representing in the extreme an annihilation of existence. That something stands up against this force by rising up is therefore synonymous with survival — and survival implies freedom from the earth. A vertical wall which is higher than it is wide has therefore a completely different character to that of a horizontal wall: it is the manifestation of the rising — it is victorious and free.

## THE MOTIFS OF THE HEIGHT THEME

The described relation between the upper and lower parts of a wall as the lighter and heavier, respectively, is the canon for the experience of the wall's vertical expression. In this light, this impression is also involved in establishing the experience or the relation between inside and outside.

However, the theme of tripartition can be interpreted in many ways. Four

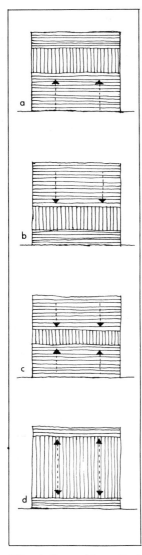

165 a-d. Theme of the motifs of height and their expressions: (a) the rising motif, (b) the sinking motif, (c) the split motif, (d) the opening motif.

motifs can be seen as dissimilar in principle. We can refer to these as (a) the *rising* motif, (b) the *sinking* motif, (c) the *split* motif and (d) the *opening* motif (Fig. 165 a-d).

In the first two motifs, the middle field is of a constant size and domination.[9] The difference between the motifs comes about as a result of the middle section being moved either above or below the wall's centreline. The next two motifs come about as result of the variation of the middle section's width, while its placement in the middle of the wall remains the same.

## THE RISING MOTIF

In the rising motif, the middle field is pushed upward in relation to the wall's centreline. In this way, the lower field becomes the largest, the upper the most narrow, while the middle section has an in-between size. Read from above, we see that the weight increases as we approach the ground, completely in line with our experience of gravity. But read from below, we see that the surface lightens towards the top, the form rises from the ground. The expression of the rising motif lies in these two contrasting motions. A wall that rises up seems well anchored and heavy, while at the same time upright and free. It gives the observer an impression of both secure solidity and proud stature (Figs. 165 a, 166).

The Palazzo Medici in Florence (1444) is a classic example of the use of the rising motif (Fig. 167). The façade is divided into three storeys. The ground level has been given a closed and heavy character with large coarse rustication. Above, the wall has been made progressively lighter from simple stone outlines on the middle storey to a finer plaster surfacing on the upper. In addition, the windows are fewer and more simple on the ground level and are given a richer character on the upper floors.

We can see that the rising motif also presents possibilities for penetration in that the upper part is open while the lower is heavy and closed. This means that the part of the wall which meets us on ground level stops us, while the upper sections belong to the interior spaces that in this manner open outward. Solidity and pride can therefore be traced to the wall's own variation between solid and void: solidity because the lower sections make it difficult for us to penetrate, and pride because the interior spaces are elevated and open themselves outward 'from the heights'.

Typical examples of such an effect are the palaces of the Baroque after Bernini (Fig. 168). The floor is often made of massive stone, which makes the building unaccessible and heavy. The residential floors above, on the other hand, are dissolved in large windows and often joined by high columnar orders. Therefore, the character is proud and upright with the princely chambers as towering symbols of the importance of the residents.

169. The sinking motif (Norwegian folk architecture).

170 The sinking motif Palazzo Massimo alle Colonne in Rome by B. Peruzzi).

171. The sinking motif (Kunstnernes hus in Oslo by G. Blakstad & H. Munthe-Kaas).

172. The split motif (Project for Yahara Boat Club by Frank Lloyd Wright, from Kaufmann & Raeburn (eds.), *Frank Lloyd Wright, Writings and Buildings*).

## THE SINKING MOTIF

The sinking motif represents the opposite of the rising motif. The middle field is now drawn below the wall's centreline so that the section above becomes the largest, while the lower section becomes the most narrow. The result is a sinking wall: both because the upper field pushes downward with its weight, and because the narrow bottom field will be perceived either as a base which is being pressed together against the ground, or as a base which is about to sink into the ground (Figs. 165b, 169).

This threat in the sinking motif is consciously emphasized in certain buildings. A typical example is Baldassare Peruzzi's façade for Palazzo Massimi in Rome (1535) (Fig. 170). The rules for Classical bearing have been broken. Instead of letting the columns rise freely over a heavy base, now it is the columns which have been bound and pressed downward by a high and heavy wall above. Another example whose character lies in the tension between pressure and resistance, is the Artist's House in Oslo, by G. Blakstad & H. Munthe-Kaas (1930) (Fig. 171). The building is dominated by a block-like top section with a brick fascia. This rests on white pillars which hold up a large baldachin which runs the entire length of the building. The baldachin tips effortlessly upward in contrast to the weight of the top which sinks downward.

## THE SPLIT MOTIF

As opposed to the rising and sinking in which the middle field has a constant size and a varying position, the split and opening motifs are varied by the changing size of the middle field, while its positioning remains the same.

In the case of the split motif, the middle section is made narrow in relation to the upper and lower fields which both become large and dominating. The result is a middle section which seems to be pressed from both above and below in that the lower field seems to rise, while the upper field seems to sink (Fig. 165c). In the extreme, then, the effect can be both crowded and threatening. Crowded because the middle field separates contrasting forces, and threatening because the split appears to be on the verge of 'snapping' together at any time.

The split motif results in a closed façade. Such a wall terminates the motion at the ground level, while the upper wall sinks and closes. Two examples of the split motif can be mentioned. Many of Frank Lloyd Wright's buildings have narrow, horizontal strip windows between downward sloping roofs and high wall planes (Fig. 172). In this manner, the interior is expressed as being on the verge of enclosure: It is as if the energy from within

173. The split motif (sports complex in Oslo).

174. The opening motif (entrance to the University of Oslo by Chr. H. Grosch).
175. The opening motif (detail from the entrance the University of Oslo).

is 'threatened' by two opposing forces which give the entire relationship between inside and outside an unresolved tension.

Another example in the spirit of Wright is a brick entry motif which leads into a sports hall in Oslo (Fig. 173). Here too the middle section is comprised of a narrow band of windows. The main form is long and low, with a heavy character. The heaviness is further accentuated by the rustication of the lower section. The pressure from above is also emphasized, in that the windows seem to be forced down into the rustication. The door, which is located in the middle of the surface, acts as a contrast to the closed nature in the rest of the wall. As a whole, it is an expressive image of the solid/void dialogue.

## THE OPENING MOTIF

In the opening motif, the middle section is broadened and made more dominating in relation to the narrow fields above and below. The result is a wall that seems to expand at the middle by rising and pressing the upper field further upward, while at the same time it pushes the lower field further downward. The expression is both rising and proud, but also opening and accessible for our penetration at the ground level (Fig. 165 d).

Two examples can be mentioned. The opening motif is often consciously used in Classical architecture as an entrance or façade motif. The University of Oslo, designed by Chr. H. Grosch in cooperation with Karl Friedrich Schinkel (1854), is dominated by the large temple front, its pediment borne by four Ionic columns (Figs. 174, 175). The columns rest heavily on a low compressed stair and rise up powerfully toward the roof with its ascending tympanum. The façade appears appropriately triumphal and upright.[10] But it also seems receptive and open, as a public entrance must.

The opening motif can also be interpreted as splitting. A typical example is Giulio Romano's house in Mantova (1544) (Fig. 176). In line with Mannerism's taste for contrast, the entire façade expresses a struggle between ascent and descent. The descent of the lower storey is revealed in two ways: firstly, the square windows are located below the centreline of the base's surface, and secondly, the cellar windows seem like lowered full-size windows.

The rising character of the upper field is a result of the roof appearing as if it is about to be lifted off the wall below. This comes about through the interpretation of the frieze in the entablature as something non-bearing and open: The static reality of the field is reinterpreted by means of its garlands and round attic windows. Instead of resting heavily on the wall below, the roof is on the verge of floating overhead because the entablature is split in two. This conflict between ascent and descent is repeated in the architec-

176. The opening motif (Romano House in Mantova by G. Romano).

ture of the entire middle field. The field is divided by a row of high arches. Inside each arch are smaller windows, which are notably lower than the height of the arch. In this fashion, the arches rise in relation to the windows which sink: put another way, two motions in the same surface which make preparations for that which is above and below respectively.

# THE DEPTH THEME

Wall-form expressions may seem infinite, stretching from main, overall forms and their divisions right down to details such as texture and structure. Equally varied are the ways in which the inside-outside relationship is experienced. From this we understand that these experiences regarding both the walls' breadth and height are dependent on how they are built in relation to such categories. For instance, the expressiveness of the city gate of Lugo (Fig. 156) as an example of the split motif, was dependent on the relation between main form (convexity), building system (massiveness), and material (blocks of stones). The same was true of the rising motif, which was exemplified by baroque palaces (Fig. 168) in which the expressiveness was dependent on the contrast between two building systems, i.e. the massive system of the ground floor and skeleton system of the top floors.

In the following study of the *depth theme* we will examine these categories in order to explain the expressiveness of the relationship between the spaces in front of and behind the wall. The categories will be divided into four themes: (1) the main form, (2) the building system, (3) the openings and (4) the articulation (Fig. 177, a-d). Each theme represents a principal set of motifs and variations representing the archetypes of the wall.

The first group deals with the wall's *main form* (Fig. 177, a). This means how conditions such as height and width, slanting and curving influence the impression of the relative strength between inside and outside.

The second group covers *building systems* and deals with how wall forms are constructed (Fig. 177, b). Is the wall built as a solid slab, as a composite skeleton, or as a combination of both? Moreover, how will these systems affect our impression of the transition between inside and outside?

The third group concerns the *openings* (Fig. 177, c). Here we must differentiate between two types of openings, *door* and *window,* each of which affects our impression of the inside-outside relation differently. Both door and window are perceived as holes in the wall. Their effect, however, depends upon the form and profile of the hole, the location of the door or window area, and the frame around the hole (Fig. 177, d).

The fourth group, *articulation,* affects all three previous groups and concerns the importance of dimensions, the way in which various parts are joined together, the division of the wall, as well as texture and colours. In the following we shall begin by describing the expressions of motion, weight and substance conveyed in the main wall forms and continue with

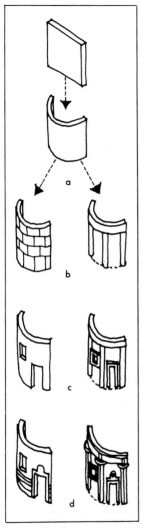

177 a-d. The themes of the wall: (a) main form, (b) construction system (massive-skeleton), (c) openings (doors — windows), (d) articulation, (dimensions — connections — divisions — textures — colours).

the wall's building systems. In connection with the latter, we shall cover the impression given by the use of various types of articulation. The wall's main form and its building system are to be seen as a 'background' for the openings. These consist of windows and doors, which will be the last group we shall examine, and these too will be seen in relation to various types of articulation.

141

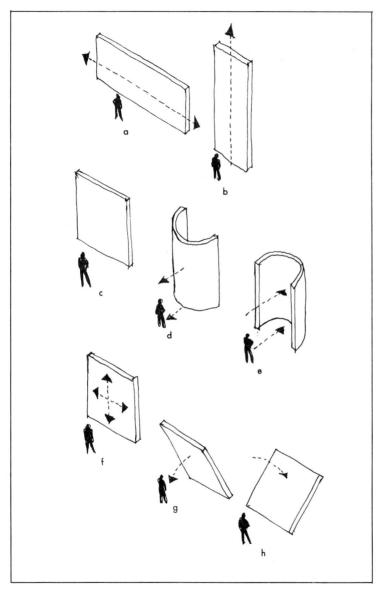

178 a-h. The main forms of the wall: (a) horizontal, (b) vertical, (c) flat, (d) convex, (e) concave, (f) straight, (g) leaning toward, (h) leaning away.

# MAIN FORMS

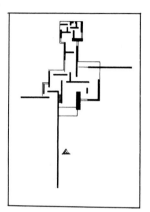

179. The horizontal wall and the motion alongside.

A wall area, in principle, may be formed within eight different motifs (Fig. 178, a-h).

The first two are concerned with the relation between width and height, in that the wall's main form is either *horizontal* or *vertical*. The next three motifs deal with the relation to depth, which covers the *flat*, the *convex*, and the *concave* main forms. The final three motifs deal with the slant of the wall, which means that it may be *upright*, lean *toward us* or *away from us*.

All eight motifs are first and foremost actual representations of fundamental motion situations, which we may characterize by using prepositions and words specifying directions. The first two describe a 'follow along' and an 'upward' motion respectively. The next three convey a 'halting', 'advancing' and 'retreating' motion. The last three depict a 'neutral' motion, a 'tilting away' and 'downward' motion, and a 'leaning towards' and 'over' motion. Assuming that we stand in approximately the same position in front of the walls, they will arouse motion impulses corresponding to these terms, which in turn create highly different impressions of the inside-outside relationship in depth. These, added to definite weight impressions and associated with corresponding environmental forms, will convey a specific overall expression for each of the eight wall forms.

## THE HORIZONTAL WALL

The horizontal wall expresses *weight* against the ground. Its horizontality gives a compressed and compact first impression. It will, therefore, have a basically closed and delimiting character (Fig. 178, a).

The motion impulses aroused by this wall type will also increase its closed character. Because it stretches out horizontally the impulse is to follow *along* beside it in either direction. This phenomenon might be compared to a street that defines a space and as it stretches away before us entices us to follow along with it (Fig. 179). Such a space conveys no urge to pause, to turn and enter. A horizontal wall is, therefore, actually an obstacle, because the interior it hides is not our concern. It does not penetrate the wall to make its presence known but is led past us.

A directional space invites us to enter through the ends. For this reason too, our attention will be drawn to either side as if seeking an entrance 'around the corner', which is where the interior will meet us.

180. Horizontal and vertical walls in combination: the horizontal is 'closed', the vertical is 'open' (project for a villa by E. V. Langlet, from Nordin, *Träbyggande under 1800-talet*).

181. The vertical wall and the vertical space (Medieval house from Amsterdam).

# THE VERTICAL WALL

Whereas the horizontal wall rejects and shuts out, rather like the invisible wall between two passing strangers, the *vertical* wall is communicative. There are three main reasons for this.

The first is its weight expression. The horizontal wall weighs down upon the ground and shuts off, whereas the vertical will always seem lighter because of its rising effect. This wall seems to lift itself upwards and open up vertically.

The second reason is the motion expressed in the vertical wall. The wall itself illustrates the vertical, which marks point and line. Whereas the horizontal wall spreads movements, the vertical rising wall collects them (Fig. 178, b). The horizontal wall draws attention to the corners at each end, while the rising wall concentrates attention around the centre of the area. And, the centre in an area is the 'open' part, the place which communicates with the surroundings. Throughout architectural history we find many examples of the exploitation of characteristic differences in vertically and horizontally oriented walls. The Swedish architect, E.V. Langlet's theories from 1867 are typical in this respect and are revealed in several contemporary houses.[11] In most of them the vertical wall is also the open wall. It is here the main entrance is to be found and here stairs, verandas and balconies are concentrated (Fig. 180). The horizontal side wings, on the other hand, are more compact and inaccessible with fewer windows and larger areas of solid wall. Here the more private and closed off spaces are situated.

The third main reason for the vertical wall's communicative content is that, like a tower, such a wall is the image of the erect, standing figure. Not only does it attract our attention but also corresponds to certain anthropomorphic conceptions of 'great men'. Just like two people who stand talking, the vertical wall concerns us directly and personally either as something threatening or conversational. The first may often be the case with tall houses in an open landscape. Like some dominating landmark they are the focus of all attention, whereas horizontal rows of houses will direct our attention on past and away.

# THE FLAT WALL

The flat wall tells us nothing about the inside-outside relationship. It merely closes off (Fig. 178, c). A stiff and impassive plane, it is like neutral theatre backdrop where activities take place both in front and behind. It is just like a projection screen, according to the Norwegian architect Kjell Lund, and may be compared to drawings on white paper where: 'the drawings and

182. The convex wall (NAF Building in Oslo by F.S. Platou).

183. The concave wall (Baroque palace in Munich by J. K. Schlaun).

146

the paper constitute a whole — the black gives value to the white and the white gives value to the black'.[12]

By itself, the flat wall is just a background. In order to express itself, it is dependent on how the surface is treated and the openings are placed (Fig. 181).

The flat wall in which stress and counter-stress are in balance is, therefore, a typical man-made product, maintains Hugo Häring. The curved wall, on the other hand, is related to nature itself.[13] In what he says, Häring emphasizes the essence of what we *see* in nature's own formations — in the mountain, in plant life, and in the human body. The curve constitutes the sum of counteracting forces in the life process itself. The convex curve restrains the dominance of forces from within, while the concave curve receives the dominating forces from without.

## THE CONVEX WALL

When facing a convex wall one visualizes the interior space behind it as strong and dominating. This impression is conveyed either in the form of an expanding movement toward us or as an enfolding movement protecting the interior space from us (Fig. 178, d).

In the first case, we feel as if the interior space itself resists our approach. We are kept at a distance, stopped by the interior's own force.

An example of this effect is found in the large curved façade of the Norwegian Automobile Association in Oslo by F.S. Platou (1974) (Fig. 182). It is a corner building at the end of a wide street. Thus, the convex façade has a double effect, because the curve is not only a projecting goal for the street but also 'splits' the course of the street. Let us imagine ourselves walking along beside it. There is a feeling of being led by the form itself. The wall guides us around the corner, we say, and thereby indicates that the movement is not our own volition. This experience might be compared to the difference there is in moving around *amongst* the undulating walls of Reima Pietilä's student residence (1967) and in following *along* beside them on the outside. In the first case the walls seem to fit us like a glove. It is we and our own movements which generate the flowing motions of the space. Outside, on the other hand, our movements seem to be guided by the inside space itself, which has dictated the form along which we are following.

The convex form, in other words, seems always to be filled with something. 'Convexity tends to win out over concavity', according to E. Rubin.[14] Arnheim maintains that, like children, we perceive the convex as a solid and concrete thing. In contrast the concave is perceived more as a background for things.[15]

Consequently, the strength indicated by convexity corresponds to the

184. The wall as an embracing form (project for Piazza St. Pietro, Rome, in the shape of extended arms, from Hausmann, *Baukunst des Barock*).

form's own substance. In this manner, the convex surface of a stone represents the delimitation of that inner weight which is the nature of stone. Similarly, the curve of a tree trunk, a muscle or a column, will display the essence of its form — for the tree, sap, for the muscle, blood, and for the column, an inner cohesive core providing structural integrity. Therefore, a convex wall will be characterized not only by an outward expansion but also by an inward-looking concentration.

## THE CONCAVE WALL

When we face a concave wall, the feeling is one of being received, the interior space seems to yield to our forward movement (see p. 105 f). As a consequence, the wall is a visualization of two expressions: the embracing and receiving, and the yielding and pliant (Figs. 178e, 183).

A person receiving us with open arms represents friendliness and security. Arms are clasped in order to hold one firmly and to give nearness and protection (Fig. 184). The cave is a space conveying a similar feeling. The harbour too is one of nature's forms which depicts the protective aspect of the concave curve. The harbour is a haven of safety in stormy weather giving security by its very form. 'The harbour in fact, represents one of the most commonplace types and in many languages the word 'harbour' is synonymous with safety and belonging'.[16] In this sense, the concave wall expresses benevolent expansiveness — an outgoing gesture *from the inside*.

But as stated above, concavity also depicts an inward penetration *from the outside*. Again the cave is a symbol of this. Its form may be interpreted as the result of an outside force — the solid mountain has yielded to a blow from without.

Seen in this way, the grotto with its spring is deeply meaningful as a symbol of concavity's duality (Fig. 185). The cave-like form of the grotto reflects an intrusion whereas the water trickling forth is what this form 'gives' from within.

A combination of the convex and concave wall results in the broken or *undulating* wall. The undulating wall acts in its own particular way, in which the heavier and lighter parts balance each other in a continuous motion *along* the wall. This curving expanse reflects both interior and exterior space but is at the same time independent of both, because neither gets the upper hand and breaks through. As with the water's surface, where each movement immediately exacts its counter-movement, the undulating wall keeps a dynamic balance between inside and outside.

Sigfried Giedion emphasized the undulating wall as one of architecture's basic features or 'constituent facts'.[17] It dominated the Baroque, a typical sign of that period's sense of a continuous spatial treatment. But, it is also

149

185. The grotto as a receptive and giving form (Fontana del Prigione in Rome, from Morton, *Waters of Rome*).

186. The undulating wall and the continuity along the surface (Finnish pavilion in New York by A. Aalto, from Joedicke, *Geschichte der Modernen, Architektur*).

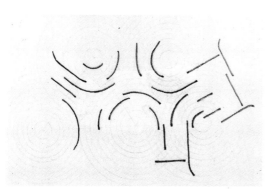

187. The undulating wall as a divided surface (Casa Andreis by Portoghesi/Gigliotti, from Norberg-Schulz, *Existence, Space and Architecture*).

188. The forward leaning wall (folk architecture, from Cornell, *Byggnadstekniken*).

used frequently in modern architecture, as seen in many of Alvar Aalto's buildings (Fig. 186). His Finnish pavillion at the New York World's Fair (1939) is a good example of the use of the undulating wall's qualities.

> An inclined wooden screen three stories high embraces the interior space in a freely drawn curve. The screen consists of three sections, each cantilevered over the other; at the same time the whole structure leans forward, intensifying thereby the impression of continuous movement.[18]

Another variation of the undulating wall is to be found in the architecture of Paolo Portoghesi and Vittorio Gigliotti. Here, as a rule, the walls are interpreted as divided waves, with continuity assured by concave segments and arches with intervening open slits for doors and windows (Fig. 187). The result is an interior which presses forth between inwardly curving sections. In an expansive sense the interior is opened towards the outside. The inside-outside relationship, however, is not so uncomplicated as it was with the directional wall planes of the 1920s in which the overlapping of exterior and interior space was free and in equilibrium (Fig. 179). Portoghesi and Gigliotti restrain the exterior space. Tense curves simultaneously affirm and deny the impact of the surroundings. So, concavity is a necessary corrective to openness. Space is directed outward, but at the same time the walls protect against any inward movement. Hence, the walls' function as a delimiting element is emphasized, but without expressing rejection, because within each concave form there is a receptive and pliant gesture of 'welcome' to the surrounding environment.

## THE SLANTING WALL

The vertical wall, just like the flat wall, balances between contrary motion tendencies. Thus, a wall section still upright, but which we know is about to fall, will convey an insecure, tense feeling. Will the wall fall our way and destroy us or the other way and we are 'saved'? In these two intuitive reactions we find the expressions of the slan0ed wall's two basic variants (Fig. 178 g, h).

A wall that seems to tilt over us is *threatening* (Figs. 178g, 188). This sensation may be illustrated by the way people react to the leaning tower of Pisa (1174). Visitors very seldom pause immediately beneath the leaning side. They feel safe only when at a certain distance and preferably on the opposite side of the tilt. The wall that leans out over us is, therefore, seldom found in architecture. A well-known example, nevertheless, is Alvar/Aalto's exhibition wall from the New York World's Fair (see over) (Fig. 186). There the form's boldness results from the way in which it leans out over the floor. With this solution Aalto exploited an ever-present technical problem in all

151

exhibition architecture. Now all photographs could be clearly seen from below. He used this solution to create an expressive architecture in which the threatening aspect was converted to one of tense excitement. Imagine a corresponding wall but flat in form without curves and horizontal divisions; we would feel ourselves to be in an uncomfortable and dangerous space. Aalto, however, by using a few simple effects transformed this basic impression. First the curves: they accentuate motions around us and *alongside* us and moderate the falling aspect by breaking it up. So, the sections: these divide the wall into three broad bands and thereby lighten the whole. This is further developed by the way the sections are composed of vertical struts against a pale background, which makes the whole seem to float above the floor. This last aspect is accentuated in that the wall stands all of three metres above the ground without visible supports or columns.

A wall leaning over us obviously threatens the space where we stand. On the other hand, the wall that tilts away from us no longer concerns us but threatens whatever is within the space on the other side (Fig. 178, h). Its expression, however, is completely dependent upon its articulation. It may be formed in such a way that it is perceived as a heavy, massive form, such as we find in sloping stone bastions from the Renaissance (Fig. 189). Or, it may have a planar character like that of the shed roof (p. 365 ff). In both cases the form indicates a *closed* interior space. In the first case owing to the compact and inaccessible nature of the interior, the wall denies 'penetration' and encourages 'scaling'. In the second case, the effect is that of a pitched roof which extends to the ground, thereby 'turning its back' on the exterior space (see p. 369 f).

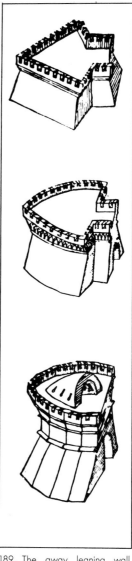

189. The away leaning wall (Renaissance fortress, from Giedion, *Space, Time and Architecture*).

152

# BUILDING SYSTEMS: MASSIVE SYSTEM, SKELETON SYSTEM, INFILL SYSTEM AND LAYER SYSTEM

The wall's main form is affected by various building systems. The expression of motion, weight, and substance in these systems can transform the impact of the main form.

By the term *building system,* we mean how the wall indicates the way in which it is built. In this context there are four motifs which predominate (Fig. 190, a-d):

(a) the massive system
(b) the skeleton system
(c) the infill system
(d) the layer system

In the *massive system,* the wall is built as a solid whole. This signifies that it is a compact mass from outer to inner surface and that all its parts are of equal value. In principle, there are two ways of building a massive wall. It may be formed as a solid mass (*the moulded wall*) or built of individual blocks laid one upon the other (*the masonry wall*). Equal distribution means that the structural capacity, both in terms of its own weight and that of the roof, is evenly spread throughout the whole of the wall.

In the *skeleton system* the wall is divided into separate units, each having a different role in transmitting vertical load. The basic unit of this system is a frame in which the lintel (the supported element) rest on two posts (the supporting element). In this system, therefore, support is guided in specific paths leaving the remainder of the area open.

In the *infill system* the supporting element is the frame. This system requires a main, primary skeleton to support the roof, while the opening is covered by a secondary wall, which may be either massive or skeletal. An infill wall presupposes that the secondary wall is subject to the main skeleton and that both are roughly on the same plane.

The *layer system* is composed of wall sections, juxtaposed in depth. Support may be carried out by either the front or rear sections or all sections together. There are four main variations in this system. If the wall has only two sections, one variant is plane behind plane, another is skeleton behind skeleton. The next two variations consist of a combination of skeleton and plane. In one, the skeleton is in front of the plane and in the other it is behind it.

The massive and skeletal systems are simple and unmixed, whereas infill

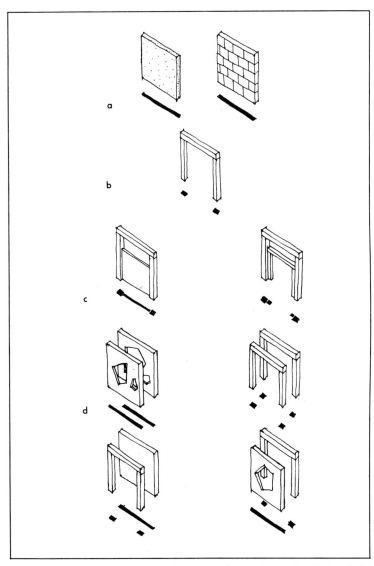

190 a-d.  The wall's constructive system: (a) planar-wall system (cast wall — block wall), (b) skeletal system, (c) infill system (planar element in the skeleton — skeleton in the skeleton), (d) layer system (planar element in front of planar element — skeleton in front of skeleton — skeleton in front of planar element — planar element in front of skeleton).

and layer systems are combinations of the first two. In the inside-outside relationship this means first of all that all variations of the system are dependent upon the fundamental expression to be found in the massive system and in the skeletal system respectively. In the impression given by the infill and layer system there is the added factor of the way in which the elements are combined.

We shall see that the differences in expression between the massive and skeletal systems are determined by differences in support, which means that the relation between exterior and interior strength is affected by the systems' vertical *expression of weight*. As for the infill and layer systems, there is, in addition, an *expression of motion* in depth as the eye is led inwards in different ways depending on the relationship between the layers.

In the following we shall first examine the infill and the layer systems in order to show how important their motion expressions are for the inside-outside relationship. Thereafter, emphasis will be on the massive and skeletal systems in order to find out how their expressions of weight affect our impression of the wall's enclosure.

Following that we shall weigh the importance of *articulation* for these qualities: first in relation to the elements in the massive system and subsequently to those in the skeletal system.

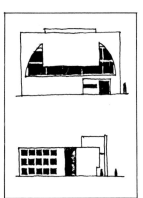

194. Plane in front of plane (Kresge College by Ch. Moore, photo by M. Baer).

195. Skeleton in front of skeleton (Piazza d'Italia by Ch. Moore, from *A.D. 5/6*, 1980).

193. Plane in front of plane (project for a city hall in an Ohio city by R. Venturi, after Venturi, *Complexity and Contradiction in Architecture*).

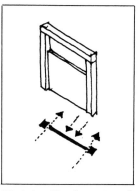

196. Skeleton in front of skeleton (Romanesque wall system, from Koepf, *Baukunst in Fünf Jahrtausenden*).

191. In the infill wall, exterior wall meets the interior wall in the same plane. The infill element belongs to the interior space while the surrounding framework belongs to the exterior space.

156

# THE INFILL SYSTEM AND LAYER SYSTEM

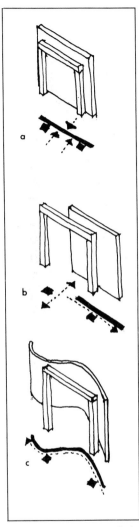

192 a-c. In the layered wall, the outer and inner wall lie in parallel planes. Thus, the tension between them is a factor of whether they are, (a) adjoining, (b) pulled apart, or (c) formed independently of one another.

The *infill wall* indicates a *balance* between inside and outside (Fig. 191). This is because the framework signifies opening from the outside inward, while the infill element that is flush with the skeletal framework signifies a closed off interior. This is particularly apparent when the infill section is solid and contrast determines the opening-closing effect.

In the *layer wall*, this balance between inside and outside is substituted by a *stage by stage* motion inwards. This means that the outer wall, which belongs to the exterior, and the inner wall, which belongs to the interior, are combined in such a way that they delimit the space independently. Furthermore, the buffer zone between them may vary in depth and thus 'participation' in the spatial effect depends on whether the wall sections are adjoining or separated (Fig. 192, a-c).

The following examples will illustrate how the inside-outside relation varies according to which of the layer motifs is used.

## PLANE ON PLANE

A modern example of a façade in which two solid planes are juxtaposed is Robert Venturi's project for a town hall in North Canton, Ohio (1965) (Figs. 193, 194).

The outer plane is a large free-standing screen with a wide entryway and an enormous arch as the only hole. Behind this is the next layer, the office building wall with a plain, regular window system. The walls are separated to allow for a walkway between them. This solution responds to the inside-outside relationship on all of three levels. The frontal façade, with its large simple figures, is meant to relate to the more distant environment, the city's squares and streets. The walkway forms an intermediate layer between these and the building itself as it stands drawn back with its uniform window pattern.

## SKELETON ON SKELETON

The next variation is one skeleton placed in front of another (Fig. 195).

This has been much used in Gothic (Fig. 196) but also in Classical architecture, both of which exploit the possibilities of this motif to give a layered opening into a wall. An example is Andrea Palladio's Palazzo

157

198. Skeleton in front of plane (Palazzo Rucellai in Florence by L.B. Alberti).

201. Plane in front of skeleton (from Bryggen in Bergen, Norway).

197. Skeleton in front of skeleton (Palazzo Valmarana by A. Palladio from Koepf, *Baukunst in Fünf Jahrtausenden*).

Valmarana, Vicenca (1566) (Fig. 197). Giant pilasters in the forefront, extending from plinth to cornice, determine the scale of both the street and the house. Behind the pilasters are two storeys in which the upper storey appears to be supported by lesser pilasters partially recessed behind the greater. Behind these again but still on the first floor lies yet another skeletal wall of Tuscan pilasters supporting a recessed mezzanine. Finally, even further in are deep reliefs and windows forming the fourth and final layer.

The purpose of these recessed layers is the same as in Venturi's project, that is, to attain a gradual transition between inside and outside. But, the effect is different. One plane section in front of another results in an additive juxtaposition of the outer and inner plane, and this is very effective, especially when facing a large, open urban space as in this Ohio city. Superimposed skeletons, however, give a greater perspective depth. An example of this can be found in the narrow street facing Palazzo Valmarana. Here, the Palazzo's main façade helps to widen and open up the street.

## SKELETON ON PLANE

To continue with the next layer variation, the skeleton placed in front of the plane, we find that the effect created is a contrast between an open, public frontal wall and a closed, private rear wall. The variant is the most widely used system in architectural history. It was reintroduced for the first time since Antiquity by Leone Battista Alberti in his Palazzo Rucellai, Florence (1451) (Fig. 198). The system's characteristics already appear in the classical temple (Fig. 199). With free-standing columns forming an open colonnade outside the massive cella wall, the duality stands out clearly. A closed inner world for the gods alone was surrounded by a wall of widely placed columns, which established contract with the outside world.

The contrasting effect of the variant is often emphasized in the wall's articulation itself. In Filippo Brunelleschi's Foundling Hospital façade, Florence (1419), it is emphasized by the way the strict, precise and dark arcades facing the square clearly belong to the public sphere. In contrast, the massive wall behind, with its 'unsystematic' openings indicates another and more private world within the walls (Fig. 200).

## PLANE ON SKELETON

We come finally to the fourth variation of the layered wall. In this combination a solid plane is placed in front of a skeletal section (Fig. 201). One of two things is necessary to enable us to comprehend the variant.

In the first place, the plane must be either perforated or transparent to allow us to *see* the skeleton behind. The latter is true of the curtain wall,

199. Skeleton in front of plane (Hadrian's Temple in Rome, from L'Orange/Thiis-Evensen, *Oldtidens bygningsverden*).

200. Skeleton in front of plane (Foster Home in Florence by F. Brunelleschi).

202. Plane in front of skeleton (curtain wall enveloping stair tower, Werkbund, by W. Gropius, from Giedion, *Space, Time and Architecture*).

160

which is in principle a glass front attached to an inner structural skeleton (Fig. 202).

The other prerequisite is that the outer plane be membrane-like in character or in other words seem thin and non-supporting. Once again the curtain wall is an example. As a protective skin it cannot stand on its own but is completely dependent upon the inner framework. Just as the skin on our own bodies, every membrane-like wall will indicate an inner supporting structure.

204. The planar system as an enclosing wall (a block wall from Palazzo Pitti in Florence by F. Brunelleschi).

205. The skeletal system as an open wall (Snyderman House in Indiana, by P. Eisenmann).

# THE MASSIVE SYSTEM AND
# THE SKELETON SYSTEM

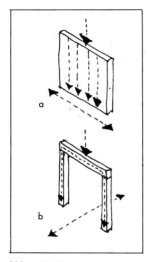

203. a-b. The planar system is both delimiting and supporting: (a) it encloss while the skeletal system separates between delimitation and support, (b) it opens.

We have seen that the massive wall is both supporting and delimiting, whereas the skeletal wall differentiates between delimiting and supporting. In the inside-outside relation this means that the massive wall lends weight to the spatial boundary itself and thereby closes the space (Figs. 203a, 204).

The skeletal system, on the other hand, concentrates support in a primary load-bearing system which frees and lightens the spatial boundary and thus *opens* the space (Figs. 203b, 205).

Throughout architectural history, not only *de facto* but also symbolically, the weight expressed in these systems has been responsible for the opening and closing of the wall.

## THE MASSIVE WALL AND CLOSURE

The closure effect of the massive wall has been emphasized in buildings in which the main purpose is to isolate and protect the inside space. The massive wall, therefore, is particularly associated with concepts of fortresses, city walls and prisons. The city wall should not only be strong in reality but strong in appearance as well.

> A material protection and at the same time a psychological defense, it was meant to arouse fear in the enemy by its terrible aspect and give the combatant a sense of security so that he could defend himself and strike as well. In the Middle Ages fortifications were essentially defensive; in the Renaissance they were both defensive and aggressive.[19]

Furthermore, in the theory of the 1800's:

> 'The exterior of a prison should be formed in the heavy and sombre style, which most forcibly impresses the spectator with gloom and terror'[20]

The material we immediately associate with a massive wall is stone. Inherently, stone has the same quality that the massive wall in its extreme form tries to attain: heavy and closed, earthbound and immovable.

## THE SKELETON WALL AND OPENING

The skeletal system is the very symbol of open space. The skeleton has the characteristics of a tree: dynamic, continuous, and ever-growing, in contrast to the heavy inertness of stone. Like a tree, the skeleton 'when built of

163

208. Interplay between the public openness of the skeletal wall and the private closure of the massive wall (Piazza Navona, painting by P. Pannini, from Hausmann, *Baukunst des Barock*).

206. The openness of the skeleton (Swiss-style villa in Oslo, Norway).

207. The openness of the skeleton (painting of portico villas from Pompeii, photo by Alinari).

wood .... gives a character of lightness' (Fig. 206).[21] The skeletal system in itself, therefore, is an expression particularly well suited to buildings with an expansive content. The villa exemplifies this type of dwelling and already in Antiquity was associated with long colonnades extending into the landscape (Fig. 207).[22] Such elements express the nature of the villa, says Alberti, 'where you have as much freedom as you have obstruction in town'.[23]

A similar desire for openness lies behind the use of the skeletal system in Gothic cathedrals. With walls broken up and with soaring columns it was built in spite of the stone. Its expansiveness lay in the spiritual truth which the building was meant to symbolize, a truth to be spread throughout 'the entire world' (see p. 57).

The open character associated with the skeletal system has the *column* as its most characteristic element. The column is regal it was said in Antiquity, '*aedificiorum purpura*'.[24] In this, not least of all, lay the acknowledgement of the column as representing the *public* aspect. It is the column that opens a building by making the walls redundant, and it is the column itself that is the intermediary of motion between outside and inside (See also columns p. 195 ff). Typically, therefore, it is the entrance façade, which is most frequently decorated with columns. This was the part facing the world, the part to be seen by the public.

It is in this context that the development of the fictive skeletal system must be understood. From the Renaissance, as first seen in Palazzo Rucellai, buildings of special importance have been decorated with entire storeys of non-structural rows of columns and beams (Fig. 198). The skeleton was an attempt to give a more public appearance to key buildings in medieval Florence, a city accustomed to heavy, inwardly orientated palaces such as Palazzo Vecchio (1340) and Palazzo Medici (1444). These buildings derived from ancient towers, fortresses and city walls.[25] The new buildings had their roots in the urbanism of Antiquity. This urbanization, brought about by the introduction of the skeletal system, is of great importance for both church and palace in the entire subsequent development of architecture. The skeletal system's expressive possibilities attain perhaps their greatest perfection in Michelangelo's Campidoglio project, in which mighty pilasters become an integral part of both building and square (See also p. 85 f) (Figs. 101, 102).

## CLOSURE/OPENING

Piazza Navona in Rome is one of the places that most clearly demonstrate the way in which skeletal and massive systems may express openness and enclosure of buildings (Fig. 208).

The piazza takes its form from a stadium built at the time of Domitian (first century) and is surrounded by buildings from both early Renaissance and high Baroque. All the private dwellings are massive and closed, compact plastered structures broken only by rows of plain windows. Inserted into this world of privacy are two churches, St. Agnese (1657) and Nostra Signora del St. Cuore (1450). Their rich systems of pilasters, attached columns, lintels and portals indicate another and more public world than that of the neighbouring buildings.

Flanking St. Agnese is Palazzo Pamphili (1650), which differs from both the private houses and the churches in its combined public and private character. The central section is opened up by pilasters while the wings retain the form of solid volumes. This partly public expression illustrates the building's function, since the house was both the residence and the symbol of the papal family.

In the following we shall concentrate in greater detail on the massive and skeletal systems by examining the effect of *articulation*. It is a question of how articulation, which particularly concerns texture and weight expression, can influence the system's basic interpretation of the inside-outside relationship.

We begin with the massive system and question the importance of thickness, surface treatment, building method, and transparency. We continue by examining the skeletal system, with the main emphasis on the articulation of columns and beams. Finally we shall study the importance of colour in relation to both systems at the same time.

# THE MASSIVE SYSTEM

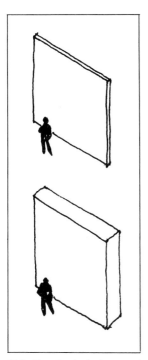

209. The plane's thickness and the expression of weight.

The inward or outward expression of the massive wall depends upon its appearance of lightness or heaviness. In other words, if a massive wall seems solid and heavy, it will impart a feeling of being 'impenetrable' and stop us, while at the same time conveying an impression of great structural capacity. On the other hand, if it seems thin and light, there seems to be no difficulty in 'breaking through', and its load-bearing capacity seems reduced.

In the massive wall four conditions determine this weight expression: *thickness, surface treatment, building method,* and *degree of transparency*.

## THICKNESS

It a massive wall seems thin, it conveys a light and therefore 'open' feeling. The reverse is true if it seems thick (Fig. 209).

A thick wall corresponds to something inert and closed in that thickness indicates compactness and thereby inner resistance. A thin wall, on the other hand, has more the character of a light film and as a result seems far more vulnerable.

Just what determines this impression of thickness?

The *main form* is important because of its overall effect on weight character and thus on how we feel the wall can be handled — this in the widest sense. As a result, a curved wall seems thicker than one which is straight, a sloping wall thicker than a vertical one, a low one thicker than a high etc.

The *openings* too are very important, because by the depth of their jambs the thickness of the wall can be clearly read. This will be treated in greater detail in the chapter on windows (See p. 253 f and p. 259 ff). ·

Furthermore, the *material* of the wall plane is important in expressing weight. Materials span all the way from natural materials such as stone, clay, and wood to processed material such as concrete, iron, glass or plastic. Some of these are moulded, as with concrete and plastic, others must be constructed, as is the case with stone and wood. Each group of materials has its own special character and, providing they are left in their natural state, give varying impressions of thickness.[26] The main reason for this is to be found in our own *experiences* with the materials regarding both their use and their quality. Hence, a wall of iron, glass, plastic or laminated

212. The plane's method of construction and the expression of weight *(Palazzo Pitti, by Brunelleschi)*.

211. The plane's method of construction and the expression of weight (half-timber construction with brick infill from Akershus Fortress in Oslo, Norway).

210. The plane's method of construction and the expression of weight.

wood will immediately be thought of as thin and membrane-like, whereas a wall of concrete or stone strikes us at once as thick.

Experience with these materials, however, has taught us that thickness does not always correspond with weight. An iron wall with the same thickness as a plastic wall will always seem heavier. Similarly, a thick wall of concrete blocks will seem considerably lighter than the thinnest steel wall.

## SURFACE

What then about the effect of the surface on the wall's expression of weight?

There are four factors which determine this: *texture, pattern, relief* and *colour.*

Colour, as we have already said, will be treated in a later chapter (See p. 240 ff). Texture may be smooth, fine or rough, while the effect of various patterns depends on three interrelated conditions, namely: the pattern's order, its range of motifs, änd its plasticity. The latter is a question of whether the pattern is flush with the wall or recessed.

## BUILDING METHOD

All four factors, texture, pattern, relief and colour affect a wall's expression of weight regardless of whether it is moulded or block constructed. Nevertheless, the building method in itself may cause different expressions of weight. To the eye, the moulded wall will have a smooth surface, while a masonry wall will reflect the pattern determined by the size of the blocks, the bonding, and the texture. If we compare two such walls, the block wall with its chequered surface will immediately convey a thicker and heavier impression than the moulded wall with its smooth surface. What is the reason for this difference? (Fig. 210).

Again we find a principal explanation in the phenomenon of how we relate to things. A smooth wall has no immediate connection with our world of everyday experience. It tells nothing of its weight or size. As a reference for scale it eludes us. Thus, frequently a smooth wall area, particularly if it is pale in colour, will seem larger than it really is. Optically it extends both upwards and outwards, which means that the surface effect is greater than the depth and weight effect.

The reverse is true of the block wall. Such a wall immediately seems denser and more compact. In contrast to the moulded wall the block wall consists of comprehensible individual parts to which we can relate (Fig. 211). A single block can be 'read'. Its weight and durability can be evaluated by how it can be grasped or held, whether it is large and unmanageable or light enough to lift and control. These familiar units are piled one upon the other to form an integrated whole. In this way, the whole becomes compre-

213. The cast wall and the neutral expression (house for an employee by C. N. Ledoux, from Christ & Schein, *L'Oeuvre et les rêves de Ladoux*).

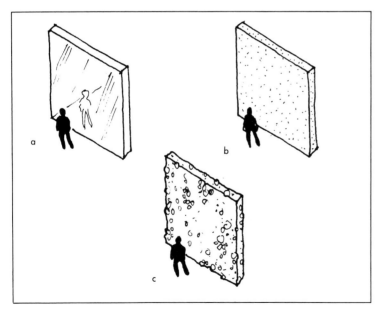

214. a-c. Three categories of texture: (a) smooth, (b) fine, (c) coarse.

hensible, which in turn means that the wall area is 'identifiable' by means of its individual parts (Fig. 212).

To simplify this analysis, we shall relate surface to each of the two wall types separately. In order to do this we assume certain factors to be constant, thus the main form of the walls described are all perpendicular and without openings.

# THE MOULDED WALL

In the history of architecture there are three variations in particular which correspond to what we mean by the moulded wall: *the stucco wall, the concrete wall,* and *the glass wall.* The glass wall will be considered separately in the concluding chapter on massive walls.

As for the concrete wall and stucco wall, only the first is cast in a strictly technical sense, while the stucco wall merely gives that impression. Stucco is usually an outer covering of an inner composite wall of brick or natural stone. Strictly speaking, concrete walls are not all isotropic planes. Frequently they are reinforced with steel which technically puts them in a mixed category between a skeleton and massive systems.

In any case, the stucco wall and the concrete wall merely represent degrees of difference within the same expressive limits and in the following will be treated as if they were alike. We shall first examine them with different *textural* treatment and then with various types of *patterns,* in the latter case those which are flush with the wall surface and those forming *reliefs.*

### TEXTURE

Elias Cornell calls moulded walls *neutral*: 'They serve as backgrounds for colonnades or create smooth sections between windows and doors' (Fig. 213).[27]

This means that the effect is primarily determined by the figures seen in connection with these surfaces. Their neutral effect, however, will be judged more particularly by the roughness of their texture. The finer the texture the more neutral the surface in the sense that in itself it gives no indication of being thin or thick but depends on openings and other forms of treatment to reveal this. A rough texture immediately conveys greater strength in the wall itself; it seems thicker and therefore provides more closure.

Textural treatment may, therefore, be divided into three categories: *smooth, fine* and *coarse.* All three correspond to specific tactile characteristics and thus to degrees of differently experienced weight and 'resistance' in the inside-outside relation (Fig. 214 a-c).

214. Smooth texture and hard expression.

215. The interplay between smooth and porous banding in a masonry wall from the 1800s (All Saints by W. Butterfield, from Hersey, *High Victorian and Gothic*).

## SMOOTH TEXTURE

The smooth wall surface seems *hard*. We experience this most frequently in glazed tiles and glossy paint (Fig. 214). Familiarity with the qualities of the material plays a part in one's experience of it. Nevertheless, smoothness as a phenomenon has a universal quality. A smooth area seems to slip away when touched; one cannot 'get hold of it', it seems unapproachable and unassailable. Smoothness becomes a protective layer giving the inner part more meaning and a strength which seems impenetrable.

## FINE TEXTURE

The finely grained wall surface seems *soft*. In a way it is exposed and 'open'; it does not seem rejecting to the touch. A fine texture is associated with porousness, thereby a warm and protected space. A space with smooth walls seems colder than a comparable space with finely textured wall surfaces.[28]

Yet, certain combinations of a smooth finish and a finely grained mat finish will give quite the opposite effect to the one described above.

This is because a smooth finish usually both reflects and shines. If the mirror effect dominates, the wall is opened up in that outside space penetrates further into the wall fabric. The same occurs in a glossy wall, because the light striking it is reflected and 'imprisoned' within the wall itself. A glossy finish in this case will be an opening instead of a closing factor (See also glass walls p. 189 f and the open floor p. 63 ff).

Examples of this effect in connection with a mat finish are found in neo-Gothic walls (Fig. 215). Areas of mat brick were often alternated with bands of dark, glazed bricks. These bands stiffen, strengthen and 'reinforce' the wall, both because they are darker and because they are harder than the rest of the wall. But, because they reflect the light and mirror the surroundings they give just the opposite effect. Glistening and shining, they break up the wall area and make it lighter, whereas the porous and mat brick areas in-between make up the massive structural substance of the building itself.

## COARSE TEXTURE

We have already mentioned that a coarse texture seems to give weight to the wall. A coarsley textured wall rejects, but in another way than does the smooth wall. Whereas the smooth wall protects something within, a coarse wall draws the inner substance to the surface in an almost 'aggressive' manner. We can be scratched by a coarse wall; it may hurt if we touch it. It represents an active resistance and so possesses its own power and weight. Such is the character of the parapet surrounding Oslo's underground stations. A coarse surface, combined with sharply edged undula-

216. Coarse texture in E. Viksjø's concrete mixtures (from the Norsk Hydro Building in Oslo, Norway).

218. Horizontal patterning and the heavy/dynamic expression (Casa unifamiliare by M. Botta, from *A.D.* 5/6, 1980).

219. Horizontal patterning and the heavy/dynamic expression (detail from the Norsk Hydro Building in Oslo).

217 a-c. The three categories of pattern motifs: (a) abstract, (b) figurative, (c) material-determined.

tions in a low wall, effectively keep people away from these large openings in the street surface.

The rough wall, in other words, indicates its own inner substance. Erling Viksjø's mixtures of concrete consisting of fine gravel and sand mottled with larger stone fragments are typical attempts to reveal the masonry wall's innermost substance (Fig. 216). At one moment the stones seem to break forth from the wall's interior, but in the next instant they seem imbedded in it. The wall's inner core, therefore, is the precondition for the effect conveyed and thus for our perception of its existence. This inner core is the concrete itself, which bonds everything together into a heavy mass.

## PATTERNS

In principle, the surface pattern on a plane wall falls within three categories (Fig. 217). The first has an abstract character dictated by independent patterns of lines, grids or curves. The second is figurative, based on representations of people, animals or things. The third is rooted in materials and building methods and indicates how a wall is built up of separate parts. We shall deal with this last category separately in the chapter on masonry walls (see p. 183 ff).

To a certain extent all three categories may: (1) be organized horizontally, vertically or diagonally, (2) appear as a pattern flush with the wall itself or, (3) be composed of various plastic reliefs. Each of these motifs whether abstract, figurative, or constructive, will give the wall a different weight expression.

## PATTERN ORDER

Patterns made up of *horizontal* compositions have an inert and heavy character. The reference is the ground, not only because the weight seems to lie heavily on it but also because motion parallels it (Fig. 218).

As an example, Viksjø's Hydro building in Oslo (1960) consists of two main volumes, the tall building itself and the base on which it stands. This base, of coarse polygonal concrete, slants outward. Both the roughness and the slant of the main form indicate the power and weight necessary to withstand the stress of the tall building above. The pattern of the base creates an important accent in the overall expression. The entire surface consists of alternating light and dark horizontal strips extending uninterrupted around the entire form. The pattern increases contact with the ground but also holds the walls of the base together as it they were taut bands restraining pressures from within (Fig. 219).

A *vertical* pattern helps to give the wall a freer character. A house is lighter if the dominating composition is vertical. It is only necessary to compare

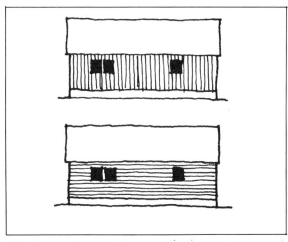

220. Houses with vertical siding (above) and horizontal siding (below).

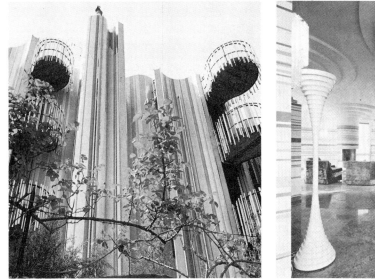

221. Vertical patterning and the rising expression (Casa Papanice by Portoghesi/Gigliotti, from Norberg-Schulz, *Alla ricerca dell'architettura perduta*).

222. Horizontal patterning and the connecting expression (inside Casa Papanica by Portoghesi/Gigliotti, from Norberg-Schulz, *Alla ricerca dell'architettura perduta*).

176

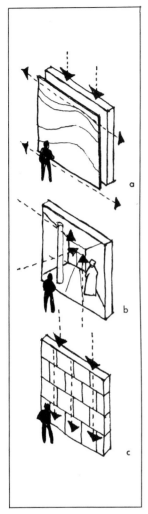

223 a-c. The effect of the pattern motifs on the wall's expression of weight: (a) abstract patterns along and *independent of* the surface, (b) figurative patterns *within* the surface, (c) material patterns which weigh the surface *downward*.

two smilar wooden houses, one with vertical and the other with horizontal siding (Fig. 220).

Another example is Paolo Portoghesi's house, Casa Papanice (1970), which is made up of concave wall planes divided by perpendicular strips of windows (Figs. 221, 222, 231). Vertical bands of coloured tiles cover the façades. The ascending bands are green, decreasing in number and becoming paler as they rise. The descending bands are blue, flecked with stripes of gold. These too decrease towards the middle, where they meet the green bands rising from below. The colour tones play a role in tying the upper and lower parts together; the green tiles continue the growth of the soil upwards, while the blue and golden tiles are a downward extension of sky and sun.

In addition, the vertical bands underscore the independence of the individual wall planes. This again accents the entire system of wall divisions around the house and hence the rhythmic opening of the exterior. That this is international may be seen when compared to the interior walls, which are covered by *horizontal* tiled bands. Here the wall planes are linked together around the interior in contrast to the way the exterior is split; the interior is closed, the exterior is opened.

## PATTERN IMAGES

All the patterns discussed above were flush with the wall's own surface, neither cutting into it nor projecting from it. Further, the examples of horizontal and vertical ordering were all illustrated by walls decorated with abstract patterns. This means that had the same structures been shown with figurative or constructive patterns the surface expression would have been different. In other words, each of the three patterns applied to the same surface will convey a greatly varied weight expression and thus a different opening and closing effect between inside and outside (Fig. 223, a-c).

*Abstract patterns* will convey lightness. They reveal nothing of how a wall is built as do constructive pattern motifs. In contrast to the latter, in which the pattern symbolizes the wall's own essential substance and load-bearing nature and hence indicates weight, abstract patterns are perceived as a membrane-like *surface* on a massive wall behind. The motions indicated by the pattern therefore seem more to exist on a covering skin, their directions following along the wall mass and not within it.

A *figurative pattern* will also give the wall a lighter character. By figurative patterns we mean murals and mosaics which cover the entire wall with figures. The effect meanwhile, depends completely upon the figural representation. In this sense, a figurative pattern may give a covering, carpet-like, non-structural effect as do Byzantine mosaics. Or, the pattern may create 'holes' in the wall, thereby opening it up as in the case of Pom-

224. Figurative pattern which opens up in depth (Pompeian architectural illusion, from L'Orange & Thiis-Evensen, *Oldtidens bygningsverden*).

peian illusionistic architectural murals. The common factor in all types of figurative patterns is that in one way or another they will always convey the effect of optical depth into the wall.

In just the same way as abstract patterns, figurative patterns will also help to disguise the wall's essential substance. To these optical effects must be added the meanings of what the patterns represent. In content these have varied throughout history. The modern abstract mural plays on spatial effects between pure colours and plan. Early Christian mosaics exploited the symbolic effects in various constellations of stylized human figures and 'sacred' colours, while in Antiquity's architectural illusions the eye was drawn deeply into the space of large painted landscapes. Pompeian murals dissolve the wall as a substantial reality, so that one is led into a magnified and open illusionistic space which makes even the smallest apartments seem spacious and airy (Fig. 224). In Byzantine pictorial tradition secular and spiritual qualities are united. A church with walls covered in life-size figures of saints and biblical scenes is transformed into a vision of the divine sphere itself. The wall ceases to exist and becomes lost in a shimmer of brightly coloured *tesserae* against a ground of gleaming gold. 'The (light) comes from above and in front, filters down over everything depicted, settling upon it, strewn like gold and silver dust from the top of the dome'.[29] The space ceases to be a conceivable reality, says Otto Demus. It is not so strange that corners are 'ignored' in the compositional whole. 'The sanctuary seems to revolve round the beholder; the multiplicity of the view forces him to turn round and round and this turning of his is imputed by his imagination to the building itself' (Fig. 225).[30] The figures, however, do not hover freely in an unstructured void. They are ordered in a hierarchic plan as in the successive stages of religious perception. At the bottom, the smallest figures form a floor level frieze, the middle level consists of over-life-size martyrs, while the topmost level is reserved for the archangels and apostles in colossal images. This ordering has nothing to do with the wall's own structural system but concerns the ideological content in the mosaics. From a heavenly scale the figures are gradually reduced to human dimensions as they descend towards the believer himself.

## PATTERN RELIEF

The patterns already discussed may also occur as *reliefs* in the wall. If we imagine that these motifs are similar in form and content but recessed instead of flush with the wall face, the wall will change from having a light membrane-like character to having a heavier and more substantial quality. As surface patterns, the three types will vary in degree of lightness. In a relief it will be just the opposite. Now the wall will show varying degrees

225. Figurative pattern which dissolves the surface and which 'ignores' the corner (detail from Convent church in Daphni, from MacDonald, *Early Christian & Byzantine Architecture*).

of weight. Here, again, the difference will depend upon whether the motif is abstract, figurative, or derived from the type of material used.

Most important, however, is the relation of the relief to the wall. In this, three situations predominate (Fig. 226, a-c): the relief may seem to be (1) attached *to* the wall (addition), (2) projecting *out of* the wall (convex), or (3) *sunk* into the wall (concave).

These three principles will, as a rule, occur in combination. For example, a relief projecting from its own slab will obviously appear to be fastened *to* the wall. In the case of the convex relief, more depends upon the contours and details, in deciding whether the relief is added to the wall or emerges from it. In addition to plasticity, texture and colour treatment must be considered. An additive relief in a colour other than that of the wall will seem even more prominent, whereas a convex relief in another colour will be given more freedom.

Despite these modifying factors we will study each type of relief and its influence upon the wall's weight expression. We shall limit our examples to those with figurative patterns.

## THE ADDITIVE RELIEF

The additive relief conveys a neutral character to the wall to which it is attached (Fig. 226, a). The relief corresponds to the principle of figure/ground and depends on articulation for its effect, assuming that the relief is visually active in contrast to a more homogeneous and uniform background.

We find an example of this in the restored reliefs depicting the Via Dolorosa on the plaster wall in St. Olav's Cathedral in Oslo. Following the principles of the Gothic wall system, these carved wooden reliefs are perceived as a superimposed layer on the wall behind. The relief, therefore, creates a transition between the observer and the background wall. Consequently, the reliefs and the background wall 'do' different things. The wall forms a physical boundary between the church and the world around. The Via Dolorosa reliefs also create a 'wall', but a purely spiritual one which holds the spectator within a world of religious perception determined by the meaning of the reliefs. It is the relief which is 'active', not only optically but in content as well, whereas the outer wall in both ways becomes a subordinate background.

## THE CONVEX RELIEF

The convex relief protrudes from the wall face.

This may give two different impressions (Fig. 226, b). In one the relief seems to be restrained by the wall itself. The relief is a part of the wall's own fabric, its forms 'undulating' within the limits of the wall. The other effect is

227. The convex relief (atelier in Munich by A. Endell, from Pothorn, *Das Grosse Buch der Baustile*).

228. The concave relief (wall section from Horus' temple in Edfu, from Lloyd, *Architettura Mediterranea Preromana*).

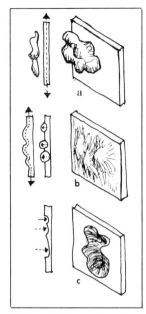

266 a-c. The three categories of relief motifs: (a) additive, (b) convex, (c) concave.

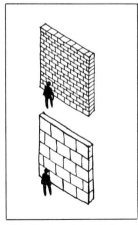

229. The size of the blocks and the expression of weight.

more as though the forms in the relief are about to *free* themselves from the wall. The wall seems about to loosen its grip on its own substance.

The overall impression becomes one of tension between these two extremes, between a modelled wall and a wall about to disintegrate. The two expressions are, in other words, degrees of difference within the same thing: an active and massive wall having its own substance, which it appears either to 'part with' or to 'imprison'.

We see an example of this dualism in an Art Nouveau façade from 1896 (Fig. 227). These organic relief patterns swirl over the entire façade, seeming at one moment to fuse with the wall and at the next to curl outwards and away from it. The same type of motifs are used in the main form of the house, the frames and window openings. In this way we see that the relief, in motif as well, is part of the wall treatment. In other words, the relief has both its origins and its basis in the wall mass itself.

### THE CONCAVE RELIEF

The concave relief lies within the body of the wall. This means that in the relief an inner substance is laid bare, an interior that is kept under control by the wall itself (Fig. 226, c). Both the exposure and containment reveal a plastic and powerful reality, giving the wall an air of massive weight.

Egyptian wall carvings are a good example of the use of concave reliefs (Fig. 228). On both the exteriors and interiors of temple walls the Egyptians carved long series of figures and symbols. The human figures, plastically modelled, were as if sunk into the wall — everything was contained within the stone itself. This impression of great weight corresponded completely with the Egyptian ideological search for permanency. Egyptian building art has always had a strong monolithic character, revealed in its colossal dimensions, tightly spaced rows of columns, and slanting block-built pylons. In this atmosphere, the concave relief adds further emphasis to the stone massif's meaning as the 'captor' of all motion and life.

## THE MASONRY WALL

From what has already been said, we see that the weight expressed by the *masonry wall* depends upon the different characteristics of its individual blocks. These may be divided into three main categories according to *size, method of joining,* and *surface.*

### SIZE OF THE BLOCKS

We judge a block to be large or small according to whether we can handle it or not. Thus, a wall built of small blocks will seem lighter than one built of large ones (Fig. 229). A brick wall, for example, is made up of small easily

183

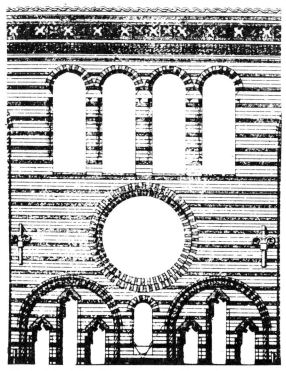

230. Brick details (from Ungewitter, *Vorlegeblaetter für Ziegel- und Steinarbeiten*).

232. Base under pressure (Frauenzuchthaus in Würz-burg, from Klopfer, *Von Palladio bis Schinkel*).

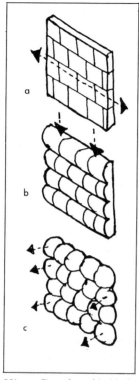

231 a-c- The surface of the blocks and their expression of weight: (a) flush with the surface, (b) protruding from the surface due to over compression, (c) protruding from the surface due to inherent character.

handled elements. Nor does such a wall seem thick because the size of the bricks on the surface is spontaneously associated with a corresponding size in depth. In just the same way, the blocks that we consider large will also be thought of as having a corresponding depth, thus giving the wall as a whole a heavy, impenetrable character. An example of the deliberate use of difference in weight between small and large blocks is classicism's corner solutions. Wall surfaces are either in plaster or brick. The corners, however, are frequently reinforced with powerful quoins, whose job it is to hold the form together.

## SURFACE OF THE BLOCKS

The second factor which can affect expression of weight is the block's *surface*. The block's main form, its texture and colour treatment affect the wall's character (Fig. 230).

As was pointed out when dealing with the moulded wall, a coarse texture will give a heavier impression than does a fine, smooth texture. Similarly, a solid, dark wall will seem heavier than a pale one. The same weight difference will occur between an ashlar wall in which the stones are flush with the wall face and a wall in which the stones jut out (Fig. 23, a-c). In the first case, the stones appear to be controlled by the surface itself. In the second case the stones seem to protrude as though from some inner thrust. In the first case, the stones are neutralized, in the second they jut forth towards the onlooker. This convexity has two effects.

One is determined by the feeling of tremendous pressure on the stones from above. The scale of Frauenzuchthaus in Würzburg (1809) must be seen in this light (Fig. 232). The entire ground floor façade consists of horizontal 'tubes', which seem to be squashed together by the weight of the upper storeys.

The other effect is determined by the way each stone behaves independently — swelling and protruding as a result of the individual stone's 'own weight' (Fig. 233).

In any case, whether the blocks project or seem squashed together, they will convey strength to the plastic wall.

## JOINING OF THE BLOCKS

The third factor affecting the masonry wall's expression of weight is the *joints*. The contours of the blocks decide this and thus in turn the pattern on the wall face. The variety of patterns may seem endless, yet they are all found within two basic structures. One is *amorphous,* the other *geometric*. By an amorphous pattern we mean one that is irregular such as when the stones have different dimensions, forms, and contours. Typical of this is An-

234. Blocks of stone adapted to the shape of the space ('Clytemnestra's Grave', photo by Photo Marburg).

233. Rustic block wall from Peru.

235. Blocks of stone in contrast to the shape of the space ('The East Gallery' in Tiryns, photo by Photo Marburg).

tiquity's polygonal walls, which seem to consists of a network of interwoven and broken lines (Fig. 233).

In the geometric block pattern there are two main characteristics (Fig. 230). First, the pattern is the result of an overall determining structure which orders the individual blocks. This is the horizontal, the vertical or the diagonal structure, each of which as we have shown earlier, gives the wall differing 'weight'. The other characteristic is the precise fitting of each individual block. Each has its allotted position, and all are exactly fitted together to make the form determined by the governing structure.

From this we conclude that a geometric ashlar wall, providing the dimensions of the blocks are reasonably alike, will seem *thinner* than an amorphous ashlar wall. This is because a geometric wall indicates an even, organized weight transfer towards the ground. In contrast, the transfer of weight in the amorphous wall is more casual, which in turn seems to require greater thickness to prevent it from falling apart.

In short, the effect of what has been described above corresponds with what may be called *abstract* and *rustic* characteristics.

## THE ABSTRACT MASONRY WALL

Great care is taken in the working and joining of the blocks in an abstract wall. The blocks are in every way *subjugated* and controlled. Small stones will always seem more subjugated than large ones, because the latter are not so easily controlled by the human hand. The individual stones are also formed by man; they are both prepared and fitted, carved and polished. In addition, abstract walls are very often characterized by symmetrical bonding patterns, which clearly organize every stone. The abstract wall is often built to fit the space it surrounds. In the ancient Greek Treasury of Atreus (1350 B.C.), each block is hewn to fit into the even curvature around this domed space (Fig. 234). It is symptomatic, therefore, that in Roman architecture with its interest in interior space, the ashlar wall was avoided. Both formally and technically the Romans built their walls as a plastic skin to comply with the motions of the interior space

## THE RUSTICATED MASONRY WALL

The character of the rusticated wall is determined in part by the nature of its material.[31] In contrast to the abstract wall, the main impression is one of sovereign independence — neither human hand, the wall itself, nor space gain 'the upper hand' over the stone blocks. In the so-called East Gallery in Tiryns (1350 B.C.) there is a constant struggle between the spatial form and the blocks (Fig. 235). The spatial form rises upwards to make way for

236. Naturalized block wall (Student dormitory by R. Pietilä, photo by Chr. Norberg-Schulz).

237. Glass wall by day: the exterior is directed inside (photo from *GA*, 2, 1979).

forward movement, while the downward stress of the individual, rusticated blocks makes the space seem about to collapse.

The most important aspect of the rusticated wall, however, is its association with nature. Its elements are as if taken straight from nature itself. And, nature is a given thing, independent and beyond the range of human control, 'L'opera di natura'.[32]

The basic qualities of the rusticated wall are best illustrated by the Cyclopean walls in Myceneaen architecture. Around the royal citadel in Mycenae (c. 1250 B.C.) the outer wall is built of huge uneven blocks forming an amorphous pattern in which each block swells out in a taut curve. The entire structure takes on the air of a gigantic pile of stones in which the stones seem ready to fall apart at any moment. 'Those walls were said to be uncertain, which were made of stones of unequal angles and sides', declares Palladio.[33] This uncertainty connected with the amorphous wall increases both its frightening and natural aspect. Over the whole is an air of the primeval, of magic, a Cyclopean masterpiece and 'the dream of the people of the forest' (Fig. 236).[34]

# THE GLASS WALL

An opaque wall will always seem heavier than a *transparent* wall. A glass wall can carry no weight and in character is 'non-existent'. The impression it conveys, therefore, is in a category by itself, quite apart from the massive wall's closed character and the skeleton wall's openness.

A clear glass wall is, of course, transparent but it also transmits light and has a mirror-effect. It is these three qualities together which determine the way in which the glass wall carries out the inside-outside connection.

In the clear glass wall, inside and outside seem to merge. The mirrored version of what is in front overlaps that which lies behind (Fig. 237). Transparency and mirror-effect, therefore, unite inside and outside like projections on a screen. In the following, we shall treat them separately in considering the influence of glass on the inside and on the outside.

## INSIDE

The character of whatever lies behind a glass wall is transformed when the wall is removed. The reason is that the clear glass wall takes on a quality, not based on itself alone but in relation to what it picks up and transforms. And, of what is seen behind the glass wall, it is light and colour which the glass 'catches' and transforms. Light and colour, however, are always a part of things, a part of what we see in there. Light and colour accent the wall face and enwrap the figure. Through glass, which can never be completely flat but always wavy, all this is transformed. Colours glow, as in

189

238. Glass wall by night: the interior is directed outside (house by G. Grung, photo by G. Grung).

stones seen through water, light is broken up into points, and rays and things vibrate and come alive, all depending on how we focus our gaze.

Things seen through glass convey a feeling of distance. The motif appears to have a life of its own, different to what it would be if measured without glass in front. At the same time things seem very close. In a way they are within the glass itself, the way a landscape appears in a highly varnished painting. This duality lends an ephemeral air to what we see behind the glass; the glass makes whatever is inside seem to withdraw and come forward at the same time.

## OUTSIDE

Within the glass is a transformed interior but also an *illusion* of the exterior. Glass mirrors the outside and the actual space is enlarged by its own reflection. Thus, in the glass wall, time and space are united as Sigfried Giedion says when referring to the Bauhaus building in Dessau:

> . . . there is the extensive transparency that permits interior and exterior to be seen simultaneously... variety of levels of reference, or of points of reference, and simultaneity — the conception of space-time, in short. [35]

## OUTSIDE-INSIDE

Effects in glass, which include the visual relation of strength between outside and inside, are dependent upon day and night, lightness and darkness. In the daytime they become two spaces in ever-changing balance. Exterior and interior struggle for mastery in that both are seen as overlapping parts. But, if the interior light is intensified, exterior space is weakened. Just the opposite takes place with strong daylight — now the inside disappears and the outside space invades the interior. Or, if the glass wall is transluscent but not transparent and also depending upon whether the glass is dark or light, the reflection of the exterior will be either strong or weak. At night, on the other hand, it is the interior that is drawn outwards (Fig. 238). The shining interior becomes a 'gift' to the night.

240. The skeletal system: grid (detail from the Bauthaus by W. Gropius, photo by Chr. Norberg-Schulz).

241. The skeletal system: pattern achieved by the combination of arcades and colonnades (detail from a building in Czechoslovakia).

242. The skeletal system: pattern achieved by the combination of a massive element and a colonnade (Palazzo Vidoni-Caffarelli by Rafael).

192

# THE SKELETON SYSTEM

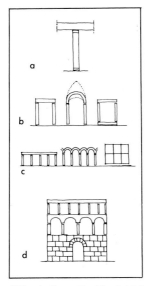

239 a-d. The motifs of the skeletal system: (a) column and beam, (b) frame (straight — arched — quadrangle), (c) row (colonnade — arcade — grid), (d) pattern.

We have already shown that the skeletal system opens the inside-outside connection and that its composite character, in principle, appears lighter than the isotropic wall. The light and open character of this system, however, just as for the massive wall, depends upon its main form and articulation.

The main form varies, but within a limited set of elements. These are determined by the skeleton's construction, which can be interpreted as a certain combination of elements at four different levels (Fig. 239, a-d).

The basic level comprises the primary elements, *column* and *beam*. The column is the vertical supporting member, and the beam is the horizontal supported member.

These in combination form the next level of the construction, the *frame*, in that two columns are joined by a beam. Frames may be formed in very different ways, but their variations all fall within three motifs primarily determined by the form of the beam. The first is the *straight* frame with a horizontal beam, the second is the *arched* frame, in which the beam may be semicircular, pointed or flat. The third motif, a variation of the straight frame is the quadrangle, in which beam, columns, and sill form an unbroken rectangle.

In the next stage several of these units are repeated to form a row. Based on the above forms we find three row motifs: the *colonnade* with straight beams, the *arcade* with arched beams, and the *grid* of equal quadrangles.

The fourth and final level is determined by the way the repetitive row motifs are integrated in a *pattern* within the same wall. These patterns may be formed in different ways. One of the repetitive motifs alone may cover an entire wall, as in the Greek temple (colonnade) and the modern curtain-wall (grid) (Fig. 240). In another variation the rows may be combined in the same wall as in Classicism's layering of colonnade above arcade (Fig. 241). The repetitive motifs may be combined with massive wall area as, for example, in the Doge's Palace, Venice, in which a solid wall is supported by lower rows of columns. The latter system may be reversed, as in the Palazzo Vidoni-Caffarelli, where columns rise above a massive socle. The systems may even be juxtaposed in depth etc. (Figs. 205, 242).

From the above description it becomes clear that two sets of elements are present in all combinations within the skeletal system. First of all come column and beam, followed by the frame motifs which they create and which in turn form the basis for rows and patterns.

244.  The inherent security of the column ('The Death of Samson' by G. Doré, from Doré, *Bibelen i Billeder*).

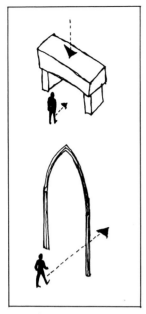

243. The supportive expression of the skeletal system: 'insecure' and 'secure'.

In examining the skeletal system, in terms of opening and closing, it is necessary to analyse the archetypes that constitute columns, beams, and frames.

## THE SKELETON SYSTEM'S EXPRESSION OF SUPPORT AND MOTION

If we imagine ourselves facing a skeletal wall, it will be the weight and substance effect — just as for the massive wall — which influences our desire 'to enter'. In the skeletal wall this means a unified directional expression, which is particularly determined by how we experience the system's ability to carry a load (support expression) and the way the system directs our passage in (motion expression).

Support expression may mean that certain skeletons seem heavy and overloaded so we hesitate to enter. Others may seem strong and light so that we feel no 'danger' in entering (Fig. 243). Support expression is particularly determined by the system's plastic character, which in turn is decided by how individual columns and beams are articulated and joined together. The question is, when will a beam best withstand stress: when it is pointed, arched, curved or straight? And, when does a column seem strongest: when it is high or low, straight or 'swollen', dark or light?

The other factor influencing the inside-outside relationship is the way in which the skeletal system impels our movements. This motion impulse is largely caused by the intervening spaces in the system. It concerns the treatment of the columns, as to whether they are quadratic or round, rough or smooth, and also whether the form of the frame's opening is wide, narrow or high, the beam straight or arched, etc. The repetitive motifs, too, are important in creating movement impulses in us, because any directional pull depends on the form, extent and rhythm of the row of columns.

Thus, sensations aroused by the skeleton system are determined by a combination of impressions. The support expression conveys security, while the system's directional aspect invites motion impulses.

In the following we shall separate these two factors by first examining support expression, thereafter the motion inviting expression, and then apply these to column, frame, and beam respectively.

# THE COLUMN
## THE COLUMN'S EXPRESSION OF SUPPORT

The column's expression is to be found in its alternating pattern of rising and sinking. We recognize a corresponding interaction in our supporting function. In its broadest sense it reveals itself in our 'Willensenergie', strength of

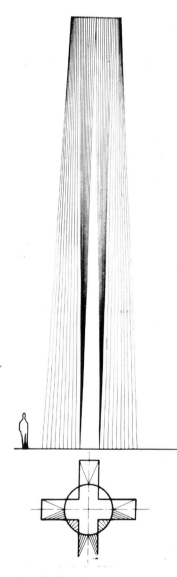

246. The column's dynamism (column and ribs from Palazzo del Lavoro in Torino by P. L. Nervi).

245. The form of a column (column from Palazzo del Lavoro by P. L. Nervi, from Nervi, *Aesthetics and Technology in Building*).

247. Column form (detail from Palazzo Cancelleria in Rome).

will, says Theodor Lipps: 'Because within ourselves arises a corresponding action pattern and thereby a feeling of self which is a natural part of that same action'.[36]

Identification with the column is, therefore, an absolute necessity, because within the ability of the column to give support lies the presumption of safety. If the column gives way, both it and whatever it supports collapses and 'crushes us'. The tension in Milton's Samson is ours; Samson and the column are as one:

> . . . these two massy pillars with horrible convulsion to and fro
> He tugged, he shook, till down they came and drew
> The whole roof after them, with burst of thunder
> Upon the heads of all who sate beneath (Fig. 244).[37]

This organic interplay of strength in the column is clearly illustrated in Pier Luigi Nervi's concrete forms. His column shafts clearly describe the dynamics of strength in the vertical, from downward stress to upward thrust. The principle underlying these colums is always the same. It is an integral part of the nature of concrete, says Nervi, in its plastic and static unity, 'which because of the monolithic nature of construction in reinforced concrete, holds together the various parts of the structure'.[38] The alternate rising and sinking is a continuous process in the column shaft itself between two different cross-sections, one in the upper and one in the lower part. 'The transition between each section is obtained by joining with straight lines the corresponding points of the two extreme sections'.[39] The most usual method is to expand the form at the bottom while compressing it at the top. The principle is most clearly revealed in the enormous pillars of the Palazzo del Lavoro in Turin from 1961 (Fig. 245). At the bottom the columns are in the form of a cross, at the top they are round with a diameter half that of the bottom. The entire form is a visible expression of balance and unity. The lower part expands to withstand lateral stress, and the top is concentrated to tie the roof ribs together (Fig. 246).

EXPRESSION OF SUPPORT: THE COLUMN'S THREE PARTS
From this description we see that the column may be divided into three 'energy sections'.

The uppermost is the column head or *capital*, which receives the load of roof or beam. The bottom part is the foot or *base,* which makes the transition to ground or floor. Between these two extremities stretches the third section, the *column shaft,* the intermediary of the rising and sinking action (Fig. 247).

In the following we shall examine the Classical column. We assume that all the examples support the same load. First let us look at the column shaft

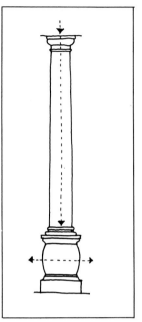

250. Column and 'bulging' pedestal.

249. Column form: the slender column of the Gothic style (Rouen Cathedral, from Frankl, *Gothic Architecture.*).

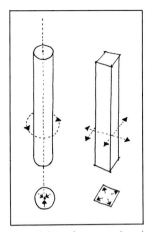

248. Column form: round and square columns.

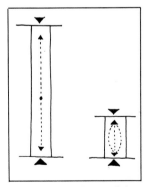

251 a-b. long column and short column.

separately in order to study the importance such factors as cross-section, height, thickness and entasis (swelling) have for its expression of support. Then we shall examine how certain forms of capital and base extend this expression further to roof and ground.

## EXPRESSION OF SUPPORT: ROUND AND SQUARE SHAFTS

In comparing two column shafts having the same height and volume, but with round and square cross-sections, the circular shaft appears slimmer and stronger than the quadratic (Fig. 248).

The circular shaft appears *stronger* because it is a closed form, concentrated inwardly upon itself. 'The curved surface conveys an impression of concentration, a circling around a central point, a lasting unity in itself'.[40]

In contrast, the square pillar is a composite form. It is easy to imagine that its surfaces and corners can 'come apart' because of the unequal distance to a central unifying core.

The round column's concentration around a point conveys a *slimmer* impression than does the pillar. Its form circles unambiguously around the vertical line of the core, and verticality indicates upward thrust and height, which is the underlying principle in any form of growth energy.

This difference in dynamics between a round and a square column shaft has been exploited throughout the history of architecture. An example is the tall free-standing Gothic columns, which are almost always circular or spiral, never square. Had they been square, they would have lost their characteristic toughness. They would seem too weak and flimsy, rather like easily broken 'sticks' (Fig. 249). As another example we find that square columns with swelling are seldom found. The reason is evident. A pillar with a convex curved profile will seem about to sink, while a round column with the same treatment simply gains extra flexibility. An illustration of the first is Borromini's use of the bulging pedestal, here to be understood as a small pillar, beneath a powerful round column (Fig. 250). The expression cannot be mistaken. The entire form appears to be pressed down as if by the column above.

## EXPRESSION OF SUPPORT: SHORT AND TALL SHAFTS

The relatively short column appears to be squashed together by a combination of stress from the roof and resistance from the ground (Fig. 251, b). It reflects the two opposing forces which affect it vertically. The shorter the column, the thicker and broader it seems. Width increases the visual mass and with it the weight of the column.

If we imagine the same column but considerably taller, it will assume an air of *independence* (Fig. 251, a). A tall column, in other words has enough visual mass to give it its own centre of gravity. From this centre vectors will

254. V-column in the *Galerie des Machines* in Paris (from Giedion, *Space, Time and Architecture*).

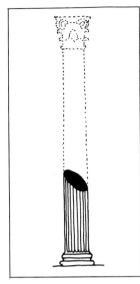

252. The 'broken' column.

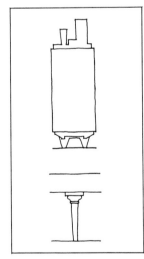

253. V-columns that support L'Unité d'Habitation (above), and V-columns that support the roof at Knossos (below).

spring in two directions, towards the ground and towards the roof. Whereas the short column appears tied down, the tall column gives an impression of freedom, the active conqueror of its surroundings above and below.[41]

Examples of the visual impact of this are the triumphal columns of Roman Antiquity. In their very form these soaring 'heavenly arrows' visibly express the divine elevation of emperors and heroes *super ceteros mortales*. Another illustration confirming this triumphal content is romanticism's burial motif, the *broken* column. The column stump stands above the grave as an earthly symbol of life itself, which in its course stood forth in the full column's vertical dynamism (Fig. 252).

EXPRESSION OF SUPPORT: SHAFT ENTASIS

Entasis creates an even curvature in the shaft, which may be either above or below the column's mid-point. "

If the swelling is *above*, it means that the upper part of the column is thicker and therefore heavier than the lower part. We find this in both Cretan palaces from the seventeenth century B.C. and in modern piloti such as those of Le Corbusier's l'Unité d'Habitation from the twentieth century (Fig. 253).

The main effect of such columns is that of downward led stress, particularly if they carry a great weight. Here too lies the V-column's expression. Because the entire mass balances on a small point at the bottom, an immediate impression of insecurity and danger is conveyed. It is to this the critics were referring in calling the proportions of 'Gallerie des Machines' (Paris, 1889), an error in judgement, 'This lack of proportion produces a bad effect; the girder is not balanced; it has no base... The eye is not reassured' (Fig. 254).[42]

Thus immediately we 'reverse' the actual support aspect and read the form from the ground up. In other words, we identify ourselves with the column's own thrust power and 'help' it to withstand the load above. 'Moving downward, the trusses become increasingly attenuated until they appear scarcely to touch the ground; moving upward, they spread and gain weight and power'.[43]

In the Classical column the swelling is *below* the middle point making it broader at the bottom and narrower at the top. It follows, therefore, that the centre of gravity is closer to the ground. The column seems to push itself off the ground while simultaneously rising upwards. Fundamentally, the Classical column is characterized by its firm anchoring, corresponding to the actual dynamic surge in the column's mass itself. The primary impression, however, depends upon two other conditions in the column's main form.

256. Columns from the 'Basilica' at Paestum.

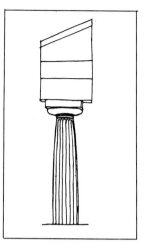

255. Column entasis (column from the 'Basilica' at Paestum).

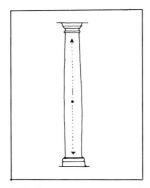

257. Column entasis: a typical Classical column.

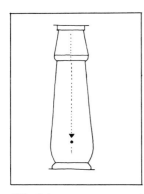

258. Column entasis: a typical Egyptian column.

One involves the way in which the swelling continues on down towards the ground, the other concerns the height of the column.

If the column shaft *diminishes* as it nears the ground, the impression of pressure and sinking is intensified. Typical in this respect is the archaic Doric as exemplified at Paestum, where the column shaft seems ready to give way at any moment under the enormous pressure from above (Fig. 255). But this downward stress impression is also dependent upon the distance of the swelling from the mid-point. If it is right down at ground level as in many Egyptian column types, the sinking characteristic has a more self-contained content. Now it is the column's *own* weight and not the weight it supports which appears to cause the swelling. The shaft takes on an almost 'soft' and self-burdened character, quite different from the tense will-power of the Doric (Figs. 256, 257).

The column's height, furthermore, is important in the effect of entasis. If the column is short and wide, this swelling will accentuate the *sinking* character. In Fagerborg Church, Oslo, by H. Schytte-Berg (1903), the interior columns are formed as just such short, compressed volumes. The intention has been to create a Romanesque atmosphere, an interior hall which, in combination with the heavy roof trusses pressing down upon the surrounding walls, is a manifestation in stone of Lutheran gravity itself.

On the other hand, if the column is tall and slim as in the Corinthian order, entasis will accentuate its *rising* quality. For the Corinthian order Palladio prescribed a proportion of 1:3.[44] The lower third of the column profile is perpendicular, giving it the appearance of resting drum-like on the ground. Above this point the column narrows gradually to a form characterized by an accelerating rise to meet the load above. In comparison, a similar column without entasis has a stiff and spindly look. A column with entasis appears, therefore, to be *stronger* than one without, precisely because it replies to the overhead load by swelling in compliance, while at the same time the accelerating upward thrust masters that same pressure (Fig. 258).

This double content of downward stress and upward thrust contained in the swelling is fully balanced in the developed Doric column. This column, shorter and wider than the Corinthian, is heavier also and therefore visually expresses its ability to support a heavier load. The downward pressure is made visible in the shaft's bulging entasis. At the same time, greater weight means greater strength in the column's own support capacity. Seen thus entasis expresses not only downward pressure but equally the flexibility in the shaft's counter thrust as it rises to meet the entablature and roof.

## EXPRESSION OF SUPPORT: SURFACE OF SHAFT

The column's basic form is in itself not alone in conveying the visible aspect of its support capacity. Surface colour and articulation are additional factors. By means of different colour treatment a thick Doric column in its white marble splendour appears larger but at the same time lighter and thereby 'weaker' than the same column in a dark colour. The latter in turn seems reduced in size but at the same time gives an impression of greater compactness and support capacity. The reverse is true of a slim column. The graceful iron skeletons of the 1800's for example, would appear thinner if painted black rather than white. The latter treatment would enlarge the skeleton and make it visually thicker.

Texture too affects the column's expression of support. Rustication and rough cutting will as a rule give the shaft greater 'weight'. In the squat stone pillars of Stonehenge it is precisely the coarseness of their surfaces that is of essential importance in the whole megalithic atmosphere. At the other extreme a smooth surface will also seem to strengthen the form. Now, however, the impression of strength is quite unlike the above, in that it is decided by a flint-like hardness. H.P. Berlage has interpreted just this effect in designing the columns in the main hall of the Amsterdam Stock Exchange (1902). The primary columns supporting the greatest weight are highly polished and 'hard'. The secondary columns, on the other hand, have a rough surface compared to the others, giving them more texture and 'softness'.

Treatment in relief may also change the column's appearance of strength. The most common surface treatment of this kind is *fluting*.

Doric, Ionic, and Corinthian columns all have these vertically grooved shafts. Their effect is twofold. On the one hand, they may outline verticality in itself and thereby accentuate the upward thrust of the shaft form. On the other hand, they can be a factor in emphasizing exactly the opposite, which is the shaft's own essential substance and weight. The dominating characteristic depends upon the thickness or slimness of the column and whether the fluting is deep or shallow. On the elegant Corinthian column the flutes are narrow and deep, separated by flat edges (Fig. 259). These grooves appear as deep cuts in the body of the shaft itself while the edges outline the actual surface (Fig. 260, a). This effect of concentrated vertical lines accentuates the entire uprightness of the form.

In the thicker Doric column the fluting is quite different. Here the grooves are broad and shallow, with sharp edges in between. It is as if this fluting does noe 'penetrate' the body of the shaft itself but remains an exterior decoration on the form's mass (Fig. 260, b). This serves merely to accentuate its plastic character, which becomes quite clear when compared to similar columns *without* fluting such as those of the temple at Segesta (400 B.C.). The smooth columns here seem stiff and lifeless in comparison with fluted ones, whose softly shadowed grooves emphasize all the inner flexibility of the shaft.

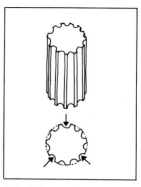

259. Column surface treatment: example of Corinthian fluting.

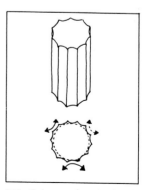

260. Column surface treatment: example of Doric fluting.

204

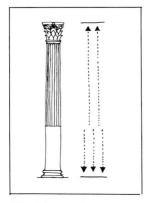

261. Column surface treatment with examples of combinations of smooth and fluted surfaces.

Confirmation of the effect that arises with and without fluting is to be found in columns where the shaft is *both* fluted and smooth. Examples of this combination are already to be found in Antiquity, particularly in the slim Corinthian column. It is done by filling in the grooves in the lower third of the column shaft so that the surface becomes approximately even. A possible reason could be that the flute edgings were particularly exposed to wear and tear on the lower part of the column. This pattern, however, has been maintained even where columns are raised on high pedestals. Is the reason then of a visual nature? As we have shown above, the lower part has approximately the same diameter top and bottom. It is only when the fluting begins that the entasis is intensified. The following impression is clearly conveyed by the different surfaces: the lower part becomes even heavier, the upper section even steeper. The resulting contrast emphasizes the dynamics in the column's own expression of support, which is the struggle between sinking and rising (Fig. 261).

## EXPRESSION OF SUPPORT AND THE COLUMN'S HEAD AND FOOT: CAPITAL AND BASE

In the transition of column to ground and roof, the form given to these connecting elements is decisive for the effect of the column's dynamics on its surroundings. In classical architecture this is a question of how capital and base are designed. Vitruvius stated three ways of forming these members: the *Doric,* the *Ionic,* and the *Corinthian*, each of which should correspond to a definite ratio of proportions in the column shaft (Fig. 262). These three orders formed the basis of an extensive architectural school of thought. The main content in his teachings was based on the wish to differentiate between various weight and strength relationships in the column's visual support capacity. This differentiation has played an important role in traditional classical architecture, both in the interpretation of specific building tasks and in the formulation of their various parts and details (Figs. 263, 264, 265).[45]

## EXPRESSION OF SUPPORT: THE DORIC COLUMN

Of the three orders, as already stated, the Doric column is the heaviest in character.

The Doric order portrays masculine strength says Vitruvius: '... The Doric column, as used in buildings ... exhibits the proportions, strength and beauty of the body of a man'.[46]

It follows, therefore, that the Doric was a suitable style for temples dedicated to heroes and male gods. 'The temples of Minerva, Mars and Hercules will be Doric, since the virile strength of these gods makes daintiness entirely inappropriate to their houses'.[47]

262. Doric, Ionic and Corinthian orders (diagram after Uhde, *Die Architekturformen des Klassischen Altertums*).

263. Doric, Ionic and Corinthian orders as articulating elements: the major column is Corinthian, the inner columns are Ionic, while the outer columns are Doric (temple in Bassai, from Berve etc., *Greek Temples and Shrines*).

264. The column meets the ground (corner columns from Rome, photo by I. K. Barstad).

265. The column meets the ground (base from temple in Bassai, from Charbonneaux, *Das Klassische Griechenland*).

206

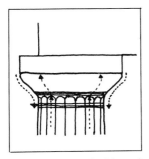

266. Doric capital (classical type).

270. Pre-Ionic capital (diagram from Robertson, *Greek and Roman Architecture*).

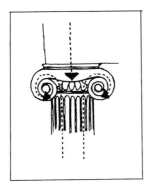

271. Ionic capital (classic type).

As a result, the Doric has been used through the ages in strong and rusticated buildings ' ... such as city gates, fortresses, citadels, treasuries, arsenals, prisons, ports and similar military installations'.[48]

The form given to base and capital was intended as a part of this visual expression of weight.

The Doric capital comprises two parts. Immediately beneath the architrave is a square slab, the *abacus,* and beneath it the head of the column itself, the *echinus,* which is in the form of a convex circular cushion. The Doric column has no base in the usual meaning of the term. The fluted shaft is led straight down to the ground with no emphasis on the transition.

The form at both places reflects the balanced tension between the column's upward thrust and downward stress. The lack of a base accentuates the power of both tendencies simultaneously. Viewed from the bottom up it is as if the column springs directly from the horizontal level, strong and uncompromising. Fluting emphasizes the dynamics of this growth. Read in reverse, the impression is exactly the opposite: the column is forced directly into the ground by the heavy pressure from above. This balance between rising and sinking also occurs in the fully developed Doric capital. In the column capitals of 'Poseidon's' temple at Paestum (c. 450 B.C.), for example, the two tendencies overlap in the *echinus* itself (Fig. 266). The *rising* tendency is emphasized by continuing the shaft fluting part of the way into the neck of the capital and terminating it by a row of fillets (ánuli) immediately beneath the cushion. The *sinking* impression is accentuated by terminating the capital a short distance down the shaft itself with a similar row of fillets. In this way the two tendencies overlap and are united.

The curvature between neck and cushion is also decisive for this double tension in the capital. In the classical capital the curve is even and upright in contrast to the archaic capital, where it is broken by a deep groove immediately beneath the cushion (Figs. 255, 256). Here the column profile narrows sharply towards the top while the cushion bulges outwards over it like a slightly flattened inner tube. The cushion's form emphasizes the effect of downward pressure. The shaft, on the other hand, accents the upward thrust in that the diminution of the upper half 'sharpens' and accelerates the verticality. Altogether, the archaic column is a greater visualization of a dramatic *collision* of opposing forces rather than a *fusion* of them, as we have seen in the fully developed classical column.

## EXPRESSION OF SUPPORT: THE IONIC COLUMN

The Ionic column takes its place midway between the heavy Doric and the slim Corinthian. It personifies the feminine qualities says Vitruvius. It is, however, the mature woman who is represented in the calm elegance of the Ionic. Whereas the Corinthian column depicted youthful feminine spontaneity, the Ionic was the style of the more serene goddesses.

> The construction of temples of the Ionic order to Juno, Diana, Father Bacchus and other gods of that kind, will be in keeping with the middle position which they hold, for the building of such will be an appropriate combination of the severity of the Doric and the delicacy of the Corinthian.[49]

In the Doric order we saw how entasis was clearly visible as an interpretation of a powerful balance between thrust and stress. This struggle between survival and resistance is less apparent in the Ionic column. The impression here is of something accomplished and sure. First of all, the Ionic column is slimmer than the Doric and the diminution not as great.[50] Combined with slimness we find a shaft rising unconcernedly upwards. In the second place, both Ionic and Corinthian columns have a base that divides shaft and ground and thereby blocks any further continuation. This 'buffer' absorbs the jolt of the shaft meeting the ground but at the same time, like a springy counter-power, initiates the upward thrust. The effect, however, depends upon whether the base appears to belong to the column or the ground. If the base is formed as part of the ground, it is as if the ground itself rises to push the column upwards, giving an overall rising effect. The reverse is true if the column pushes downwards — a sinking effect occurs (Fig. 267, a, b).

This upward or downward spring-like action is made clear by the form of the details. In considering the classical Ionic, we see that the base is divided into two main parts. At the bottom is a square slab (plinth) which neutralizes the transition between level ground and the round base and column above. The round part consists of two convex mouldings *(tori)* above and below a concave groove (Fig. 268).

The bulging cushion-like mouldings illustrate the effect of *downward* stress. The lower ring, therefore, which receives the greater pressure, protrudes most. On the other hand, the concave groove depicts the way in which the form thrusts itself *upwards*. This means that the lower and deeper the horizontal groove is, the heavier seems the pressure from above. Inversely, the higher and more upright the groove, the stronger seems the 'thrust-off' towards the top (Fig. 269).

The Ionic capital conveys a 'soft compliancy'. In contrast to the Doric order's conflict-filled struggle against the weight above, the Ionic capital appears to yield to this pressure and settles obediently but resiliently against the roof-bearing architrave. Whereas the Doric capital draws attention to an overlapping of contrasting powers, the Ionic capital appears at first glance to be *split* by the pressure from above in the way its two spiral volutes curl outwards in opposite directions beneath the weight of the entab-

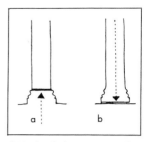

267 a-b. The base as a part of (a) the ground, and (b) the column.

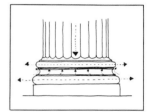

268. Ionic (Attic) base.

269. Ionic base with broad and narrow cavettos.

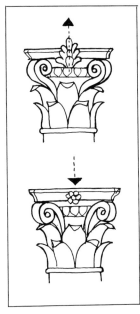

272. Capitals from F. Borromini's St. Carlo alle Quatro Fontane (Above with vertical scrolls and below with horizontal scrolls).

lature. In older proto-Ionic capital forms it is even more apparent that the volutes are a result of such a splitting in the upper part of the rising column shaft itself (Fig. 270). In the classical capital the form is seen as a resilient cushion in which the volutes form its parallel sides. The other two sides, which face the spectator, show a convex downward curl illustrating clearly and directly the strength of the pressure from above, a pressure identical to that which causes the capital to coil (Fig. 271). The entire capital thus reflects both the reception and resiliency in the column's contact with the architrave and roof.

An interesting variation of the Ionic volute pattern, confirming the above description, is Borromini's formulation of the columns in the interior of San Carlo alle Quattro Fontane (1641). In contrast to the other interior columns, whose volutes are of the usual reclining type, the eight columns carrying the dome have capitals with active upright volutes (Fig. 272). The reclining volutes *terminate* the verticality in the column shaft, while the upright volutes *continue* it further up and into the roof system's ribs and arches.

## EXPRESSION OF SUPPORT: THE CORINTHIAN COLUMN

The Corinthian column is usually slimmer than the Ionic but otherwise has similar fluting and base. The capital, however, is different and in its form a direct response to the verticality in the shaft itself. Whereas both Doric and Ionic capitals illustrate the *alternation* of thrust and stress in the column's support capacity, the Corinthian capital appears to state unequivocally upward thrust alone.

This is already apparent in the capital's ornamentation. The entire capital is covered with rows of naturalistic acanthus leaves giving the form an organic and non-supporting appearance. The verticality in the shaft is interpreted as a free growth, unhampered by architrave and roof, 'bursting forth' playfully against the roof moulding. While both Doric and Ionic capitals are compressed or divided by the load above, the Corinthian thrusts on upwards as though having nothing to support (Fig. 273).

This unfettered and dynamic impression is caused not only by the overlapping acanthus foliage but also by the concave inward swing of the abacus and the diagonal outward swing of the corner volutes (Fig. 274). The volutes dynamically lead the entire capital out into space in contrast to both the Ionic and Doric capitals where the form is strictly imprisoned within the architrave above. In the concave grooves between the volutes, however, there are indications of another diametrically opposed motion, which seems to be caused by some external pressure. It is as if the form itself pulls back to make way for a further growth of the underlying foliage, which may climb over the abacus and even right up into the entablature itself (Figs. 275, 276).

277. Corinthian triumphal columns (reconstruction of *Forum Romanum,* from Dal Maso, *Rome of the Caesars*).

276. Corinthian variation (detail from Nicholai Church in Leipzig, from Klopfer, *Von Palladio bis Schinkel*).

273. Corinthian capital in motion (drawing by G. Neumann, from *Domus,* 610, 1980).

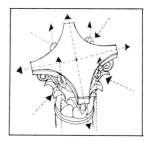

274. Corinthian capital (classical type).

278. Stone pillars at Stonehenge (from Hitchcock (ed.), *World Architecture*).

279. Apparent column height and the effect of the length of the colonnade (Parthenon).

275. Corinthian capital (Rococo variation from the Bishop's residence in Würzburg by L. von Hildebrandt, from Forssman, *Dorisch, jonisch, korintisch*).

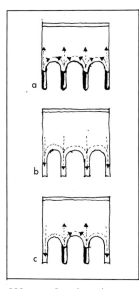

280 a-c. Round and square columns and the supportive expression of the wall: (a) rising from below, (b) sinking from above, (c) alternation between rising at the middle and sinking at the corners.

This non-supporting and vertical effect in the Corinthian is well exploited throughout the history of architecture. The Corinthian was considered to be the most 'delightful' of the three orders and was used in particularly important and prominent buildings. 'It is reserved for particularly elegant buildings meant to be impressive by their nobility of character and splendid ornamentation'.[51]

This usage was due not only to the capital's rich ornamentation but doubtless also to the entire vertical emphasis in the column's form. Such a column portrays victory over all stress and resistance. It springs freely aloft as if in triumph. The triumphal column of Antiquity was, therefore, preferably Corinthian and supported no more than a statue of the exalted one. Thus the column's inherent verticality became also a meaningful part of the entire monument's content, which was the victor's 'triumph and power' (Fig. 277).

## EXPRESSION OF SUPPORT: THE RELATION BETWEEN INSIDE AND OUTSIDE

In general, the heavier, shorter and more tightly formed the skeleton system is, the more closed off it appears.

The distance between the squat megaliths of Stonehenge may be just as great as between the clustered pillars in a Gothic nave (Figs. 52, 278). The diameter may also be the same, but their height and texture are vitally different. For this reason, Stonehenge 'shuts out' while Gothic 'opens'.

A column may also seem taller than it really is if the row in which it stands is taller than it is wide and is compared to one which is wider. We see, therefore, how the eight frontal columns of the Parthenon stretch skywards to a greater extent than the seventeen columns on each flank (Fig. 279).

Various surface treatments of columns are also used to differentiate between inside and outside. In historicism it was quite usual to use coarse and closely placed granite columns in an outer wall while the same column in the interior was of highly polished and colourful, veined marble. The latter gave the form a composite and flamboyant character contrasting sharply to the more natural, exterior columns serving as buffers against exterior space.

The difference in the expression of support between a round column and square column is also intentionally used to convey the impression of varying motions in the wall. Let us imagine a comparatively high wall supported by three round arches, in one case by square columns and in the other by round columns (Fig. 280, a-c).

The square columns, which in their form are a part of the wall, passively receive the weight that seems evenly distributed by the rounded arches. If these columns are replaced by round columns, the sinking effect is coun-

281. Variation of column orders. Doric outermost, Ionic innermost (Attalo's Stoa in Athens).

282. The columnar orders in super-position: Doric, Ionic, Corinthian (Colosseum in Rome, from Koepf, *Baukunst in Fünf Jahrtausenden*).

tered by a *rising* effect. The result is a contrast between the upward thrust of columns and arches and the downward stress of the wall. If round and square columns are combined, the central arch being supported by round columns and the corners by square columns, the result will be a rising mid-section and two sinking corner parts, which means that the wall opens up in the middle and shuts at the corners (Fig. 280, c).

The varying character of the classical orders is also used to differentiate between inside and outside. The Corinthian and Ionic orders are more open than the Doric. Again we take the University buildings in Oslo as a typical example. In the mid-section, where one enters, the columns are not only round but Ionic as well. The applied pillars on either side, on the other hand, are Doric. The columns are used to enhance the width in a case like this, in which an opening section is framed by closing sections.

This differentiation takes place in depth also, and in the same way. In Palladio's Palazzo Valmarana, Vicenza (1566), the outermost giant pilasters are Corinthian (Fig. 197). These are festive columns opening the wall's outer layer towards the world. In contrast, the innermost layer of pillars, really part of the wall, are Doric. In classical Athens this order is reversed. In both the Propylaea leading in to the Acropolis (431 B.C.) and the Stoa of Attalos facing the Agora (150 B.C.) the outer columns are heavy Doric — a protective wall against exterior space. Within, however, the columns are in the lighter Ionic (Fig. 281).

The orders are superimposed as well, thereby indicating differences in the wall's stress pattern. One of the earliest examples of superimposition in such a context is Rome's Colosseum (A.D. 82) (Fig. 282). The building is a massive arched wall construction in four storeys, each storey having fictive skeletal frames around its arches. At the bottom is the Doric order, above it the Ionic while the two upper stories are Continthian. The ground storey is the lowest of the four, its columns are without pedestals and stand directly on the ground. The two storeys above are equal in height while the top storey is the highest. The entire fabric of the building may be read in even stages from the ground up. The heavy Doric base is surmounted by the more graceful and gradually lighter Ionic and Corinthian storeys with the slimmest version at the top. In symbolic form, the columns summarize weight differences in the supporting wall. The skeletal system delineates these differences and in so doing makes visible and expresses the rising in an otherwise homogeneous and uniform building. The amphitheatre's heavy muscularity is transformed into something proud and erect, which at a glance prepares the spectator for what he is about to encounter within: hero and soldier in proud combat for emperor and people.

283. Round columns and freedom of motion (from The Ministry of Health in Rio de Janeriro by Le Corbusier, from Le Corbusier, *Oeuvre compléte 1910–65*).

284. Square columns and directional motion (The Supreme Court in Chandigarh by Le Corbusier) from Le Corbusier, *Oeuvre complète 1910—65*).

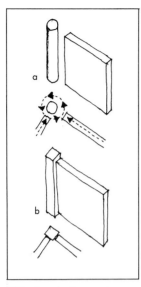

285. Round column and square column and their relationship to other elements: (a) the round column is free, (b) the square column is attached.

## THE COLUMN'S EXPRESSION OF MOTION

In our introduction to the free-standing column we pointed out that its expression of support concerned the *plastic* treatment of the column form.

This will also affect its expression of motion. Its size, for example, whether tall, short or thick, will arouse different motion impulses. The tall column with accent on verticality will convey an arresting rather than a directional impulse. With verticality and centre so strongly emphasized, a spontaneous feeling of reserve will arise in the passer-by (see the vertical wall p. 145 f). A thick column stops us in another way. Its sheer plastic mass brings us physically to a halt, in contrast to the short, normal column, which, because it is our 'equal', allows for easier passage.

The column's aspect of motion, however, is largely determined by the form's *outer surfaces*. In consequence, the smooth and the rough column have different directional capabilities. We slip easily past a smooth column but a rough one disturbs and 'brakes' our passage (See rough and smooth surfaces p. 171 ff). In this connection the cross-section is especially important. Consequently, in the following we shall limit our study to the most important motion effects conveyed by square and round columns.

## EXPRESSION OF MOTION: ROUND AND SQUARE COLUMNS

The round column lends freedom to the surroundings — a square column directs them. In approaching a round column we have a choice of either proceeding along and past it or along and around it (Fig. 283). In approaching a square column we encounter a mass which, if it does not stop us completely, leads us along beside it in a definite direction. The round column conveys freedom, the square column restricts it. This corresponds to their own forms. The round column is an independent individual, in all parts equal and self-contained. The square column, on the other hand, has sides leading along its centre and corners that point away from this centre. When it is rectangular, an inequality arises; the longer sides dominate the shorter (Fig. 284).

## ROUND COLUMN AND SQUARE COLUMN: SURROUNDING SPACES

Freedom and restriction are also the impressions made by the round column and the square column (or pier if rectangular), in the *context* of their immediate surroundings.

The round column is released from its surroundings because nothing can be joined to it. The square column on the other hand, has four sides to which walls and slabs may be added (Fig. 285). A round column in a wall stands out because the wall is straight and the column curved. The pillar is perceived as a part of the wall itself, or rather 'what remains of the wall'.[52]

215

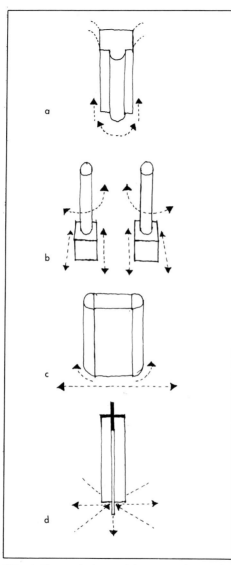

288 a-d. The round column and the square column combined: (a) round and square joined, (b) round and square on top of one another, (c) a cross between round and square, (d) round and square abstracted (cruciform column).

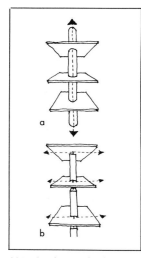

286 a-b. The round column and the square column and their relationship to vertical space: (a) the round column is free, (b) the space column is additive.

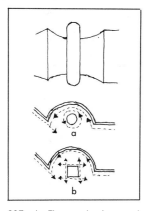

287 a-b. The round column and the square column and their relationship to horizontal space: (a) the round column sets free and focuses surrounding elements, (b) the square column leads and binds them.

This freedom and restriction also concerns the surrounding spaces. In principle, round columns lend freedom to space, both vertically and horizontally. We find an example of the first in the relation between column and floor slab in Le Corbusier's pioneer projects. The columns have the same diameter from top to bottom and are without base or capital. There is nothing to prevent the columns from continuing on through the slab in both directions (Fig. 286, a). Nor do the slabs seem attached to the column shafts, they seem almost movable, as if they could be slid up and down the columns. If these same columns had been square instead, the overall impression would be one of additive isolated units (Fig. 286, b) The slabs between the storeys would appear to be whole units, unpenetrated but carried by superimposed supports.

Horizontally as well, in relation to its environmental space, the round column allows for freedom. A modern example is the office building of the Norwegian University Press in Oslo (1980) designed by the architectural firm of Jan and Jon (Fig. 287, a ). The great columns which extend through all the storeys are surrounded by curving and sharply cornered walls, decorations and mouldings. Areas are created which are not just random parts in an undulating whole. They become specific places, because the columns themselves create focal points. If the columns had been quadratic, a situation of conflict would have arisen — a conflict between the curving freedom of the walls, on the one hand, and the columns' directionality on the other (Fig. 287, b).

ROUND AND SQUARE COLUMNS IN COMBINATION.

Round and square columns may be combined in many ways.

They may be *juxtaposed,* as we have seen in the case of the Colosseum. This variant conveys a stage by stage inward motion from an open skeletal layer on the outside to a more closed pillar and wall system further in (Fig. 288, a). Round and square columns may also be *superimposed* as in the column mounted on a pedestal. This combination conveys verticality in the upper part and a leading horizontality below (Fig. 288, b). Round and square columns may also be *combined* to create a new form. This we find when two semicircular columns are attached to opposite sides of a square column(Fig. 288, c). This symbiosis encourages the impulse both to proceed along the unit and to go around it. A square column may also have its corners sheered at an angle or rounded, which in turn gives the double effect of directional and centralizing motion.

A special variation of the combined column is the *cruciform column* (Fig. 288, d). In section it is a cross, something quite apart from the above examples. It is not meant as a combination of round and square columns but rather as a fusion of their individual qualities; the column focuses, the pillar

294. The deformed frame (Loggia del Capitaniato by Palladio, from Vendetti, *The loggia del Capitaniato*).

295. The deformed frame (Loggia del Capitaniato by Palladio, from Vendetti, *The loggia del Capitaniato*).

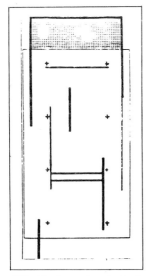

289. Cruciform column in directio nal space (Barcelona Pavilion by Mies van der Rohe, from Johnson, *Mies van der Rohe*).

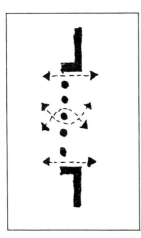

290. Round column as entrance motif (diagram of entrance to The University of Oslo).

directs. Mies van der Rohe's use of this type in his Barcelona pavilion (1929) shows that its combined qualities are to be seen as an accentuation of the building's own spatial system (Fig. 289). This spatial system combines strictly ordered rows of supporting columns with expansively free wall planes connecting outside and inside. Just like the walls, the columns are to be interpreted as an arrangement of freely arranged horizontal planes. At the same time, however, they point inwards towards a unifying core at the crossing point. Thus, the qualities of both the column system and the plane system are revealed in concentrated form; the columns order the space and hold it together; the wall planes direct and spread it.

## ROUND COLUMN AND SQUARE COLUMN AND THE RELATION BETWEEN INSIDE AND OUTSIDE

Round and square columns differ in terms of their relationship to the concept of inside and outside. Let us take two examples, beginning with the main entrance to the University in Oslo (Fig. 174). This entrance is formed like a temple front with four free-standing round columns framed by a square column at each corner (see also p. 137 f). The walls on either side are divided into a system of giant pilasters. The corner columns are meant as conclusions to the projecting side walls, which frame the round columns while at the same time creating the transition between these and the shallow wall pilasters on each side. Whereas the square columns and pilasters are seen as part of the delimiting wall, the round columns are intermediaries of the connection between inside and outside (Fig. 290). One passes easily around and past them. They form the actual transfer point for the continuous flow of people moving freely between the fore-court and the great staircase.

A square column, however, does not necessarily hinder inward movement, it may also emphasize it. If a square column is slab-like it may either halt or guide movements, depending upon whether it stands across or parallel to the entrance direction. In Le Corbusier's Supreme Court in Chandigarh (1953), piers paralleling the direction of entry are used to make the entrance inviting (Fig. 284, see p. 295). The building is long and narrow with the approach to its broad side. As we have shown earlier, such a horizontal form has a rejecting effect on further forward movement. Consequently, the architect creates a contrasting motion to this transverse breadth by freeing three of the colossal piers which support the roof. In this way one is led alongside the piers and straight into the mighty stairs and ramps within.

298. The relationship between the beam and the columns (Cathedral in Carpi by B. Peruzzi, from Wittkower, *Architectural Principles in the Age of Humanism*).

293. A diagonally stiffened frame (Gothic buttressing, from Macaulay, *The Cathedral*).

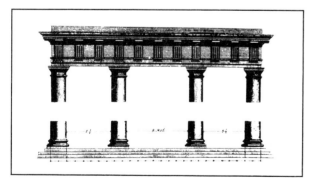

297. The relationship between the columns and the beam (Doric frame, with larger intercolumnation at the centre, by L.B. Alberti, from Alberti, *Ten Books on Architecture*).

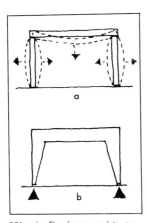

291 a-b. The frame and its tendency to deflect and buckle: (a) diagram of the phenomenon, (b) C. Siegel's stiffened solution (Siegel's diagram, from Siegel), Strukturformen der modernen Architektur).

292. A diagonally stiffened frame (proposed portal into The University Press in Oslo by Jan & Jon).

# THE FRAME
## THE FRAME'S EXPRESSION OF SUPPORT

The frame is a complete figure (Fig. 291, a).

In the combination of column and beam lies the expression of support. For all frames, the main problem in both vertical and lateral stress is to prevent combinations of the beam deflection and inward or outward buckling of the two columns.

A simple diagram by Curt Siegel illustrates this factor and its importance for the form of the frame (Fig. 291, b).[53] The danger of beam deflection is avoided by giving the beam sufficient size and cross section in relation to the span and by using appropriate materials. As for the columns, the danger of cracking or splaying is prevented by firm foundations. To prevent failure when the foundation is immovable, the upper part of the column is strengthened by being made thicker in the transition to the beam.

Providing a frame with acceptable stiffness and load-bearing capacity has represented a major problem throughout architectural history (Fig. 292). A good example is the Gothic buttressing system (Fig. 293). Buttress form is impossible to understand unless directly associated with the roof and its lateral stress. In cross-section the Gothic church nave is seen as a frame construction in which the pointed arch and buttress together form the beam. The arch as a form and not least of all the pointed arch, is a direct answer to the problem of effective deflection deterrence in a stone construction with maximum span (see p. 228 f). The buttresses illustrate strategic points of transition and anchoring which transmit lateral stress. Tall, towering superstructures topped by pinnacles and finials supply extra weight and reinforcement at the points where arch and buttress meet. The buttress itself is enlarged in stages in the descent in order to offset diagonal stress.

In a way, this support expression at the junctures above visualizes the entire Gothic ideology. Gothic construction was meant to depict *triumph*. This was a triumph over falling and earthbound forces, which in concentrated form were imprisoned and conquered for the sole purpose of illustrating the very opposite — the ascending and heaven-bent.

In other periods, the wish was not to express triumph and conquest but quite the opposite — collapse and pessimism. This was done by weakening the skeleton at precisely the same points that would otherwise have been strengthened. Such tendencies were particularly seen in Mannerist architecture. In Giulio Romano's Palazzo del Té, Mantua (1526) it is the architrave which is weakened. Here the keystones appear to slip down in the very centre where the sagging tendency is greatest (Fig. 294). In Andrea Palladio's loggia del Capitanio, Vicenca (1571), the architrave is broken at the same point, this time by the windows, which are pushed right up into

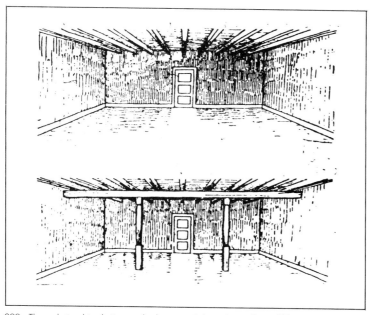

299. The relationship between the beam and the columns (from Phleps, *Vom Wesen der Architektur*).

300. The relationship between the beam and the columns (a modern concrete parking garage).

296. The deformed frame (sketch detail from Fontana di Trevi in Rome, by Salvi).

301. The relationship between the beam and the wall (beam resting on glass, from Ekeberghallen in Oslo).

the architrave (Fig. 295). The outer pilasters of Nicolò Salvi's Fontana di Trevi, Rome (1762), are a Baroque example of a similar weakening of firm foundation. They are 'broken' just where they meet the solid stone on which they stand (Fig. 296).

## EXPRESSION OF SUPPORT: COORDINATION OF BEAM AND COLUMNS

From what has been said already it is clear that columns and beam must be in accord if the motif is to appear secure. Thus, the beam and columns must be suitably proportioned to both the width and height of the frame's opening seen in relation to our shared experiences with the materials used.

An example of this is to be found in a colonnade by Alberti in which the centre inter-columniation is greater than those on either side (Fig. 297). We see that the dimensions of the architrave are not scaled to the narrower side openings but to the central bay, where the tendency to deflection is greatest both visually and in reality. On such grounds, according to Rudolph Wittkower, Palladio could have criticized Baldassare Peruzzi's fictive façade system for the cathedral in Capri (1515) (Fig. 298). There, the only support for the long transversal main beam are two small corner pilasters and no apparent support in the middle, a 'necessity' to prevent optical deflection.

Herman Phleps maintains the same by pointing out the spontaneous relief one feels when a long and heavy beam is supported in the middle — even if this is statically unnecessary (Fig. 299). Frame constructions in many modern halls also lack such a reassuring corrective. Enormous concrete girders, technically strong enough because of inner reinforcement, are only supported at each end by thin pillars. To accept such a construction automatically we must be aware of the hidden reinforcement. This means, in fact, that general reactions to what is considered 'good' form have become dependent on knowledge (Figs. 300, 301).

## THE BEAM

The above examples show that in the coordination of frame elements the *beam* is particularly important for the expression of support. It is the beam's form, dimensions and span which tell us whether or not the supporting columns are suited to their task — and not the other way round. Two mighty columns, therefore, may carry an undersized beam without any indication of danger and collapse. Danger is first apparent when a heavy, oversized beam is supported by columns that are too slender (Fig. 302, a, b).

In the following, therefore, we shall limit our study to the support expression of the beam. We repeat that we shall base this discussion on the

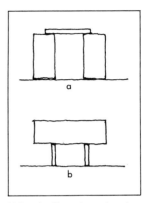

302 a-b. The relationship between the beam and the columns: (a) over-dimensioned columns, (b) over-dimensioned beam.

303. The curve of a straight beam (bridge in Schwarzenburg, Switzerland, by R. Maillart, from Bihalji-Merin (ed.), *Brücken der Welt*).

306. The curve and midpoint/endpoint correction of a straight beam (door from Hatton Garden in London, from Amery (ed.), *Period Houses and their Details*).

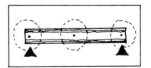

308. The curve and midpoint/endpoint correction of a beam (brick warehouses from Amsterdam).

304. The curve and correction points of a straight beam: end points, midpoints, upper- or lower edges.

224

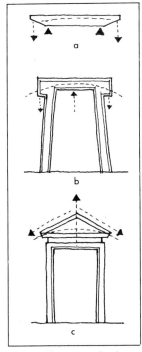

305 a-c. The curve and end point correction of a straight beam: (a) concrete beam by Siegel, (b) the Doric 'ears', (c) the Classical pediment.

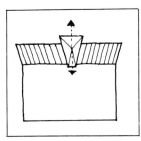

307. The curve and midpoint correction of a straight beam (keystone).

*straight beam* in both its classical and modern variations and the *arched beam* with the pointed arch, segmental arch, and flat arch as its most typical variations.

### EXPRESSION OF SUPPORT: THE STRAIGHT BEAM

Of the various beam forms, the straight beam is both in appearance and reality the one most prone to deflection.

To offset this tendency and to convey a 'secure' impression, optical correctives have been used. The entire form may be given a slight curve, or particularly unsure points along the beam accentuated.

The first solution may be compared to the form of the Greek temple floor. Given a very slight convex curve the sinking tendency of the *stylobate* was counteracted and the entire structure seemed to rise upwards towards heaven. This same principle is also used in modern design, especially in the case of bridges with lengthy spans (Fig. 303). For reasons more visual than technical, the course of the bridge itself is raised to offset an otherwise slack and insecure line movement.[54]

The other solution concerns optical correctives at the beam ends, midpoint and upper and lower edges (Fig. 304).

As we have already pointed out, the support expression of all straight beams depends upon the distance between the supporting points. If the span seems too great the horizontal line may be made more taut by *extending* the beam beyond the support points on each side. These extensions, both visually and in reality, will function as counter weights which relieve the stress in the middle (Fig. 305, a).

This effect is a possible explanation of the so-called 'ears' of the Doric door frame (Fig. 305, b). Combined with slightly inward slanting posts a plain rectangle is transformed into a vibrant curve with all the sturdiness of the Doric order. The classical triangular pediment may also convey the same effect (Fig. 305, c). The weight of the triangle's raking cornices in falling on the outer ends of the straight cornice give this horizontal element an upward bent effect.

A triangle, in itself a stiffening form, gives an additional vertical effect to the whole composition. This theme has been used in endless variations, especially in the Renaissance and Baroque periods (Fig. 306). (See also the triangle as a roof form p. 335 ff).

Another method of counteracting this visual deflection is to emphasize the beam's *keystone* (Fig. 307). This is often done in brick beams and very clearly so in Dutch buildings of the 1800's in which the voussoirs (the wedge-shaped stones) are held in place by a larger keystone. Frequently this keystone protrudes both outwards and upwards in the form of large wedges and consoles (Fig. 308). This triangular form helps to lift the

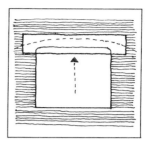

310. The curve and lower edge correction of a straight beam (routed moulding).

309. The curve of a beam and an excessively heavy keystone (from the Palace of Justice in Rome by G. Calderini, photo by Chr. Norberg-Schulz).

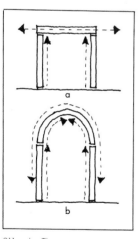

311 a-b. The supportive expression of a beam: (a) straight beam (vertical and horizontal addition), (b) arched beam (vertical and horizontal unification).

226

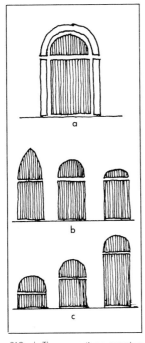

312 a-b. The supportive expression of an arched beam and the form of its opening: (a) arch section and column section, (b) the shapes of the arch section (pointed, semicircular, shallow), (c) the shapes of the column section (horizontal, square, vertical).

middle section, while at the same time the sturdy concrete gives visual strength to an otherwise weak point in the form. In this motif, it is quite evident that the slightest change in position and dimensions of the keystone can convey the completely *opposite* effect (Fig. 309). In buildings by both Nicholas Hawksmoor and Giulio Romano, enormous slipped keystones give a threatening rather than a rising effect.

The third method of counteracting visual deflection is by the use of various *mouldings* along the upper and lower edges of the beam. The simplest method in this respect is the use of horizontal fluting on the beam's underside (Fig. 310). This motif, used particularly in the Gothic period and in the 1800's, gives the effect of removing part of the mass where the stress is greatest, while by arching the corners at the same time the entire form is given a necessary vertical lift.

## EXPRESSION OF SUPPORT: THE ARCHED BEAM

The arch is the solution to the problem of deflection. Its upward curve resists deflection and is the ultimate consequence of the correctives in the straight beam and the goal for forms and lines of articulation.

In a straight frame, verticals and horizontals are in contrast. Columns and beam are parts added to one another. In an arched frame the accent is vertical because the horizontal element is 'cancelled'. Columns and beam are joined (Fig. 311, a, b). Thus, in an arched frame the supporting element will always dominate the vertical stress element. Basically, therefore, the arched frame is 'secure' and the straight frame 'insecure'.

We find that the support expression of the arched frame is more dependent on the relation between columns and beam than is the straight frame. This relationship is in turn mainly determined by two aspects of the frame's form.

The first aspect concerns the form of the *opening* as outlined by its surrounding borders. This form consists of two secondary figures, one within the arch opening at the top and the other within the limits of the columns below (Fig. 312, a-c). As already stated, arch forms are variations on the basic types of pointed, rounded and flat. The rectangle bounded by columns is dictated by the height and distance between these columns and will vary accordingly, but here too within certain fundamental variations: the horizontal, the vertical, and the quadratic rectangle. Thus, the same arch supported by very tall or by very short columns will convey quite different expressions of support. The first will seem 'free' and rising, the other heavy and sinking.

The other aspect of importance for the effect of the frame is the *plastic* form given to the arch and columns. Concerning the arch, as already noted, there are three places in particular which are important: the top of the arch, the upper and lower edges, and the transition to the columns.

In the following, the rectangle between the columns will remain unchanged so that we may study the primary effects of the arch form independently. We shall take as our point of departure the principal forms of arch openings, while the role played by various kinds of plastic treatment of both arches and columns will be considered in connection with individual examples.

### EXPRESSION OF SUPPORT: THE POINTED ARCH

Of all the archetypes of the arch, the pointed arch is the most 'non-bearing'.

The principle behind the connection of column and arch in the Gothic pointed arch is vertical integration, in which arch opening and column opening merge to form an extended, unified whole (Figs. 293, 313).

In the Gothic nave verticality is already indicated by the slenderness and height of the columns. The columns become clusters of pipe-like perpendiculars interspersed with deep grooves, which convey a dynamic rising stretch of light and dark lines. There may be no sign at all of the transition to the arch as frequently seen in late Gothic. Most usual, nevertheless, is the spreading foliate capital, which with its organic character further emphasizes the growth of the form. Within the arch are two characteristics which extend this verticality, the steep *sides* and the *point* at which they meet.

The sides of the arches are seen as a continuation of the columns' own structure, as if the columns themselves were bending in towards one another (Fig. 314).[55] This unity has both technical and spatial reasons. Technically, the desire was for maximum vertical stress in order to alleviate lateral stress and the need of overly thich walls. Spatially, the capital marking the transition from column to arch could be placed far down the shaft without destroying the main form. In this way, narrow and wide pointed arches could be combined and still maintain common springing points and height.

The point of the arch itself emphasizes the verticality of the form. It seems to tear the very wall it supports (see window p. 263). The point also indicates that the arch does not stop within itself but continues on upward. The arch form, which is constructed by the overlapping segments of two circles, shows that its conclusion lies *outside* the frame (Fig. 315). The principle behind the continuity of a round arch is that it leads evenly back to the same level at which it began — the form 'closes'. Just the opposite happens in the pointed arch were continuity is broken at the top point — the form 'opens'.

We realize that the uncompromising upward rise of the pointed arch was not created as a load-bearer. The intention was rather to give a symbolic

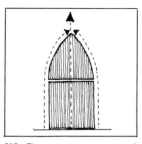

313. The supportive expression of a pointed arch: the formal expression of the pointed arch is integrative.

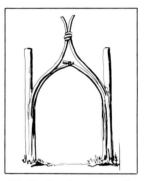

314. The formal expression of a pointed arch: arch sides bound together (after Rykwert, *On Adam's House in Paradise*).

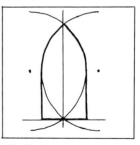

315. The formal expression of a pointed arch: arch sides are parts of two circles which overlap each other.

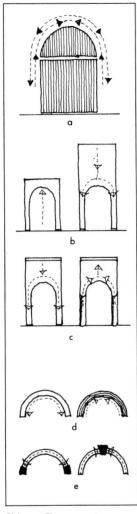

316 a-e. The supportive expression of a semicircular arch: (a) the formal expression of the semicircular arch is additive, (b), (c) the semicircular arch and column support, (d), (e) the semicircular arch and articulation (moulding, end points, keystone).

send-off, a continuation beyond itself of verticality, the very principle of the heavenly ascension. This concept was of such importance in sacred architecture's use of the pointed arch that buttresses, the visible solution to the stress problem, were placed outside the spiritual space. The Gothic pointed arch, in other words, was not developed to visualize the realities of the forces of gravity but, on the contrary, its purpose was to defy this world, not to follow it.

## EXPRESSION OF SUPPORT: THE ROUND ARCH

Whereas integration is the keynote in the relation between arch opening and column opening in the pointed frame, addition is the keynote in construction of the round arch frame. This form is seen as a combination of a complete semicircle and a complete rectangle (Fig. 316, a). This means that the frame is composed of independent but balanced upper and lower elements (Fig. 317).

The support expression of the arch is also in balance between to tendencies. In contrast to the accentuated rising aspect of the pointed arch, the true semicircle may be interpreted as either sinking or rising. Read from the bottom, the form may give the effect of a tense curve supporting the load from above (Fig. 316, a). Read from the top this same curve may appear to be an equal distributor of vertical stress. Consequently, determination of the dominating tendency depends on three conditions: the size of the load the arch appears to carry, the form of the columns, and the form and articulation of the arch itself.

An example of major stress on the arch is found in the openings carrying the clerestory walls in Ottonian churches (Fig. 318). The overly heavy wall presses downwards, and the arches distribute the motion towards the ground. In other arches which support no great weight, as for example in the interior of Brunelleschi's St. Lorenzo, Florence (1421), the stress is vertical and motion is led upwards (Fig. 316, b).

The columns beneath the arch are equally important in the expression of support (Fig. 316, c). If a round arch is supported by square columns that must be interpreted as parts of the wall, the motion has a downward direction. If it is supported by round columns, which in themselves are independent vertical forms, motion is led upwards (see p. 212 f).

The articulation of the arch itself may also have a corresponding effect (Fig. 316, d, e). If an arch is smooth and unarticulated, it will seem compact and heavy, with downward pressure predominating. If carved profiles and mouldings parallel the curve of the arch, the accent is on its light and composite character, which adds vigour to a rising effect. Of equal importance are the springing points of the arch. Only an exact semicircle assures a balanced effect between rising and sinking. If the segment is made smaller,

316 f Semicircular arch and the angle of intersection with column field.

317. Semicircular arch (from courtyard in The Palazzo della Cancelleria, Rome).

318. Semicircular arch under load (detail from apartment building, Oslo).

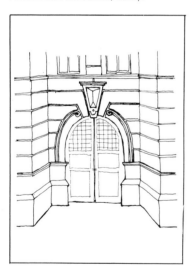

319. Semicircular arch and keystone (detail from apartment building, Oslo).

320. Semicircular arch as triumphal symbol (reconstruction of Titus' triumphal arch in Rome, from Fletcher, *A History of Architecture*).

230

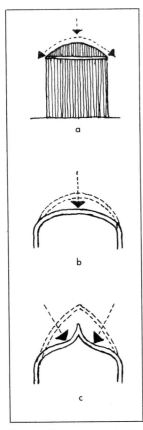

321 a-c. The supportive expression of a shallow arch: the formal expression of a shallow arch is determined by a deformation of the semicircular arch (Jugend arch) or of the pointed arch (Tudor arch).

a break will occur in the transition to the columns, and the frame will seem pressed both downwards and outwards by the weight from the top. The opposite effect is achieved if the arch is extended vertically down towards the columns. The arch seems to rise in an involuntary response to the verticals beneath (Fig. 316, f).

Another treatment of the arch itself which is vital to its expression of support is the keystone. It is the last unit to be inserted when constructing an arch and assures the form's static and functional integrity. It is pressed downwards as well as sideways against the arch flanks. One effect of this is that the arch sides seem to move in the opposite direction. On both sides they spring towards the burden at the top as if to hold it in a 'vice' (Fig. 319). In short, an arch with a keystone rises.

Until now we have considered the arch as a vertical intermediary between up and down. Its task, however, also concerns the form *horizontally*. Just like a bridge, it connects two sides by vaulting the gap between. The arch, again just like the bridge, contains a general spirit of triumph and victory. These aspects of the arch are exploited in a meaningful way in Antiquity's triumphal arches (Fig. 320). These triumphal arches were imperial symbols of victory: the eternal power of imperator and empire made manifest.[56] In these constructions bearing the emperor's statue, the round arch was the central motif and indicated merely by its form the content of its message. The arch is usually decorated with accentuated keystones. These were embellished with sacred symbols and figures, a direct reference to the heavenly allusion of arch and vault (see p. 305 f). Above the arch proper, and thus 'within' heaven itself hover two celestial Victories pointing their long victory staffs directly up towards the keystone. Aided by these godesses of victory the entire arch seems to rise towards the keystone with its message of divine triumph.

## EXPRESSION OF SUPPORT: THE FLAT ARCH

A typical characteristic of the pointed arch was the extension of the columns into the upper part of the opening and their integration into a dynamic form. In the round arch frame this relationship was in balance; motion between the two elements was variable — at times upwards and at other times downwards. In contrast to these, motion in the flat arch is an unequivocal sinking. It conveys a feeling of pressure from above (Figs. 321 a, 322). Of these flat arches, the Tudor and the Art Nouveau types are the most typical. Both are to be seen as deformations of the two arch types examined above. The Tudor arch has its source in the pointed arch and the Art Nouveau arch in the round arch (Fig. 321, c, d). The Tudor arch can be interpreted as a profane version of the sacred pointed arch. It was particularly widespread in England during the sixteenth century and frequently used

323. Shallow arch (loggia with Tudor arches, from Koepf, *Baukunst in Fünf Jahrtausenden*).

322. Shallow arch (detail from prison in Pittsburg by H.H. Richardson inspired by the 'Bridge of Sighs' in Venice. Photo from van Rensselaer, *Henry Hobson Richardson and His Works*).

324. Shallow arch (entry arch in Jugend style, from machine hall at Sollern II/IV coal mine in Dortmund-Bövinghausen, by B. Möhring).

326. Shallow arch and continuation (room by H. Guimard, from Naylor, *Hector Guimard*).

325. Shallow arch and plasticism (sketch of an entrance, by J. Hoffmann, From Tschudi-Madsen, *Sources of Art Nouveau*).

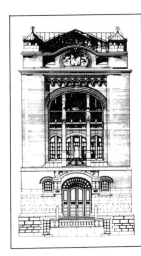

327. Shallow arch and tension (entrance to The Museum of History in Oslo, by H. Bull, from Thiis-Evensen, *Henrik Bull*).

in private homes and other secular buildings in an intended contrast to the more sacred pointed arch (Fig. 323). Earthly forces press down on the taut sides of the pointed arch causing the whole form to collapse. This collapse in the Tudor arch, however, is never total. The counter movement of its sharp point rising in the centre allows the arch to 'survive' despite the pressure. Considered thus, the Tudor arch points to a synthesis of vertical and horizontal, and as such is part of the transition from Gothic to the Renaissance.

The Art Nouveau arch is typical of the new ideas emerging at the close of the nineteenth century. This 'new art' was thought if as being freed from earlier style-bound forms but nevertheless its sources were deeply rooted in history. The Middle Ages, Rococo and The Baroque were all forefathers to its special characteristics. Thus the Art Nouveau arch is a paraphrase of Romanesque heaviness and Gothic flamboyance (Fig. 324).

The Art Nouveau arch is a continuous unbroken form, as may be seen in Josef Hoffmann's arched doorway (1898, Fig. 325). Hector Guimard's work must be interpreted in the same way. His arches grow from their columns as plants from their stems to join in a lightly swaying downward curving crown of foliage (Fig. 326).

This combination of suppleness and downward curves in these organic wrought iron forms is also expressed in a completely different context. In The Romanesque rusticated wall, the Art Nouveau arch is a visualization of the entire form's suppleness. Much of Henrik Bull's work confirms his understanding of this content. In the Museum of History, Oslo (1902), he allows his arch around the entrance to be the gauge for the entire body of the building (Fig. 327). The entrance is set in the central part of the building, which has a rusticated base storev. Above this the wall is opened by a large staircase window between two towers. The projecting section is finished off at the top by a curved attic decorated with the royal coat of arms. The arch above the main entrance is pressed flat by a severe and heavy moulding marking the transition to the window area. The articulation of the arch maintains this character. Beneath each end of the arch stands a pair of squat columns on a thick, broad console. Above them and between the edge of the arch and the bordering moulding are two owls, not erect and scowling but wide-eyed and with flapping wings (Fig. 328).

The large arched opening leading to the staircase is also pressed flat by the heavy moulding. The arch is squashed down in the middle and bulges out at the corners. In this opening stretched between two massive corner towers we find a wholeness full of contrasts, an expanding opening held in check by the two verticals. Even the royal coat-of-arms above is set in a distorted form. In this case it is a circle squashed by two tautly drawn mouldings.

328. Shallow arch and plasticism (detail from entrance to The Museum of History in Oslo, by H. Bull).

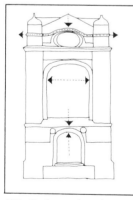

329. Shallow arch and tension (diagram of entrance to The Museum of History in Oslo , by H. Bull).

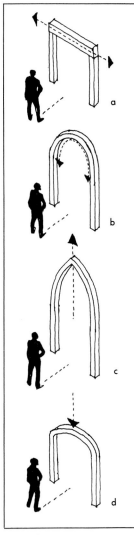

330 a-d. The expression of a beam: (a) straight and impaired motion, (b) semicircular arch and penetrating motion, (c) pointed arch and rising motion, (d) shallow arch and closing motion.

It is clear that the Art Nouveau arch is used to illustrate the inside-outside conflict itself (Fig. 329). The lower part clearly shows the conflict that arises by inserting a large opening in the most closed part of a wall. It symbolizes exterior pressure, while the window area above reveals an inner expansion. At the very top, it is the weight of the roof which converts the form into a set of compressed curves.

### THE BEAM'S EXPRESSION OF MOTION

We have seen how the visual problem of sinking has been solved in vastly different ways by various beam forms. With the same articulation we saw that the straight beam is the 'weakest', the pointed arch the 'freest', and the round arch in 'balance', whereas the flat arch is 'compressed'.

The same beam forms also elicit highly varying motion impulses in us (Fig. 330, a-d). A frame with a straight beam will be more of a barrier between inside and outside than one with a curved beam. Within the arched variations, the round arch is the most open, whereas the pointed and the flat arch, each in its own way, lessen the penetrative effect. Why?

A straight beam will accent a horizontal motion crosswise to the penetrative motion. Just as in the case of the horizontal wall, and as we shall see later, the horizontal window (see p. 261), a motion paralleling the construction is indicated, a motion that interrupts our intended entry.

The arched beam seems to be lifted by the opening itself. The arch makes the entire frame rise to outline a vertical form, and this verticality indicates a direction which, as already stated, initiates direct communication between inside and outside.

Of the three arch forms, the round arch most clearly emphasizes the act of entering in itself. Our own head in the centre of the semicircular curve, which means that the opening outlined by the arch is caused by us alone and not by external forces.

In the pointed arch the self-centred quality found in the round arch disappears. Here the form points upwards and away from us. The opening is less directly concerned with us and our intended entry. The form is the result of something 'up there', something beyond our own action which is to be led inside.

In the flat arch the form is distorted in the opposite way. The weight supported by the arch presses downwards, conveying a potential closing of the entrance passage itself.

### EXPRESSION OF MOTION: COLONNADE AND ARCADE

The principal difference in the expression of motion between the straight and the arched beam is most clearly seen when the frame is repeated and

332. Straight beam and arched beam combined ('Palladian motif', detail from the Basilica in Vicenza by A. Palladio).

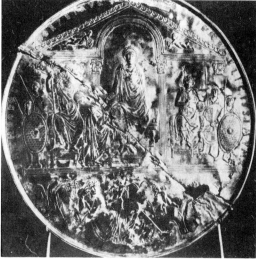

333. Straight beam and arched beam combined (silver *missorium* from Madrid with emperor in the middle and his sons at either side).

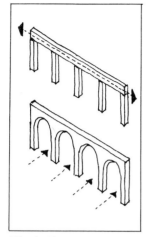

331 a-b. The expression in (a) a colonnade and (b) an arcade.

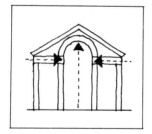

334. Diagram of silver *missorium* from Madrid.

becomes a row. As we have seen, it is the straight frame that forms a colonnade and the arched frame that forms an arcade (Fig. 331, a, b).

In a colonnade the beam becomes one continuous horizontal moulding which accents the principal motion that parallels the colonnade. This motion seems to take place behind and within the row of columns themselves, a characteristic which further accents the limitation in the form. Despite the apertures between the columns, a straight beam gives less direct communication between inside and outside.

The arcade consists of a row of individual openings in which the arches both separate and isolate each opening, which becomes a self-contained unit. Despite the horizontal extension, the arched beam gives greater communication between inside and outside.

Thus, an arcade indicates a *penetrative* motion, the colonnade a *lateral* motion.

A classical example of these differences combined in a meaningful way is the so-called Palladian motif (Fig. 332). The motif comprises three openings, the central one spanned by an arch and those on either side by straight beams. The centre area is used as the entrance, while the side usually consists of full-length windows. The side apertures, in other words, are intended to keep us within the columns, while the central area is for passage in and out.

The duality of the Palladian motif may be confirmed by ancient precedents. In the silver *missorium* in Madrid (388) the motif is given ideological meaning, in that the straight frame and the arched frame convey different depths of contact between the onlooker and the persons portrayed in the opening (Fig. 333).

Emperor Theodosius I commands the centre area beneath the arch. His sons sit on either side. The figure of the emperor is the largest, the sons are somewhat smaller. The arched opening emphasizes these dimensions. The person of the emperor appears to be 'led forth' beneath the arched frame — he becomes more direct and inviting. The flat beam, on the other hand, holds the sons back in relation to the middle. These beams, with their lateral motion, point directly at the emperor, thereby accenting the ideological basis of the composition in the figure of the emperor itself. It is he who is the unifying force and the centre of the world (Fig. 334) (see also gables p. 352).[57]

Differences in the expression of motion between arcade and colonnade are also used to distinguist between dissimilar spatial forms.

An example of this is the ancient complex of St. Peter's, Rome (333) (Figs. 35, 335 a, b). The mighty nave leads directly to the high altar in the apse, which is the meaning and goal of the entire interior. The architraves above the columns are made straight in order to emphasize unequivocally the

336. Column alternation (St. Maria in Cosmedin).

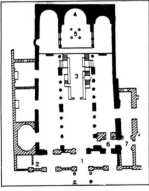

337. Column alternation (plan of St. Maria in Cosmedin, from *Roma e Dintorni*).

238

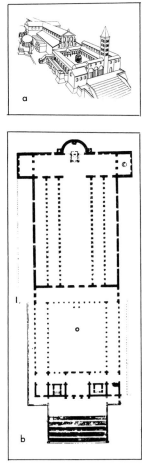

335 a-b. Arcade and colonnade in combination (diagram of motion patterns in St. Peter's, Rome).

linear and extended length of the form all the way to its finish. The quadratic peristyle surrounding the courtyard in front of the church is in the form of an arcade. In the middle of the square is a well, the centre of the courtyard's liturgical content. From this point of view the arcade is an answer to the central form itself, just as the colonnade was to the rectangular form. With its tall arches the space opens equally in towards the centre as if reflecting the rays radiating from the central point. At only two places is the continuity broken: in the east by the raised baldachin leading into the church and in the west by the three-arched entrance to the entire complex.

In this way the differences between straight and arched openings help to tie the two spatial forms together. The entrance opens directly out towards the incoming throngs. Once within the peristyle all attention is focused on the central well then led further in a straight line through the narrow baldachin and into the church nave. Here the straight architrave takes over and leads the eye directly into the curve of the apse. In this way all of four stages in a pilgrim's progress are united. From the outside world one passes to the next stage of baptism and preparation and from there to follow the path of humility to the goal itself, the altar as the symbol of Christ.

It is obvious, of course, that these directional tendencies found in arcades and colonnades are merely a base from which each individual case will be weakened or strengthened by different kinds of articulation. The rows of columns may be long or tall, the intercolumniation equal or in a rhythmic sequence, or they may be combined and overlapped, etc. An important factor in this context is the column's form. If the columns of a colonnade are round, the transverse direction is increased at the cost of the lateral effect of the main form and architrave. If the columns are square, just the opposite takes place — the accent is on the barrier effect and the row will be perceived more as a wall with 'holes'.

The architectural development of column rows, as we are able to follow it from the earliest basilicas, shows in fact that a rhythmic alternation of round and square columns was an important means of attaining varied spatial effects.[58] In the inner arcade of St. Maria in Cosmedin, Rome (sixth century) (Fig. 336) a wide buttressing column with a square cross-section is introduced for every three round columns.[59] These pillars both break the arcade's natural transverse motion and emphasize the principal direction of the nave. At the same time they aid in dividing the space into three zones (Fig. 337). These divisions are functional, because each zone has a different 'value'. The lowest zone is closest to the entrance and signifies entry or preparation. The middle zone, which is broken up by choir stalls and lecterns, is the area in which the congregation worships and gives praise. At the top is the choir zone itself, to be entered only by the clergy and used for the preparation of the sacrament.

# THE COLOURS

'Plain drawing is an abstraction ... because everything in nature contains colours. Only when the colours are rich is the form worthy of merit'.[60]

Through colour and light the world is made known to us. Colour is the device that indicates the structure of our surroundings, because everything is composed of colours.

Colours, therefore, embody specific meanings. In many cultures black and yellow symbolize sorrow. Red means danger, while green is identified with growth. On the water faucet hot is marked with red and cold with blue. In language too, colours convey particular meanings: 'when I look at him I see red', 'at night all cats are grey', 'the black heart', etc. These miscellaneous examples suffice to justify the following question. Is the perception of a colour's meaning relative and conventional or does the individual colour have a given and unchangeable meaning?

If the question is to be answered, it is necessary to consider some of the widespread research that has been done on the significance of colour. Of the visual phenomena it is colour which has attracted the greatest attention, particularly in recent times. Colour studies may be divided into two areas. The first, already tackled by Newton in his 'Opticks' from 1704, concerns mainly the physical and chemical content of colours — what Goethe called the 'atomistic' view of colour. It is Goethe in particular who has studied colours from the other viewpoint. Using the term 'Die sinnlich-sittliche Wirkung', he is among those seeking to analyse the psychic effects of colour.[61] In this connection it is maintained that certain colours and colour combinations will cause specific emotional states which, in certain situations, are decisive for our psychic and motor reactions. This has been experienced, not least of all, by artists throughout the ages, in that architects, designers, and textile artists have been absorbed by the principles of colours' compositional and harmonious nature.

## THE EXPRESSION OF COLOURS AND THE IMPORTANCE OF COMPOSITION, ASSOCIATION AND PERSON

By comparing the viewpoints which have emerged in this field of research it is clear that especially three factors are considered to be particularly influential in determining the effect of colours.[62] One is *composition*, by which is meant that the effect of a particular colour depends on whether it is modified or enhanced by neighbouring colours. Artists know that colours do not act alone but have their effect in concert with other colours. 'Of different colours equally perfect, that will appear most excellent which is seen near its direct contrary: a pale colour against red, a black upon white, blue near yellow, green near red'.[63] Modern researchers also, such as Erich Raab, stress the importance of interdependence in the effects of individual colours:

> The pleasure aroused by a certain combination of colours depends upon the individual colour tones in combination, (2) the pleasure conveyed by the whole composition cannot be predicted on a basis of individual colours. The impression is also partly qualified by the gestalt-effect and the quantity of the colour distribution.[64]

The second factor of importance in the effect of colour is *association*. This means that the effect of a colour will depend upon whatever it is compared with. This association with the environment is partly dependent upon conditioning and conceptual habits. The comparison may be limited to the colours *alone* as, for example, when one says that red stands for blood or fire while green signifies the fresh growth of nature. On the other hand, the effect may depend upon the *form* with which a colour is associated, whether it is abstract (circle, square, organic, etc.) or descriptive (nature, animal, human, etc.).[65] M.J. Friedländer says accordingly: 'Only coloured form exists and correspondingly, only formed colour'.[66]

The third precondition in the effect of colour is the *person* himself. This implies that personal characteristics, sex, age and status all take part in 'filtering' the meaning in colour. Aristotle maintained in fact that certain colours are preferred by specific personality types: red by the 'bon vivant', purple by the snob, yellow by the schemer, and blue by the intelligent.[67] A modern researcher such as G.J. von Allesch doubts, furthermore, that colour effect can be understood at all without an exact knowledge of the recipient's personality.[68] Based on statistical investigations, Raab sees a direct correlation between certain colour combinations and the observer's sex, as for example: 'Men prefer the colour combination red/blue while women (but in a less pronounced way) prefer the combinations red/yellow and green/yellow'.[69]

## THE EXPRESSION OF COLOURS AS MOTION, WEIGHT, AND SUBSTANCE

In terms of the generation of their effects, colours do not differ from other phenomena. Just as in other architectural elements the effect of colour is a factor of varying preconceptions.

But do colours also have an existential expression?

Many researchers maintain that each colour is presumed to have its own particular expression, which is basic and invariable.[70]

339. Colour and articulation of the skeleton (half-timber building from Celle in northern Germany).

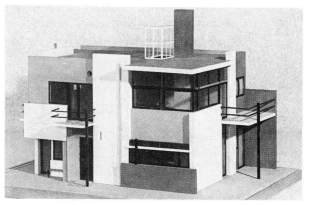

338. Colour and articulation of plastic form (Egyptian temple in Edfu, from Uhde, *Die Architekturformen des Klassischen Altertums*).

340. Colour and articulation of the surface (model of Schroeder House by G.T. Rietveld).

If we look at our introductory examples, we find that there is an inner structural similarity in the feeling expressed and the phenomenon that is symbolized. Black is chosen for sorrow for just like black, sorrow is heavy, deep and rejecting.[71] Yellow is chosen because it can be associated with our reactions to light and sun — and light is sacred in the sense that it describes that other world of which the deceased is now a part. Furthermore, physical heat is aggressive; it burns you and is intense in the way red is said to be. Blue, however, is cool and chilling just like cold water. The existential expression of colours is, therefore, once more to be found in connection with our basic physical reactions to the environment.

Rudolph Arnheim has summarized these expressions in the term, the *dynamics* of colours.[72] By this is meant the inherent expression of motion in colour characterized by such terms and 'distance', 'nearness', 'extension', 'contraction', 'expansion', etc.

There are particularly two conditions which give these expressions.

First, we find that colours differ in *weight and size.* Hue, saturation and brightness all posses varying dëgrees of 'material form'. They are preceived as having 'weight' and 'size', which is to say that thay are directly compared with other experiences of weight and physical reality.

Secondly, we may sense that colours have different *temperatures.* Some colours are described as 'warm', others as 'cold', qualities also instrumental in relating them to our experiences and to physical reality.

Colours are not only important as an aid in emphasizing details in a building's structure (Figs. 338, 339, 340). As a dynamic phenomenon colours are also instrumental in giving a space motion and thus have a direct bearing on the relation between inside and outside. In connection with walls, it is important to explore the qualities of colours which convey varying impressions of weight, size and temperature.

## HUE, BRIGHTNESS AND SATURATION

The expression of motion in colours is decided, in principle, by the interaction of three qualities.

First is the *hue,* which distinguishes the colour type. In general we recognize three primary colours: yellow, red, and blue. The complementary colours are orange, green, and violet.

The second is *brightness,* which describes hues according to their tendency towards white or black.

The third quality is *saturation* or density, which is a measurement of the strength or weakness of a colour.

In considering the relationship of these three qualities it will be found that saturation is independent of hue. Thus, all colours may be either strong or weak. Brightness, on the other hand, is more closely associated with the hue itself. Accordingly, yellow will tend towards white, while blue tends towards black. It follows that there is an inner relation in the qualities of pale and yellow and of dark and blue. In all cases the three qualities will affect each other mutually. Furthermore, if one of them is to be examined, the other two must remain constant. The following account is based on this necessary limitation.

## BRIGHTNESS AND SATURATION AS WEIGHT

It is the degree of brightness and saturation in a colour which makes the wall it covers seem heavy or light, larger or smaller.

There are, of course, other qualities in colours which may give a corresponding effect. As has already been said, hue is important in that yellow and blue also convey lightness and darkness. The same applies to the association evoked. A pale brown colour will, accordingly, seem heavier than a pale blue, since brown is associated with the earth and blue with the sky. Correspondingly, saturation and brightness convey a feeling of warmth or coldness. A pale and unsaturated colour, therefore, tends to appear cool and chilly while a dark colour tends towards closeness and warmth.

Degrees of weight and size, nevertheless, are the most typical impressions conveyed by differences in the brightness and saturation of colours. What effect then does this have on the inside-outside relationship? Pale and unsaturated colours share the quality of giving a surface the appearance of *lightness and openness*. Dark and saturated colours share in giving a feeling of *weight and closure*.[73]

The explanation of these fundamental effects is once again to be found in our common experiences. Both that which is pale and that which is unsaturated are by nature light and airy, having within them expansive and outgoing qualities just as light and day. That which is dark, however, draws together and becomes denser — it becomes smaller but also harder and more impenetrable, somehow like night. One's nature is liberated by white and constrained by black. Pale colours, therefore, are 'friendlier' than dark ones. Dark colours inhibit our natural life develoment.

> Darkness is without light and thus prevents the possibility of any meaningful activity in the world. It is first when man renounces the daylight clarity of the world and entrusts himself with uncertainty to darkness that it displays itself in its own character.[74]

Saturation and brightness, however, convey openness and closure in quite different ways.

An unsaturated colour, be it pale or dark, has about it an air of lightness which conveys an impression of opening in depth. A wall is given texture when covered by an unsaturated colour. The pigments are loosely connected to each other, one sees between and 'behind' them. The wall 'opens up' and is made lighter as in a three-dimensional curtain.

In a saturated colour, on the other hand, the pigments are pressed more densely together — the wall it covers becomes solid and strong, giving the appearance of a plainer two-dimensional expanse.

The lightness occurring with the use of a pale colour does not lie in a depth effect but in a *weight* effect. It means that this characteristic of weight or lightness lies always in and along the surface itself. A dark colour, therefore, will increase, but a pale colour lessens the area's own expression of weight.

It is the degree of *transparency* and *self-weight* which tells. The same factors play their part in giving an *area* different *dimensional* effects. In this connection Goethe maintained that a dark object appears smaller than the same object when light. He claimed that a black shape on a white ground appears to be one-fifth less in size than a white shape on a black ground. He points out, at the same time, the accepted fact that black clothes have a slimming effect while white have just the opposite.[75] (See also relation of colour and column p. 204). Thus, basically, a light coloured house will seem larger and more open than the same house in dark colours, which in turn will appear more closed and 'withdrawn'.

The same applies in the dividing of walls. A wall several storeys high, all in the same colour, degree of saturation and brightness, gives the effect of a stiff slab without transition to ground or roof. If, however, the storeys differ in the degree of brightness and saturation, a darker lower section and paler upper part will make the wall sit well against the ground while at the same time conveying a lighter effect as it rises upwards (see also rising effect p. 135). If the process is reversed, the wall will appear to be pressed downwards from above (see sinking effect motif p. 135).

In the next stage let us imagine a skeletal system fastened to the wall and presuppose the whole to be treated in the same colour but with skeleton and wall given different degrees of brightness and saturation.

In the first alternative the skeleton is pale and the wall behind dark. This combination gives an impression of *depth*. The light coloured skeleton expands forward and out — the dark wall behind contracts and draws inward. This shows the difference in the function of the two parts. The skeleton is active and expansive in contrast to the wall's more closing-off role. The skeleton system, as the more prominent and public element, is emphasized as a part of the exterior space, while it is the private character of the wall behind which is accented.

In the second alternative, the skeleton is made dark and the wall light.

245

341. Differentiated surface (Nobel Institute in Oslo).

342. Differentiated skeleton/background (apartment building in Oslo).

343. Differentiated skeleton/background (apartment building in Oslo).

344. Differentiated skeleton/background (church façade from Sutri, drawing from photograph).

Now the two systems 'meet' in that the skeleton contracts and is drawn backwards, while the wall opens up and expands forward. The wall becomes independent and the skeleton appears to be 'stuck on'.

We have seen that the effect of brightness and saturation on a wall's expression of strength and weight differs in the case of height and that of depth.

The effect on *height* follows the principles described above in that the dark appears heavy and forbidding while the paler area seems lighter and more open.

Seen in *depth*, the reverse may take place. As shown above, pale hues will lend strength to wall elements without necessarily giving them a 'heavy' character. Dark colours, furthermore, will in certain circumstances appear as 'holes' in the wall surface and thereby open up the wall rather than close it, which the relation beween weight and dark would otherwise lead one to expect.

Classical palace and tenement architecture is a good example of how such variations in lighter and darker areas add to a rich interpretation of just this inside-outside relationship (Figs. 341, 342, 343).

As presupposed above, the examples have had the *same* hue throughout. If this too is varied, the picture immediately becomes more complicated. If we visualize for a moment an imaginary wall in which wall and skeleton have the same degree of brightness and saturation but different colours, one colour may appear heavier and stronger than the other. This may be seen in the illustration of a church façade in Sutri, Italy (Fig. 344). The pilasters are in grey tuff, the wall itself in reddish tuff. The pilasters stand out immediately as the strong and supporting elements because the colour grey is associated with a harder stone, whereas the intervening walls are identified with a more porous and brick-like stone type. The impression in this case is different, governed as it is by association, but, it will be seen as well that colours contain essentially different weight values. With that we turn to the importance of *hues* in the relation between inside and outside.

## HUES AS SUBSTANCE

While a colour's degree of saturation and brightness first and foremost give a surface its character of varying weight and size, hue will be a primary factor in deciding the varying degress of *heat* and *cold* in the same surface.[76]

By this it is meant that certain colours cause definite psychic reactions which correspond in structure to our physical reactions to heat and cold. Heat incites and intensifies, whereas cold freezes and stiffens like something dead.

This psychic reaction has been measured as a purely physical condition.

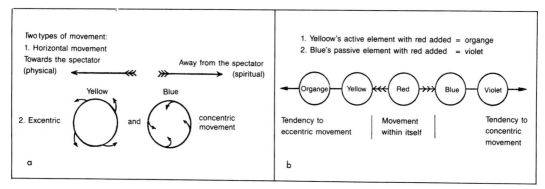

F. Birren, accordingly, has established that saturated and warm colours affect the automatic nervous system in such a way that blood pressure rises and the pulse quickens.[77] Subjectively one experiences a rise in temperature. With cold and unsaturated colours blood pressure sinks and the pulse slows. The temperature seems to fall.

J. Itten also reports similar reactions.[78] Two identical work-rooms, one in blue-green and the other in red-orange, showed a difference in experienced temperature of as much as 3 to 4 degrees, although the temperature in both rooms was exactly the same (15°C).

What effect then does this have on the wall's open or closed character?

To find an answer we might compare our experience of heat and cold with our spontaneous reactions to 'extroverted' and 'introverted' people. A warm person invites us to approach while a cold person makes us stop and withdraw. Our reactions simply mirror qualities in the person himself. The cold person behaves as if he himself felt cold — unwilling, reserved and closed. The warm person, on the other hand, has a vitality that advances towards us. The same holds true for colours. Warm colours seem to invite us, cold colours keep us at a distance. The relationship may be determined dynamically, in terms of motion in depth: *with* us, *before* us, or *from* us. In the following we will examine the principal motion content in each individual hue and thereby indicate the influence of hues on the wall's welcoming or rejecting qualities. We will follow Wassily Kandinsky's descriptions. Among researchers and artists it is perhaps Kandinsky who most clearly has stated the visual possibilities of colour hues.[79]

## HUES AS MOTION

For Kandinsky the dynamics in the contrast between warm and cold colours is 'the first great antithesis'.[80] The other contrast is to be found between white and black, between light and dark colours. The degree of lightness

345 a-b. W. Kandinsky's colour-dynamic model (from Kandinsky, *Concerning the Spiritual in Art*).

and darkness can lend nuances but not change the intensity of the dynamics in warm and cold colours. If the colours are pale, they become insubstantial or dissolved, they have 'no resistance'. If they are dark they become denser, more concrete and assume weight.

Kandinsky maintains furthermore that the colours yellow and blue constitute the extreme on the scale of dynamics. The warm colours, tending towards yellow, will advance towards the spectator, whereas cold colours, tending towards blue, will retreat. Areas of colour will also vary in relation to themselves. Yellowish tones will show eccentric motion, bluish tones concentric. 'Yellow easily becomes sharp and never shows depth. Conversely, blue can never shine forth and up' (Fig. 345 a, b).[81]

In a motion context red and green are found between the two colour extremes yellow and blue. The colour red moves 'within itself' says Kandinsky — its power is to be found in a sort of contained potential: '...red does not have the irresponsible appeal of yellow ... it glows maturely within itself and does not shine forth aimlessly'.[82] The colour green also has its own inherent quality, but this is one of repose. The contrast of its complementary colours yellow and blue is balanced in a motionless calm. Pure green is the most restful colour lacking any undertone of joy, grief or passion.[83] In contrast to grey, which Kandinsky considers a 'hopelessly motionless' colour because it has its source in the lack of tonality in white and black, green in different mixtures is able to break into either forward or backward motion because of its position between two active colours.

This is true too of the other colours. By mixing, primary qualities may be subdued or strengthened. With the addition of yellow, red will radiate as orange, if black is added to red it will sink towards brown. The latter colour is 'immovable'.[84] When blue is added to yellow, the yellow colour will be checked and 'die away'.[85]

We see from this that colour hues are of great importance in the impression of a building's welcoming aspect to the world outside. If all the colours of a house are in their purest form, with the same degree of saturation and brightness and without undue influence from their environment, they will 'stimulate us' very differently. The grey wall may give a deadly sensation, convey an insignificant, empty impression as if the house were unoccupied. A green wall may emanate a restful expression and give the house a sort of lived-in character. The red wall may impart a stirring and intense clang, a wall that attracts on the strength of its own supremacy. The yellow wall will shine brightly towards us like an invitation to a sunny place, whereas the blue wall will retreat in cool reservation. The white wall is immaculate. It may convey an expression of elegance, as in Le Corbusier's early villas, or of innocence and friendliness, as in the white idyllic seaside houses of southern Norway (Figs. 346, 347).

346. The 'heavy' inland architecture (Langbråta drawn by Th. Kittelsen, from *Theodor Kittelsen i tekst, tegninger og malerier,* Oslo 1957).

347. The 'lightweight' coastal architecture (a house in Arendal, Norway).

# OPENINGS

## THE WINDOW

### THE WINDOW AND INSIDE-OUTSIDE RELATIONSHIP

The wall's fourth and final theme is that of *openings.*

An opening in a wall occurs when the wall's structural system is interrupted either in the form of a *hole* in a plane wall or a change of *rhythm* in a skeletal wall (Fig. 348).

The aperture need not be a true one in order to be perceived as an opening. Blind windows or a false door are also openings (Fig. 349). The precondition is that the wall acts as a ground, while the openings stand out as figures.

The window and the door are two types of openings which function very differently in the relation between inside and outside. The basic difference is that the window is meant to be looked through and to admit light, whereas the door is primarily to be gone through.[86] While the door is determined by its relation to what is *outside,* the window is the symbol of what is *inside.* Just as the eye, it expresses the interior's outlook over exterior space, while as a light source it bears witness to the fact that light is necessary for the use of the interior.

This means that the window, regardless of form, size and location, will always be an expression of the interior to the world at large. Consequently, it is the windows which announce our mode of life, according to Loudon:

> A cottage with one bedroom, a living-room and a bathroom ought to express these three rooms by using windows of three different sizes. Windows can also express differences in floor plans, the presence of stairs and other aspects of the plan.[87]

In other words, regardless of the *reason* for using a small or large window, it will by its size alone describe the relation of inside to outside. It is invariably the 'struggle' between interior space and exterior space which the window expresses, a question of whether the interior seems to be drawn outwards or whether it remains protected within the dividing wall.

In the following we shall examine the elements in a window composition which determine the window's importance in opening or closing the space. Each element will be treated individually and in introducing them they will be described and given a technical/functional foundation. We shall then explain their potential expression in relation to the expression of motion, weight, and substance.

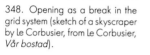

348. Opening as a break in the grid system (sketch of a skyscraper by Le Corbusier, from Le Corbusier, *Vår bostad*).

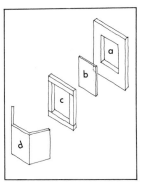

350 a-d. Window motifs: (a) hole, (b) face, (c) frame, (d) bay.

349. Opening as blind window (from an apartment building in Oslo. Photo by T. Lange).

352. Vertical opening: Gothic window (from Teyn Church in Prague).

353. Horizontal opening: the functionalistic window (from a 'band city' outside of Amsterdam).

354. Centralized opening (from the Governmental Centre in Dacca by L.I. Kahn, from Norberg-Schulz/Digerud, *Louis I. Kahn, idea e immagine*).

356. Right-angled profile (from Notre Dame du Haut by Le Corbusier.

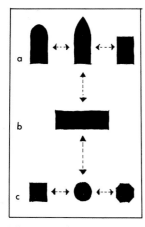

351 a-c. Window openings: (a) vertical opening (circular arch — pointed arch — straight arch), (b) horizontal opening, (c) central-ized opening (square — circular — polygonal).

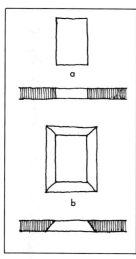

355 a-b. The opening's profile: (a) right-angled profile, (b) di-agonal profile.

This study will be based on the window as a hole in a planar wall. The skeletal system will be discussed only in connection with the articulation of the window elements.

## WINDOW MOTIFS

Four elements in the window's composition exert their effect either in com-bination or individually. These are (a) the *opening* in the wall, (b) the *face* in the opening, (c) the *frame* around the opening, (d) the space in front of the opening (the *bay*) (Fig. 350, a-d).

### THE HOLE

The primary element is the hole. Two main factors, *form* and *profile,* deter-mine its importance in the inside-outside relation.

The form is based on three variations (Fig. 351, a-c). The first is the *verti-cal* window with upright orientation. Traditionally, the verticality effects a variation of three motifs all determined by the form of the lintel, whether it is a *round arch, pointed arch* or *straight arch.* The second form is the *horizontal* window, which in principle conveys a sideways motion. The third form is the *centralized* window, which is essentially neutral, marks a point, and may vary from a square to a circle.

Throughout architectural history the vertical window has been the type most used. It was preferred because it met two different factors: the limited width of the span in a post and beam system and the desire for the largest possible opening to admit maximum light (Fig. 352).

The horizontal window is particularly associated with the Functionalism of the 1920's. One of its origins was the desire to open space horizontally (Fig. 353). This was made technically possible by the introduction of rein-forced concrete, allowing a greater span above openings.

The central window is less determined by technical factors than both the vertical and the horizontal window. A well-known exception is Louis Kahn's circular openings in his building complex in the capital of Bangladesh (1962—1974). Because of frequent earthquakes the round form was necessary to offset shear forces in the building mass (Fig. 354).

### THE PROFILE

The profile outlining the opening can be straight or diagonal (Fig. 355, a, b).

By a straight profile we mean one that is cut into the wall at right angles (Fig. 356). By a diagonal profile we mean that the sides of the form slant inwards to a smaller light aperture. Such a reveal can be formed in many ways. Typical examples stretch all the way from simple rounded-off forms

357. Diagonal profile: formed plastically (Casa Milá in Barcelona by A. Gaudi).

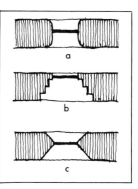

359 a-c. Diagonal profile: (a) plastically formed, (b) stepped, (c) angled.

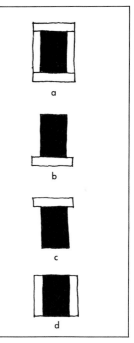

362 a-d. The frame's components: (a) complete, (b) sill, (c) lintel (d) jambs.

254

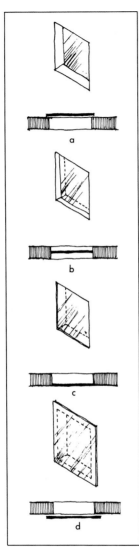

360 a-d. Location of window face: (a) inside the opening, (b) in the middle of the opening, (c) outermost in the opening, (d) outside the opening.

as often seen in plastic wall constructions (Fig. 357), through deep and richly decorated stepped profiles found in Romanesque and Gothic niche openings right up to smooth, deep diagonal reveals such as those in Le Corbusier's Notre Dame du Haut, Ronchamp (Figs. 358, 359 a-c).

## THE FACE

The next element in a window composition is the window face. This includes the frame and system of transoms and mullions breaking up the face. It also includes the covering, which may be of glass or other transluscent materials such as parchment, paper and certain types of stone. The same applies to coverings made of more solid materials such as shutters, Venetian blinds, and curtains, but also open grille and lattice systems.

The window face is a collective expression for all transparent or other types of covering which close the window opening.

As well as the structure of the face itself, its location within the opening is of importance. Whether alone or in combination the layers of the face will always be found within four extreme positions (Fig. 360, a-d): (a) inside the opening, (b) in the middle of the opening, (c) outermost in the opening, (d) outside the opening.

## THE FRAME

The next element in a window composition is the frame.

The relation of the frame to the wall opening itself is decisive in the extreme variations. Here there are particularly three motifs which stand out (Fig. 361, a-c).

The first is the frame that lies within the opening. In the second motif the frame is free of the opening in so far as it is attached to the wall around and outside the opening. In the third motif the frame becomes part of a larger skeletal system in front of the wall. In both the second and third motifs the frame's location means that it may vary in size and form independently of the opening's form. The frame is freed. This independence may be found in depth, height and width.

Within all three motifs discussed above, four possible interpretations stand out. Each of these is determined by the part of the frame which decides the visual effect (Fig. 362, a-d).

These four variations may appear each in its own 'pure' style or in combination. By a pure interpretation we mean that the frame motif is seen against an otherwise plain diagonal or straight cut reveal around the opening.

In the first interpretation the frame is complete, i.e. the lintel, sill, and jambs, with no one part dominating, form an unbroken contour around the window.

358. Diagonal profile: formed as simple angled surfaces (from Notre Dame du Haut by Le Corbusier).

363. The complete classical frame with an accentuated sill in the form of a straight, arched or triangular pediment (frame around a bust of Palladio, from *Cevese, Palladio*).

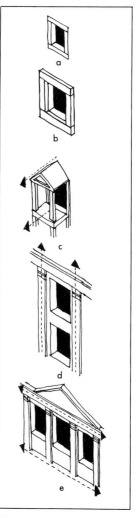

361 a-e. Location of the frame: (a) within the opening, (b) around the opening, (c) in front of the wall and extended past the opening (depth), (d) in front of the wall and over the opening (height), (e) in front of the wall and to the side of the opening (breadth).

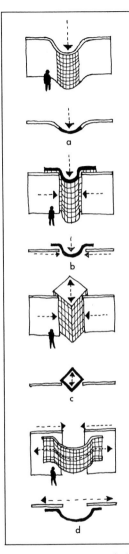

364 a-d. Bay window motifs: (a) as a bulge in the wall, (b) out of a split in the wall, (c) as overlapping element in the wall, (d) as attached to the wall.

In the next two variations, either the *lintel* or *sill* alone is the dominating element.

In the final variant it is the *jambs* which convey the main impression.

In the above examples, the basic variations were in their 'pure' form. The most usual, however, is combined interpretations in which the basis is a plain surrounding frame but in which lintel or still, together or individually, dominates the overall impression (Fig. 363).

## THE BAY WINDOW

When a window occurs as a frame, it will, at the same time, be perceived as a *space*. A frame describes a separate spatial volume with its own ceiling, floor and wall. Its boundaries are within the hole. The word 'aedicula', which indeed describes a frame, means a 'little house'. If the frame is fastened to the wall around an opening, either as an independent element or as part of a skeletal system, it also suggests a potential space, but in this case one in front of the opening.

In spite of this, the window as space is considered to be in a separate category within window architecture. It appears in the form of a *bay window*. In the bay window both window face and frame are secondary elements of the main form. The bay window's four variants, however, are completely determined by their relationship to both the window opening itself and to the wall in which it is located (Fig. 364, a-d).

In the first variant the bay window appears an an outward bulge in the wall itself. In other words, the wall of the bay window is a part of the overall wall system.

The second variant is seen when the bay window form bursts through the wall, irrespective of whether the wall is built as an open skeleton or as a closed massif. In such cases the bay window seems to push its way through great slashes in the wall or out between pilasters and columns.

In the third variation, the bay window must be seen as an overlapping space that both protrudes from the wall and is drawn into it.

The fourth variant appears when the bay window is attached to the wall in front of the opening as an independent volume. One method of doing this is to place the bay window on its own support in front of the wall. Another way is to fasten it to the wall by the use of exposed consoles or with overlapping 'wings'.

## THE EXPRESSION OF THE WINDOW

The next question is: what do the hole, the face, the frame and the bay express in relation to motion, weight, and substance, and what is their importance for the way in which the connection between outside and inside is experienced?

365. Window without frame (Column house in Retz by E.-L. Boullée, from Arthaud, *Dream Palaces...*).

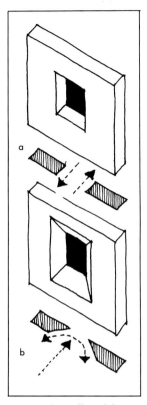

366 a-b. The profile and the motion expressions of the opening: (a) the profile emphasizes motion from the outside, (b) the profile weakens the motion from the outside.

## THE HOLE

'Houses with windows which are merely holes in the wall are like empty skulls' (Fig. 365).[88]

This was said by John Ruskin and reveals the essence of the effect of a window as a naked hole. A window that is only a gaping hole in the wall transforms the wall to a lifeless skin around a dead and empty interior. The hole is not the result of an interior force, rather it seems to have been punched in from the outside.

So, a house with gaping openings will always remind us of a ruin. The interior no longer seems like private property but rather a deserted, empty space — a common property. A space without window frames and glass is physically unprotected as well. Wind and weather play havoc with what the wall is supposed to protect. Thus, an empty window is merely a hole and influences the entire meaning of the wall. It loses its function of protection and becomes lifeless.

## THE PROFILE

The impression that the motion is from the outside inwards can be heightened or lessened by the opening's profiles or reveals.

A cut at right angles to the wall emphasizes motion from the outside (Fig. 366, a). The strength of the wall is weakened, it 'offers no resistance'. With a straight profile it is as if the wall's own substance deflects the incision. The entire wall takes on a thin character, a stiff plane with no muscular strength.

On the other hand, a diagonally cut opening will 'resist' motion from outside (Fig. 366, b). The narrowing of the hole itself shows that the wall is about to close. It is given added weight and substance as well, because the diagonal reveal conveys an impression of greater thickness than the wall actually possesses.[89]

In the diagonally cut opening the hole itself appears to lie deeper in the wall than does the right angle cut opening. It is less accessible and is protected within the wall itself. In some cases these qualities serve to differentiate between door and window. In Sudanese folk architecture windows are not only small but plastically rounded and deeply inset. The door, however, is often cut straight into the wall. Thus the door demonstrates its association with motion from the outside inwards while the window belongs to the protected interior.

## THE FORM

We repeat that the window is immediately perceived as an expression of interior expansion towards the outside. We saw from the above that when the window is in the form of a naked hole, that impression was weakened,

372. The vertical and the centralized window (La Tourette, in Eveux, France by Le Corbusier).

368. The vertical window and the open context between inside and outside (from an apartment building in Oslo).

370. The horizontal window and the dividing expression between inside and outside (from southern Harildstad in Gudbandsdalen, Norway).

371. The centralized window and the directed expression (detail from house in Oslo by E. Collett).

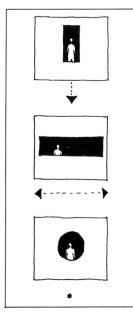

367. Window forms and the relationship between inside and outside.

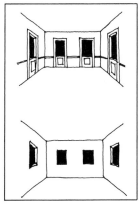

369. The varying relationship between inside and outside when the windows have a dado and when the windows do not have a dado.

because the interior was dead and the exterior alive. Further distinctions resulted from the treatment given to the reveals. When we consider the importance of the *form* as interpreter of motion from the inside outwards, we find mainly two determining conditions.

One condition is determined by the form's own expression of motion. By this is meant the various impacts revealed by the vertical, horizontal and centralized window (Fig. 367).

The other concerns the effect of these forms on the wall's own expression of motion, depending on their location and size. In combination they can strengthen or weaken one another.

### THE FORM'S OWN EXPRESSION OF MOTION

In the wall face we saw that the vertical form initiated arresting and inviting movements (see p. 145). The upright window will accentuate this motion coming *from the inside* and thus strengthen contact with exterior space. There are two main reasons for this. First of all, the form is that of a person standing and looking out. The other reason may be explained by the way the form conveys the possibility that one may enter. Considered in this way the vertical window is related to the door. This type of window, therefore, is frequently interpreted as a door partly filled in with panels, balustrades or wrought-iron railings (Fig. 368). This motif also appears in interiors. In the period of Historicism, apartment house windows were 'opened' right down to the floor with deep panel areas. The entire form is associated with French windows which, as a combination of something to both look through and walk through convey a direct and strong feeling of the interdependence of inside and outside (Fig. 369).

We pointed out above that the horizontal wall encourages lateral motion (see p. 143). As a window, the horizontal or oblong form will suggest a motion that cuts across the inside to outside contact. It is as if the people inside do not concern us directly; they seem to pass in front of us and past us (Fig. 379). Stopping is an exception defied by the form.

A wall with equal height and width, we maintained, conveys a neutral and reserved motion impulse (see p. 145). As a window opening the impression becomes the exact opposite, because the centalized form conveys the feeling of a hole caused by a direct and penetrating motion from the interior. For example, a round window not only resembles an eye but by its form is a direct rendering of concentrated 'peering out' (Fig. 371).[90]

Le Corbusier's La Tourette (1959) is an example of a building in which all the three window forms mentioned are used (Fig. 372). From the interior they lead the eye towards the landscape in three different ways according to the type of space from which one looks out. The horizontal window indicates the corridor behind. As narrow bands along the surface they outline

261

373. The horizontal window (from La Tourette, in Eveux, France, by Le Corbusier).

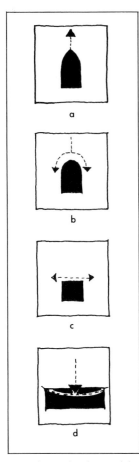

374 a-d. Window form and the relationship to the wall: (a) pointed form tears the wall, (b) circular form causes both the rising and sinking of the wall, (c) the straight form can have a neutral effect, or (d) cause the sinking of the wall.

the boundaries around the building's interior (Fig. 373). By way of contrast, the windows of the study rooms are small centralized peepholes, while the openings into the common rooms are larger sheets of glass in which verticality is accentuated by the vertical mullions. For the monks inside, the study windows frame a concentrated section of the landscape, the common room windows allow a total impression of the unity of heaven and earth, while the corridors carry the eye horizontally along the silhouette of the landscape.

## THE FORM AND THE WALL'S EXPRESSION OF MOTION

From what has already been said, we know that the reason for the impression of motion conveyed by the form is to a great extent determined by the directionalities of the form itself. In this way, the vertically oriented window accentuates verticality, the horizontally oriented window stresses horizontality, while the centralized window emphasizes the point and thereby a right-angled motion in depth. Wherever the window is placed, these directional factors will influence the relation between window and wall. The design of windows, however, is also important for the way in which motion in the wall itself is to be perceived. 'These holes are often the destruction of form, they must be made an accentuation of form', says Le Corbusier (Fig. 374, a-d).[91] If we consider the influence of the vertical window on the wall in which it is situated, we realize the importance of whether the window finishes in a pointed arch, round arch or a straight lintel.

A pointed arch 'slashes' the wall above it, because the vertical line does not finish within the form but continues past it. The round arch supports weight from above and leads it equally to each side. In that sense the round arch indicates a more composite motion than the pointed arch. It expresses pressure from above in addition to a certain upward push from below. The semicircle, as part of a centralized form, emphasizes a horizontal motion *through* the wall from within. The pointed arch, on the other hand, exaggerates upward motion, thereby subduing motion through the wall and contact between inside and outside. In the Gothic cathedral there is a purpose in this. The entire interior is isolated and made more sacred; it is cut off from horizontal communication despite the skeletal wall and translucent glass. The symbolism of the vertical has determined the window form and is meant to create an eloquent image of the church for the outside world. If the window if finished off with a straight lintel, it means that its expression of motion is determined by width in relation to height. If the width is relatively great, motion through the wall is reduced, because the accent is on crosswise motion. This also applies when the width is so great that the

263

375. Window form and the relationship to the wall: the window and the wall system follow each other (from Palazzo Valmarana by Palladio).

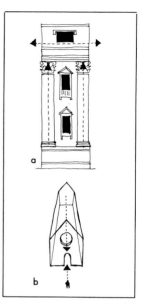

377 a-b. Window form and the relationship to the wall: (a) contrast between the wall's vertical and horizontal motions (diagram of St. Peter's wall system), and (b) accentuation of the entrance and the motions of the interior space (diagram of the rose window in the medieval church).

376. Window form and the relationship to the wall: the window and the wall system are separate (from an apartment building in Oslo, photo by T. Lange).

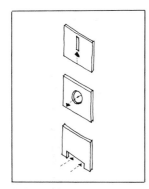

378. Window form and the importance of the location in the wall.

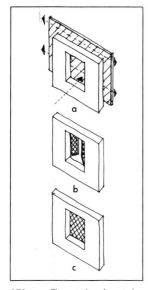

379 a-c. The window face is located innermost in the opening: (a) wall and surface exist as two independent layers, in which the exterior space dominates the interior space. The face can be further separated with contrasting patterns or colours (b, c).

danger of deflection in the middle arises, thus opening the way for the wall's 'collapse'.

Interplay of wall and window will sometimes cause wall motion and window motion to accent one another, while at other times it leads to a contrast between them (Figs. 375, 376).

An example of the first is to be found in the vertical window, which accents a tall wall as seen in skeletal walls of the Gothic cathedral. Horizontal windows, in just the same way, can extend and add weight to the horizontal wall. This added weight is exploited by Michelangelo in the attic storey of St. Peter's. The horizontal windows cause this storey to sit heavily on the tall pilasters below (Fig. 377, a). An extended, stretched-out look is also typical of Functionalism's bands of windows, which give a horizontal accent to the motion of the entire wall.

An example of a contrast between window form and wall is the Gothic rose window, which suggests motion not *within* the wall but *through* it. All verticality in the façade design stands suddenly in sharp contrast to the rose window's horizontal impulse. This latter is in keeping with the motion of entry below and creates a closer and more direct rapport with the length of the nave (Fig. 377, b).

The window's location also affects the wall's expression of weight. A horizontal window placed low in the wall increases the sinking effect and a vertical window high up increases the rising effect, while a centralized window conveys ambiguity (Fig. 378). A window form's own particular motion expression may be lost, depending on where the window is placed in the wall. The horizontal window, as we have said, indicates a lateral motion crossing the outward impulse. People behind the wall are restrained by it — they follow alongside the wall. This effect, however, is reversed if the window extends down to the floor. Then it is the floor which becomes the directing element and in a continuous process leads the inside out and outside in.

## THE FACE

The window's form and profile showed the relation of the opening to the surrounding wall, whereas the role played by the window face mainly depends upon its relation to the opening in which it is located.

The wall face and window face are seen as the boundaries of two different spaces (Fig. 379, a). The wall face is the boundary towards the exterior and is perceived as the outer shell of the house. The window face, on the other hand, is a boundary relating to the interior, because through the window we glimpse the interior's own life, which is held in check by the membrane of the window.

380. The window face is located innermost in the opening: wall and face are separated — the wall becomes an outer skin (from Tribune Review Building in Pennsylvania by L.I. Kahn, from Giurgola/Mehta, *Louis I. Kahn*).

383. The window face is located outermost and the door is located innermost in the masonry wall (neo-classical house in Oslo).

266

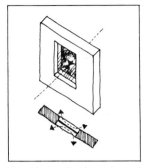

381. The window face is located in the middle of the opening: the exterior and interior are in balance.

This means that the four choices of location for the window face — inside or in the middle of the opening, outermost in or outside the opening — convey highly different impressions of relative interior and exterior strength. In the following descriptions, wall thickness will be held constant.

## THE FACE INSIDE THE OPENING

With a window face inside the opening the wall face and window face will be perceived as parts of two independent layers extending freely alongside one another (Fig. 379, a).

This phenomenon corresponds to what we have said about the hole (see p. 259). Through the opening we look into an inner detached world, which might be compared to watching swimmers glide past us when looking through a side window in a pool. The motif is interpreted in many ways. Interior curtains and shutters show the independence of the window face to the hole in the same way as when mullions and transoms create a crisscross pattern in the hole's own form. (Fig. 379, a-c). The window face gives the effect of being part of an independent membrane around a separate interior behind the stiff wall. In addition, when the window face is sunk deeply in the wall, the depth of the wall is revealed in the opening itself. Thus, it seems that the hole is caused not by the interior but by a force from the outside which cuts through the wall to reveal an inside world bounded by the window face (Fig. 380).

## THE FACE IN THE MIDDLE OF THE OPENING

When the window face is placed in the middle of the opening, the effect is one of inside and outside meeting at the halfway mark. The window face seems to be pushed out from the interior but is halted half way by a counter movement from the exterior, all of which can be read in the opening's depth (Fig. 381).

To experience this, the face must be transparent and so reveal both the front and rear part of the embrasure. Or, that an accentuated frame around the face shows its position within the hole. Here again, the relation between the form of the hole and the way in which the face is located will determine whether an outward or invard motion 'prevails'.

## THE FACE OUTERMOST IN THE OPENING

In placing the window face outermost in the opening the interior space appears to extend right out to the wall face (Fig. 382).

This can result in two effects. In the first, the entire volume of the building seems 'overladen'. This is because the outer wall surface and the inner substance meet in a common face conveying a feeling of interior space trying to break out. The effect is aimed at in neo-Classicism (Fig. 383). According

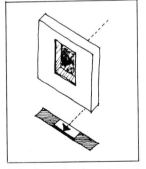

382. The window face is located outermost in the opening: The interior is led out.

384. The window face is located outermost in the opening: the wall and surface
are flush — the wall becomes 'thin' (from an
apartment building in Oslo).

387. The window face is located outermost while the door is located innermost in the
masonry wall (neo-classical house in Oslo, by N. Beer).

385. The window face is located in front of the opening: wall and surface are separated — the
wall becomes 'powerful' (from S. Lewerentz's 'Klippan' in Helsinki).

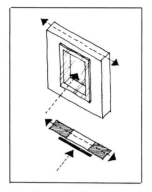

386. The window face is located in front of the opening: the exterior restricts the interior.

to its tenets a building should appear as a combination of stereometric masses. Herein lies the reason for large hipped roofs with no projection, plain wall faces, and Doric articulation. Windows are kept small and quadratic, usually flush with the wall. The location of the window face supports the architectural intention and gives the effect of a solid and 'inflated' building mass.

The other effect of placing the window face outermost in the opening gives the wall, especially when the windows are relatively large, the impression of being a thin 'skin'. The main reason for this is that wall and window face are seen as one and the same. Thus, it is not without reason that Functionalists placed glass windows outermost in the opening. The walls should appear as thin planes, a sort of non-supporting cloak wrapped around an open and expansive interior (Fig. 384).

## THE FACE OUTSIDE THE OPENING

The final variation, where the window face is fastened to the wall outside the aperture, gives the impression of a face belonging to the exterior space. In Sigurd Lewerentz's brick architecture from the 1950s, glass faces cover the openings like 'bandages' and seem to hold back the interior space (Fig.385). The wall flows freely behind them and thus seems in a way to have regained both individuality and strength (Fig. 386).

From what has been said hitherto we realize that variation in window face location can be a factor in the wall's character as a whole and in the relation between inside and outside.

A neo-Classical façade from the 1920's in Oslo is organized according to the vertical tripartition (see p. 119) (Fig. 387). The central area is divided into two storeys with small quadratic windows, their faces outermost in the opening wall. Doors have been placed in both corner sections. The French windows in the upper storey give onto narrow balconies, which rest on the frames surrounding the doors on the ground floor. All the doors are set deeply in the doorways.

The effect is immediate. The treatment of the centre area conveys an urge to expand. The interior seems to strain forward from within because of the windows' centralized forms and the flush position of the glass faces. The corner sections, on the other hand, seem massive and heavy. An important reason for this is the deep doorways, which reveal the thickness of the wall. Another reason is the location of the doors themselves, which emphasizes the difference between door and window. In line with the outer wall face the window leads motion outward from within, while the deep-set doors reveal their purpose of leading us in from outside (Fig. 388). In framing the ground floor doors, two contrary motions are emphasized at the same time. The deep-set door conveys a penetrating motion, the frame conveys

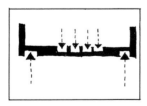

388. Pattern of motion in the façade of a neo-classical building in Oslo, see Fig. 387.

391. A farm house with and without frames around the openings (after Venturi, *Complexity and Contradiction in Architecture*).

389. The window frame accentuates the opening and separates it from the wall (from Enerhaugen in Oslo, Norwegian Folk Museum).

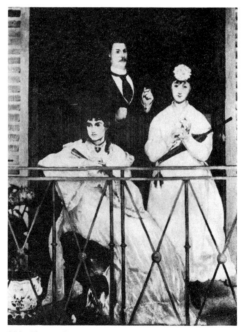

390. The window frame accentuates the framed motif ('The Balcony', painting by E. Manet, from Janson & Janson, *Maleriets historie*).

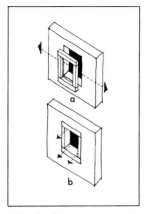

392 a-b. The motion expression of the frame components: (a) the frame in front of the wall, (b) the frame within the wall.

an emanating motion. This last element brings us to our next theme, which is the *frame's* role in the way we experience the role of the window for the relation between inside and outside.

## THE FRAME

A frame surrounds and creates the setting for a window face, just as four walls surround and create a room. This implies that the frame accents and emphasizes whatever it surrounds in relation to its environment.

The frame also draws a boundary between the window face and the walls around, which means that it isolates and protects what it surrounds. Thus, every frame has a double effect in both accenting and separating a motif (Fig. 389).

This again leads us to perceive the framed motif as being more important than its surroundings. The frame, therefore, is used to accentuate important objects, people and situations. When one receives a gift of a drawing or a painting, it is a sign of appreciation to promise to 'frame it'. A painting, according to Alberti, is an excerpt of a symbolic reality and like the window it frames another and more elevated world. In his well-known balcony painting, Edouard Manet concentrates and emphasizes a group of people by using the edges of the door to frame the figures (Fig. 390).

For us this means that a frame will accentuate what we see when looking in through a window. The frame, on other words, increases the importance of the *inside* space and in a way brings it towards the spectator on the outside.

This is clearly demonstrated when similar windows in the same wall are framed or unframed. In our example, the upper storey windows and the door beneath are merely unframed holes (Fig. 391). They show that the outside is forcing its way in, while the framed windows on either side accent an inside being led out.

## THE FRAME PARTS AND THEIR EXPRESSION OF MOTION

The expression of motion depends upon the actual composition of the frame.

From what has already been said we know that in relation to the opening, the frame's location is essential for the interpretation. We have pointed out the three basic motifs which can be distinguished by this relationship (see p. 255 f). Each gives the frame a different degree of importance in guiding motion, depending upon whether it is placed within or outside the opening. If, however, its location is outside the opening, the frame's variations are a function of a separate space *in front of* the wall. It is not until it

271

395. A city house with the sill as the dominating motif (by F. Furness, Philadelphia, Pennsylvania, from Venturi, *Complexity and Contradiction in Architecture*).

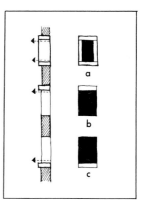

393 a-c. The motion expression of the frame components: (a) complete frame, (b) lintel, (c) sill.

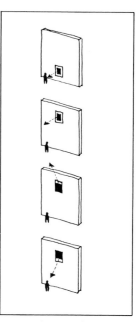

394. The frame motifs and motion expression in relationship to the location in the wall.

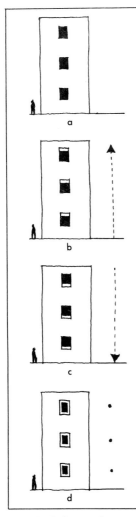

396 a-d. The frame and its motion effect on the wall's expression: (a) windows without frames (neutral), (b) windows with lintels (rising), (c) windows with sills (sinking), (d) windows with complete frames (expanding).

is within the wall that the frame is determined by the interior space and so becomes its mediator to the outside (Fig. 392, a, b).

In the following, therefore, we shall limit ourselves to discussing the variations within this last motif and study examples in which the frame appears as a *complete* form or only as a *head* or *sill*. Each of these variations will result in essentially different ways in which the interior is directed outward. These differences are based on our perception of the frame as marking the boundary around a space. This shows that the interior by means of its frame communicates with the outside in different directions, because the frame elements describe ceiling, floor and walls (Fig. 393, a-c).

The *complete* frame expresses a straight forward motion. The entire space, with ceiling, walls and floor, seems to reach towards the outside.

Windows in which the accent is on the *head* lead the ceiling out and up — the motion becomes vertical and rising.

If the window has only a *sill*, it is as though the interior space is being 'emptied out' and down whereby a sinking motion prevails.

There are nuances in these effects depending upon the location of the window in the wall. A completely framed ground floor window indicates direct communication between the spectator and the interior. If, however, the same window is in a higher storey, it is as if the frame accents a communication above the head of the spectator and this no longer concerns him. This feeling of distance and lack of association is increased if the window has an accentuated head but will decrease when the sill is emphasized. In the latter case it is rather that the interior is on its way down to meet the spectator (Figs. 394, 395).

## FRAME PARTS AND THE WALL

We realize that these variations may affect the expression of motion in the wall itself.

Let us imagine three identical windows above one another in a wall. These can alter the entire rising and sinking effect of the wall according to how the openings are framed. If all the windows have heads only, in principle the wall conveys a rising effect (Fig. 395, b), with sills only the effect is one of sinking (Fig. 396, c), while the wall with complete frames on all windows will be practically motionless (Fig. 396, d). If these variations are combined in different ways, the wall flight can be made to 'pulsate'. Let us picture a complete frame on the lowest window and this window surmounted by two other windows with heads only. The overall effect will be one of a rising from the second window (Fig. 396, e). If the two upper windows are given sills instead, the motion is reversed. They now sink towards the complete frame at the bottom (Fig. 396, f). Similarly, a wall with a complete frame on the lowest window, one with a sill only at the top, and one

397. The form of the lintels and the wall's expression: alternation between straight pediments on the lower level, arched and triangular pediments on the middle level and triangular pediments on the upper level (Palazzo Farnese in Rome by G. da Sangallo and Michelangelo, from Linn, *Storgårdskvarteret*).

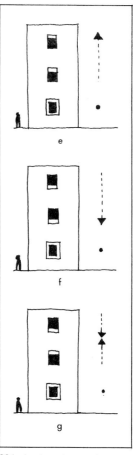

396. (e-g) windows with dissimilar frame motif (pulsating).

399. Complexity of the frame: various frames combined in the same wall (from an apartment building in Oslo).

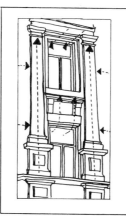

400. The form of the frame motifs and the wall's motion expression: diagram from an apartment building in Oslo, see Fig. 399.

274

398. The form of the pediments and the wall's motion expression: diagram of the frame system at Palazzo Farnese.

with only a head in the middle will convey a rhythm alternating between immobility, rising and sinking. This is a more 'traditional' interpretation of the wall in the way it responds to the roof's pressure and to its firm attachment to the ground (Fig. 396, g).

Again it is important to emphasize that the effects described may be given different interpretations and nuances depending on the *articulation* of the frame forms. Some examples follow. In a window with slanted sills the sinking effect is accented (Fig. 395). Correspondingly, we see that the rich crowning pediments of Classical architecture were the result of wanting to give the windows a rising effect. The most usual pediment types are the triangular and segmental, which each in its own way has a different rising effect. The triangular pediment continues the upward rise, while the segmental closes and rounds off the form. These qualities were used with intent and purpose in façade composition in order to provide changing rhythm both horizontally and vertically. An early example is Antonio da Sangallo's and Michelangelo's Palazzo Farnese (1534—1548) (Fig. 397). Within this strict block form, the different window pediments make the otherwise similar storeys rise stage by stage up towards the heavy cornice. On the ground floor the pediments are straight and give a flat, pressed down effect in keeping with the massive character of this part of the building. The next storey conveys a rising effect, but with alternating segmental and triangular pediments demonstrating in a way its indeterminate position between top and bottom. The entire top storey, on the other hand, rises upwards in a row of sharp triangular pediments in which even the bases of the triangles are broken by the arch of the window (Fig. 398).

THE COMPLEXITY OF THE FRAME

Finally we shall study an example illustrating the complex changes which occur in the inside/outside relation when several frames are combined and when they are placed both within and on the outside of the actual window opening.

Our example shows part of a window-wall section in a three-storey apartment house in Oslo from the 1880's (Fig. 399). The windows are equal in size but framed differently. The lowest window (not shown) is set in a ground floor heavy wall, the two above are placed between high colossal pilasters. The colossal pilasters belong to the outside space, emphasizing the main motion in the exterior building mass and linking the roof and the ground floor. At the same time they are a part of the expression of the window opening, in that the pilasters seem to 'draw aside' to make way for the opening between them (Fig. 400). There is motion from the *outside* in the top window, because it has no frame and is stepped inwards into the body of the wall. The window beneath, on the other hand, opens up from

401. Bay window as a bulge in the wall (from a factory at Tøyen in Oslo).

the *inside,* because the head guides the interior out and up by means of its powerful lintel. In contrast to the outward and inward motions above, the deep-set ground floor window announces another and more withdrawn space, well protected by a sturdy wall.

The composition above is taken from the Baroque and was used during that period to symbolize the building's function. The public nature of the great pilasters indicated the owner's noble status, whereas the different window frames were meant to show the type of room lying within. At the lowest level were shops and storerooms which, being at street level, required protection. The first floor, 'piano nobile', contained the reception and entertainment rooms with an extroverted and public reference. On the third floor were the more private bedrooms and servants' quarters.

The composition of the façade was also a logical solution to a location facing a narrow, dark street. The pilasters 'open' the street space to either side, giving it more optical breadth while at the same time guiding the eye up towards the light (see p. 159). The latter also explains the form of the windows. The darkest areas at street level are repeated in the closed ground floor and the gradual lightening upwards corresponds to the rising effect of the middle storey, while the strongest light is 'received' by the top storey windows.

## THE BAY WINDOW

We conclude by examining the importance of the bay window in our experience of the inside-outside relationship.

A bay window is to be understood as an expanding window. Its purpose is to appropriate exterior space both optically and in terms of light. Thus, the expression of the bay window is a question of whether the wall resists or gives way to this expansion from within.

The first bay window motif describes how the wall resists spatial expansion. The bay window pushes against the wall from within. The wall is bent by an inner power, which it controls and holds back, an expression giving the wall a character of both strength and flexibility (Fig. 364, a). The bay window and wall are in fact the same thing, and their encounter takes place within the body of the wall itself. The motif, therefore, is often found in buildings where the main emphasis is on the plasticity of the walls themselves. This is found in the Amsterdam school, in which architectural expression and the expression of mass are one and the same, so bay windows are formed as undulating membranes around expanding interior space (Fig. 401).[92]

In the next bay window motif connection between interior space and the wall is *broken.* The conflict between expansion and control is revealed by

402. Bay window extending from a split in the wall (from an apartment building in Oslo).

403. Bay window extending trom a split in the wall (from an apartment building in Oslo).

404. Bay window overlapping the wall (from Sea Ranch in California by Ch. Moore et al., from Futagawa (ed.), *MLTW*).

the way the bay window seems to burst through the wall opening. Inside space and outside space now have separate surfaces, each with its own purpose. The exterior space attempts to fill in the opening, while the bay window tries to open it (Fig. 364, b). A bay window of this type reveals the conflict in the architecture of the wall: a struggle between immobility and motion, *pro et contra*. In architecture this conflict is usually understood by exploiting contrasts in the composition. This may be found between curved and straight forms, as in cases where a straight wall directly encounters a curved bay window (Fig. 402). It also occurs in building systems where the wall is massive and the bay window skeletal (Fig. 403) and also between volumes where the bay window is slanted in relation to a straight wall.

In the third motif we see how the bay window describes a separate space which both *breaks into* the wall and *springs out* of it (Fig. 364, c). Whereas the first two motifs demonstrated that the bay window presses from the inside, this bay window overlaps both from within and without. We shall look at two examples. In 'Sea Ranch' designed by Charles Moore et al. (1965), a corner bay window projects from one of the wooden houses (Fig. 404). With its corners and slanted roof this bay window must be seen as an independent enclosure which both juts out of the interior space and breaks into it by taking a large piece of the corner. The other example is from the Maritime Museum in Oslo, designed by Trond Eliassen and Birger Lambertz-Nilssen (1974). A deep gash has been made in the corner facing the fjord and deep within it is a slanting bay window which projects from one of the sides. The bay window penetrates into the wall and projects from it. Both these examples derive their meaning from their seaside locations. The bay windows are a part of these windswept outposts in which the protruding part of the form is an actualization of defiance of the elements, while at the same time the retracted part shows the need for protection behind the wall itself.

In the fourth bay window type the wall passes freely behind the bay (Fig. 364, d). The bay window appears to be a box hung on the wall from the outside. Expansion from the interior is caught and imprisoned by an exterior enclosure fastened to the wall, which may be compared to Charles Moore's 'saddlebags'.

The wall in the first motif resembles a flexible membrane; in the second it gives the impression of being a contradictory narrowing element, and in the third of being an open element with neither wall nor bay dominating. In this last case, however, the wall is totally independent of the bay window. Therein lies the possibility of interpreting the wall as the superior element, as something stiff and strong in contrast to its lighter 'appendage' (Fig. 405). This point is more clearly expressed in the great mountain monasteries in Athos, Greece. These massive megalithic structures crown

405. Bay window as a room attached to the wall (19th century buildings in Amsterdam).

the island's craggy landscape like unassailable bastions. The characteristic covered galleries stretch along the top of the wall just like open skeletal windows. These open passages and massive walls complement one another; the very massiveness of the walls is accentuated by the lightness of the galleries and their openness is in turn emphasized by the closed walls.

406. The welcome at the entrance ('Velkommen', painting by E. Soot).

407. Entrance surrounded by painted windows and wreaths (Sudanese folk architecture).

# THE ENTRANCE

## THE ENTRANCE AND INSIDE-OUTSIDE RELATIONSHIP

The entrance is a thing through which one passes and belongs to the space outside (see p. 251 ff).

To go in is to experience entering, and in this lies an existential description of the *transition* itself — the distance between qualitatively different places — between inside and outside. It is by entering that one succombs both physically and mentally and 'occupies' the architecture with all its fundamental meanings. The symbolic value of entering and of the entrance is revealed in both the rituals and behaviour of most cultures. To carry the bride over the threshold, to bid welcome and farewell at the entrance is still customary in western European countries (Fig. 406). A glance at recently built residential areas shows the importance still attached to the entrance, even in a ritual-free society. Lamps, flower boxes, the old wagon wheel and ornate stone work accentuate broad, hardwood doors, all meant to give the residents individual identity. Formerly the entrance could illustrate the concept of eternity itself. 'The Lord shall preserve thy going out and thy coming in from this time forth, and even for evermore'.[93] A blood sacrifice was placed beneath the threshold to protect the interior, and the door casing was smeared with blood so that 'the angel of wrath' would pass by that house (Fig. 407).[94]

By comparing the most diverse buildings throughout architectural history we find certain specific motifs which through constant recurrence accentuate the very action of entering. They appear with varying degrees of strength, alone or together, and are found in both monumental and folk architecture.

These motifs concern two elements in the entrance design. The first is the *opening* itself and includes its form, profile, and the door. The other element is the surrounding *frame* and concerns the space around the doorway.

## DOORWAY MOTIFS

The *form* of the doorway follows the same principles as those of the window. It differs, however, because the window may be allowed a freer form. The door depends more upon the human figure and usually appears as an upright rectangle. Just as for the window the head will vary, according to style and purpose, between straight, curved or pointed, and the reveals too will alternate between straight and diagonal.

408. Wrought iron gate (entry by M.L. Leray, from Battersby, *Art Nouveau*).

409. Solid wood door (apartment building entry door from Venice).

413. Frame motif (St. Maria in Campitelli in Rome by C. Rainaldi, from Sedlmayr, *Epochen und Werke*).

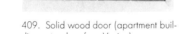

412. Frame motif (from a farm in Gudbrandsdalen in Norway).

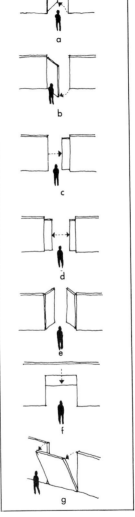

410 a-g. The doorway motifs: (a) away, (b) towards, (c) sliding, (d) double sliding, (e) double swinging, (f) lowered, (g) drawbridge.

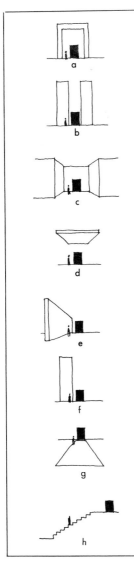

411 a-h. Door casing motifs: (a) frame, (b) split, (c) niche, (d) shelter, (e) directional wall, (f) side tower, (g) path, (h) stair.

The door face or *door itself* may vary in construction, material, and location to the same degree as the window face (Figs. 408, 409). Of particular importance, however, is the way the door opens (Fig. 410, a-g). A door can be opened in four ways: away from us, towards us, around us (revolving door) and sideways (sliding door). It may be either a single or a double door (two leaves). Likewise, the single door may be hinged on the right or the left but also at the top or bottom. Two familiar variations of the latter are the portcullis, flush with the wall and hinged at the top, and the drawbridge, hinged at the bottom and lowered from above.

## DOOR-CASING MOTIFS

The motifs used as casings *around* the door-opening are all variations on the wall's own archetypes. It is customary to take into account eight such entrance motifs, for which we shall use the following terms (Fig. 411, a-h). First is the *frame* or portal motif. This motif constitutes the primary form in the wall's skeletal system (see p. 193). It runs the gamut from naive ornamentation around doors found in rural and folk architecture (Fig. 412) to mighty column and cornice combinations in Baroque church façades (Fig. 413). The next motif, the *split* or twin-tower motif, may stretch from simple gateposts leading into the gardens of private homes (Fig. 414) to monumental Egyptian temple pylons and tall west-front towers in Gothic cathedrals (Fig. 415). The third motif, the *deep-set* or niche motif, (Fig. 416) occurs on a smaller scale, as when the door sits deeply in the opening itself (Fig. 417) and on a larger scale when projecting side wings create deep courtyards in front of the opening (Fig. 418). The *convex* motif makes the opposite impression to the niche motif and occurs when the façade springs forth either as an undulation or a risalit. The dominating feature in the *shelter* motif is its varying roof forms but it may also take the form of tall towers. The latter is typical for entrances at the foot of church and palace towers. We meet the first type in both column-supported anterooms and suspended baldachins (Figs. 419, 420). The *directional wall* motif has the same effect as the horizontal wall form (see p. 143) and appears as low half-walls leading to the entrance in Frank Lloyd Wright's houses or as high stone slabs leading straight into Mies van der Rohe's pioneer houses (Fig. 421). The *side tower* motif is found especially within Romanesque architectural tradition and takes the form of a tower on one side of the entrance (Fig. 422). The last motifs, the *path* and *stair* motif have also been examined earlier in connection with floor architecture (see p. 89 ff) (Fig. 423). As shown, it is the stair motif which permits particularly rich variations ranging from the plain *stoep* in front of Dutch bourgeoisie houses to broad series of stairs in the Baroque style (Figs. 424, 425).

414. Split motif (double-tower motif) (garden entrance to Villa Borghese in Rome).

415. Split motif (double-tower motif) (Egyptian pylons in front of the temple at Edfu).

418. Niche motif (terrace between two wings into the Cultural Centre in Risør, Norway by E. Anker & A. Hølaas).

416. Niche motif (entrance facing street intersection in Nancy, France).

417. Niche motif (entrance facing Damstredet in Oslo).

419. Shelter motif (covered entrance in front of Bergamo Cathedral).

421. Directional wall motif (from the Barcelona Pavillion by Mies van der Rohe, from Johnson, *Mies van der Rohe*).

420. Shelter motif (canopy in front of Stazione Termini in Rome by L. Calini and E. Montuori).

423. Street motif (pavement in Bergamo).

422. Side-tower motif (project from the 1850s by A.J. Downing, from Downing, *The Architecture of Country Houses*).

424. Stair motif (stair up to St. Marino in Montemagno).

425. Stair motif (from an apartment building in Oslo).

All the motifs that have been mentioned can be traced to both practical and technical considerations. Thus we see that the size of the door is often determined by the number of people to pass through (see difference between main entrance and auxiliary entrance) while the form may be the result of what is to be transported through the door (Fig. 426). Similarly, the frame or casing is the result of the need for added support and stiffening around the opening itself, while the baldachin solves the problem of protection both for those entering and for the interior space from sun and rain, while stairs are necessary to allow movement from one level to another.

Historical usage shows that they have an inherent value in themselves which far exceeds the purely practical. The reason is that the motifs reveal basically different ways of *entering*.

Concerning the form of the door opening, we have in connection with the window, drawn attention to the fact that breadth, height, and arch form take part in interpreting 'the speed' of the entering motion (see p. 259 ff). The door itself and the direction in which it swings contribute in turn to the degree of strength experienced in this motion relation between inside and outside. The phenomenon may be explained thus: the door swinging outwards brings the interior space out *towards* us, the inward swinging door leads the outside space inside *from* us, and the sliding door opens *between* us and the interior space. In the same manner the portcullis and the drawbridge bring the interior space down *on top of* us.

The casings around doors may be described in a similar manner. The frame motif conveys the feeling of entering *through* something, the split motif of passing *between* something, the deep-set motif of entering *into* something, the baldachin motif of passing *under* something, the directional motif of entering by following *alongside* something, the side-tower motif of entering by passing *by* something, the path and stair motifs, respectively, of entering *on* something and entering *up* or *down*.

Thus, different types of motion can be compared to prepositions in language, words that describe our physical orientation in relation to concrete objects in our surroundings. Regardless of cultural background, all of us have experienced different types of movement. They are universal and as a result immediately recognizable. This means that consciously or unconsciously we transfer our experiences to the motif we see. In other words, we 'enter' mentally before doing so physically (see also p. 29). The motifs, therefore, have been important in the preparation for entry, a process that may begin long before one reaches the entrance itself. For just this reason several motifs in combination are frequently used in the same façade in order to interpret the various stages on the way towards the goal. The Gothic cathedral may serve as an example. From a distance its soaring twin towers

426. Form of the door opening: form adapted to mule with packs (photo by Norberg-Schulz).

427. The size of the door opening: the largest frame is adapted to the façade's public image, while the smaller is adapted to private expression (cliff grave from Petra, from Springer, *Handbuch der Kunstgeschichte*).

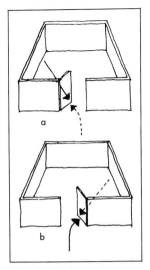

428 a-b. The door and its opening: (a) hinged on the left, (b), hinged on the right.

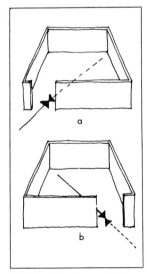

429 a-b. The door and its location: (a) on the left, (b) on the right.

announce the entrance to the church. Upon arrival at the square in front of the building the pointed arch around the door 'takes command', and finally it is the arched niche which concludes the outside space.

We have shown earlier that certain types of motion, embodied by certain motifs arouse in us corresponding sensations (see p. 29 ff). Buildings throughout acrhitectural history appear to show that this expressive content has been understood and exploited.

## DOORWAYS

'Build high the door and broad the gate. The king of honour cometh here'.[95] The quotation shows that not only the form of the door opening but also its relative size conveys a definite impression of the relation between inside and outside (Fig. 427). A large door opening is both generous and public; generous because it lays bare the interior and extends towards the person entering and public because the opening seems calculated for the passage of large crowds or socially important people. The height of the door is particularly important for the impression of size. If a door is low and one must bend to enter, a basically submissive movement is created. This is the expressive content of the low door. In Japan, entrances to tea-houses frequently measure no more than a square metre and are placed about 60 cm above the ground. One enters on one's knees, bowing at the same time, an action intended to put the visitor in a state of humility. The same impression is conveyed by the low slit through which one enters Emanuel Vigeland's mausoleum in Oslo (1926). One bows one's head, not just to the space within but equally to the artist himself, whose urn is immediately above the door.

The door itself may be seen as a movable part of the surrounding wall. In this sense the way it swings is an actualization of the relative dynamic strength of inside and outside. Thus, the outward-swinging door gives an impression of rejection; the interior space is shoved at us and makes us back away. Conversely, an inward-swinging door gives substance to our movement inwards; it lends added action and follows up this movement. This characteristic differs according to whether the door is hinged on the right or left. If it is hinged on the right, entry is a strong action in which the stronger hand opens the door and the interior space is actively shoved 'to the side' (Fig. 428 a,b). If it is hinged on the left, the active element is reduced because now one encounters the strong part of the *space*. If we imagine two identical spaces with the entrance on one wall, on the right and left respectively, it will seem more difficult to enter from the right than from the left. The reason is to be found in the spaces' own elements of strength, which in the right-hand case is what one meets and which offer

430. Frame motif (Constantine's triumphal arch in Rome).

431. Split motif (double-tower motif) (rear entry to Notre Dame du Haut by Le Corbusier).

more opposition to entering than if one enters from the left (Fig. 429 a, b).

The portcullis lowered from directly above conveys a threatening impression. Even more rejecting is the drawbridge, because it threatens the entire space in front of the opening in just the same way as the slanting wall (see p. 151 f). Medieval fortresses usually had both partcullis and drawbridge which made an effective rejection, both visually and in reality, doubly certain and quite in accord with the intention of these complexes.

## DOOR CASINGS

We have pointed out that casing motifs emphasize the wall's own themes. The same applies to the sensations which they arouse. In the following we shall look at some examples which illustrate this relationship.[96]

## THE FRAME MOTIF

We have maintained earlier that the casing or frame was both the setting and an accentuation of whatever was within it. As an entrance motif this means that it accentuates the person about to enter. The frame/casing thus has an idealizing content. That this is fully understood is shown in the triumphal arches of Antiquity, which, detached from architectural connections, bear witness to emperor's *res gestae* (see p. 231) (Fig. 430). The same may be said of the enormous portals in Baroque façades, which opening out towards the city to announce 'the church triumphant' (Fig. 413). All in all the casing and the portal are classic motifs in buildings that have their origin in socities holding clearly idealistic views of mankind.

## THE TWIN-TOWER MOTIF

The twin-tower motif, as shown earlier, conveys an impression of dignity and strength. This is because the motif is a visualization of an almost claustrophobic feeling which arises whenever we find ourselves between elements expressing power (Fig. 431). Verticality is such a powerful symbol, its structure indicates a strength which we immediately recognize with our own bodies. For this very reason the Phoenicians called the mountainous cliffs on either side of the Straits of Gibraltar, the Pillars of Hercules.[97] Similarly, the columns on either side of the entrance to the Temple in Jerusalem were called 'Jachin and Boas', meaning stability and strength.[98] In the split between the towering flanks man becomes 'small'. Thus, the motif is much used in sacred architecture. Between the pylons of Egypt's temples, stylized mountains joined together by the arc of the sun, man as a person is powerless, at the mercy of the gods (Fig. 432). The same is expressed in the towered west walls of medieval churches. Here the motif evokes humility beneath a heaven stretching above and between the two tower peaks.

433. Shelter motif (the shelter is created by a bracing arch, from the Bergamo Cathedral).

432. Lowered doors in a medieval fortress tower (from Caboga, *Die mittelalterliche Burg*).

## THE NICHE MOTIF

The niche motif conveys a feeling of being both received and embraced (see p. 149 f). The basis of this quality is that the motif conveys the feeling that architecture yields before us. In other words it illustrates the intrusion of exterior space, which in turn means that interior space yields to the space before us. Basically, the motif conveys an intimate touch, which may explain its revival as an entrance motif in many mass-produced houses. The Baroque *cour d'honneur* has, therefore, been compared to a welcoming gesture. Lorenzo Bernini said that he recognized the arms of man in the wings of palaces, and Emil Langlet wrote that the wings of the Norwegian Parliament, like 'outstretched arms' were meant to welcome the 'representatives of the people' (Fig. 183).[99]

## THE SHELTER MOTIF

The shelter motif has a protective air and conveys an impression of being the building's offering gesture to one who enters. The shelter is a visualization of an anteroom giving a three-dimensional preparation to the act of entry (Fig. 433). This preparation may consists of creating hesitation before entering, a psychological 'halt' as in the anteroom of the Pantheon. But, the preparation may also convey the feeling of being led in, as beneath Le Corbusier's baldachin over the entrance to Villa Stein (1927).

## THE DIRECTIONAL WALL MOTIF

The directional wall motif leads us forward with a feeling of security but also of dependence. This is because the motif is based on asymmetry and the contrast between the vertical and the horizontal. One 'keeps close to' the vertical. This is emphasized in Mies van der Rohe's brick house project (Fig. 434). The relationship between the large, open space and the wall leading straight to the entrance makes entering an almost forced action. Without the wall one is lost in an open space and feels drawn to follow its uncompromising and unbroken course right up to the entrance door.

## THE SIDE-TOWER MOTIF

The side-tower motif is essentially the same as the directional wall motif, but despite this it differs in the way it dramatizes verticality and thus the feeling of security. In placing the entrance beside this accentuated point where the vertical line and the ground meet, the entrance motion is given a surprising and contrasting effect. This effect is one of the reasons the motif was so popular in the romantic period. The side-tower's expressive content is exploited in modern architecture as well, as in Le Corbusier's Notre Dame du Haut (Figs. 358, 435). A conflict in plastic form is created by the

434. Directional motif (brick country house by Mies van der Rohe, from Johnson, *Mies van der Rohe*).

435. Side-tower motif (Schroeder House in Utrecht by B.T. Rietweld).

wall's upward slant from the tower and the decline of the heavy roof towards it, but all of this is kept in balance by the tower. Thus, it is safe both to be close to the tower and to enter along side it.

## THE PATH AND STAIR MOTIF

Path and stair-motif. Earlier we have pointed out that the path-motif is a visualization of one's own action radius. The path leads but at the same time expresses an independent action. By means of the path one can conquer the world, says Bollnow. In other words, the path is active and purposeful as well as goal orientated. We find this conquering quality accentuated in Egyptian temple axes which lead into the interior without interruption. Corresponding features are found in Baroque architecture and similarly in the ramp leading into Le Corbusier's Carpenter Centre (1963) (Fig. 39).

Stairs are a path dramatized. Their diagonal direction suggests the same tension as does their function, which is to connect two different levels, up and down. Herein lies their content as well, because of the different value attached to up and down in our action radius. If stairs lead us upwards from below, we expect to reach something important. If, on the contrary, we are led downwards, our movements take on an air of 'being tolerated'. For this reason stairs convey a feeling of both contact and distance. The stair-motif, therefore, is particularly emphasized in monumental architecture, an architecture aimed at responding to common interests and the elevation of common ideals (Fig. 424).

436. The roof as experience (photo *Aftenposten*).

# THE ROOF

438. The roof rises (detail from Rockefeller Center in New York, from Kouwentoven, *The Columbia Historical Portrait of New York*).

439. The roof sinks. Illusionary collapse (from Pommersfelden Palace, painted by G. Marcihni, from Zucker, *Fascination of Decay*).

440 a-c. The roof's form and its relationship to shape and articulation of the space: (a) the roof is neutral, (b) the roof uplifts, (c) the roof is directional (from *Wohnen* I, 1980)

# WHAT THE ROOF DOES

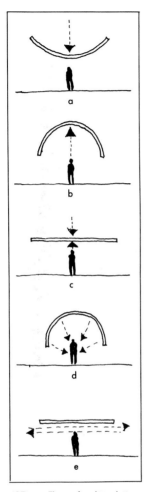

In our environment the roof is two-dimensional.

In the inside-outside relationship this means that the roof protects an interior space against an exterior space, a space which is both *over* and *around* it. The space above is the vertical dimension, the sky. The surrounding space is the horizontal dimension, the ground's surface (Fig. 436).

In relation to the sky, a roof may *accept* the sky, which means that it guides a downward motion from above. On the other hand if the roof *resists* the sky, the motion will be directed upwards from below. A roof may also be *balanced* between downward and upward motion (Figs. 437 a-c, 438, 439).

In relation to exterior space a roof may direct motion inwards toward a centre and thereby *close* the space or outward along a line and thus *open* the space. Both effects may operate simultaneously (Figs. 437 d, e, 440 a-c).

437 a-e. The roof and its relationship to the sky above: It is able to (a) receive the sky, (b) resist the sky, (c) balance the sky. The roof and its relationship to the surroundings: It is able to (d) close the space, excluding the surroundings, (e) open the space, including the surroundings.

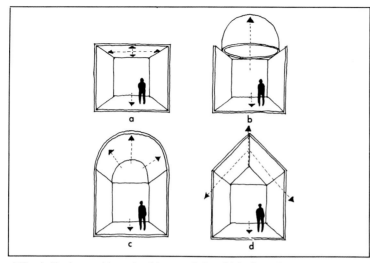

442 a-d. The themes of the roof and the space below: (a) the flat roof is neutral, (b) the dome centralizes, (c) the barrel vault is directional, (d) the gable roof both directs and closes.

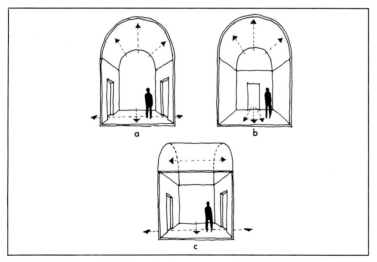

444 a-b. The themes of the roof and the relationship to the articulation of space: (a) barrel vault in contrast to the openings, but in correspondence with the form of the space, (b) barrel vault in correspondence with the openings and the form of the space, (c) barrel vault in correspondence with the openings, but in contrast to the form of the space.

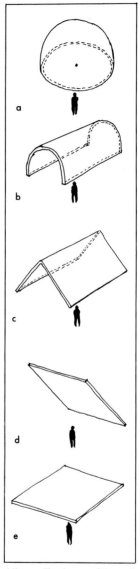

441 a-e. The themes of the roof: (a) dome, (b) barrel vault, (c) gable roof, (d) shed roof, (e) flat roof.

302

# THE ROOF THEMES

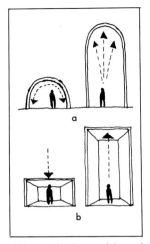

443 a-b. The themes of the roof and wall height.

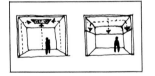

445 a-b. The themes of the roof and the relationship to the articulation of the wall: (a) the walls extend upward to the flat roof (rising effect), (b) the roof extends downward along the walls (sinking effect).

Throughout architectural history we find a series of shelter forms which each in its own way is a variation, vertically and horizontally, of these expressive components.

On closer examination we find that these variations are based on just five themes: (a) the *dome,* (b) the *barrel vault* (c) the *gable roof,* (d) the *shed roof,* (e) the *flat roof* (Fig. 441 a-e).

Each of these archetypes conveys specific expressions with regard to motion, weight, and substance, which in turn influence our experience of the space beneath. In describing the expression of these various forms, the terms sinking, rising and neutral will be used when referring to verticality, while the terms centralizing and directional will be used when referring to horizontality.

These impressions, however, depend upon three conditions, each of which will influence the main expression of each theme. The first concerns the *spatial form* created by the walls, the second pertains to the *height* of the walls, and the third has to do with the *articulation* of the walls.

When it concerns spatial form, a dome over a square will, for example, convey a far different impression than a dome over a round space. A barrel-vaulted roof over a long, narrow space will give a different effect than if placed over a short, wide space etc. Seen in this way, roof form and spatial form will affect each other mutually (Fig. 442 a-d).

When it is a question of the wall's height, a dome above low walls will convey a close and protected feeling, whereas the same dome set on high walls will give a rising effect. A corresponding effect is conveyed by a flat roof. Placed on low walls it may seem threatening, but raised slightly it will seem light and airy (Fig. 443 a, b).

When it comes to articulation, the openings in the wall are of great importance in determining the motion effect. In a barrel-vaulted corridor the placement of the openings in either the sides or ends will influence the apparent length of the corridor (Fig. 444 a-c). Of equal consequence is the articulation of the transition between the two elements. In the case of the roof, it is a question of whether the roof form appears to bear *down on* the walls or to rise *up from* them. As for the walls, the question is whether the wall architecture is carried upward into the roof form or whether the roof architecture is drawn down along the walls (Fig. 445 a, b).

In the following we shall examine the five roof themes individually. We shall, first of all attempt to describe expressions of motion and weight in order to determine their impact. Thereafter we shall study examples showing different motifs and their variations. The use of various forms, articulation, lighting and colour will increase or lessen the expressiveness of the themes and their importance for our perception of the 'struggle' of interior space against the powers of the environment.

# THE DOME

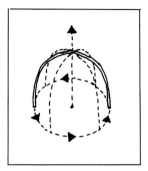

446. The dome is generated by the rotation of an arch around a vertical axis.

## THE EXPRESSION OF THE DOME

As a form the dome is to be understood as a roof covering based on the principle of an arch in rotation around a vertical axis (Fig. 446). The plan of the dome is circular; its form is vertical and has a continuously curved surface. The key words in describing the basic characteristics of the dome are, therefore, *centrality, continuity,* and *rising* (Fig. 447).

What then is expressed by the dome?

The dome is associated with numerous and diverse conceptions and forms.[1] Common to all of them is their reference to conceptions of the cosmos. The main reason for this is that the dome is a reminder of the sky and in its very form a replica of the heavenly sphere we have above and around us. The primitive house, accordingly, was regarded as a miniature of the universe itself (Fig. 448).[2] This association may be seen in the word 'dome', derived from the Latin 'domus' which means 'house'.[3]

As a form also, the dome contains within itself the fundamental qualities which are typical both of the sky with its elevating character and of the house with its protective associations. In that the dome ascends in a circle around a vertical line, it is by inclination potentially related to the sky. But, because it also arches above and around us, it conveys a feeling of both safety and protection, which again by its very nature is related to the conception of dwelling, to the house itself. This aspect is particularly discernible in the primitive hut in which walls and roof were fused into one encompassing and continuous unit. The word cupola which is akin to the Sanskrit word 'kupah', which means 'cave', suggests the same.[4] The dome gives an enclosing feeling of safety, which corresponds to the effect of an all-encompassing and protective universal space. But, the dome is also centralized. Its focus is the centre of the space where existence is calmed. The dome, therefore, indicates the very essence of what we mean by being *inside,* which in turn is the prerequisite for all security and life.

## DOME MOTIFS

There are three main outstanding types of domes in which all these qualities are combined but in different ways and with different emphasis. These motifs may be compared to similar arch forms (see p. 227 ff). As a result, we speak of the *conical* or elliptical dome (pointed arch), the *spherical* or

447. A dome's characteristics are centrality, continuity and rising (from Glyptoteket in Copenhagen by V. Dahlerup).

448. Dome of primeval house as an image of the universe (Trulli House from Apulia, from Rudofsky, *The Prodigious Builders*).

450. The conical form and the first round huts made of branch forms ('The first building' drawn by Viollet-le-Duc, from Rykwert, *On Adam's House in Paradise*).

451. The flat form as a baldachin over a holy person (High Priest under a baldachin, from Baldwin Smith, *The Dome*).

306

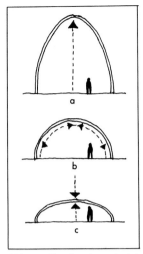

449 a-c. The dome's motifs; (a) conical, (b) spherical, (c) flat.

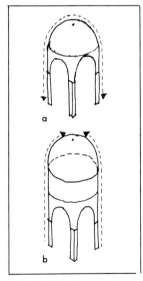

452 a-b. (a) Dome resting on pendentives, (b) dome resting on tambour inserted between dome and pendentives.

semicircular dome (semicircular arch) and the *flat* or segmental dome (flat arch) (Fig. 449, a-c).

The three dome motifs represent three stages in an historical-technical development. E. Baldwin Smith, accordingly, judges the *conical* form to be the earliest and establishes its possible derivation from man's first primitive round huts.[5] The form has its origin in the flexible or naturally bent reed and branch forms which were fastened together at the top with interwoven bands (Fig. 450). This form was subsequently transferred to stone as for example in the *tholos* of Mediterranean countries and in primitive folk architecture in Italy, Africa and Nubia (Fig. 448).

The *spherical* form is thought to be a result of mathematical and ideological speculation. As a form, the sphere corresponds to the conception of perfection in that the form illustrates complete and absolute harmony, '… the most perfect and the most like itself'.[6] In its construction too the sphere had advantages recognized by, amongst others, the Romans, who built in concrete and brick and had developed efficient and standardized building methods.

The *flat* dome derives from tent-shaped shelters and has been used throughout history particularly as tabernacles and baldachins to mark important and 'sacred' places (Fig. 451). The four corner columns carrying the cupola are thought to have their origin in the poles of movable nomadic tents. In modern times the flat dome is used in roofs of reinforced concrete, and thanks to the rigidity of steel a much flatter span than those of high stone domes is made possible.

As we have seen, all three dome motifs are centralized and have approximately the same degree of curving continuity. The main difference between the three is first and foremost the difference in their degree of rising. The motifs, accordingly, will express the dome theme's rising effect in the following ways: by *accentuating* the rising effect as the conical dome does, by *neutralizing* it as seen in the spherical dome, or by *counteracting* it as does the flat dome. Seen thus, the dissimilar degrees of rising may convey equally different effects, which vary between having a rising or 'hovering' effect, a balancing or 'struggling' effect, or one of giving and 'protecting'.

## FORM OF THE DOME

We realize, nevertheless, that it is not the dome alone but its articulation as well which is essential in conveying its effecr. This includes not only the detailed form of the dome itself but perhaps more particularly the form given to the transition between roof and walls.

In joining a dome and a square space, the problem of transition may in principle be solved in two different ways (Fig. 452 a,b). Firstly, the dome is

453. Sedlmayr's example of 'übergreifende' domes without tambours from the late-Roman period (from Sedlmayr, *Epochen und Werke*).

456. Bramante's proposed tambour dome over St. Peter's: neutralized rising (from Wölfflin, *Renaissance and Baroque*).

308

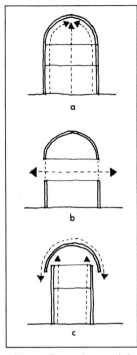

454 a-c. The tambour and the relationship between the dome and the walls: (a) accentuated rising, (b) neutralized rising, (c) resisted rising.

455. Michelangelo's proposed tambour dome over St. Peter's: accentuated rising (from Koepf, *Baukunst in Jahrtausenden*).

set directly on doubly curved pendentives, which distribute the dome surface evenly over the space beneath by way of the four corners.

In the other case, a cylindrical drum is inserted between the dome and pendentives.

Basically, the pendentive solution gives the roof a sinking character. If the dome rests on four columns, it enfolds the space within its grasp like a baldachin lowered from above. Hans Sedlmayr calls this solution 'übergreifende' and shows that it reached its height of development in the early Christian period (Fig. 453).[7]

The drum solution lends a rising character to the roof. The dome is given an extra shove from below which lifts the roof up and above the lower wall zones. The rising effect, however, may be increased or decreased according to the articulation of the drum. In this context there are three alternatives in particular which stand out (Fig. 454, a-c).

In the first, the rising effect conveyed by the basic form is *emphasized* in that the drum unites an upper and lower space. The dome interior of St. Peter's Basilica in Rome (1590) is an example of this (Fig. 455). Here the drum is broken up by alternating pairs of pilasters and window openings. These pilasters continue and become dome ribbing by way of projecting parts in the dividing dome ring. In this way the entire verticality of the form is accentuated and is further emphasized by the drum windows between the pilasters. They 'free' the dome from the walls below and give it an even greater rising effect in accord with the open oculus in the crown.

In the second alternative, the drum divides walls and dome thereby *neutralizing* the rising effect of the main form. St. Peter's dome may again serve as an example, but this time as we find it in Donato Bramante's project about one hundred years earlier (Fig. 456). The interior of the drum in this case is composed of a closely set circle of columns supporting a perfectly spherical dome with no articulation whatsoever. On the exterior we find a corresponding colonnade but here the dome is encircled at the bottom by stepped horizontal buttressing resting on the cornice.

In comparing the exterior and interior forms an obvious difference may be seen. The exterior of the dome is heavy. With its horizontal stepped buttressing it rests on the colonnade beneath. Inside, on the other hand, the dome neither weighs down nor rises. It 'hovers' above the colonnading like something immaterial.

In the last variation the rising effect is *counteracted* because the drum conveys the impression that the dome is lowered down over the interior space. One way of creating this impression is to hide the transition between dome and walls. In other words, the dome continues down behind the drum, which in turn rises into the dome. An example of this is the vaulting over Francesco Borromini's San Carlo alle Quattro Fontane, in which the

457. Boullée's project for a tambour dome over Madeleine: resisted rising (from Rosenau, *Boullée & Visionary Architecture*).

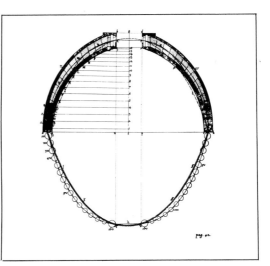

458. The conical dome follows a catenary curve (Poleni's chain experiment, from Cornell, *Bygnadstekniken*).

459. The conical dome as an exterior motif (Kalubé, from Baldwin Smith, *The Dome*).

460. The conical outer dome over flat inner dome (The church of the Holy Trinity, in Oslo, section drawn by W. von Hanno, from Berg, *Trefoldighetskirken. Kirken bygges.*)

dome ring is hidden by a 'crown' of foliage and flowers. Another illustration is Etienne-Louis Boullée's project for the Church of the Madeleine (1785) (Fig. 457). Here the drum is transformed into a free-standing screen which projects upwards into the dome space. The dome is painted with heavenly visions which combined with the arcade convey a feeling of infinite space.

> The painting of the vaulting extends down onto the rear wall from which the columns jut out, with the result that the expanse of the Heavens and the glory that adorns the vaulting and cupola become immense.[8]

In the following we shall return to individual dome motifs. We shall treat them separately and with the help of examples show how the expression is interpreted by various types of articulation.

## THE CONICAL DOME

The conical dome emphasizes the *rising* effect.

This applies technically also in the sense that a conical dome when its section approaches the shape of a catenary curve is the 'lightest' of the dome forms because its stress is led downwards through its own form with minimal horizontal stress. Giovanni Poleni demonstrated this principle in his chain experiment (1748), in which he allowed the catenary curve, illustrated by a hanging chain, to describe the silhouette of St. Peter's dome (1590) (Fig. 458). The same principle was used in Filippo Brunelleschi's Florence Cathedral dome (1420). In this Gothic silhouette the horizontal stress was minimal, with the result that both the dome itself and the walls beneath could be made thinner than if the form had been spherical. Corresponding ideas lie behind the construction of modern paraboloids. Great compound curved concrete shells reach the ground supported by thin arched pillars, giving the form a floating effect undisturbed by slanting horizontal buttressing.

The dynamics in these examples lies not only in the construction method but equally in the dome form itself. The contours rise continuously just as in the Gothic arch, and all lines converge at the apex in a point. This rising effect is probably one of the main reasons for the frequent use of the conical dome for exteriors whereas it is less prevalent in interiors (Fig. 459). A typical example is the double dome, in which the outer dome may well be the rising, conical type while the inner dome is either spherical or flat (Fig. 460). An important reason for this difference between the exterior and interior dome is visually determined. A spherical outer dome, when seen from below would have given a sinking impression. We know that originally Michelangelo planned a spherical dome over St. Peter's Basilica in Rome (1569).[9] Later (1590) Giacomo della Porta gave the dome a markedly

464.  The spherical inner dome (the Pantheon in Rome).

463.  The spherical dome and ideal calm (Tempietto in Rome by D. Bramante, photo by Alinari).

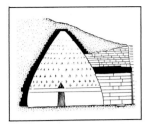

461. The conical inner dome (Atreus' burial chamber in Mycenae, from Baldwin Smith, *The Dome*).

conical form which resulted in a lively verticality both in the dome and in the building itself (Fig. 455).

The conical dome is seldom found as an interior vault. One reason could be that its form gives the space a diminishing and funnel-like effect as it rises. In this sense both the spherical and flat type are more 'immediate' and in closer harmony with the roof's function as a canopy and as an upper completion of the space. An example of an attempt to minimize this vertical effect in a conical inner space is to be found in the Treasury of Atreus at Mycenae (c. 1350 B.C.), where the bronze covered heavenly dome is drawn down over the walls (Fig. 461).

# THE SPHERICAL DOME

The spherical dome is *balanced* between rising and sinking.

Just as the semicircular arch, when read from the bottom up, appears to rise but read from the top downwards seems to sink, the hemisphere too is a form that balances between up and down. Basically, the spherical dome is at *rest* (Fig. 462). The type was very much used during the Renaissance, a period which sought after a balanced relation between elementary geometric forms (Fig. 463). Several early Renaissance examples reveal domes which were frequently without any articulation. In this way the form's neutrality was clear and undisguised. Thus the spherical dome in itself is not decisive in determining the chief dynamics of the space below but is dependent upon articulation in order to convey an impression of rising, floating or sinking.

### THE PANTHEON

A classic example of the spherical dome in which all these fundamental motions are in balance is the Pantheon in Rome, built by the Emperor Hadrian (A.D. 124) (Fig. 464). This dome combined with the drum-like walls beneath creates a space famous for its perfect balance. Here all forces are equalized in a perfect calm, completely in keeping with the intention of the space as a symbol of unity between spiritual and human power in an all-encompassing universe. 'One bows beneath a magical power emanating from the stars, from their movements and constellations, a power which is centred in this hall'.[10]

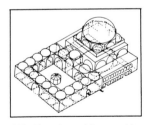

462. The spherical dome and the isolated addition (dome system in Selimiyeh in Edirne by Sinan, from Norwich (ed.), *Verdensarkitekturen*).

### THE PANTHEON AND THE ADDITIVE DOME

The dome of the Pantheon is to be understood as a coffered vault. In keeping with Classical tradition and the flat coffered ceiling, familiar to us from Greek temples, the vault too is an element which basically rests *on* the walls. 'The walls are given, thereupon the upper conclusion becomes an additional other form'.[11]

Thus, despite the fact that the roof is an addition to the walls, it is simultaneously both united to and separated from the walls. The combination of all these factors affects the spectator and creates the overall impression of the space. The impression, however, varies in magnitude according to the position of the observer beneath the dome.

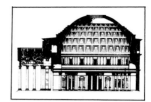

465. Section through the Pantheon (from Pothorn, *Das Grosse Buch der Baustile*).

## THE PANTHEON AND THE INTEGRATED DOME

The dome and its walls are united vertically, horizontally and perspectively (Fig. 465 a-c).

Besides the equality in height of dome and walls, it is particularly the interplay of the rings of coffering and the oculus which convey this effect.

The vault is divided into squares by the coffering and becomes a network of vertical and horizontal lines. In this way attention is drawn to the fundamental characteristic of all domes, which is the combination of an encompassing and a rising effect. We find the same characteristics in the division of the walls beneath. The horizontal lines are repeated in the moulding cornices, which divide a high main storey and a low attic storey, whereas the vertical lines recur in the upright columns surrounding the main level of the space.

In this way walls and dome are united *vertically* by means of the column lines. These again are picked up by the vertical dome ribs and led up to the *oculus,* which in turn opens up and expands freely towards the sky (Fig. 465, a). This, combined with the diminution of the coffers towards the apex creates an effect of walls and dome rising towards the light. The verticality, however, may be read in reverse. The *oculus,* true enough, when regarded as a hole is an opening which guides the inner space outward. But, seen as a light source it conducts the sunlight from outside to inside. In a compact cone the light is cast down from the dome's crown. Now the ribs have become the sun's own 'accomplices' and like a cluster of constructed rays guide the light down upon the spectator.

The upper and lower spaces are integrated *horizontally* also (Fig. 465, b). The wall mouldings and the roof ribs may be seen as a continuous system of rings gradually becoming more concentrated as they approach the dome opening as though the space is about to seal itself off at the crown. Regarded in this way the space may be read from the bottom up, but, the dome opening in counteracting this closure makes it possible to read these same rings from the top down as well. With their centre in the *oculus* they spread down over the space in ever-expanding rings just as when one casts a pebble into still water.

*Perspectively,* upper and lower parts are also united (Fig. 465, c). This ef-

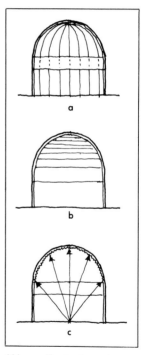

466 a-c. The Pantheon dome is linked to the space below in the following three ways: (a) vertically, (b) horizontally, (c) in perspective.

314

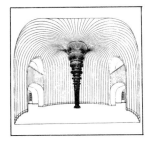

467. The flat dome and sinking (drawing by H. Scharoun, from Pehnt, *Expressionist Architecture*).

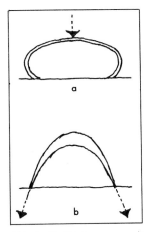

468 a-b. The flat dome as a result of (a) pressure from above, (b) expansion from below.

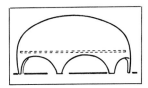

469. The flat dome and sinking (drawing of the University Synagogue in Jerusalem, by E. Rau, from Siegel, *Strukturformen der modernen Architektur*).

fect is accomplished by the way the roof coffers are calculated from a starting point in the centre of the floor — thus their perspective gradually straightens the further one looks upwards into the vault. This means that the roof is connected to the centre of the space by a network of sight lines. In other words, the roof is controlled by the person in the centre. This person is the emperor, he who sits in judgement at the central point of the space and commands the universe. 'Viewed from here the hovering vault seems to be drawn toward the observer'.[12]

## THE PANTHEON AND THE SEPARATED DOME

Vault space and wall space, as we have seen, are merged in several ways. But, the upper and lower parts are two separate elements. This is underlined by the attic storey, which acts as a dividing insertion between the main storey and vault. This applies, however, to the form of the attic before its reconstruction in the eighteenth century. The present form, with deep blind niches and intervening solid panelled areas, gives the storey a strong plastic character, causing the dome to rest heavily on the main storey beneath. This zone, originally, consisted of rows of small pilasters evenly encircling the entire space. The pilasters were unrelated both to the rib system above and to the columns beneath, thereby breaking into the continuity of the two levels. Statically as well, the attic storey was experienced as a disrupting zone. The small columns conveyed a non-supporting air of lightness in sharp contrast to the plastic realism of both the dome and main storey. The result was a hovering dome — a dome which in utter calmness and raised high above the world announced its content of 'templum deorum omnium'.[13]

## THE FLAT DOME

The flat dome seems *weighted down* in contrast to the conical dome with its rising effect and the spherical dome in its tranquility (Figs. 466).

The flattening of the form is due to a weight coming either from above, which presses the form flat, or from below, which hinders the rising effect. Both will convey an effect of tension. In the first case we sense the ability of dome and walls to withstand downward pressure, whereas in the second case we read the capacity of dome and walls to restrain expansion from below (Fig. 467, 468). The first tendency may be compared to a drop of liquid which, owing to its intrinsic weight, is flattened on top and bulges out at the sides. An example of such a form is the shell dome of the University Synagogue in Jerusalem (1958) designed by Ezra Rau (Fig. 469). The other tendency could be compared to an inflated sail anchored to the

470. The flat dome (Palazetto dello Sport in Rome by P.L. Nervi, from Nervi, *Aesthetics and Technology in Building*).

472. The flat dome in rotation (Palazetto dello Sport in Rome, from Nervi, *Aesthetics and Technology in Building*).

ground with posts and guy lines. This is exemplified in antiquity's renditions of baldachins over thrones and altars (Fig. 451).

In the following we shall limit our analysis to two examples of the flat dome, specifically, the modern domes over two sports stadiums in Rome. Both are designed by Pier Luigi Nervi (1955 and 1959).

## THE SPORTS STADIUMS IN ROME

At first glance Nervi's sports stadiums resemble one another in both form and structure.

Both have the same function, both are round and covered by large flat domes. In both cases the domes are constructed with visible supports and ribs and in both, the spectator benches and arena are below ground level. Even so, there are some important differences. Whereas the small sports stadium, the so-called Palazzetto, appears muscular and 'combative', the large Sports Stadium seems hovering and 'ordering'. Each illustrates the expression of the flat dome, the first by its pressed down effect and the latter by its expansiveness.

## THE SPORTS STADIUMS: EXTERIORS

The differences between these two stadiums are already apparent on their exteriors.

The Palazzetto is fundamentally associated with the *ground* (Fig. 470). The interior space is sunk into it while at the same time the exterior supports spring up from it. Y-shaped supports surrounding the Palazzetto give evidence of an unusual upward thrust from below. This contributing strength is not necessitated by the weight of the thin dome covering with its undulating scallops in the transition to the supports below. It is rather the dome's *form* which requires this expression of power in that these supple buttresses must be there to 'convince' us that the flat span will hold. From this point of view the Palazzetto expresses a struggle against the vault's own weight.

In the large Sports Stadium the dome supports are hidden by a circular glass wall (Fig. 471). In this way the visible interplay of forces between the dome and ground is interrupted so that the roof appears to hover above the glittering membrane. The glass ring itself is divorced from the ground in that the ground storey is set back slightly in relation to the glass wall above. Twelve free-standing staircaises spring directly out from the wall ring and bring the hovering dome structure into a light contact with the ground. These serve to emphasize even more the non-supporting character of the form. This is enhanced by still another factor: the location of the building. The large Sports Stadium is situated at the end of a broad boulevard and crowns a high ridge just outside Rome. In this way the ridge itself is used as a further means of elevating the structure towards the sky.

471. The flat dome (the Palazzo dello Sport in Rome by P.L. Nervi, *Aesthetics and Technology in Building*).

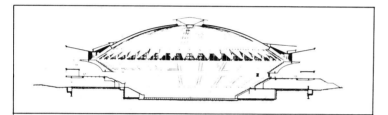

473. The flat dome in stasis (from the interior of the Palazzo dello Sport, from Nervi, *Aesthetics and Technology in Building*).

474. The relationship between the dome and the floor in the Palazzo dello sport, from Nervi, *Aesthetics and Technology in Building*.

The exterior differences continue in the interiors of these domed buildings.

In both cases the vault ribbing remains visible. It is questionable whether the ribs are statically necessary for the support of the dome. They do, however, have the practical advantage of hiding and conducting lighting fixtures, pipes and air-conditioning ducts. Apart from these considerations it is obvious that the ribs are of visual importance. Without them the enormous vault surfaces could seem both threatening and overdimensioned. Now the roofs are experienced as being 'secure' because the ribs 'form a pattern that suggests the isostatic lines of the principal stress'.[14]

The rib pattern, however, differs in the two buildings. The rib network in the Palazzetto is restless (Fig. 472). By means of rhombic formed coffers interspersed with large criss-crossing arches the surface is set into motion in an endless rotation around the lantern at the top. The transition to the Y-shaped supports is also questionable in that the clusters of straight ribs which carry the billowing cloaks must be joined to the network of curved lines in the dome surface above. The main impression is of a roof in a plastic 'struggle' — a roof which like a whirling disc must remain in motion or fall down.

In the large Sports Stadium the character of the rib pattern is one of supreme calm (Fig. 473). Effortlessly and uncompromisingly the ribs ascend in uninterrupted lines to the lantern eye at the zenith. From below, the dome is lifted up by slender V-shaped supports with the ribs radiating directly from them. Sitting inside the Palazzetto it is impossible to see how the roof meets the ground. In the large Sports Stadium the supports are brought right into the interior space and seem to spring directly from the upper tiers of the stadium benches.[15] These rows of benches form a separate gallery raised above the rest of the seats below.

This impression is consciously accented by the use of light and shadow. The roof ribs are V-shaped in section. In a broad belt at the bottom immediately above the V-shaped supports and again at the top around the lantern, the ribs are solid and unperforated. In the intermediate zone the ribs are perforated by large openings. The lighting is placed here and gives the entire section of the construction a feather-light effect, while the upper and lower areas appear darkened and heavy.

The overall effect of this articulation is strong and convincing. The dark zones 'draw' the dome together at both top and bottom. At the top the dome becomes more compact as it reaches its zenith around the light aperture and again at the bottom as it nears the dark tiers of benches to which it is anchored and thus hovers above a dividing belt of light. The resulting effect is one of a flat dome with an extra curvature in the illuminated area, which imparts a rising effect to the whole body and like a full sail lifts entire zones of the space beneath. The dynamics of the roof become more strongly emphasized when seen in relation to the sinking effect in the arena below. Seen in contrast, the distinctive quality of each part strengthens the other, so that the sunken floor and rising roof depend upon one another to reach a state of dramatic tension (Fig. 474).

# DOME VARIATIONS

In our survey above we saw that all dome examples were of *true* domes. By this is meant that they all were circular in plan, had a continuous surface, and were upright.

Throughout architectural history, however, there are many roof forms *resembling* domes, in other words, forms that contain one or several of the qualities characterizing the true dome.

These may be divided into two main groups. The first may be called *modified* dome roofs. By this is meant roof forms which are basically true domes but which have undergone changes of various kinds. The other group may be called *dome-like* roofs, meaning roof forms which basically are either true barrel vault, gable or flat roof and have been altered in such a way as to give them some of the dome's characteristics.

In the following we shall examine modified dome roofs as a separate category while the second group will be covered in connection with other roof forms.

Modified domes may be divided into two sub-groups in which the main reason for the alteration will be given. The first we call the *hanging* or inverted dome and the other the *modelled* dome.

# THE HANGING DOME

The main difference between a hanging dome and a true dome is that the hanging dome conveys a *falling* impression. Such a form may impart a threatening effect, a feeling that a thin membrane is being pressed down by a powerful thrust from above. We shall give two examples of how this primary effect varies according to the dome's articulation and juncture with the walls.

The hanging dome of St. Hallvard's Church in Oslo, designed by architects Kjell Lund and Niels Slaatto (1966), is essentially just such a powerful 'threat' to the circular interior (Fig. 475). The surrounding walls are of brick, whereas the dome is cast in reinforced concrete, with the pattern of the formwork left visible. This pattern leads downward towards the dome's lowest point and gives added motion to the sinking effect of the basic form. The feeling of weight is further intensified by the way in which the roof rests

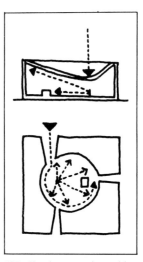

475. The hanging dome (diagram of St. Hallvard Monastery, by K. Lund and N. Slaatto, section and plan).

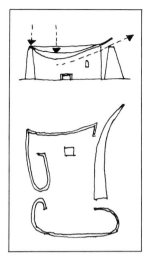

476. The hanging dome (diagram of Notre Dame du Haut by Le Corbusier, section and plan).

directly on the walls with no indication of joining whatsoever. In this way the walls are given accented importance in the load-bearing process, which in combination with the roof gives the total space a distinctive strength.

In the space below a hanging dome it is only beneath the lowest point that a sensation of direct 'danger' is felt. In contrast, from any other position it is as if the roof surface lifts the space and opens it outwards in all directions. In St. Hallvard's Church this effect is exploited in order to give the ceremonial room a further meaning. The lowest point lies well behind the centre of the space while the altar is placed at the opposite end, giving an impression that the entire space ascends towards the choir. Thus, the threatening effect of the roof is a condition for the redeeming effect of the altar, which in addition becomes the 'rescue station' of the interior both optically and symbolically.

In Le Corbusier's Notre Dame du Haut (1954), the hanging roof is both threatening and hovering at the same time. The space is not circular as in St. Hallvard's but trapezoidal, opening fan-like as it nears the altar (Fig. 476). In section too, the space opens towards the altar. The floor sinks and the roof rises. The lowest point of the roof and its sharpest curvature is opposite the choir and immediately above the church entrance. The curve of the roof surface gradually flattens as it rises towards the choir wall at the east end. But, the roof rises transversely as well, to the south, i.e. towards a wall from which the light streams in through deep window openings (Fig. 99). The roof is separated from the walls by a narrow light slit over both the choir and south walls, while in the rest of the church it rests heavily on the walls where they are lowest. Weight and lightness are thereby combined in the same form. Heaven is both 'near' and 'distant' and as such, is a subtle reminder of Le Corbusier's intention for this space as a place of *concentration* as well as *meditation*. Christian Norberg-Schulz says accordingly:

> The hanging roof is both a heavy weight which concentrates the interior and reminds man of his precarious situation on earth, and a light 'heavenly' veil, which floats over the walls. [16]

## THE MODELLED DOME

The modelled dome differs from the basic form in both plan and profile. In the true dome the plan is a circle and the profile is evenly curved. We have seen the problems involved in connecting it with spaces beneath, and how these have had to be solved by means of transitional elements such as drums and pendentives.

With the modelled dome, all types of spatial forms can be directly joined

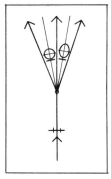

477. The oval dome as an optical corrective (diagram of Piazza del Popolo with the two 'gate' domes, drawn by Chr. Norberg-Schulz).

478. The oval dome as an optical corrective (Piazza del Popolo in Rome, etching by G.B. Piranesi).

482. The modulated dome (dome over St. Ivo in Rome by F. Borromini, from Portoghesi, *Roma Barocca. Storia di una civiltà architettonica*).

481. The broken dome (Uranienborg Terrasse 2, in Oslo).

322

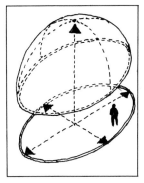

479. The oval dome as a mediator of directionalities in an oval plan (diagram of St. Anna dei Palafrenieri in Rome by Vignola).

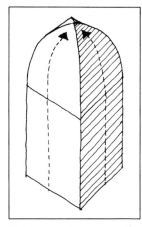

480. The broken dome (diagram).

to the roof, thereby uniting upper and lower areas. This may be interpreted in two ways, either that motions in the lower part are gradually gathered together and brought to rest by the dome above or that the dome little by little dissolves as it nears the walls. In this context there are two main types, the directionalized and the broken dome.

Most typical of the *directionalized* domes is the oval. The relation of the oval dome to exterior space has frequently been of an optical nature. A case in point is the dome of St. Maria di Montesanto in Rome by Carlo Rainaldi (1657). This building with its neighbouring church forms the gate to the city's Corso from the north. Rainaldi designed both with the intention that they should appear as symmetrical buildings framing the entrance to the avenue. As the building lots were unequal in width, he used oval form to correct the perspective, so that from a distance the domes appeared to be equally broad and round (Figs. 477, 478).

The other important role of directionalized domes is related to oval or direction-orientated interiors. The earliest example we find of an elongated dome covering an oval space is in Giacomo da Vignola's church, St. Anna dei Palafrenieri in Rome (1572). The oval unites a centre and a path into one form (se Il Campidoglio p. 85 f). This means that the horizontally extended lines of the lower space are brought together in the centre of the roof area above. Thus, the organizing principles, point and line, are each relegated to a separate level within the same space. The lower part, which is the 'world', emphasizes a *path,* whereas the upper part, which is 'heaven', marks a *goal* (Fig. 479).

The *broken* dome is the other variation of the modelled dome. In this form a polygonal plan is joined to a spherical cover. The simplest variation is the plan in which the dome surmounts a square. This variation has been widely used in French Baroque to crown tower-like projecting parts of buildings. Such square domes are typical exterior motifs. This is because the form unites four separate façades (Figs. 480, 481). It is not formed in rotation around an axis but by two intersecting diagonal arches. The dome surfaces are stretched between these and are flush with the walls beneath. The four façades, thereby, appear to be drawn upwards into the roof, gradually becoming more curved and pointed before converging at the top. The result is a form that is both centralized and directional, making it easier to combine with other spatial forms around it.

A more complicated variation illustrating the possibilities of the modelled or shaped dome is found in Francesco Borromini's church, St. Ivo alla Sapienza (begun 1642) (Fig. 482). The plan is developed around a hexagon with alternating concave and convex wall areas. This pulsating rhythm of expansion and contraction continuous up into the dome until finally all motion is brought to a standstill around the lantern at the top.

483. The modulated dome and the modulated wall (detail from St. Ivo, from Portoghesi, *Roma Barocca. Storia di una civiltà architettonica*).

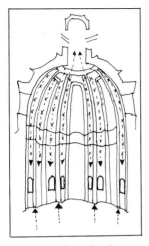

484. The relationship between up and down in St. Ivo (diagram).

485. Pyramid roof (diagram of a Dutch farm house).

The space strives upwards from below towards the light (Fig. 483). Even the windows in the lower part of the dome narrow upwards to add to the vertical effect. The pilasters and ribs emphasize the unity of the upper and lower parts and flow in continuous unbroken lines from floor to lantern. The space, however, not only rises upwards but also flows downwards. But, now symbolic elements prevail. A heavenly light shining from the lantern materializes in showers of stars between the ribbing of the dome. We must imagine these symbolic rays of light streaming further down the walls to mark twelve niches between the pilasters at the bottom intended to hold statues of the apostles. Viewed in such terms, the interior of St. Ivo conveys a dynamic union of an upper and lower part, each with an essentially different meaning. The muscular and plastic lower part rises upwards, an image of man's own pursuit of the Divine, while at the same time the Divine Spirit is directed downwards from above in the form of light and stars, an inspiration reminiscent of the tongues of fire descending upon the apostles in the Pentecostal miracle (Fig. 484).

Another variation of the broken dome is the pyramid and the spire. In these, all curvature has disappeared, but both vertical and centralized characteristics remain.

The pyramid roof is frequently used as an outer covering over an interior dome space. It is easily built of wood and has been important as a plain tower cap, particularly in Carolingian and Romanesque architecture. These tower caps were often quite low, corresponding to their width in a relation of 1:2, so that the effect was both cubic and restful, completely in keeping with the character expressed in the building's massif as well. Seen thus, pyramid roofs became not only a capping but also a part of the tower beneath.

The pyramid roof is also used in Dutch architecture (Fig. 485). As large forms they gather all the functions of a farm under one roof, thereby avoiding the need for outbuildings on the precious land. An additional reason for this use was the necessity for protection from the gusty winds which sweep over the flat landscape. All these requirements are recognizable in the form of the pyramid roof itself. The pyramid rests heavily on the ground and defines the boundaries of the house around a collective point. But, the pyramid rises also and points directly upwards and is equally collective in its erect and upright bearing. Both aspects are equally important in an endless horizontal landscape in which it is necessary to both anchor and mark, to collect or gather around a low centre as well as upwards around a vertical.

Whereas the pyramid is in repose, the spire stretches upwards as its height is far greater than its width. Whether it consists of four or more surfaces, the broken form creates lines and angles which in combination with its height convey a distinctly linear appearance. One could imagine the same spire shaped as a round cone, in which case it would immediately convey a heavier and more plastic effect. In this sense one might say that the broken spire 'grows', an aspect which the neo-Gothic interpreted quite literally by allowing the ribbing to be formed as stems sprouting leaf-like projections (Fig. 486). The spire is the 'dome' of the Gothic and forms the natural conclusion to the verticality of the building itself.

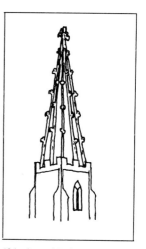

486. Spire (Gothic spire by J. Hall, from Rykwert, *On Adam's House in Paradise*).

# THE BARREL VAULT

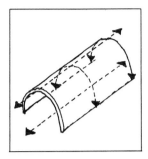

487. A barrel vault is formed by numerous arches lined up side by side.

## THE EXPRESSION OF THE BARREL VAULT

We have seen that the dome form was the result of an arch in rotation around an axis.

The form of the barrel vault is formed by a series of arches set at intervals along a line. Otherwise, it has the same qualities as the dome (Fig. 487). The primary effect, therefore, is one of emphasized horizontal motion while at the same time the eye is directed upwards. 'Above all, it conveys an impression of movement, by seeming to be ever in a state of new formation, so much so that given certain proportions it seems actually to rise upwards' (Fig. 488).[17]

Two conditions in particular are important in conveying this directional expression. The first is contained in the roof's cylinder effect. Made up as it is of a half cylinder, the barrel vault allows the space to open up at each end but closes it evenly on the sides. The second condition is that roof and wall are continuously joined both statically and optically. This means that the side walls are supporting elements and therefore enclosing, whereas the short walls, not having this function may be removed (Fig. 489).

## BARREL VAULT MOTIFS

We have seen that there are several factors not only in the form of the barrel vault but also in its relation to the walls beneath, all of which may influence the directional effect of a tunnelled space. We shall now examine these factors individually by dividing them into three main groups. The first deals with the *proportions* of the space and covers the relationships of length, width, and height. The second group deals with the *modelling* of the space, which means the effect conveyed by various arch forms and other plastic treatment. The third will cover the *articulation* of the vault, which involves the effect of certain types of openings and divisions. There after, we shall examine the groined vault, which is the result of two intersecting barrel vaults.

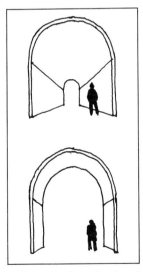

490. Barrel vault and the effect of its length on a space.

### THE PROPORTIONS

The directional effect of a barrel vault will be far greater in a lengthy space than in a short one (Fig. 490). The same applies if a straight barrel-vaulted space is compared to one which is curved.

489. Barrel vaults (reconstruction of Porticus Aemilia in Rome, from MacDonald, *The Architecture of the Roman Empire*).

488. Barrel vault (from the vestibule in Palazzo Farnese, from Wölfflin, *Renaissance and Baroque*).

491. Barrel vault and the effect of its curvature on a space (St. Constanza in Rome, photo by Deutsches Archaelogisches Institut Rom).

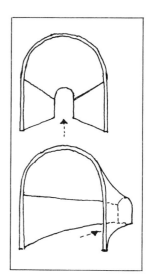

492. Barrel vault and the effect of its curvature on a space.

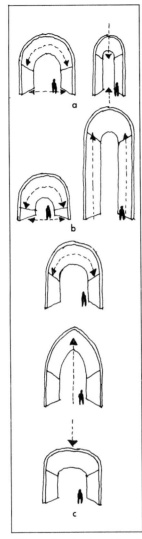

493 a-c. Barrel vault and the effect of (a) the breadth of the space, (b) the height of the wall, (c) the modulation of the vault.

A straight space will be in 'balance'. Upon entering a barrel-vaulted corridor we find that the motions of the space and our own movements coincide. In a curved corridor, on the other hand, a conflict between them arises. This reaction is purely physical in that centrifugal force leads us out of the curve and straight forward, whereas the space with its barrel vaulting leads us around in a swing. Take, for example, the circular ambulatory of St. Costanza in Rome (c. A.D. 340). Here it is the *space* which assumes command, and the influence of the barrel vault in this respect is of corresponding significance (Fig. 491). This expression of being guided or led has a greater effect in a curved space than in an axial one. In the former the roof exerts an influencing power while in the latter it is primarily a part of the effect (Fig. 492).

To carry the thought further, if the width of a barrel-vaulted space is varied, the following may occur. In a wide space the transverse motion will compete with the longitudinal motion so that the feeling of being led will be weakened.[18] In a narrow space the depth effect becomes more important, while at the same time the vault comes closer to the observer. Whereas the roof in the wide space was high, swinging up and around, the vault of the narrow space is lower, thereby accenting the cylinder and with it forward motion (Fig. 493, a-c).

A somewhat similar effect occurs if two barrel-vaulted spaces are given different heights but length and width remain unchanged. If the walls are low, the lines of perspective and the depth effect are intensified. This, combined with the nearness of the barrel vault, which seems to encircle the onlooker as in a tube, accelerates the forward motion. In contrast, a high vault will seem distant and far, with walls drawing attention upward and not forward.

## THE MODELLING

The same dynamic tendencies which were examined above may be obtained by other means as well. Although we were aware that height, width, and depth varied, the *form* of the barrel vault itself remained constant. If this too changes, the expression becomes even more complicated. Considered thus, a flat, circular, and a pointed vault will result in quite different effects (Fig. 493, c). A pointed vault will increase the height tendency and lessen the effect of depth, whereas a flat barrel vault will accent the transverse at the cost of this effect. The spherical vault causes the space to rise, encloses it and gives it direction, controlling all these tendencies in a sort of dynamic balance.

Furthermore, the form of the section is of importance. An example is the so-called hyperbolic paraboloid. The curves in such a form are created by the use of parabolas which hang between two vertical parabolas and

329

494. Barrel vault and the effect of its modulation (parabolic barrel vault in Zürich by R. Maillart and H. Leuzinger).

495. Barrel vault and the effect of articulation (Bibliothèque Nationale project, by E.-L. Boullée, from Rosenau, *Boullée & Visionary Architecture*).

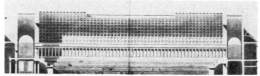

496. Section through Bibliothèque Nationale project (from Rosenau, *Boullée & Visionary Architecture*).

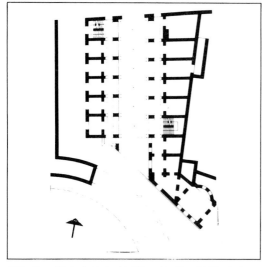

500. Plan of Trajan's Market Hall (from MacDonald, *The Architecture of the Roman Empire*).

499. Directionality of a groin vault (Trajan's Market Hall in Rome).

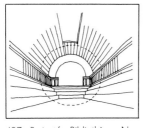

497. Project for Bibliothèque Nationale in Paris and the principle of the cylinder.

which in section also form parabolic curves. In such a space one is always 'on the move' through a pulsating unrest of contractions, expansions and accelerations (Fig. 494).

### THE ARTICULATION

In addition to proportions and modelling, articulation takes its place as the third influential factor.

As an example, let us look at Etienne Louis Boullée's project for a national library (1792) (Figs. 495, 496).

This vast space is based on the cylinder (Fig. 497). In the upper part of the form, the barrel vault is the guiding element in the main direction of the space. The vault coffering accents the main directional lines. The elongated skylight also adds to the horizontal motion and at each end the space is opened by huge arches. In the lower part the rest of the cylinder is formed by surrounding galleries. These rise from the central floor like tiers of seats around the arena of a Roman circus: Along the top of these stretches a severe colonnade, which is cut off at the ends so that the space is not closed off longitudinally. All in all, a space is created in which the details intensify the main tendency of the vault. In this strongly dynamic space it might be thought difficult to 'relax'. This, however, is managed by a distinctive transition between vault and wall. The colonnades along the top of the galleries do not support the vault above. On the contrary, these colonnades are free-standing screens in front of the vault which continues on down *behind* them. Thus, the same effect is gained as in Boullée's Madeleine dome — the roof sinks downwards. In this way the cylinder effect is offset and the place dynamically defined. This, in combination with the light streaming from above, gives the entire space dramatic tension.

## BARREL-VAULT VARIATIONS

### GROINED VAULT

In the above we have considered various forms of a plain barrel vault. We shall now examine an important barrel vault combination. The most common type occurs when two barrel vaults intersect. The resulting groined vault combines the characteristics of both the dome and the barrel vault and allows for rich possibilities in directing space both horizontally and vertically (Fig. 498). As an example of how this is exploited in order to interpret definite functions, we shall examine Trajan's Market in Rome (c. A.D. 100).

The hall of Trajan's Market is long and narrow (39 m x 6 m) and is flanked on both sides by rows of small shops *(tabernae)* (Figs. 499, 500).

498. Directionality of a groin vault.

Access to the hall from the surrounding city is through the short ends. The roof rises high above the low tabernae and is in principle an elongated barrel vault, which is intersected by lesser barrel vaults lying side by side. These have the same ridge-line as the longitudinal vault. The intersecting vaults are the same width as the tabernae beneath and act as light shafts above the shop roofs.

The result is a combination of directional tendencies in the roof which is reflected in corresponding motions in the space beneath (Fig. 501,a-c). The longitudinal vault emphasizes the intention of the space as a passage from one part of the city to another. From the exterior the vault stands forths as a strong and inviting entrance motif (see p. ??). The expression of length, however, is not the sole governing influence. In moving through the hall, each crossing may be interpreted as an independent baldachin in which the intersecting lines as well as the gradual narrowing of the vaults radiate towards a centre. In this way forward motion is 'halted' so that at the next moment attention is diverted to the shops on either side. From this point of view, the hall unites three tendencies in all: the main longitudinal direction and transversal direction lines draw attention to space *outside* the hall while the intersecting points between them are the centres of baldachins which accent points *inside* the hall.[19]

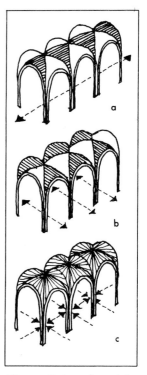

501 a-c. Groin vaults and the directionalities in Trajan's Market Hall: (a) passage, (b) transverse motion, (c) centralized.

# THE GABLE ROOF

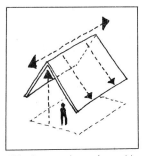

502. Directionalities of a gable roof: vertical, horizontal and diagonal.

## THE EXPRESSION OF THE GABLE ROOF

The gable roof is the result of the need to rid the roof surface of rain. 'The form of the roof, too, was altered, for being on account of its flatness, unfit to throw off the rains … it was raised in the middle … after the form of a gable roof'. Thus simply did William Chambers explain the origin of the gable roof (Figs. 502, 503).[20] Filarete, just as simply, asserted that it was Adam who formed the first roof by placing his hands over his head to protect himself from rain and sun (Fig. 504). This gesture took the form of a triangle, the same triangle which with the column and beam constituted the basic elements in Marc Laugier's vision of the first architecture (Fig. 505). Together they form an *aedicula*, little house', which is the very essence of all classical architecture (see 'the frame' pp. 271 ff). Palladio, too, considered the gable as one of the original architectural elements. The pedlment, therefore, which graced temples and public buildings was a primeval motif, a survival from the first primitive house.[21]

We have already described certain aspects of the gable roof's open and closed qualities . These may be summarized in three points: (1) it is the gable of the roof which opens the connection between outside and inside; (2) the gable roof encloses along its sides in that the two sloping surfaces cut off the relation between inside and outside along both ground and ridge lines, (3) there is upward motion in the gable as it rises towards the ridge line. In other words, the gable roof expands vertically at its apex, it expands *horisontally* in the lengthwise direction of the ridge, and it sinks *diagonally* along its surfaces.[22] The basis for the expressions conveyed by this form is too be found within these qualities.

## GABLE ROOF MOTIFS
### THE RISING ASPECT OF THE GABLE ROOF

The *ascending* quality in the gable roof causes the space to rise upwards. In this connection, a Gothic sharply angled ceiling has been characterized by Andrew S. Downing as follows:

> The superior effect of this ceiling arises, partly, from its carrying the eye upwards and thus recognizing the principle of perpendicular rather than horizontal support, as well as causing it to appear higher than it really is; and, also from a certain airy lightness, found

333

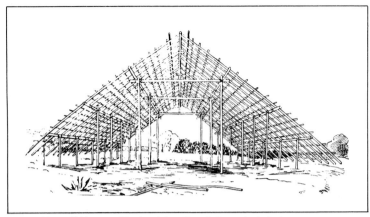

503. Gable roof (African webbed roof, from Cornell, *Bygnadstekniken*).

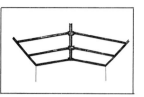

506. Rising of the gable roof: accentuation of the ridge (Gothic ceiling, from Downing, *The Architecture of Country Houses*).

504. Gable roof as the original form for protection (drawing of Adam, after Filarete, from Rykwert, *On Adam's House in Paradise*).

505. Gable roof as the original roof form (primeval house drawn by M.-A. Laugier, *Essai sur l'architecture*).

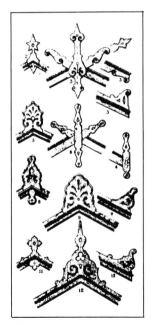

507. Rising aspect of the gable roof: gable ornaments by Löfvenskiöld (from E. Nordin, *Träbyggande under 1800-talet*).

509. Rising aspect of the gable roof: The column accentuates the apex (King's Gate at Mycenae).

513. The falling aspect of the gable roof: gable as protection (child's drawing of the phenomenon of the 'house', after Bloomer & Moore, *Body, Memory, and Architecture*).

in a ceiling in which the lines rise, however slightly, but never in the one entirely flat (Fig. 506).[23]

In the same way, the exterior gable peak will point and not 'gather in' as does the arch. Throughout architectural history this quality has been emphasized by the use of the most diverse ridge decorations, from figures of the gods and rosettes in Antiquity's *acroteria* to spires and flower garlands in the Swiss style gable tower (Fig. 507). The former cause even the hills of Rome to rise, writes Martial in his panegyric on the *fastigium* atop Domitian's palace on the Palatine: 'It pierces heaven, and hidden amid the lustrous stars its peak echoes sunlight to the thunder in the cloud below'.[24]

This heaven-bound quality in the gable's triangular form is embodied in the phenomenon 'Irminsul'. Irminsul is the *universalis columna* connecting earth and the heavens and is associated with the central post in the earliest versions of the gable roof (Fig. 508).[25] We find it as the motif above the royal portal (the Lion's Gate) in Mycenae (c. 1250) (Fig. 509), as well as in decorated totem poles on the hut façades of west coast Canadian Indians (Fig. 510). The latter show fully the lengths to which man is willing to go in order to emphasize verticality in the gable roof.

## THE SINKING ASPECT OF THE GABLE ROOF

The *sinking* aspect of the sloping surfaces lends a protective quality to the roof. The roof of the Greek temple has been compared to the eagle's wings, enfolding and protecting the treasures of the inner sanctuary. 'The eagle is the symbol of Zeus and in the temple gable, interpreted this way, it is as if the entire Olympian world descends to enfold the building within its powerful wing-span' (Figs. 511, 512).[26]

Modern studies reveal that the pitched roof may convey a feeling of safety and security. Accordingly, Richard D. Cramer maintains that in the United Kingdom it is the gable roof and not the flat roof which psychologically is felt to be a protective form (Fig. 513).[27] The pitched roof, therefore, has become the symbol of what is meant by a *home*. The same results were reached in another study in which various house forms were chosen according to the degree of comfort and 'cosiness' expressed by the roof.[28]

## THE DIRECTIONAL ASPECT OF THE GABLE ROOF

The *directional* quality of the gable roof becomes apparent, on the one hand, by the frequent emphasis on the gable façade itself and, on the other hand, by the importance given to the ridgepole and the roof ridge.

The gable is used quite intentionally as a façade. It stands as the symbol of an opening out of or into a building, usually in connection with entrances or large window areas (Fig. 514).

The roof ridge, too, is directionally important. In the interior it is the ridge-

508. Rising aspect of the gable roof: Mid-post('Irminsul') accentuates the apex (Neolithic grave building from Switzerland, from Hauglid, *Norske Stavkirker*).

510. Rising aspect of the gable roof: The totem pole accentuates the apex (building from Canada's west coast, from Cornell, *Bygnadstekniken*).

512. The falling aspect of the gable roof: the Greek temple pediment ('Heras' temple at Paestum).

514. The directional aspect of the gable roof: gable as opening motif (Nakauchi House in Yamato Kosiyama by T. Watanabe, from *A.D. 5/6-1980*).

511. The falling aspect of the gable roof: the eagle's wingspan as a mystical precedent for the temple pediment.

515. The directional aspect of the gabled interior: the ridge beam (from Phleps, *Der Blockbau*).

516. The directional aspect of the gabled exterior: the ridge capping and dragon heads (Borgund Stave Church, measured by H. Bull).

338

517. The sinking console roof.

pole itself which guides a horizontal movement towards each gabled end. Figuratively also, this element is a connecting axis. As 'Firstbaum' it represented the axis of the earth itself, uniting the two poles of the north and south (Figs. 508, 515). On the exterior it may be the ridge itself which is formed in such a way as to accent horizontal motion. An example of this is the grimacing dragon heads at the ridge ends of Norwegian stave churches. These are attached to undulating decorative bands along the ridge itself (Fig. 516). The entire body of the dragon seems to writhe its way with great speed along the length of the ridge like a defending animal ready to spring outwards against unearthly evil spirits. The dynamic essence of the gable is contained in these dragon heads, as is its meaning, in that the vertical, horizontal and diagonal tendencies are all combined in one protective symbol.

In the following we shall study examples of the way in which various forms can emphasize the three dynamic directionalities of the gable roof. We will look at the effect of formal variations in addition to articulative variations both in the roof surface itself and in the transition between roof surface and walls. This will be treated first of all in relation to the gable roof as an interior motif and then as an exterior façade motif. Finally we shall examine the hip roof as an example of the most important variation of the gable roof.

### THE GABLE ROOF AS AN INTERIOR MOTIF

As we shall demonstrate later in connection with the gable façade, motion in the gable roof depends on effect, the *angle* of the ridge peak. The following description, therefore, will be limited to showing how an almost identical form can convey either a sinking, rising or directional character depending upon its articulation or attachment to the walls. We shall, furthermore, limit ourselves to examples taken from Norwegian wood architecture.

### THE SINKING AND DIRECTIONAL INTERIOR

Two interiors may serve as examples of the sinking and the directional aspect of the gable roof.

The principle behind the first aspect may be illustrated by the *console* ceiling. Such a ceiling rests on consoles or brackets placed at some distance down the wall (Fig. 517). They are found frequently in Gothic halls in the form of dark brown, richly carved trusses springing from whitewashed or painted stone walls. This solution had a constructional advantage in that the exaggeratedly high wall massifs acted as supports for the diagonal stress of the roof trusses. With that, the effect of these large

519. The enclosing aspect of the gable roof, supported by purlins (from Phleps, *Der Blockbau*).

520. The rising aspect of the gable roof: supported by rafters (from Phleps, *Der Blockbau*).

518. The sinking aspect of the gable roof (Hampton Court, Great Hall, from Hitchcock (ed.), *World Architecture*).

521. The directional aspect of the gable roof: rafters and double purlins (Raulandstuen from Uvdal at the Norwegian Folk Museum, Oslo).

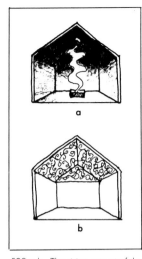

522 a-b. The rising aspect of the gable roof: (a) smoke vent and open fire. The smoke sooted the ceiling, which was decorated with chalk designs. Thus, the roof and walls were established as individual elements (b).

roof constructions was emphasized by the way the entire ceiling seemed to 'glide' down the walls so that wall space and ceiling space became intermingled (Fig. 518). The result was a heavy and majestic, an even threatening impression, clearly distinguishing these secular halls from the spiritual character typical of the verticality in contemporary churches.

The other example which illustrates an enclosing gable roof is found in Norwegian log-timber houses with so-called *purlin* roofs *(åstak)* (Fig. 519). The roof is carried lengthwise by large log purlins *(åser)* which correspond in number to every second log in the gable end walls. The principle is that the roof and long walls are joined *horizontally* in that the lengthwise wall logs seem to 'roll' up into the ceiling and on down to the walls on the other side. The continuity in this form destroys any impression of planar surfaces, thereby creating dynamics similar to that of the barrel vault.

## THE RISING INTERIOR

The rising aspect of the gable form is emphasized by the pattern of the lines in the *rafter ceiling* (Fig. 520). In the first place, the supporting rafters are upright and in the Norwegian rural house rise straight up to meet at the ridge forming sharp angles contasting with the horizontally laid log walls beneath. Secondly, the layer of smooth planks overlaying the rafters has a neutralizing effect giving an impression of 'open' areas between the members.

This basic effect in the rafter ceiling may be reduced or intensified according to variations in the construction. If a ridgepole is introduced it is as though the form closes — the rising effect is brought to a standstill while at the same time the length of the roof is emphasized. If one enters through the short end, to meet such a ceiling, as is the case in the traditional Norwegian 'three-room plan', the log ridgepole will accentuate the act of entering. The same applies if the log ceiling beams are situated otherwise, as in the large Rauland house in Uvdal (c. 1300) (Fig. 521). Here, there is no ridgepole but rather two double beams about halfway down each side of the rafter roof. These so-called 'bear-backs' give the necessary support to the construction while simultaneously accenting the act of entering from the two small side rooms at the gable end. Without the ridgepole the effect is as though the other two sets of beams 'move aside', away from the ridgepole. This, in fact, is the case because the room originally had an open smoke vent in the roof.

The smoke vent is actually the element that most strongly emphasizes the rising tendency in the rural house rafter ceiling. The effect was as if a gable roof was transformed into a 'dome' concentrated around a central, vertical shaft of light with increasing darkness in the lower parts of the encircling walls (Fig. 522, a). In the imagination the smoke might be a visualization

524. The rising aspect of the gable roof: the double rafter roof of the Stave Church (Gol Stave Church, from Bugge/Norberg-Schulz, *Stav og laft*).

525. The rising aspect of the gable roof: ancient rafter roof (St. Paolo fuori le Mura near Rome, from Pothorn, *Das Grosse Buch der Baustile*).

523. The rising aspect of the gable roof: staves in Stave Church and the uninterrupted transition to the ceiling rafters (Kaupanger Stave Church, reconstructed by Bjerknes, from Hauglid, *Norske Stavkirker. Dekor og utstyr*).

of the upward vertical surge, while the smoke blanket beneath the roof, in blotting out the constructional and horizontal lines, transformed the whole to a softly outlined vault beneath a shining crown. That this vault-like effect was comprehended may be seen clearly in the chalk-painted decorations in the ceiling area. Both the gable wall and ceiling surfaces were often covered with continuous patterns of vine foliage, the white lines standing out against the soot-darkened background. The entire upper ceiling zone down to the first horizontal wall logs was treated as an entity, with all parts given equal value, a principle we recognize in ceiling decor done with *rosemaling* (a style of decorative painting) (Fig. 522, b). The Viku house from Oppdal has even been given wide moulding around the walls providing added plasticity in the transition to the ceiling area.

In the rural house examples given above, we saw that although the roof gave a rising effect, the walls were horizontal and prone. This conveyed an additive effect between ceiling and wall. In other words, the upper and lower zones were disconnected, they lacked continuity.

Conversely, in *stave churches* the columns are led directly into the roof rafters. This is particularly noticeable in Kaupanger Church (c. 1190) (Fig. 523), but these columns extend right up to the roof in other stave churches too, springing even if they are interrupted on the way by breastsummers, St. Andrew cross struts, and capitals. The Gothic form was the inspiration and ideal of the stave church. The dominant factor, therefore, was verticality, to which the sharply pointed raftered roof was the logical conclusion (Fig. 524). The stave church's rafter roof consists of two sets of rafters, the lower ones crossing each other diagonally like 'scissors'. Just below this crossing is a horizontal beam frequently supported by a collar beam. As they near the roof cornice, the rafters are strengthened and unified by U-shaped frames. These resemble inverted arches and give all sides around the roof a pointed form, not only crosswise but also from the long sides and up.

From the lowest arches the entire roof seems to rise with accelerating speed in layers of increasingly pointed rafters. All in all it is as if the roof projects itself upwards level after level towards the ridge line. This was also a characteristic of the open raftered ceilings of Antiquity's basilica. The space was not closed in by a tight lid but rose through its network of beams and rafters steadily upward in a light and airy 'heaven' (Fig. 525). The lighting emphasized this effect. In the stave church as well as in the basilica the light enters through small windows in the clerestory beneath the cornice. This led to the illumination of the lower space while the ceiling space remained in semi-darkness. Thus resulted an emphasized impression of a roof absorbed into a distant mystical and unattainable world.

526. Pointed gable (Tromsdalen Church by I. Hovig, photo by K. Aune).

528. The blunt gable (log storehouse from Ål in Hallingdal, measured drawing by Chr. Christie).

527. The blunt gable (from eastern Tyrol, from Swoboda, *Alte Holzbaukunst in Österreich*).

We have already pointed out that the gable can have essentially different expressions, depending on the roof angle. Three variations in particular stand out: (1) the *pointed* gable found in the stave-church and neo-Gothic gables, (2) the *shallow* gable found in the Swiss chalet and the American shingle-style house, and (3) the *balanced* variation as expressed in the crowning pediments of the classical temple and the Roman aedicula.

The *pointed* gable accents the verticality of the gable roof. Steeply pitched roofs may be used for practical reasons as well. Such roofs are suitable in terminating high, narrow buildings where the site is narrow and deep as we find in Dutch buildings. And, in Christian IV's urban code it is stated that city roofs must be pointed, 'so that in case of fire the firebrands would not as easily remain'.[29]

The pointed gable, however, is also used because of its expressiveness. It is a daring architectural motif in the way it actively breaks and thrusts upwards from the environment. In Dutch streets it is the gable which gives each house its individual identity. And, against the steep roof expanses covering stave church galleries, it is these pointed gables which have sufficient strength in themselves to accent the entrance and transept (Fig. 514).

The verticality of the pointed gable gives the form its own distinctive meaning. The 'Irminsul' ideology is accented and with it the sacred dimension. It is for this reason that the pointed gable is so frequently used in church architecture as seen not only in the Gothic cathedral and the stave church, but also in modern triangular churches such as the 'Arctic Cathedral' in Tromsø, northern Norway, by Inge Hovig (1965) (Fig. 526). The latter demonstrates clearly the expressive use of the pointed gable, which here rises upwards in one great frontal sweep while simultaneously being dramatically drawn right down to the ground on either side. In this way the building is directed towards Heaven *and* is protective at the same time — it is both 'temple' and 'fortress'.

The *shallow* gable accents the sinking expression in the gable roof. Such flattened gables are typical of houses with extensive width if, for example, they are situated in a hilly landscape as in the case of the Swiss chalet (Fig. 527). The Norwegian rural storehouse, too, has a wide flattened gable mainly because the covered upstairs gallery is broad and outflung and also because any great roof height was considered unnecessary (Fig. 528). Besides, the sod covering required a gently pitched roof. In addition, the shallow gable was important in restraining the impression of height. The roof lent weight and width to the upstairs covered gallery so that these storehouses fitted snuggly into the landscape.

The weighty impression conveyed by the blunt gable is found also in the

529. The blunt gable and the heavy expression: (a) Artemis' Temple at Corfu (from Charbonneaux, *Das archaische Griechenland*).

530. The blunt gable and the protective expression (Low House in Bristol by McKim, Mead and White, from Scully, *The Shingle Style*).

531. The blunt gable and the balanced expression (The Temple of Mars, from Palladio, *The Four Books of Architecture*).

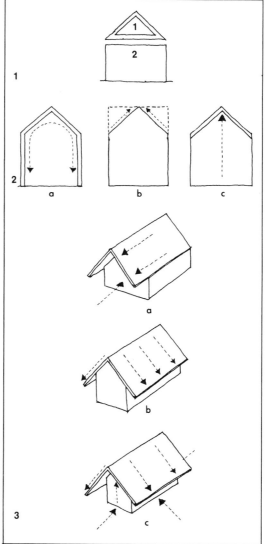

532.1-3 The gable and its relationship to the walls below: (1) gable with added wall, (2) gable and integrated wall: (a) frame, (b) plane, (c) edge, (3) gable and contrasting wall: (a) directional, (b) sunken, (c) retracted.

346

earliest Greek temples (Fig. 529). In these, the roof pitch is markedly gentle, so much that both the gable and the high entablature seem to press down on the columns beneath. Viewed in such terms, the columns' bulging form is a logical answer to the entire sinking aspect of the gable roof (see columns p. 201 f). This sinking aspect in the shallow gable also accentuates its protective impression. Its general character is secular and enfolding as is so clearly apparent in many American shingle-style houses (Fig. 530). Modern architecture also uses the shallow gable in the same manner and in this case as a solution to the question of putting the entire house 'under one sheltering roof'.[30]

In the *balanced* gable, rising and sinking aspects are almost equalized. Typical examples are the pediments of later Roman temples, which, combined with slimmer and taller columns, give the building as a whole a lighter character than its precursors. The roof does not weigh down upon its walls but sits upon them as an independent unit. It is this characteristic that is renewed in the Renaissance canon in which balance was the ideal and the gable element took on a planar character, with no accentuation of either rising or sinking (Fig. 531).

We have seen that the gable motif does not act independently but must be considered in combination with the motion tendencies of the walls below. In other words, whether or not the gable in a façade composition is to show rising, sinking, or directional tendencies depends upon how it is linked to the walls. In this context there are three methods of joining them (Fig. 532, 1, 2, 3). In the first case, walls and gable are *separated*. Here, however, in principle, none of the main motion tendencies are accentuated in that the total effect depends upon the form given to the gable and walls individually (Fig. 532, 1). In the second method the walls are continued up *into* the gable which accents the rising tendency of the roof (Fig. 532, 2a, c). In the third case the walls are pulled back *beneath* the gable, which emphasizes its sinking aspect (Fig. 532, 3a-c).

### THE ADDITION OF GABLE AND WALL IN EXTERIOR

A typical example of the first method of joining in which gable and wall act as two separate parts is found in the Greek temple façade. The gable frames a limited and isolated zone separated from the rows of columns by a broad entablature. As said previously, the overall effect of such a combination depends on the way in which the roof and wall 'act together'.

In the Temple of Artemis at Corfu (sixth century B.C.) the general impression is one of heaviness and downward pressure because the flattened gable is 'followed up' by the underlying walls with their high entablature supported by short bulging columns (Fig. 529). On the other hand, the façade of Palladio's temple of Mars, conveys a taller, slimmer more upright effect.

533. Frame gable (retail building in Lillehammer, Norway, by Fougner Architects, completed 1977).

534. Planar gable (Amsterdam canal buildings, from Meischke, *Het nederlanse Woonhuis*).

535. Edge gable (a warehouse, after Semper, *Der Stil in den technischen und tektonischen Künsten oder praktische Ästhetik*).

Here, the gable is more pointed, the entablature narrower, and the columns are in the slender Corinthian style (Fig. 531).

We have previously pointed out the importance of the temple roof as a symbol of the *heavens*. At the other extreme, the *stylobate* or floor has been compared to the earth's surface. We know too from Vitruvius that the column symbolized man and the human body.[31] Considered in such terms, collectively the main façade of the temple embodies and represents the three levels: earth, man, and the heavens. These three worlds, although separated, nevertheless stand in a balanced relationship to one another, an attitude typical of Greek individualism. These conditions, however, may shift between a state of equal balance, as in the classical and Roman temple, and a state of imbalance in which heaviness and pressure predominate, as in archaic temples. Considered thus, the archaic temple may well reflect the uncertainties of the age which we find in the *polis* of the eighth and seventh centuries B.C., whereas the fully developed temple in its own way reflects the triumphant assurance of Hellenism and the Roman Empire.[32]

## THE INTEGRATION OF GABLE AND WALL IN EXTERIOR

The gable's rising tendency is accented by the way in which it is joined to the walls. This is mainly done in the following three ways (Fig. 532, 2a-c).

In the first method they are joined in such a way that the gable profile and wall corners form a *frame*, which makes a setting for the form. In the second variation they are unified in that wall and gable form an unbroken *plane* with the upper corners cut off to form a point. In the third case the form is created in that the upper part is concluded with a *bargeboard*.

The common factor in all three variations is the disappearance or disruption of the horizontal element in the triangle, so that wall and gable form one continuous surface right up to the ridge point.

The first variation is frequently seen in Scandinavian apartment houses from the 1940—50s (Fig. 533). This is connected with the increased use of prefabricated concrete framework elements and clearly limits the visual rising aspect of these concentrated exteriors.

The second type is to be found in the free-standing screen-like fronts. The screen principle opens the possibility for a free treatment of the gable profile which we find so richly exemplified precisely in the Dutch city house (Fig. 534). Typical of the Dutch example is its urban quality. It is independent of the rooms behind and may, therefore, vary in form and size according to the city space in front.

The third type is a combination of the first two in that the wall seems to lift the entire roof edge up in a sharp angle (Fig. 535). Some of the earliest examples of deviation from the classical triangular gable are the temple fa-

536. Double gable (temple from Termessos, from L'Orange & Thiis-Evensen, *Oldtidens bygningsverden*).

538. Double gable (St. Maria della Pace in Rome, by P. da Cortona, from Koepf, *Baukunst in Fünf Jahrtausenden*).

540. Broken gable (Zwinger Pavillion by D. Pöppelmann, from Koepf, *Baukunst in Fünf Jahrtausenden*).

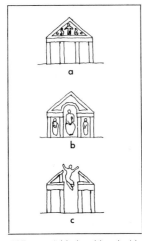

537 a-c. Added gable, double gable, and broken gable as expressions of the relationship between man and the heavens: (a) classical Greek gable, (b) Late-Roman gable, (c) Baroque gable (St. Andrea).

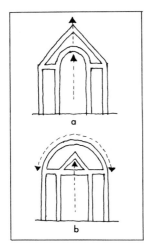

539 a-b. Double gable: (a) triangle over arch, (b) arch over triangle.

çades in Termessos and in Baalbek (Fig. 536). Here, the entablature is broken in the middle by an arch which curves up into the pediment. This means that the lower part, which is the 'human' zone, climbs up into the *tympanum*, which symbolizes 'the heavens' (see Palladio motif p. 237 f). In some versions it is the emperor who occupies the central field beneath the arch and is thereby emphasized as the personification of the elevated and deified, a demi-god who unites earth and the heavens in 'Imperium Sacrum' (Figs. 333, 537 b). In the Baroque period this same motif appears again in the form of the so-called double-gable. The pediment consists of an arch framed by an outer triangle (Figs. 538, 539 a, b). This combination signifies an increasingly rising tendency as the arch initiates a motion that continues into the pointed part of the pediment above. Just the opposite may be imagined — the arch above and the triangle below, as was much practised during the Renaissance (Fig. 539 b). Now, the rising tendency is cut off by the arch above (see p. 275).

In more extreme variations of this same form the gable point is broken as well. Here, it is as if the powerful upward thrust is given free rein, sometimes so markedly that the pediment point swings outward to either side (Fig. 540). In Lorenzo Bernini's St. Andrea al Quirinale (1678), the open area is filled with a hovering, apotheosized St. Andrew. The result is a depiction of man transcendent, man *both* in this world and the next. This is found in the glorifying pediments of Antiquity, whereas in Greek temples man was *only* of this world, firmly attached to the columns and the earth beneath the pediment (Fig. 537 a-c).

## THE CONTRAST BETWEEN GABLE AND WALL IN EXTERIOR

If the wall is drawn back beneath the roof gable, the roof will project and overhang. The resulting impressions conveyed will vary greatly, depending on whether the roof overhang is: (a) only on the gable end, (b) only on the sides, (c) both places simultaneously (Fig. 532, 3a-c). These effects are determined by whether the roof seems to direct the inner space out or whether the inner space seems to withdraw in beneath the roof. Different combinations lead to an architecture in which the roof may create rich variations on the theme of the inside-outside relationship.

The first variation will convey a *directional* effect in as much as the roof directs the inner space out through the open gable end (Fig. 532, 3a). Such overhangs are found often as coverings over typical transitional spaces such as verandas, balconies and entrances. The primeval house in architecture, the *megaron,* has a projecting gable over its entrance in the short end. In recent Norwegian wood architecture, additional emphasis is frequently laid on this directional aspect of gable projection. These houses are usually long and narrow with horizontal rows of windows and horizon-

541. Directional gable roof (summer house at Sjusjøen, Norway, By. A. Vesterlid).

542. Sunken gable roof (house in Swiss style by A.J. Downing, from Downing, *The Architecture of Country Houses*).

543. Hip roof (Sør-Fron Church in Gudbrandsdalen, Norway).

352

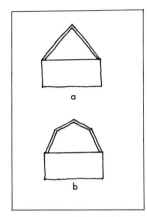

544 a-b. (a) gable roof, (b) gambrel roof.

tal panelling. In combination with large protruding roof beams, these overhanging gable ends give an accentuated horizontal character, dynamically uniting inside and outside, quite in keeping with Modernism's principle of open space (Fig. 541).

The two following variations accentuate the gable roof's *protective* character. In the first, where we find the overhang only on the long sides, the emphasis is on the sinking aspect of the space. This roof type does not direct the interior space out but 'gathers it in' as if under two outspread wings (Fig. 532, 3b). In the other variation the roof has an equal overhang on all sides. Here, the emphasis is not only on the outwardly directed aspect of the roof but also on the impression of walls being *drawn in* as under a protecting shield (Figs. 532, 3c, 542).

The typical effect of the projecting gable is the horizontal interplay between inside and outside. In contrast to an accentuation of the rising and collecting aspect, the directing quality of the gable roof will consequently cause a *spreading* effect between the building and its surroundings. For this reason this form is used particularly in connection with free-standing buildings requiring solutions in accordance with what Downing called 'the local truth', 'To give expression of local truth to a country house, it should always show a tendency to *spread out* and extend itself on the ground, rather than to run up in the air'.[33]

## VARIATIONS OF THE GABLE ROOF
### THE HIP ROOF

The most characteristic among gable roof variations is the *hip roof* (Fig. 543).

The hip roof occurs in many combinations. The earliest examples emerge in rural architecture in central and northern Europe. Originally, however, it was in French château architecture from the seventeenth and eighteenth century that this form reached its climax, with offshoots reaching into Scandinavian classicism as late as into the twentieth century.

Before looking more closely at individual examples it would be wise to seek the underlying purpose of the hip roof. If we compare a gable roof with a so-called Mansard gable, we find that the latter allows for an extra attic story with almost the same height and width as the storeys below, and this, without having to raise the entire roof height (Fig. 544, a, b). In addition, the roof angle becomes steeper than before, a particular advantage in countries with heavy snowfall. Apart from the fact that the full-hipped roof has a useful function in covering and protecting otherwise exposed wall areas, it may in certain cases have constructional advantages as well. It is, nevertheless, the visual character of the hip roof which has been the

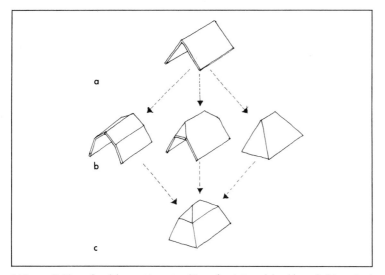

545 a-c. Gable roof and the most important hip roof variations: (a) gable roof, (b) gambrel roof, half-hip, full-hip, (c) mansard.

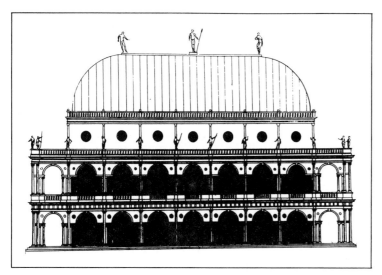

547. Dome-shaped mansard (Basilica in Vicenza, from Palladio, *The Four Books of Architecture*).

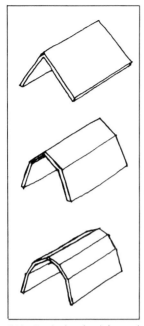

546. Gambrel roof with few and numerous facets.

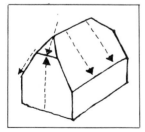

548. Directionality of the half-hip.

decisive factor in its use. The hip roof conveys a heavy and encompassing impression in which all sharp edges and projections have disappeared and the walls have been modelled into a unified volume. In this context it is typical that the Baroque period with its plastic conception of space evinced particular interest in the aesthetic possibilities of the hip roof. The hip roofs gave to French secular Baroque something which was lacking in the Italian, that is, a massiveness with expressive characteristics comparable to those contained in church buildings.

The hip roof must be understood as a gable roof, with dome-like characteristics (see domes p. 305 ff). Dome qualities are introduced in that the gable roof is refashioned into a closed form (Fig. 545, a-c).This restructuring, in principle, may be carried out in three ways, each of which establishes its own motif with distinctive qualities. First of all is the *gambrel* variation, which means that the long sides of the gable roof are broken up into several surfaces between the roof edge and the ridge. The other two motifs occur when the gables of the short ends are pitched either in the upper part alone to form a *half-hip* or right down to the eaves to make a *full-hip*.

## THE GAMBREL ROOF

As stated above, the most typical feature of the gable roof is that it opens at the ends and closes along the sides. A gable roof will, therefore, give the space beneath direction as well as enclosure. The gambrel roof accentuates the *directing* aspect, because the divided roof areas guide the long-side walls up and around, thereby enclosing the sides more evenly. The space, in fact, approaches the cylinder form. Seen in these terms, the pure gambrel roof is more closely related to the barrel vault than to the dome, as the rising or sinking effect depends upon, among other things, both the number of pitched surfaces and the size relationship (Fig. 546). If there are sufficiently many sloped surfaces, the profile approaches a pure curve. In Palladio's large Basilica in Vicenca (1549—1614) the profile is continuous and curving, rather like an extended dome. The surrounding galleries add to the expansive strength of the form (Fig. 547).

## THE HALF-HIP

Hipping the upper part of the gable conveys a feeling that the opening in the full gable is about to be closed. This is decisive for its character in that the half-hip gives a sinking effect, as if the roof is about to be drawn down over the end walls (Fig. 548). A 'conflict' arises between a closed and a directional volume in which the rising effect of the gable end is counteracted by the slanting surface of the roof above. The half-hip roof is used in Norwegian country manors, a style that emerged in the residences of government officials which were to be found all over the country. This

549. Half-hip roof in the landscape (drawing by E. Werenskiold, from Lie, *Familien på Gilje*).

550. Steep mansard roof (Vaux-le-Vicomte by L.Le Vau, from Norwich (ed.), *Verdensarkitek-turen*).

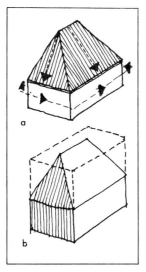

551 a-b. A hipped volume can be experienced as (a) addition of roof and wall, (b) subtraction from a cube.

demanded an architecture capable of adaptability, and the half-hip contained just this quality. Its drawn-down character kept a high house relatively low and anchored it to its place with closed and firm stability. At the same time, however, the half-hip roof opened the manor house out over the valley and countryside, the district governed from these residences (Fig. 549).

### THE FULL-HIP

Whereas the half-hip roof has different façades on the gable ends and sides, the full-hip is a centralized and closed roof in which the walls have the same height all the way around and the roof has the same pitch in all directions. Seen this way, the hipped roof is related to the pyramid roof. It contains the vertical rising and sinking character of the pyramid but also the horizontal extension of the gable roof. But, in contrast to the half-hip, this extended effect is 'tamed' and contained within sloping surfaces on all sides.

Whereas the descending effect in the half-hip conflicted with the otherwise ascending character of the gable wall, the full-hip roof maintains a poised balance between the upper and lower parts. This applies whether interpreted as an addition of elements — horizontal walls and a closed roof — or whether roof and walls are seen as parts of one volume rounded off (Fig. 551 a, b).

This 'neutral' relation between rising and sinking is, accordingly, dependent upon proportions and articulation in order to express the predominating characteristic. This applies not only to the roof form alone but to the relationship of roof form and walls.

Three sets of proportions are of special importance in this context. They comprise first of all, the *extent* of the roof, secondly the *pitch,* and thirdly the roof *profile.*

If a hip-roof is extended, the horizontality will be emphasized and also the weight and sinking expression in the form. If the hip-roof is more pointed, the form becomes a pyramid in which the rising and sinking effect appears to be in balance (see p. 327 f).

The same conditions apply to the pitch of the roof. If it is steep, the roof will stretch upwards, if it is shallow the form will seem heavy and protective. The first condition is consciously exploited in French Baroque architecture, as in Louis Le Vau's château, Vaux-le-Vicomte (1661) (Fig. 550). The corner pavilions have steeply pitched roofs, which in combination with the pilasters beneath, give the form an upward pointed tower-like effect. The connecting wings have the contained appearance of the Mansard roofs and lend strength to the spaces which tie the outflung pavilions together. At the same time the oval hall on the garden side is crowned by a dome, which, like an inflated volume, has an expanding effect.

357

552. Broken full-hip (summer house in Portør by K. Knutsen, from Tvedten/ Knutsen, *Knut Knutsen 1903—1969. En vandrer i norsk arkitektur*).

557. Full-hip and retracted walls (house in Steirmark, from Swoboda, *Alte Holzbaukunst in Österreich*).

554. Concave full-hip (house in Bergen, Norway, from Bjerknes, *Gamle borgerhus i Bergen*).

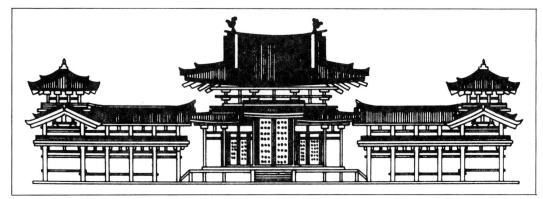

555. Concave full-hip (Fönikshallen in Japan, from Norwich (ed.), *Verdensarkitekturen*).

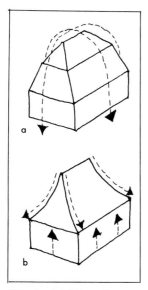

553 a-b. a) Full-hip profile: convex, b) Full-hip profile: concave.

The gently sloping and heavy full-hip is also utilized in certain types of Norwegian post-war architecture such as in Knut Knutsen's summer house in Portør (1948) (Fig. 552). Low pyramid forms, linked together at different angles, seem to press the house down into the landscape. The effect is one of reassuring protectiveness in a hard climate.

The profile of the full-hip may be either convex or concave (Fig. 553, a, b). The convex profile seems to 'arch its back', throwing a protective cover over the inside space in the manner of a dome. This is seen when the full-hip is combined with the divided surfaces of the gambrel motif. We see once again that these possibilities are exploited in French Baroque style, but in this case in order to gather together and integrate the many outstreched wings of the palace complex (see above).

The concave profile is often found in the curving hip-roof of the Rococo period (Fig. 554). Particularly characteristic is its use in the oriental pagoda. This concave curve gives the whole roof an air of soft compliance or 'sweep' and taken altogether conveys a light and hovering effect (Fig. 555). The roof seems lifted up by a thrust from below. But in another way, the downward sweep of the roof form is counteracted by the rising effect in walls, columns or brackets beneath. Thus, an explanation of the pagoda roof is of a visual nature although technical advantages have played their part.

The relation between roof and walls is just as important for the resulting effect as is the form of the roof alone. Low walls will cause the hip-roof to seem more oppressive and heavier than if the walls are high. In this context the execution of the transition beween roof and wall is particularly important. If the roof edges project far beyond the walls, the roof may seem both top-heavy and sinking. Such overhanging roofs are common in northern European rural architecture as well as in Japanese houses and the impression is always the same: an extremely sinking roof which slides down over the walls. The latter, meanwhile, seem to climb up underneath the hipping as if seeking 'protection'. The resulting combination is an architecture conveying a strong impression of shelter and safety (Figs. 556, 557).

Another important factor in the roof's rising or sinking effect is the form and placement of the windows, both in the roof itself and in the walls beneath. If windows are placed right up under the eaves the roof seems to sink down, if they are placed closer to the ground the roof seems lighter (Fig. 558). The same conditions apply whether the windows themselves are tall or low. Oslo Ladegård (present form from 1722) has a central attic storey rising high above the roof (Fig. 559). The result is one of overlapping — a wall that springs upwards with a simultaneous and contrasting sinking of the roof on either side. The 'flexibility' of the walls is emphasized by tall windows and a high foundation, while the sinking effect of the roof is en-

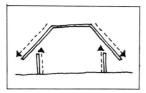

556. Full-hip and retracted walls.

559. Full-hip and the relationship to dormer storey and windows (Ladegården in Oslo).

561. Hip roof and dormer storey (Damplassen, a square in Oslo, by H. Hals).

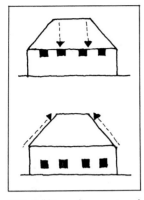

558. Full-hip and expression of motion in relation to window placement.

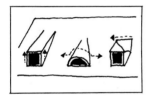

560. Hip roof and the role of the dormer shape.

hanced by a marked projection of the cornice. On the other hand, tall chimneys at the ridge points stress an upward-pointing tendency. The total effect, therefore, alternates between tall and stately at one moment and heavy the next, a visible reminder of the building's function as a symbol of pride and strength.

Windows may be built into the roof area in the form of dormers. The form of the dormers is decisive. Accordingly, a dormer that lifts up only a part of the roof will convey a downward motion, while the more plastic 'eye'-shaped dormer will give the roof a greater effect of plasticity and weight (Fig. 560).

Decisive also is whether or not the dormer windows resemble the windows below. Around Damplassen, a square in Oslo, designed by Harald Hals (1919), the form of the wall windows is repeated in the dormer windows immediately above (Fig. 561). The houses around this square appear to be two-storey buildings, whereas in reality they contain three storeys, since the dormers conceal additional attic apartments. The similarity of the windows indicates this, but at the same time announces the importance of the roof. In that the windows are drawn upwards, the roof seems to be pulled downwards. As a result, the entire roof area appears heavier and more protective. This gives the square a stronger surrounding frame, while at the same time the whole feeling of security contained in the function of dwelling is more clearly expressed.

563. Shed roof and asymmetrical space ('Air-conditioning' in Haiderabad, Sind, from Pothorn, *Das Grosse Buch der Baustile*).

564. Shed roof and Pygmy house (after Camesasca (ed.), *History of the House*).

362

# THE SHED ROOF

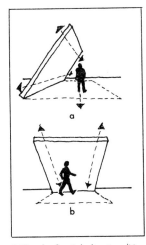

562 a-b. Spatial directionalities of shed roof: (a) longitudinal, (b) transverse.

## THE EXPRESSION OF THE SHED ROOF

Characteristic of all the roof types we have examined so far is the predominant impression of *balance*. The dome, barrel vault, gable roof and as we shall see later, the flat roof too, create motions balanced around verticality, horizontality or both simultaneously. As spaces they also presented balanced structures. The dome enclosed on all sides and the flat roof opened on all sides, whereas both barrel vault and gable roof closed the sides equally while at the same time opening both ends.

The shed roof is one half of a gable roof and is pitched in one direction only. It creates, therefore, an *asymmetric* space (Fig. 562 a, b). By this is meant that in moving along the length of the slope or traversing it, the feeling in both cases will be of a transitional stage between two conditions (Fig. 563). *Lengthwise* the diagonality will accent the roof's tension between rising and sinking, between vertical and horizontal. *Transversely* the shed roof will both open and close, both rise towards the exterior space and sink towards the ground.

Wind shelters such as those we find used by, amongst others the African Pygmy, illustrate the fundamental nature of the shed roof. These woven and leaf-covered frames are set right against the ground on one side and held up by obliquely planted poles on the other (Fig. 564). The innermost, lowest part shuts off and protects from the ground-sweeping winds, while at the same time the pitch leads the rain away. From this point of view the sinking content is important as a protection from the elements. The rising factor is equally important, but here, as a means of social contact. Pygmy society consists of small tribal units of six to eight members, each having its own hut.[34] These huts are gathered in a half-circle, with the open sides of the shelters facing inwards towards a common fire. In this way tribal solidarity is both emphasized and made visible.

## SHED ROOF MOTIFS
## THE SHED ROOF AS A TRANSITIONAL FORM

The shed roof's importance as a transitional form between opening and closing made it particularly suitable as an entrance motif. In the form of baldachins or vestibules it effects the transition between inside and outside, between the building and outdoor space (see entrance motifs p. 295 f).

566. Curved shed roof (City Stadium in Florence by P.L. Nervi, from Joedicke, *Geschichte der modernen Architektur*).

567. Undulating shed roof (Stazione Termini in Rome by L. Calini and E. Montuori, from Norwich (ed.), *Verdensarkitekturen*).

565. The shape and rising of a shed roof and its impact on the sense of opening.

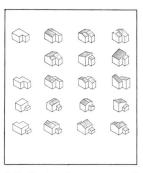

568. Shed roof as interpreter of combinations of building volumes (from *Byggekunst* 4, 1976).

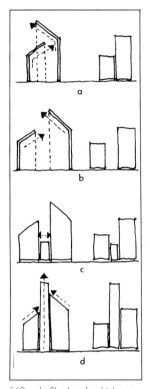

569 a-d. Shed roofs which open toward each other: (a) overlapping between the volumes, (b) distance between the volumes, (c) wedge between the volumes, (d) vertical element between the volumes. This compared to the relationship between the volumes without shed roofs (right side).

Above the entrance door to Le Corbusier's Villa Stein (1927), the baldachin slants upwards towards the outside space. This means that the roof opens towards the visitor, to receive and guide him in.

Both the angle of the rise and the form of the slanting roof are important in their effect on the observer. In cross-section the form may vary by curving upwards or downwards (Fig. 565). Seen from the outside the shed roof which curves downwards in a convex arc will close the space and modify the opening. The opposite will take place if this same roof curves concavely so that the inside space is 'pushed out' towards the onlooker. Examples of the first solution are to be found in many modern grandstand canopies. Perhaps the best known is the roof of the grandstand in Florence by Pier Luigi Nervi (1932) (Fig. 566). The roof soars boldly upwards in a slight arc giving the spectators on the tiered bench rows beneath the feeling of sitting in an enclosed space and not just within a wide-open funnel-shaped area. At the same time it is as though the form enfolds and holds together this outdoor space, thereby establishing a closer contact between the sports event and the spectator.

Another well-known combination of opening and space-creating characteristics of the shed roof is the undulating canopy in front of Rome's main railway station, Stazione Termini (1950), designed by L. Calini and E. Montuori (Fig. 567). Towards the square, the slanted surface flings itself audaciously aloft in a grand welcoming gesture towards the city. Nearing the building, the roof bulges upward again to create an area for the booking hall, which combined with the upward swing towards the city, gives the entrance space an air of rich and pulsating dynamism.

## THE SHED ROOF AS A PART OF A FORM

As a transitional space the shed roof should be understood in the broadest sense as a *fragment*. By this is meant that it is not only half of a gable roof but also a form capable of developing 'out of itself'. If two shed roofs are put side by side, first with the two higher sides facing one another and then reversed, the resulting effects will differ greatly (Fig. 568).

## OPENING TOWARDS ONE ANOTHER

In the first case the two spaces will appear to open towards one another. They belong together despite their size and the distance between them (Fig. 569, a-d). This means that the volume of each unit in any combination whatsoever may be chosen to suit function and landscape, without the composition losing its unity and falling apart (Fig. 570).

This principle is widely used in modern American architecture. 'Sea Ranch' (1965), designed by Charles Moore and others, is a well-known ex-

571.  Shed roof and adaption to the landscape (Sea Ranch by Ch. Moore et al., from Futagawa (ed.), *MLTW/Moore, Lyndon, Turnbull, Whitaker*).

573.  Shed roof and adaption to the landscape ('Murondins' by Le Corbusier, from Le Corbusier, *Oeuvre complète*).

572.  Shed roof and open and closed interiors (Murondins' by Le Corbusier, from Le Corbusier, *Oeuvre compléte*).

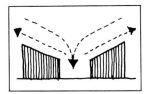

574. Shed roofs with opening away from each other.

ample (Fig. 571). Here, the shed roof makes the individual units settle into the hilly landscape and form groups around inner courtyards. The main volume has several 'offshoots' in the form of shed-type bay-windows and projections. These attachments may be placed anywhere on larger columns without loss of cohesion. Thus, unity of form is obtained without compromising the desire for a free plan — a unity previously attained by resorting to symmetry and balance.

If a smaller shed roof is set within a larger one, as in Le Corbusier's 'Murondins' project (1940), the resulting effect is an interior both closed and open (Figs. 569 a, 572). The smaller volume is encased by the larger and closes the space, while the larger rises above it to open the space. This combination creates a dynamic integration while at the same time the exterior is broken up and 'fits naturally into the landscape, allowing picturesque grouping' (Fig. 573).[35]

If shed roofs are placed a short distance from one another, the composition seems to be *split* because their interpendence is otherwise so strong (Fig. 569, b). This tension is usually resolved by introducing between them a form that is either higher or lower than both sheds.

If the form is lower, the split effect itself is accented because the intermediate form conveys the impression of a 'wedge' pressing the two units apart (Fig. 569, c). This explains the tension in the façade of Robert Venturi's 'Beach House' (1959), in which the accented motion of the entrance breaks open the form and makes way for the act of entering (Fig. 116) (see p. 93 f).

When the intermediate form is higher, as also illustrated in the 'Beach House', the unity of the forms is underscored. The form between the two shed roofs both divides and unites the elements. It separates them by blocking the opening tendency of shed roofs. At the same time, however, it draws them together by turning their rising tendency into a straight vertical line (Fig. 569, d).

### OPENING AWAY FROM ONE ANOTHER

If shed roofs are placed with their lowest sides facing, the units are closed off from one another but open in the opposite direction. This variation creates a modelled *exterior space*. Whereas the first alternative primarily lent tension to the interior by excluding the space outside, this variation creates a tension-filled exterior space which either opens from the bottom or closes from the top (Fig. 574). The following is an example in which both these effects are exploited.

The Cultural Centre in Risør, southern Norway, designed by Erik Anker and Andreas Hølaas (1978), has a courtyard main entrance framed by two wings (see p. 295) (Fig. 575). The shed roofs, sloping downwards

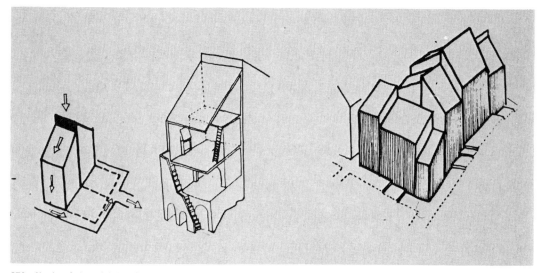

570. Shed roofs that 'glide' in relation to each other, depending on terrain and function (diagram of building volumes from the village of Castello, Isola del Giglio in Italy).

575. The shed roof closes the space downward toward the courtyard, while it opens upward toward the sky and the hills in the background (Culture Centre in Risør, Norway, by E. Anker & A. Hølaas).

to the low walls, lend an air of intimacy to the courtyard. This modifies the size of the house so that the exterior space adapts well to the scale of the narrow streets of the town. This solution also joins the Centre to other characteristics in the local environment. A steep and dominating rock ridge rises immediately behind the building. The use of the shed roof around the courtyard gives the entire space an effect of opening towards the heights behind and drawing them into the overall impression. From this point of view, the shed roof is an agent in making the building a part of both the town and the surrounding landscape.

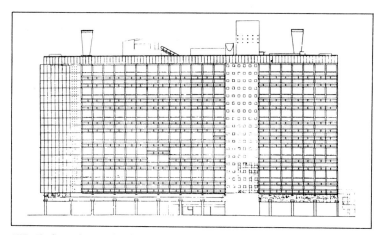

577. The flat roof is 'populated' (Unité d'Habitation in Marseilles by Le Corbusier, from Le Corbusier, *Oeuvre complète*).

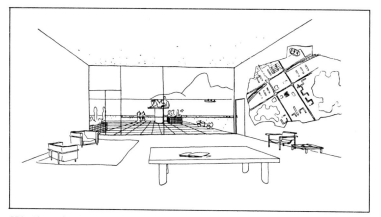

578. Flat roof and neutral articulation (from the Ministry of Education in Rio de Janeiro, from Le Corbusier, *Oeuvre complète*).

# THE FLAT ROOF

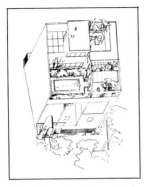

576. Flat roof as terrace (Villa Mayer in Paris by Le Corbusier, from Le Corbusier, *Oeuvre complète*).

## THE EXPRESSION OF THE FLAT ROOF

The flat roof belongs to the countries of the sunny south — a roof never weighted down by snowfall.

The exterior of this roof may be compared to a raised floor on which one can walk. In Greek villages the roof is the outdoor terrace itself. For Le Corbusier the flat roof replaced the true ground on which the building stood (Fig. 576). A dome or even a shed roof is self-sufficient. A flat roof, on the contrary, must be 'inhabited' in order to assert itself at all. Typical of this is Le Corbusier's roof landscape on l'Unite' d'Habitation in Marseilles (1952) (Fig. 577). By means of large plastically formed chimneys, 'houses', and benches the roof becomes active as a centre for residents and children but also as a conclusion to the entire angular building below. In the same way the Baroque roof was both flat and 'populated', but in this case by statues and figural representations on pedestals placed along the roof edges with a surrounding balustrade as a protective 'railing'.

Seen from the inside the flat roof or ceiling will direct the space equally in all directions. Motion is spread horizontally and in the relationship of above and below the flat roof is like a rigid lid (Fig. 442, a). Consequently, the flat roof is basically unaffected by the environment and in principle without expression. Throughout architectural history varying attempts have been made to create 'places' on flat roofs and thereby in the space beneath. These interventions may be divided into three main groups according to the treatment applied. The first concerns the *articulation* of the *surface*, the second concerns the *transition* to the walls, and the third group concerns the *modelling* of the roof form itself.

## THE FLAT ROOF AND SURFACE ARTICULATION

The white concrete roof of Functionalism illustrates the most neutral articulation of the flat roof. The intention was that roof and white walls should merge with only the angle of the junction to mark the transition. This accorded with Cubism's demand for simple and concise volumes in which no part stood out from the whole (Fig. 578).

Other types of surface articulation aim at counteracting the lid-like tendency of the flat roof or ceiling. These are carried out mainly in two ways. The first method emphasizes the *directional* aspect in the ceiling with the help of accented lines. The other method is to give the impression that the ceiling *rises*.

579. Flat roof and directional articulation (interior from Bjølstad, Norway, drawn by J. Meyer).

580. Flat roof in which the articulation is both directional and uplifting (coffered ceiling in the 'basilica' in Trier, from L'Orange & Thiis-Evensen, *Oldtidens bygningsverden*).

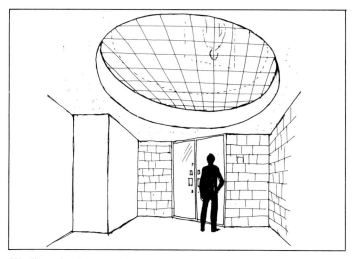

581. Flat roof and open articulation (mirrored ceiling in entrance hall of The University Press in Oslo by Jan & Jon. Diagram).

Even a roof's supporting beams may be used to convey direction (Fig. 579). In combination, therefore, a beamed ceiling will give the impression of two levels, leading in two different directions. At the same time, such a roof may also convey upward depth, particularly if the lower and upper parts are accented by using different colours.

The best example of the intentional exploitation of both these principles is the coffered ceiling (Fig. 580). The coffered ceiling is an answer to the problem of roofing large spaces and we find it, for instance, over the cella in Greek temples. The coffered ceiling may be likened to a network of equal squares framed by beams which are all laid on the same plane. Within each square is placed a gold rosette on a blue ground. We know that this motif symbolized the heavenly stars 'glimpsed' through the grid of beams. The coffered ceiling, in fact, accents both the directional and the uplifting. With their quadratic form the coffers guided the motions of the space equally in all directions. Through them the ceiling seemed to open up into the endless sky. Considered thus, the coffered ceiling is symptomatic of the Greek architectural principle which balance between the horizontal and vertical reigned.

Another method of raising a flat roof has been to decorate it with illusionistic sky and heavenly motifs. The aim of such effects, which erase the borderlines between reality and the imagined, was to break up the limiting surface of space and magnify it into a world of mythological fantasy. By the use of various painting techniques the aim was to convey an impression of perspective 'di sotto in su'.

Still another means of heightening a space has been to mirror the ceiling. In many cases it may appear as if the resulting double height causes the space to become diffused and that mirroring dissolves the entire spatial form. Two examples show an attempt made to counteract this tendency. Both are designed by the architectural firm Jan & Jon. The first is in the entrance hall of the Norwegian University Press, Oslo (1980) (Fig. 581). The space itself is a trapezoid form through which one passes diagonally. In the white ceiling an oval has been cut out. It contains deeply inset mirrors. Thus, the optical dome-like effect within the form itself is conditioned by the actual height of the space around the opening.

The other example is taken from a garden room in a house at Nesodden near Oslo (1976) (see p. 67) (Fig. 70). The entire ceiling is fragmented in mirrored surfaces which are continued down the walls. In order to combat the complete disintegration of the space, a free-standing baldachin has been placed in the centre. In this way the space becomes a bit of each: both a clearly defined space and one in the process of disintegration — all of this from a plain flat-ceilinged quadratic room.

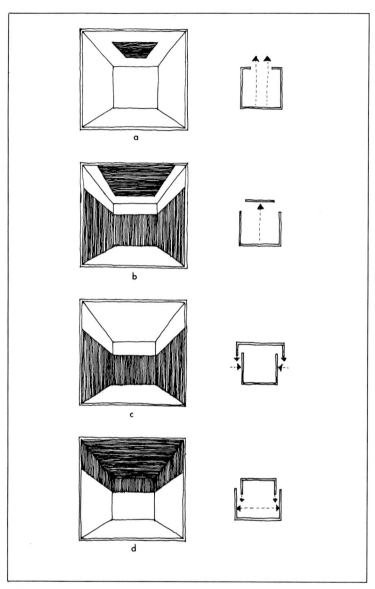

582 a-d.  Flat roof and the articulated transition between ceiling and wall: (a) opening articulation, (b) uplifting articulation, (c) expanding articulation (d) sinking articulation.

374

## THE FLAT ROOF AND THE ARTICULATION OF TRANSITION

In principle, the form of the actual transition between a flat roof and the walls may create four quite dissimilar impressions.

Presuming the height to be the same in all four examples, the transition in the first case will convey the feeling of an *open* roof, in the second of a *raised* roof, in the third of an *expanded* roof, and in the fourth case, of a *sinking* roof (Fig. 582, a-d).

The principles behind these four different impressions will be demonstrated by showing the use made of various combinations of dark and light surfaces. Our references, however, will be mainly to forms of classical mouldings.

A flat roof may seem *open* if the walls are continued without interruption part of the way into the ceiling area. The impression given is of a ceiling lying above the walls' springing level (Fig. 582 a). If the walls are light and the roof dark, a 'hole' may be created, which, combined with the extended walls, gives the space an effect of opening upward. This effect may be compared to the one obtained in the classical console cornice carried by either brackets or beams projecting directly from the walls. Such cornices have their origin in palace façade architecture and served also to draw a boundary line between the street space and the open sky. Indeed, it is often more appropriate to compare Baroque rooms to covered courtyards than to enclosed interiors.

A flat roof, furthermore, may seem *raised* or 'hovering' if the roof zone appears to be detached from the walls below. If we imagine both roof and walls to be in the same dark hue but between them a paler 'belt' extending partly into the roof area and partly into the walls, the surface will seem to rise (Fig. 582 b). A corresponding effect is conveyed by the concave moulding enriched with ornaments and flower garlands. Against the wall the groove is often concluded with a prominent row of dentils and against the roof with a similar number of convex profiles. The richly ornamented stucco-work will, however, lend to the entire concave area a non-structural sense so that the upper and lower mouldings tend to belong to the ceiling or to the wall rather than to the cornice itself. In this way ceiling and walls are separated, and the ceiling is 'detached'.

A flat ceiling may appear to be enlarged and *'expanded'* if the ceiling and the belt just beneath are pale while the walls up as far as this belt are dark and low (Fig. 582 c). A contrast between ceiling and wall arises here in that the walls seem to contract around the observer while the ceiling zone appears to expand. The overall impression becomes one of a lid too large for its box (see p. 309). This phenomenon is frequently met when attempts are made to lower the height of a room and make it more intimate by extending wallpaper and panelling part way down the walls.

583. Flat roof and sinking articulation (room in 'bracketed style' by. A.J. Downing, *The Ar-chitecture of Country Houses*).

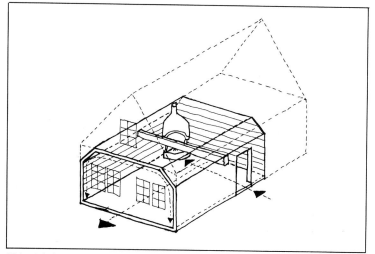

584. Krukefarm, Gudbrandsdal, Norway. Diagram.

376

All the above examples have one quality in common, that of a flat ceiling appearing to open up and lighten the inside space beneath. Our final example will show how the ceiling wall transition may convey an *oppressive* or sinking effect. The phenomenon is the same as we found with the gable roof (see p. 341) and may occur if a dark ceiling area is drawn partly down over paler walls (Fig. 582 d). Now the walls will expand while the ceiling contracts as though the cover is too 'small' in relation to the space beneath. We find examples of such transitions in cases where the ceiling glides without interruption partially down the walls in a series of convex and concave mouldings. A concrete example in this connection is a ceiling in the 'Bracketed Style' (Fig. 583). Here, the transition to the walls is made by means of slanted areas which surround the space and are finished off at the bottom by a narrow border projecting from the walls. All of this is supported by double beams which cross one another to end in brackets fastened part way down the wall. The result is a dome-like flat roof, which is drawn down into the space, so that the entire room becomes more compact and intimate.

### THE FLAT ROOF AND THE ARTICULATION OF THE FORM

A flat ceiling may easily appear to sink in the middle, specially if the area is large and low slung. As we have previously noted in connection with the floor and straight beam, attempts have been made to counteract this tendency by gently arching the element (see p. 221 ff). With its sloping upper edges, our last example illustrated how this tendency was surmounted by plastic treatment of the form itself. Two other examples are worth mentioning, particularly because the modelling underscores the idea and meaning of the space.

The drawing-room of the house at Kruke farm, Gudbrandsdal in Norway, is a large room approximately 7 X 7 metres and has a relatively low ceiling height (Fig. 584). The log walls are broken only by small-paned casement windows. The entrance is at one corner across from the large soapstone fireplace in the corner on the other side of the room. A stout cross-beam accents the connection between them. The panelled ceiling forms a large smooth surface at a relatively low height. A ceiling of this kind would have seemed heavy and sagging if the following steps had not been taken. Along the two side walls and crossing the line of entrance, the ceiling slants down towards the walls. In this way the ceiling is raised optically; it appears to be higher and at the same time the ceiling and walls are more clearly united. Another effect is also achieved. As the ceiling is slanted on only two sides, the space is given an accented direction. This parallels the roof ridge of the house. In this way the angled ceiling becomes a part of both the inside and outside. It is a part of the exterior space

585. Flat roof and articulated form (exterior of 'Fosse Ardeatine', Rome).

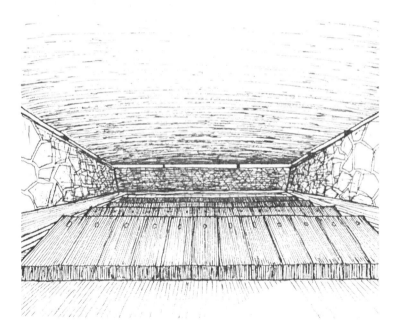

586. Flat roof and articulated form (interior of 'Fosse Ardeatine', Rome).

by reflecting the direction of the house out towards the large valley. But, it is first of all a part of the character of the inside space. The log walls enfold and frame the room space. The form of the ceiling follows up this tendency and gives the whole an intimacy and compactness which it would otherwise have lacked. This compactness is the first thing that meets the eye upon entering, a sight which in addition to the fireplace conveys a feeling of protection and safety — the very essence of what is meant by being inside.

Our final example has a completely different function than that of the living room space just described. The space is a mausoleum housing the sarcophagi of 335 war victims, situated on the Via Appia in Rome (Figs. 585, 586). Fosse Ardeatine, (1949) is a memorial to the Italian partisans who, in 1944, were imprisoned in a cave and killed. 'Sarcophagus' and 'cave' are, therefore, the key words for an understanding of the exterior of the building. On the crest of gently sloping earthen embankments lies a high concrete wall about 40 X 60 m. The impression is one of an immovable weight pressing down towards the ground — an allusion both to the sarcophagus lid and to the imprisonment which was the victims' fate. This feeling of primeval weight is retained as one enters. But, once inside, the atmosphere is completely transformed. One is faced with an almost endless space beneath a cosmic roof. The floor is sunk several steps down to the level of the more than three hundred sarcophagi. These black coffins are laid in rows of pairs slanting upwards towards each other to form pointed crests. The low surrounding walls slant outwards and are built of large irregular blocks of tuff. Over the whole is flung the great roof — slightly vaulted and resting on small elements which separate it from the walls by means of a narrow, surrounding light slit.

The impact is powerful and the symbolism clear. The floor and sarcophagi are like an undulating black 'ocean' into which one descends. The coarse massive walls appear dimly as the very earth itself into which the whole has been lowered. Above arch the detached and floating 'heavens'. Even the *sounds* within the space add to this impression. The chirping of birds and the rustling of the surrounding forests are amplified by the resonance of the vaults. The entire space collectively conveys a total image of 'the world' in which the heavens, sea, and earth are the setting for man's span of existence between life and death.

379

Photo: Otto Hagel.

# CONCLUSION

589. Architectural construction: masonry (from Notre Dame du Haut, by Le Corbusier).

590. Architectural construction: log system (detail from storage house at Sevle, photo by Norberg-Schulz).

We began this discussion by pointing out that our immediate reactions to architecture are qualitative in nature. Buildings and rooms are spontaneously classified as 'intimate', 'monumental', 'bleak', 'Spartan', etc. These reactions can be founded on private or social experiences which as we pointed out, do not necessarily have anything to do with the structure of the building itself. The *shared experience,* on the other hand, is directly connected to the form itself, and, as a spontaneous experience exists without conscious comparisons to other conventions. In this way, an object's formal 'essence' can be immediately ascertained, often regardless of the object's function. A factory smokestack can in this manner seem sacred. Not necessarily because one interprets industrial work as holy, but because the form is vertical.

The qualitative character of architecture (intimacy, monumentality, simplicity, etc.) which is experienced on the basis of a form's individual constitution, is especially related to how architecture is *built.* (Figs. 588, 589). Therefore, user reactions of this sort must be taken seriously in the sense that the question is immediately raised of *what* it is about the form that elicits this or that response. An architect can thus arrive at effects that may be incorporated in other buildings at a later date.

The theory of archetypes is therefore an attempt at supporting such a desire by ordering the principal solutions from which a choice will always have to be made, no matter what the building task. Subsequently, it seeks to interpret the *existential expression* which these archetypes have by describing how motion, weight and substance manifest themselves in form (Figs. 590, 591). Because shared experiences are based on the same qualities, it becomes possible to control the effects of architecture (Fig. 592, a-f).

Of course, these effects do not come automatically. They depend on personal creativity in the same way as notes and chords or words and syntax are only the beginning, but also the preconditions of music and poetry.

In the preceding work, we have sought to develop a theory of archetypes on the basis of those fundamental forms which exists within the elements floor, wall, and roof. The initial point of departure has been to *classify* the archetypes in terms of themes and motifs within each element. Furthermore, the intention has been to arrive at the expression inherent in each of the archetypes. This was approached as an interpretation of what we termed the form's existential expression, which included a description of what the archetypes 'do' in terms of motion, weight and substance. This existential expression was additionally a description of the form's effect, in that we suggested that shared experience referred to the same qualities, and was therefore a recognizable expression.

In the introduction, it was suggested that the theory of archetypes was

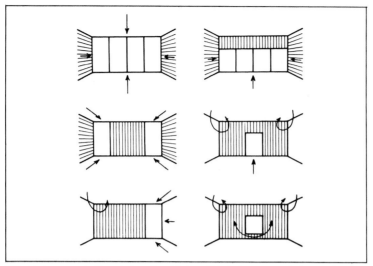

591. Motion generated by windows (from Norberg-Schulz, *Intentions in Architecture*).

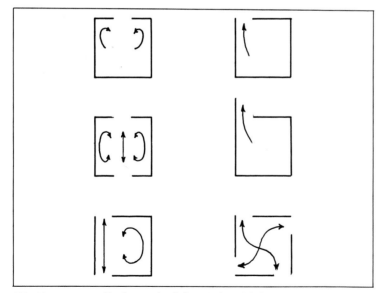

592. Motion generated by doors and walls (from Norberg-Schulz, *Intentions in Architecture*).

384

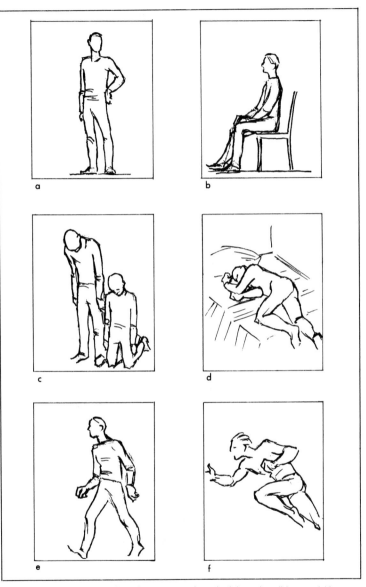

593 a-f.  Shared experiences based on motion and weight: (a) standing, (b) sitting, (c) bowing, kneeling, (d) lying, (e) walking, (f) running.

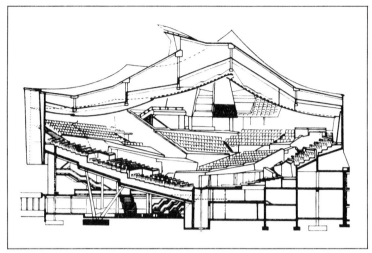

594. Architect's goal in design: the complete space (Philharmonie in Berlin by H. Scharoun, from *Philharmonie Berlin*).

595. Architecture as a cultural phenomenon (historical styles combined to symbolize an entrance for a museum. (Project by Chiswich, from Hersey, *High Victorian Gothic*).

*design-oriented*. At this juncture, it may be understood that the theory is also *analysis-oriented*. It can serve to provide a better understanding of the common denominators present in existing buildings (intentions).

But does not such a theory go against both common design practice and established historical understanding?

As regards the first point, the following question must be asked: Is it not the complete space, or the *whole*, which is both the architect's starting point and goal in design? (Fig. 593). The goal of design, of course, is synthesis, the completed building. And the starting point is nearly always linked to a vision of this whole, a concept which carries and directs the entire project 'from top to bottom'. If the theory of archetypes is followed, it would seem that design could only be thought of in the opposite manner: as with a Lego system, in which a wall, floor, and roof are put together as isolated pieces to form a whole 'from bottom to top'.

As regards the second point concerning the effectiveness of the theory as a method of analysis, the question pertains to the opposite relationship: Is not an existing building an historical reality, and in that sense, formally determined by changing historical events, which again are determined by changing architects and changing economic and cultural conditions? (Fig. 594). In other words, is it possible to speak of holistic solutions based on constants or archetypes in such a context?

In the following, we will attempt to show with the help of two examples that the theory both as a method of design and as an analysis is based on holistic concerns. The example of design is from St. Svithun's Church in Stavanger, Norway, designed by the author (1983). The analytic example is a discussion of the fundamental principles in the tradition from neoclassicism via functionalism to postmodernism.

## DESIGN AND THE THEORY OF ARCHETYPES

Every architect works in relationship to an overall idea of how a problem ought to be solved. Based on the study of a building task, he creates for himself a spatial image which he feels responds to what the building 'wants to be', both practically and expressively. Understanding of archetypes and their expressive potentialities is essential when this vision is to be turned into a realization. If one has a vision of a directional space which is thus formed in order to focus upon an important act that takes place at the end of the space, these questions quickly arise: Should both the roof, walls, and floor reinforce this directionality, and if so, how? Or should only the floor reinforce the directionality while the walls remain neutral and the roof is oriented transversely? In the first situation, is the reinforcement attained with the help of the major forms, or by breaking up and articulating

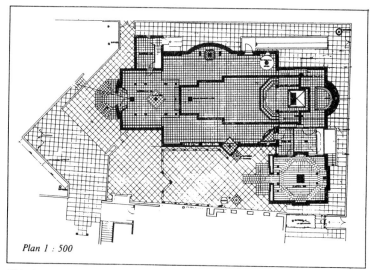

Plan 1 : 500

596. St. Svithun's Church. Plan.

597. St. Svithun's Church in Stavanger, Norway (by Th. Thiis-Evensen, axonometric drawing by Erik Norberg-Schulz).

the surfaces, or both at the same time? One is immediately faced with a complexity which touches on the very essence of architecture, and which mercilessly puts the designer to the test.

## THE CHANCEL AT ST. SVITHUN'S CHURCH

The Chancel at the Roman Catholic church of St. Svithun is the place for the most important act of the mass: communion. According to Roman Catholic beliefs, bread and wine are transformed into the body and blood of Christ during the service. The altar literally becomes a meeting place between heaven and earth. The union is called the incarnation. The chancel is to be a separate place in the church in order to mark this event. But the chancel must also be a part of the nave, which is the place for the congregation who are to receive both the word from the pulpit and the sacrament from the altar.

An overall vision of what the space ought to 'do' can be developed from this functional description. The incarnation implies a unification of up and down and suggests a reinforcement of *verticality,* which means that the roof and the floor must be brought together around the altar. The union between the chancel and the nave implies a *horizontal* interaction between the two zones. Here, the floor plays a special part as a physical mediator of this spatial contact.

Just how was this vision realized? As in any project with a specific tradition, the architect is left with a choice which has to do with the relationship between the building as a symbolic expression and the building as an existential expression. The symbolic meaning is concerned with *which* forms are selected to express a society's image of 'church', while the existential expression is concerned with *how* one interprets these symbolic images in relationship to our experience of the images in terms of motion, weight and substance.

In this instance, the symbolic meaning implied a chancel that was built up with images from ancient church forms, while retaining a modern character. The inspiration from ancient forms led to a chancel that was narrower than the nave, an altar that was vaulted by a baldachin *(ciborium),* a priest who sat behind the altar, and a rear wall with an apse (Figs. 595, 596). The 'modern' element was to be expressed in materials such as glass, steel and concrete. In terms of the existential expression, the challenge was one of reinforcing the verticality between the roof and floor in conjunction with the baldachin and the altar. Additionally, the floor, and also the apse were required to mediate the horizontal continuity between the chancel and the nave.

598. St. Svithun's Church. View towards the chancel from the gallery.

599. St. Svithun's Church and verticality. The chancel with its altar, apse and baldachin.

## VERTICALITY

The vertical continuity had to do with how the altar, baldachin and chancel roof together can attain a rising, sinking or balanced expression around a middle axis. The altar and the baldachin were located in the middle of the space so that the point of the vertical line could be accentuated. The walls of the chancel, with their white, unbroken surfaces were thought of as a neutral frame around this major theme in the centre of the space (the blue apse contradicts this notion for reasons which will be discussed later). Other furnishings, such as the chancel chairs, the tabernacle, the pulpit, etc. ring the altar for the same reason. The ascent begins with the raising of the altar level at the floor, is tranferred by the columns and glass pyramid of the baldachin, and runs out of an aperture in the roof of the chancel itself.

Throughout the church, the floor is covered with dark-red tiles. The idea was to provide a heavy, restful surface. This is accentuated by the walls being white, so that the floor becomes yet darker. The floor is conceived as the uppermost layer on top of a heavier, black mass below. This can be seen at certain places where the mass sticks up *through* the level of the floor. Around the baptismal font, the black floor is concave and given a shiny glaze. The circular opening is meant to give the impression of being lowered down into a hole of 'water'. In contrast, the floor of the chancel is raised three steps above the floor level of the nave, thereby suggesting a rise in the whole floor mass below, which continues at the level of the altar that rises 'through' the tiled floor (Fig. 597). The tiles are pulled back from the edges of the black altar level in order to 'make way' for the penetration. The altar table itself is formed as the next and final step in the rise of the mass beneath. The altar sticks up into the baldachin, which with its pyramidal roof directs the forms below into a pinnacle that points further upward. This vertical energy then bores its way through the chancel roof above as the aperture leads inwards through the surface of the roof.

The rise is accentuated by the major forms between the floor and the roof (Fig. 598). It is also emphasized by a gradually simplified detailing. The iron columns of the baldachin are constructed of perforated bases and capitals, and the shaft of the column is cruciformed in order to carve out its mass. In order to increase their lightness, the columns are separated from the level of the chancel by a slit — they do not 'rest'. The roof is constructed of transparent glass, it does not 'exist'.

In this way, the baldachin partakes in the ascent which begins with the altar as it breaks through the floor. But it can also be seen quite differently as a mediator of the light from above *downwards*. The baldachin can be regarded as 'built light' which casts itself over the altar and is diffused by the rising form. The glass surfaces of the pyramidal roof 'collect' the light

600. St. Svithun's Church and horizontality. View towards the chancel from the entrance.

601. St.Svithun's Church and horizontality. The entrance as seen from behind the altar.

from the chancel roof and make it almost tangible by means of their extremely reflective surfaces. The columns and beams are plated with gold, which is the colour of light itself, and the perforated columns, which do not touch the floor, are a part of this interpretation of sinking from above.

In this manner, the light from on high has been interpreted in the forms and colours of the baldachin. Nevertheless, the baldachin is, of course, an autonomous figure independent of up or down. It ought to be able to express the balance between the two affected forces. In this context, the form of the pyramidal roof is essential, in that it is just as tall as it is wide, and therefore 'rests'. If it had been more pointed, it would have risen; had it been more shallow, it would have fallen.

We understand that the existential expression of the forms in the verticality between rising and falling is also a visualization of the meaning of the chancel, which we call the incarnation. The altar is the earth, or man, which rises up toward the light in heaven. The light, on the other hand, shines down to meet mankind and make fertile the earth. The meeting between these two directionalities is a visualization of the conception of Christ as both god and man, expressed in the image of the communion.

## HORIZONTALITY

The horizontal motion that joins the chancel and the nave is primarily initiated by the stair up to the chancel and the apse in the end wall behind the seat of the priest.

The apse is a well-known element from ancient churches with a background in Roman architecture. It was used in order to emphasize the seats of the bishop and priests. The major form of the apse expands the chancel as a reflection of the main directionality through the church from the entrance via the centre aisle forward to the semi-circle (Figs. 595, 599, 600). In this way the zones are connected in a gradual spatial reduction from the nave via the chancel to the apse. The movement through the spaces is taken up in the form of the apse — as in the altar and the baldachin. The apse is painted a heavy blue in order to emphasize its depth. From a distance, it appears as a hole in the white surroundings. Given that the apse recedes, the contrast between it and the light altar baldachin in front will reinforce the impression that the altar baldachin projects forward.

The stair continues the projecting motion. It projects from the chancel space and overlaps between the chancel and the nave. Being a fan stair, it articulates this motion evenly in all directions. With its deep treads, this projection is slow and dignified. The pulpit desk is located on the protruding landing.

It is apparent that the apse as a focused form catches one's gaze upon entering the church. At the same time, it 'pushes' the baldachin and in turn

603. From the Chapel of St. Mary. View towards the entrance.

602. From the Chapel of St. Mary. View towards the tabernacle. The formal vocabulary is related to ancient church architecture.

the symbol of the sacrament forward towards the entrant. The stair further transmits this motion, while at the same time the pulpit and therewith the Word are presented to the devout.

St. Svithun's Church provides an example of how existential expression can determine a specific vocabulary subsequent to an overall vision of the project. In this context, the vocabulary includes symbolic forms from ancient church tradition (apse, baldachin, chancel, stair, etc.) (Figs. 601, 602). The existential expression — specific interpretations of motion, weight and substance — provides overall strength to the vision, which in this case implied the weaving together of the vertical and horizontal by means of the vocabulary.

## ANALYSIS AND THE THEORY OF ARCHETYPES

The buildings of architectural history are not primarily results of various individual contributions, but rather the individual contributions' elucidation of the same formal understanding. These formal understandings, which we call styles, hold the epochs together and give them commonality. These commonalities are clear, even quite dissimilar architects have been at work, and even though the building tasks and places have varied greatly.

What is it then that comprises these commonalities? The theory of archetypes can elucidate these interrelationships through the utilization of terminology equivalent to that which we used for our discussions of design. We must describe the styles based on the phenomena of overall vision, vocabulary, and existential expression. *The vision*, which in the case of design was the same as a conceptual foundation for a project, can be illustrated in the case of a style by the question: What is a period 'comprised' of, what is the sentiment of the period, and how is this expressed in its architecture? *The vocabulary* is concerned with those spatial types which the various periods have at their disposition. During Roman times, it was the vault; in Greek times, the skeletal system; in the Gothic it was the groin vault, etc. *The existential expression* has to do with how these types are interpreted as regards motion, weight and substance, based on the overall vision the architects have of contemporary attitudes. The development of the basilica is characteristic. As a constant spatial type, it is interpreted in numerous ways throughout history: in Roman times it was heavy, in the Gothic light, and in the Baroque 'dynamic', etc.

### THE MODERN TRADITION

As an example of the implementation of the analythical method, the development of what can be termed the primary phases of the modern tradition ought to be considered. Three styles stand in the forefront: neo-classicism,

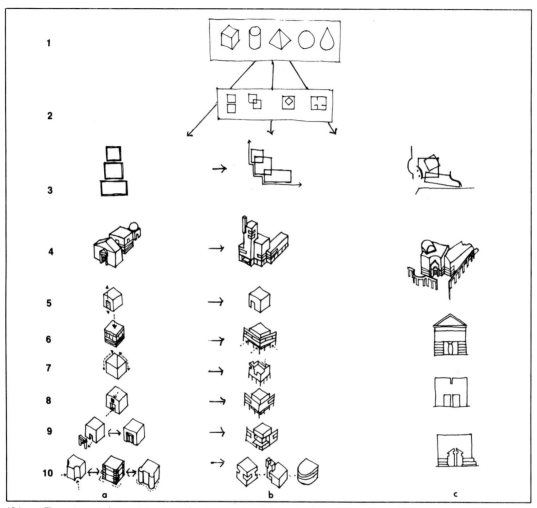

604 a-c. The major periods comprising the modern tradition, from (a) neo-classicism (1910s—20s) via (b) functionalism (1920s—30s) all the way to (c) postmodernism (1970s—80s). The periods have a common vocabulary made up of geometric volumes: the cube, cylinder, pyramid, etc., (604,1) but the interpretation of these volumes varies according to the dissimilar philosophies of each period. Neo-classicism sought *defined space* (604,3a), functionalism *open space* (604,3b) and postmodernism *complex space* (604,3c). This is due to dissimilar interpretations of the existential expression of the geometric volumes in terms of motion, weight and substance. Neo-classicism aimed for symmetry, additive forms and heaviness, functionalism aimed for asymmetry, overlapping and lightness, while postmodernism aims for all of these expressions simultaneously, in addition to its characteristic distortion (604, 4a-c). The differences are expressed in the articulation as: placement of the *opening* (5), *surface development* (6), *roof form* (7), *surface relationships* (8), *ornamentation* (9) and *corner resolutions* (10).

functionalism, and postmodernism. Neo-classicism from the second decade of this century is considered to be the final developmental advance within the traditional architecture of styles. This development was based on the Greek and Roman inheritance which had been sustained through the Renaissance and the Baroque to our own century. With its rationalist demands, functionalism from the 1920s and 1930s has been described as representing a fundamental break with this tradition. Postmodernism is the latest phase in the development of modern architecture. Its goals were first formulated in Robert Venturi's book, *Complexity and Contradiction in Architecture* from 1966.

By architects and others of the time, both functionalism and postmodernism have been viewed as completely new directions in relation to the periods they followed. Functionalism was to have broken all ties with neoclassicism, and postmodernism with functionalism. But if one studies the pioneers and prominent architectural examples of these three movements, it becomes clear that this is not the case. On the contrary, one can more accurately speak of prominent variants of a fundamental vocabulary. This vocabulary can be referred to as the basic geometrical forms, such as the sphere, cube, cylinder, and pyramid to name a few. Each of these three periods interpreted these archetypes differently, in response to dissimilar visions. As far as neo-classicism is concerned, the result was a desire for *defined space,* for functionalism it was the desire for *open space,* and for postmodernism it was the desire for *complex space.* The differences in interpretation were linked to dissimilar ways of assembling the geometric volumes (the expression of motion) and various ways of delineating spatial separation (the expression of weight and substance) (Fig. 603, a-c).

## THE GEOMETRIC VOLUMES

The use of basic geometric volumes in the modern tradition was justified by the desire to accentuate various functions each with its own space. The principle was: 'form follows function'.

History is full of examples of these sorts of 'functional volumes'. An Italian stone village is built up of clearly accentuated volumes, as is a Carolingian or a Romanesque church. In the villages the volumes manifested the individual families, in the churches spaces for the various saints, chancel, and liturgical rites.

In neo-classicism these functional volumes are transformed into the very foundation of an esthetic program. This is most clear in the revolutionary architecture from the outset of our own era, just after the French revolution. Ledoux and Boullée enter the scene with their geometric volumes such as the sphere, cube and pyramid (Figs. 604, 605). And each of these 'pure' forms also represented various functions: the sphere was the farmer's

605. Geometric volumes as an expression of function (the farmer's house (by C.L.ledoux).

606. Geometric volumes as an expression of function: river watch-man's house (by C.L. Ledoux).

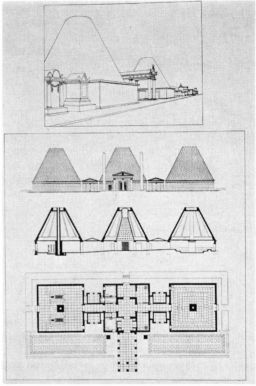

607. Geometry, symmetry and heaviness in neo-classicism (Crematorium in Malmø, Sweden, by S. Lewerentz).

house, he who lived near the earth and had his life tied to earthly goods. The pyramid was the firewood carrier's house, he who piled logs in pyramids. And the river guard's house was a cylinder, formed as a wheel like the grist mill stone further up stream in the rapids. In this manner, the geometric volumes became 'expressive discourse' — 'architecture parlante'.

The architecture of the revolution came to be a conscious reaction against the luxurious disintegration of defined volume during the Rococo period. In this way, it became a symbol of newfound sobriety after decades of joy in the parlours of the aristocracy. The same occurrence took place a century later, now with neo-classical cubism after the elegant Art Nouveau of the pre-war years. The first step is taken on the path of the modern tradition — first with neo-classicism, via functionalism to a temporary stopping point at postmodernism.

## NEO-CLASSICISM AND DEFINED SPACE

Neo-classicism's interpretation of the geometric volumes can, in spite of variations and exceptions, be summarized with the following catchwords: additive approach, mass and symmetry. Defined space is a reality — the additive approach emphasizes the individuality of the elements (Fig. 602, a). The volumes were interpreted as 'things', in that massivity and plasticity were the dominating expressions, while symmetry and articulation emphasized the balance of the elements. Each volume was considered as an isolated entity and was added to the next as an independent element. Sigurd Lewerentz's crematorium in Malmø, Sweden (1928) is an example (Fig. 606). There, the small symmetrical entrance temple is flanked by two identical cones above rectangular bases with small cubes in between. The character is heavy, precisely because each individual was to be isolated from the others with thick walls and a unifying roof.

The volumes of neo-classicism were divided into horizontal layers which interpreted the varying gravitational surge to the ground. The rustic layer was at the bottom, above it was the layer with the small, often closely mullioned windows, and on top was the crowning cornice or a pitched hip roof (Fig. 607). And around the entire volume ran unbroken profiles as if to hold the mass of the walls tightly together. The corners were often reinforced with great blocks, and the portals surrounding the doors were carried by bulging columns with over-heavy keystones in the beam above. In this way, massivity is emphasized around a finite place, a sovereign world independent of its neighbours. This is why symmetry was important, because it joined the individuals together to form a whole. In this manner, the corner stones of the new tradition were laid, as a picture of a time that desired to begin anew and accentuate and lay claim to life's true values.

608. Heaviness as an expression of neo-classicism (DNC-bank in Oslo, by Biong).

611. The lightness of functionalism (Residence in Oslo, by A. Korsmo).

610. The lightness of functionalism (Residence in Oslo).

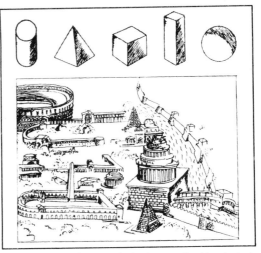

609. Geometric volumes as ideals in functionalism (drawing by Le Corbusier).

612. Overlapping of geometric volumes in functionalism (Residence in Oslo, by A. Korsmo. Axonometric drawing by A. Søreide).

## FUNCTIONALISM AND OPEN SPACE

According to Le Corbusier, the geometric volumes lived on in functionalism (Fig. 608). They were employed for a number of reasons, not the least of which was that they fit into the ideology of 'form follows function'. Thus, the geometric volumes were a part of Le Corbusier's theory of types, in that he considered them to be the ultimate product of nature's own functional selectivity. And as with nature, architecture was a question of types arising on the basis of 'well-formulated problems'.

However, functionalism's interpretation of the basic geometric volumes were completely opposite to that of neo-classicism. Now they are seen as 'containers', not as masses (Fig. 603, b). They are dissolved, as opposed to closed and introverted. Therefore, the additive method was replaced by overlapping, mass was replaced by lightness, and symmetry by asymmetry. Overlapping integrates and unifies, and results in complex transitional spaces, while the skeleton opens up as it separates between load bearing and skin, between construction and spatial definition. And while symmetry orders and delegates, asymmetry provides for flexibility and free growth.

The walls of functionalism were made white and thin like a skin that enswathed the volumes underneath (Figs. 609, 610). The walls of neo-classicism were firmly anchored to the ground; the walls of functionalism floated over the ground on high pilotis. And now the windows are transformed into long bands, and the corners are dissolved in glass as replacements for small holes and plastic reinforcement of the corners. And whereas the entrance had once been framed in Doric plasticity, it was now superseded by a floating canopy. But all the while, it is still the volume that is being interpreted. The volumes express the individual functions, while the overlapping shows that they are still a part of a greater whole, which could continually adapt itself to new demands with budding freedom (Fig. 611). This formal image is optimistic and depicts an era that opened itself to the world because it believed in it and its technological visions.

After the post WW I functionalism, the basic volumes begin to be blurred. In the post WW II period, there remain only two aspects of the pioneers' ideas: overlapping and technology. The former led to 'the great space' in which activities float as undefined currents between flexible wall elements (Fig. 612). The latter follows suit. Now the most important thing is the development of the structure surrounding the empty space. Look at the unbroken horizontal banding and the continuous strip windows from new town housing blocks of the 1960s and 1970s. What perfect proof of the post-war belief in a placeless architecture!

The sense of place was re-established by the same man who indirectly provided the inspiration for its abolition, namely Le Corbusier. This new de-

613. The esthetics of open space and technical expression in late functionalism.

614. The heavy, volumetric expression in Le Corbusier's Notre Dame du Haut.

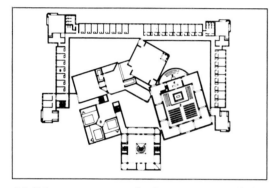

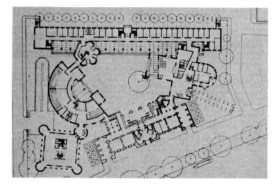

615. Volumes in contrasting conflict: Dominican monastery (by L.I. Kahn from Norberg-Schulz & Digerud, *Louis Kahn, Idea e imagine*).

616. Volumes in contrasting conflict: postmodernism (Wissensc-haftliche Sentrum in Berlin, J. by Sterling).

velopment took place with his church at Ronchamp (1955) (Figs. 613). With slanting walls, hanging roofs and plastic modulation, closed volume is re-established for defined activity. In this manner, the side-tracked development was restored to an even keel by once again concentrating on the interpretation of volumes. Robert Venturi defined the new thinking with his thoughts of 'both/and', and contradiction and complexity. In the 1970s and 1980s, these were culminated by the first projects of postmodernism.

## POSTMODERNISM AND COMPLEX SPACE

Postmodernism furthers the ideals which functionalism prepared for and revives those which functionalism left.

In functionalism, geometry volumes were overlapped at right angles. Those of postmodernism also overlap, but now mostly at acute and oblique angles. Where functionalism's interpretations were made in order to attain dynamic continuity, the goal of typical postmodernism is to impel volumes one on another in contrasting conflict (Figs. 603, c, 614, 615). Thereby the volumes are accentuated at the same time as they are unified — the isolation of classicism and the openness of functionalism are joined to a single entity. Functionalism's desire for overlapping and asymmetry answered the need for an adaptive architecture. The freedom that is implied by angling and pinwheeling is postmodernism's furtherance of the same theme. And the accidental spaces which arise in-between are also welcome additions for both expansion and input. And if there is not enough space, the volume is deformed and thereby adapted to its neighbour. The walls of functionalism were understood as a light skin that enswathed the volumes within. In postmodernism, an extra step is taken and the skin is completely detached from the volume behind. In this way the wall is 'free' and can run like an unbound screen, modulating dynamic transitions between inside and outside (Fig. 616). Functionalism replaced the plasticity of neo-classicism with lines and surfaces, and the motifs of neo-classicism were replaced by abstract form. Postmodernism contains both. The motifs are resurrected, but often as contours and lines bound to a surface, not necessarily as independent plastic forms. Thus, the powerful rustic of neo-classicism is transformed into outlines on the surface, in the same way that modulated mouldings, gables , and columns are repeated as arches and triangles cut as abstract holes in thin walls (Fig. 617).

We see that postmodernism's interpretations of the basic volumes. both in juxtaposition and in articulation, carry with them characteristics from all phases of the modern tradition. And so, it has also become a mirror of its own time, a time which seeks its identity and its roots, but which remains complex and filled with conflict.

403

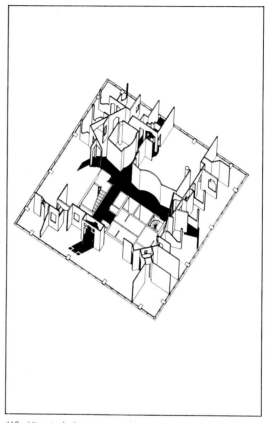

617. Dynamism in Norwegian postmodernism (axonometric drawing of the offices and hallways in Norwegian University Press, Oslo, by Jan & Jon).

618. Historical abstractions in Norwegian postmodernism (residence in Kongsvinger, by Jan & Jon.)

# FINAL WORD

We have seen that for both design and analysis, the theory of archetypes has grown out of an holistic approach. In both instances, it was either a matter of fullfilling or describing the common expressive power of architecture. As regards analysis, we find that architects during any given period are influenced by a common architectural language. They do not work in an individual vacuum, but rather are bound together by a common intention which is typical for the period. There can be individual dissimilarities and disgressions, but even these must be seen in the light of the unifying formal will of the period in order to be understood. We have seen that the modern tradition was held together by the vocabulary of the geometric volumes. The differences between the three developmental phases were a function of dissimilar interpretations of expressions of motion, weight and substance. And these differences affected the entire *space* because they grew out of a vision which had to do with the period's 'image of itself'. In such a context, considering the roof, walls, and floor as isolated parts was meaningless without having considered their place in the development of an holistic expression.

The method of approach was the samë for design. For the architect, it is essential to take advantage of the expressive potentialities of the archetypes only after considering the meaning of the whole in relationship to the content of the project.

The fundamental idea behind this work has in other words been to reinforce the creative potential of architects. This goal has been pursued by seeking the roots of architecture through a study of its expressive nature. In this, the author hopes to have contributed to a somewhat greater understanding of the role of architecture in the pursuit of more meaningful surroundings.

# NOTES

## INTRODUCTION

1. Quotation L.B. Alberti, in R. Goldwater and M. Treves (eds), *Artists on Art,* London 1976, p. 35.

2. Quotation E.-L. Boullée, in H. Rosenau, *Boullée & Visionary Architecture,* London 1974, p. 89.

3. G. Scott, *The Architecture of Humanism,* New York 1974, p. 169.

4. Le Corbusier, *Towards a New Architecture,* London 1970, p. 141 (translates by F. Etchells).

5. Ibid., p. 23.

6. See definition in Paolo Portoghesi (ed.), *Dizionario Enciclopedico d'Architettura e Urbanistica,* Rome 1968, p. 138.

7. H. Wölfflin, *Renaissance and Baroque,* London 1966, p. 77

8. F. Kafka, Der Bau, *Die Erzählungen,* Frankfurt am Main 1961, p. 379.

9. The Crystal Palace was at the time the very symbol of openness and worldly vision. The view was almost unending in both directions, and some felt that it was reminiscent of the day when all times and peoples were to be gathered at the throne of the Creator. See 'Times' 1851, in G.L. Hersey, *High Victorian Gothic. A Study in Associationism,* London 1972, p. 156.

10. Quotation L.I. Kahn, in Lobell, *Between Silence and Light. Spirit in the Architecture of Louis I Kahn,* Boulder 1979, p. 42.

## THE FLOOR

1. The imperativeness of being held up by a solid natural floor is made apparent by the fact that we always refer to this characteristic when we move across an architectural floor. It is this sub-conscious reference which makes it possible for us to feel safe even on the tenth floor with 30 metres of 'nothing' underneath us. Not until we are standing outside the building at ground level and looking up, do we understand that we have been floating high above the safety of the natural floor. Therefore, the sight of a skyscraper without a façade, in which all of the floors are expressed as thin planes, is an almost menacing reminder of the illusory concept of ground with which we live.

2. Experiences with the heavy, resolved stone which 'closes inward' are found in fairy-tale descriptions of trolls that capture and imprison people in the mountains. See the fairy tale, P. Chr. Asbjørnsen and J. Moe, De tre kongsdøtre i berget det blå, *Samlede eventyr,* 11, Oslo 1978, pp. 7–29.

3. These qualities also apply to other stone-like materials such as terra cotta and concrete. Concerning stone and mountains which rise up from beneath, see V. Lee, Empathy, in M. Weitz (ed.), *Problems in Aesthetics,* New York 1967, p. 621.

4. The immediate cause of both the bulging of the floors and the attachment to the stones is due to moist soil and frequent earthquakes.

5. E. Kaufmann and B. Raeburn (eds.), *Frank Lloyd Wright, Writings and Buildings*, New York 1970, p. 305.

6. Ibid., p. 249.

7. See Bruno Zevi's reference to the fact that Classical traditions also applied to spatial organization: B. Zevi, *Architecture as Space*, New York 1974, p. 107.

8. The exception is the chancel floor itself, which was often raised a few steps in order to be defined as a separate 'church'.

9. See the theories of James Hall concerning the relationship between trees and Gothic style: J. Rykwert, *On Adam's House in Paradise*, New York 1972, p. 82. See also K.F. Schinkel's theories on the same, in which Gothic style is compared to 'a plant which strives toward the heavens', Thiis-Evensen, *Steder...*, p. 152. In general, see E. Forssmann, *Karl F. Schinkel. Bauwerk und Baugedanken*, Munich 1981.

10. The hall-churches of the late-Gothic period take this principle of openness to an extreme by allowing the roof to become a continuous interweaving which apportions the space evenly in all directions. See P. Frankl, *Gothic Architecture*, London 1962, p. 146 (translated by D. Pevsner). See also H. Koepf, *Baukunst in fünf Jahrtausenden*, Stuttgart 1963, p. 107, and H. Sedlmayr, Die Geburt der Kathedrale, *Epochen und Werke*, I, Munich 1959, pp. 155—169, especially p. 156 about Max Dvoràk's interpretations.

11. P. Blake, *Mies van der Rohe*, New York 1966, p. 85.

12. J. Joedicke, *Geschichte der modernen Architektur*, Teufen (no year), p. 90. See also Le Corbusier, *Vår bostad*, Stockholm 1962, p. 62 (translated by L. Holm).

13. R. Venturi, *Complexity and Contradiction in Architecture*, New York 1966, p. 73.

14. See S. E. Rasmussen, *Om at opleve arkitektur*, Copenhagen 1975, p. 87.

15. See E. J. Gibson and R. D. Walk, The Visual Cliff, *Scientific American* 202, New York 1960, pp. 564—71.

16. Straus, Psychologie der Menschlichen Welt, *Gesammelte Schriften*, Berlin 1960, p. 164.

17. An example of the interpretation of the expression of a shiny black floor is given in Theodor Kittelsen's painting: 'Ekko' (1888). The black colour has a tendency to move *towards* us, wind itself around us, as it covers the walls and the roof. When it covers a horizontal plane, on the other hand, it leads us downwards, to a recess into which one is pulled and drawn, instead of being imposed upon and excluded. This is Kittelsen's in-

terpretation, in which the echo as a symbol of expansion goes beyond the boundaries of the enclosed natural space, both upwards through the gossamer mist over the mountainside, and downwards, deep into the murky waters of the lagoon. Sinking downwards into the deep water is not only a real experience which we comprehend and transfer to the floor motif. But also optically, in the shadows of reflection, we are already sunken into the deep. On a shiny black floor therefore, we become experientially 'heavy' — where the thin veneer seems to be forever on the verge of cracking or failing.

18. Shiny interior wood floors made of *hinoki* were preferred in Japanese monumental architecture. See in particular the imperial palace complex in Kyoto.

19. Concerning the sunroom, see Jan & Jon, Wenches hus, *Byggekunst* 6, Oslo 1978, p. 188.

20. Quotation R.M. Rilke, in G. Rombold, Ästhetische und antropoligische Raumqualitäten, *Kunst und Kirsche* I, Linz 1976, pp. 21—26, p. 24.

21. See concerning comparable interpretations in Le Corbusier's *La Tourette*, p. 77 herein.

22. W. Alex, *Japanese Architecture*, New York 1963, p. 41.

23. Concerning the Siena piazza, see P. Favole, *Piazza d'Italia*, Milano 1972, p. 51. See also P. Zucker, *Town and Square. From the Agora to the Village Green*, Cambridge 1959, p. 86.

24. G. Bachelard, *La poétique de l'espace,* Paris 1958, p. 40.

25. Ibid., p. 39.

26. Concerning the Trevi fountain, see Chr. Elling, *Rom. Arkitekturens liv fra Bernini til Thorvaldsen*, Copenhagen 1967, p. 315.

27. Concerning the importance of tuff for Rome's *genius loci*, see Chr. Norberg-Schulz, *Genius Loci*, London 1980, p. 144.

28. The same motif appears both with Le Corbusier and in more recent American architecture. See Le Corbusier's project for a house in Chile (1930), in Le Corbusier, *Oeuvre complète 1910—65*, Zürich 1964, *Oeuvre.. 1929—34*, p. 48, and Sea Ranch by MLTW (1966) in Ch. Moore, G. Allen, D. Lyndon, *The Place of Houses*, New York 1974, p. 31.

29. Kaufmann & Raeburn, *Frank Lloyd...*, *p.* 173.

30. Ibid., p. 42.

31. Ibid., p. 313.

32. We find the same dark line in Le Corbusier's church at La Tourette. There, it runs from the black chancel plateau and down through the nave. See J. Petit, *Un Couvent de Le Corbusier*, Paris 1961, p. 90.

33. Concerning the developmental history of the Campidoglio, see J. S. Ackermann, *The Architecture of Michelangelo*, Middlesex 1970, pp.

139—173.

34. The drive-in ramps were constructed in the 1870s.

35. Ch. de Tolnay, *Michelangelo. Sculptor, Painter, Architect,* Princeton 1975, p. 158, (translated by. G. Woodhouse).

36. Concerning the bridge as an expression of a no-man's land, in which one is abandoned to the forces of evil, see A. van Gennep, *The Rites of Passage,* London 1965, p. 145, (translated by M.G. Vizedom and G.L. Caffee).

37. Concerning the bridge which 'collects', see M. Heidegger, *Vorträge und-ufsätze,* Pfullingen 1967, II, p. 26.

38. Concerning the political and cultural symbolic meaning of the stairway, see A. Reinle, *Zeichensprache der Architektur,* Zürich 1976, p. 289.

39. A. Palladio, *The Four Books of Architecture,* I, New York 1965, p. 34, (facsimile of edition from 1738, translated by Issac Ware).

40. Quotation G. Vasari, in Wölfflin, *Renaissance and Baroque,* London 1966, p. 140.

41. As opposed to a *narrow* stair, which refers to the width of *one* person, the phenomenon of the wide stair is difficult to refer to the human body (How many is 'a lot' of people?) and is therefore more dependent on the visual relationship to the surroundings.

42. W. Kandinsky, *Punkt und Linie zu Fläche,* Bern-Bümplitz 1973 (facsimile of 1926 edition), p. 142.

43. Concerning the symbolic meaning of the stepped pyramid see H. Sedlmayr, Architektur als abbildende Kunst, *Epochen und Werke II,* Munich 1952, pp. 211—234, p. 222.

44. Quotation V. Scamozzi, in Wölfflin, *Renaissance...,* p. 45.

45. Quotation G. Vasari, in Ibid., p. 142.

46. See H. Kähler, *Rom und sein Imperium,* Baden-Baden 1964, p. 23.

47. See concerning this development, H.P. L'Orange, *Keiseren på himmeltronen,* Oslo 1949.

48. This corresponded with Le Corbusier's own principle that a building is developed from the inside-out, not otherwise. See Le Corbusier, *Towards a New Architecture,* London 1970, (translated by R. Etchells), p. 164.

49. Concerning this 'porridge-like' quality of the stair in front of St. Peter's, see Wölfflin, *Renaissance...,* p. 45.

50. See Staale Sinding-Larsen's indication concerning the practicality of the three-run stair in relationship to the desire to accommodate converging parties. St. Sinding-Larsen, The Laurenziana Vestibule as a Functional Solution, *Institutum Romanum Norvegiae, Acta, VIII,* Roma 1978, pp. 213—222.

51. See Ch. de Tolnay, *Michelangelo, Sculptor...,* p. 135, see also Venturi, *Complexity...,* p. 33.

# THE WALL

1.  Hesselgren, *Arkitekturens...*, p. 71.

2.  Both boundary continuations are dependent on the factor of proximity.

3.  Right and left have dissimilar values. In spite of our symmetric organization, with approximate equality between right and left, the right side is viewed by most cultures as being the stronger. The right hand is not only tratitionally seen, but also for 90% of mankind, experienced as the stronger, more active hand. It is the right hand that fights; the left hand is more supportive and anticipatory. In this way, the right side and right hand have a greater striking power and *weight*. Kandinsky states that the direction to the right is the way 'home' ('nach Hause'), in other words, reaches a definite point, while the left side opens up and continues out into the world ('zur Ferne'). (Kandinsky, *Punkt...*, p. 138).

    The Latin *rectus* suggests the same thing. Rectus means at a right angle, or right. In English (as in German), the word right (rechts) means both correct and right-hand. The strong sit at the right hand of God, the weak trail off to the left. The 'bad' comes from the north, the dark side, which is the left side when one turns towards the apse of the church to the east. In the West, the knife is placed on the right side of the plate: the knife is active and cutting, the one that initiates the assault, while the left side with the fork supplies and supports.

4.  Arnheim, *Art...*, p. 22.

5.  Kandinsky, *Punkt...*, p. 138.

6.  Quotation from J.W. von Goethe, in H. Klotz, *Die Frühwerke Brunelleschis und die mittelalterliche Tradition,* Berlin 1970, p. 26. A comparable tripartition was suggested by Louis Sullivan for the composition of the exteriors of skyscrapers: at the bottom is the 'base', comprised of shops and the main entrance, then the 'shaft' comprised of a variable number of identical floors (like a bee's hive), and finally, the *attica* floor in which the entire circulation system of the building is terminated. See Sullivan's statements in H. Morrison, *Louis Sullivan. Prophet of Modern Architecture,* New York 1963, p. 148.

7.  See the principle used by frame makers, who always dimension the lower part of the *passe partout* slightly larger than the upper in order to resist the 'sinking' of the image.

8.  Lee, *Empathy...*, p. 621.

9.  When we in the following speak of 'large' wall sections, this must not in all instances be perceived literally. A section can be narrow, while retaining its dominance.

10. The character of the façade was an answer to '... the sense of peace and seriousness which ought to envelop the University surroundings...'

(The Academic Collegium, 1880). Quotation from, Thiis-Evensen, *Steder...*, p. 42.

11. See E.V. Langlets 'ten rules' from 1867, quoted in E. Nordin, Träbyggande under 1800-talet, *Den nordiska trästaden*, 16, Stockholm 1972, p. 42.

12. K. Lund, Svar til Thomas Thiis-Evensen, *Arkitektnytt*, 3, Oslo 1969, p. 47.

13. See H. Lauterbach and J. Joedicke, *H. Häring. Schriften, Entwürfe, Bauten*, Stuttgart 1965, p. 13, p. 25.

14. Quotation E. Rubin, in Arnheim, *Art and...*, p. 223.

15. See Arnheim, *Art and...*, p. 220.

16. Norberg-Schulz, *Existence..*, p. 72.

17. See Giedeon, *Space...*, pp. 17—19, p. 110.

18. Ibid., p. 633.

19. G.C. Argan, *The Renaissance City*, New York 1969, p. 18.

20. N. Johnston, *The Human Cage*, New York 1973, p. 26.

21. Quotation A. J. Downing, in Scully, *The Shingle Style and the Stick Style*, New Haven 1971, p. XXXVIII.

22. See A. Boëthius, *The Golden House of Nero. Some Aspects of Roman Architecture*, Michigan 1960, pp. 95—128.

23. Alberti, *Ten Books...*, p. 100.

24. L'Orange in collaboration with Thiis-Evensen, *Oldtidens...*, p. 207.

25. St. Sinding-Larsen, A Tale of Two Cities. Florentine and Roman Visual Context for Fifteenth-Century Palaces. *Institutum Romanum Norvegiae, Acta*, VI, Rome 1975, pp. 163—212, p. 190.

26. The materials can also be copies of the originals, while retaining their visual quality.

27. E. Cornell, *Om rummet och arkitekturens väsen*, Gothenburg 1966, p. 24.

28. A room which is surrounded by smooth walls also provides reverberation and in that way 'opens' and expands the space, while porous walls absorb the sound and thereby 'tighten' and contract the space.

29. H. Torp, *Mosaikkene i St. Georg-rotunden*, Oslo 1963, p. 60.

30. O. Demus, *Byzantine Mosaic Decoration: Aspects of Monumental Art in Byzantium*, London 1953, p. 34.

31. Of course, this is not always meant literally. A block wall can also be manipulated in order to appear 'natural'. See for example the carved stone in front of Fontana di Trevi in Rome (Fig. 92).

32. The statement is from Sebastian Serlio and stands in contrast to the concept of 'opera di mano', which covers manipulated elements such as columns and ornaments. See E. Forssman, *Dorisch, jonisch, korintisch*, Stockholm 1961, p. 38.

33. Palladio, *The Four...*, I, Chapter IX, p. 8.

34. Quotation from R. Pietilä, in Norberg-Schulz, *Genius...*, p. 200.

35. Giedeon, *Space...*, p. 493.

36. Th. Lipps, Raumästhetik und geometrisch-optische Täuschungen, *Schriften der Gesellschaft für psycholigische Forschung*, II, Leipzig 1897, pp. 305—726, p. 308.

37. J. Milton, Samson Agonistes, *The Poems of John Milton*, London 1961, lines 1648—52.

38. P.L. Nervi, *Aesthetics and Technology in Building*, Massachusetts 1965, p. 22.

39. Ibid,. p. 23.

40. Lipps, *Raumästhetik...*, p. 311.

41. '...es liegt in der menschlichen Natur immer weiter, ja über ihr Ziel forzuschreiten; und so war es auch natürlich, das in dem Verhältniss der Säulendicke zur Höhe das Auge immer das Schlankere suchte, und der Geist mehr Hoheit und Freiheit dadurch zu empfinden glaubte'. Quotation J. W. von Goethe, in E. Grumach, *Goethe und die Antike*, I, Berlin 1949, p. 422.

42. Giedion, *Space...*, p. 271.

43. Ibid.

44. Palladio, *The Four...*, I, Chapter XVII.

45. Concerning the meaning of the columnar orders in the 16th-18th centuries, see Forssman, *Dorisch...*, especially pp. 27—32.

46. Vitruvius, *The Ten...*, IV, Chapter 1, 6.

47. Ibid., I, Chapter II, 5.

48. Quotation S. Serlio, in Forssman, *Dorisch...*, p. 51.

49. Vitruvius, *The Ten...*, I, Chapter II, 5.

50. In the Doric order, the column's height was six times its diameter, in the Ionic, the relationship was eight times its diameter. See Vitruvius, *The Ten...*, IV, Chapter 1, 6—7.

51. M.-A. Laugier, *Essai sur l'architecture*, Paris 1753, p. 97.

52. H. Sedlmayr, Das erste mittelalterliche Architektursystem, *Epochen...*, I, pp. 80—139, p. 82.

53. C. Siegel, *Strukturformen der modernen Architektur*, Munich 1965, p. 89.

54. In conjunction with instruction in bridge structures for engineers at The Norwegian Technical College in Trondheim, the need for a certain extra height at the midspan of the bridge in emphasized in order that the bridge may seem 'more secure' (verbal reference).

55. Such was also the understanding of the neo-Gothic theoreticians who contended that the Gothic arch was created by crossing branches bent from two tree trunks. See James Hall's theories, in J. Rykwert, *On*

*Adam's...*, p. 82.

56. Concerning the construction and symbolism of the triumphal arch, see H.P. L'Orange in cooperation with A. von Gerkan, *Der spätantike Bildschmuck des Konstantinsbogens,* Berlin 1939.

57. See L'Orange, *Keiseren...*, p. 54.

58. Concerning column alternation, see H. Pothorn, *Das grosse Buch der Baustile,* Munich 1979, p. 188.

59. The introduction of the massive piers can also have been necessary in order to support the entire construction.

60. Quotation P. Cezanne, in K. B. Sandved (ed.), *Kunstens verden,* Oslo 1959, p. 382.

61. J.W. von Goethe, *Zur Farbenlehre,* Leipzig 1926 (Foreword by G. Ipson), p. 218.

62. In the following, we will talk about the colours alone. Of course, together with dissimilar surface, texture, lighting, etc., the effect will vary.

63. Quotation L. da Vinci, in F. Birren, *Colours & Human Response,* New York 1978, p. 55.

64. E. Raab, *Bildkomplexität, Farbe und ästhetischer Eindruck,* Graz 1976, p. 83.

65. Pointed forms are often linked with light colours and high-pitched sounds, while round forms are likely to be associated with dark colours and low-pitched sounds. See M.D. Vernon, *The Psychology of Perception,* Harmondsworth 1963, p. 84.

66. M.J. Friedländer, *Von Kunst und Kennerschaft,* Zürich 1946, p. 37. Concerning the association effect of colour and its possible meaning in a therapeutic context, see J. Burrell, *Therapeutic Architecture and the 19th Century,* Essex 1972, p. 90.

67. From Aristotle's, The Characters of Theophrastus, in Birren, *Colour & Human...*, p. 80.

68. See G.J. von Allesch, Die ästhetische Erscheinungweise der Farben, *Psychologische Forschung,* VI, Berlin 1925, pp. 1—91 and 215—281.

69. Raab, *Bildkomplexität...*, pp. 83—84.

70. In addition to J.W. Goethe (op. cit.) and W. Kandinsky (see note 79), F. Stefanescu-Guanga, and later in Scandinavia, Gregor Paulsson, have also contributed to the development of the common expression of colour. See F. Stefanescu-Guanga, Experimentelle Untersuchungen zur Gefühlsbetonung der Farben, *Psychologische Studien,* VII, Leipzig 1912, pp. 284—332, especially p. 331, and G. Poulsson, *Konstverkets byggnad,* Stockholm 1942, p. 60.

71. In other words, when one selects yellow or white in order to symbolize sorrow as is the case in certain cultures, it does not mean that the relationship between colour and phenomenon is solely relative and culturally de-

termined, rather that there are other aspects of sorrow which one has wished to emphasize. Pure sorrow is in principle always heavy and black, but the perception of death for example, as a liberated existence, can 'defy' pure sorrow and transform it into joy. This is what Queen Wilhelmina had in mind when she ordered all those joining in her own funeral procession to be clothed in white: 'Long before his death, my husband and I had often talked about the meaning of death and subsequent eternal life. We were both certain that death is the entry into life and therefore promised each other that our funeral should be completely in white', Queen Wilhelmina, *Ensom men ikke alene,* Oslo 1959 (translator unknown).

72. R. Arnheim, *Art...,* p. 322.

73. See Hesselgren, *Arkitekturens...,* p. 201 and p. 224.

74. Bollnow, *Mensch...,* p. 224.

75. See Arnheim, *Art...,* p. 331.

76. In order that the differences be clear, it is necessary that all of the colours compared have the same value and purity. If not, those qualities interfere and create other effects.

77. F. Birren, *Color Psychology and Color Therapy,* New York 1950, p. 109.

78. I. Itten, *Kunst der Farbe. Subjektives Erleben und objektives Erkenner als Wege zur Kunst,* Ravenberg 1961, p. 45.

79. W. Kandinsky, *Über das Geistige in der Kunst,* Bern-Bümplitz 1959.

80. Ibid., p. 87.

81. Ibid., p. 93.

82. Ibid., p. 99.

83. Ibid., p. 94.

84. Ibid., p. 101.

85. Kandinsky's theories concerning the dynamic effects of colour have been verified by a number of researchers through studies of the physical reactions to various colours. We have already mentioned Birren's and Itten's tests concerning blood circulation (notes 77 and 78). Kurt Goldstein's study shows that we even move differently in response to the influence of colour, in that he asserts that colours with long wavelengths (warm colours such as yellow and red) elicit an extroverted reaction, while those with short wavelengths (cold colours such as blue and green) elicit an introverted reaction: The entire organism swings outward toward the world or inward toward oneself depending on the influence of colour. See K. Goldstein, Some Experimental Observations Concerning the Influence of Colours on the Function of the Organism, *Occupational Therapy and Rehabilitation,* 21, Baltimore 1942, pp. 147—151.

86. That a door can also act as a source of light is obvious. An example of a conscious combination of the qualities of the door and the window can

be seen in the so-called Dutch door, which is a double door the bottom half of which can be closed while the upper can be open in order to provide light.

87. Hersey, *High Victorian...*, p. 15.

88. Ruskin, *The Seven...*, p. 26.

89. These two principles can be compared to a dent and a gash in the body of a car. The dent expresses the resistance of the wall against external force, the gash expresses a fatal encroachment.

90. This term 'Bishop's Eye' has been used for a rosette window, see Swaan, *The Gothic...*, p. 94.

91. Le Corbusier, *Towards...*, p. 39.

92. See especially the De Dageraad complex by P. Kramer (1923), in D. Sharp., *Modern Architecture and Expressionism*, New York 1960, p. 131.

93. Psalm 121, 8.

94. Concerning threshold casualties, see W. Schencke, *Hva jorden gjemte*, Kristiania 1911, p. 64. Concerning the cult symbolic meaning of the entrance, see additionally: H. Hudspeth, The Cult of the Door amongst the Miao in South-West China, *Folklore*, 33, London 1922, pp. 406—410, Gennep, *The Rites...*, and B. Goldman, *The Sacred Portal*, Detroit 1966. See also Eliade, *Det hellige...*, p. 104.

95. Psalm by G. Weissel, No. 76, *landstads reviderte salmebok*, Oslo 1956, p. 114.

96. See Th. Thiis-Evensen, Inngangsmotivet, *Byggekunst*, 4, Oslo 1977, pp. 115—118. See also V. Huebner, Fiktiva ingångar, *Magasin Tessin*, I, Lund 1980, pp. 27—34. Also D. Lyndon, Stairs, *GA-Houses*, 8, Tokyo 1981, p.8.

97. W.R. Lethaby, *Architecture, Mysticism and Myth*, London 1974 (facsimile of original edition from 1891), p. 176.

98. Ibid. p. 191. See also an example of more recent use of the same entry motif, in Sedlmayr, Die Schauseite..., *Epochen...*, II, p. 174.

99. Thiis-Evensen, *Steder..*, p. 54. See B. Astrup, *Stortingsbygnaden, Christiania. Dens förhistoria och tilblivelse samt analys av dess arkitektur*, Oslo 1972, p. 129.

# THE ROOF

1. See Baldwin Smith, *The Dome...*, especially the chapter entitled Domical Origins, pp. 3—10. In this chapter, he refers to how dome forms have been compared to objects such as pine cones, the cosmic egg, bee hives, etc.

2. See the portrayal of a house as *imago mundi,* in Eliade, *Det hellige...,* p. 33.

3. Baldwin Smith, *The Dome...,* p. 5.

4. A. Reichlin, Cupola, P. Portoghesi (ed.), *Dizionario..,* II, p. 120.

5. Baldwin Smith, *The Dome...,* p. 8.

6. Quotation Platon in *Timaios,* in P. E. Schramm, *Sphaira, Globus, Reichsapfel,* Stuttgart 1958, p. 8.

7. Sedlmayr, Das erste..., *Epochen...,* I, p. 80.

8. Quotation E.-L. Boullée, in Rosenau, *Boullée...,* p. 93.

9. See R. Wittkower, Zur Peterskuppel Michelangelos, *Zeitschrift für Kunstgeschichte,* II, Munich 1933, pp. 348—380, especially p. 363.

10. L'Orange/Thiis-Evensen, *Oldtidens...,* p. 116.

11. Sedlmayr, Das erste..., *Epochen..,* I, p. 87.

12. MacDonald, *The Architecture...,* p. 115.

13. Quotation Dio Cassius, in ibid., p. 118.

14. Nervi, *Aesthetics and Technology in Building,* Massachusetts 1965, p. 7.

15. This is solely the optical impression of the supportive function. The actual distribution to the ground is led along solid cross-supports which are concealed inside the outer corridor ring around the middle hall.

16. Norberg-Schulz, *Meaning...,* p. 408.

17. Wölfflin, *Renaissance...,* p. 115.

18. By a 'broad' space, it is meant that the breadth of the space is equal to or greater than the length.

19. Thiis-Evensen, Aula Forensis, *AHO-skrift,* Oslo 1971, p. 2.

20. Quotation W. Chambers, in Rykwert, *On Adam's...,* p. 71.

21. Palladio, *The Four...,* Preface.

22. Typically, in Norwegian the pitched surface of the roof is referred to as the 'takfall' ('the fall of the roof').

23. A.J. Downing, *The Architecture of Country Houses,* New York 1969, (facsimile of edition from 1850), p. 385.

24. Quotation Martial, in MacDonald, *The Architecture...,* p. 62.

25. J. Trier, First, *Nachrichten von der Gesellschaft der Wissenschaften zu Göttungen,* Phil.-Hist., IV, NF III. 4, 1940, p. 117.

26. L'Orange, *Tempelet...,* p. 7.

27. R.D. Cramer, Images of Home, *AIA Journal,* September, Washington D.C. 1960, p. 40—49, p. 42.

28. W. Cowburn, Popular Housing, *Arena: Journal of the Architectural Association,* September/October, London 1966, p. 81.

29. From Royal Court letter dated 4, October 1624, in A. Collett, *Gamle Christiania Billeder,* Christiania 1893, p. 72.

30. Scully, *The Shingle...,* p. 118.

31. Vitruvius, *The Ten Books...*, p. 14.

32. T. Parsons, *Societies. Evolutionary and Comparative Perspectives,* New York 1966, p. 86, p. 103.

33. Downing, *The Architecture of...*, p. 33.

34. See D. Fraser, *Village Planning in the Primitive World,* London 1962, p. 15. See also E. Camesasca (ed.), *History of the House,* London 1971, p. 13 (translated by I. Quigly).

35. Le Corbusier, *Oeuvre..., 1938—1940,* p. 97.

36. The vestibule into the Biblioteca Laurenziana by Michelangelo (completed 1560), is an example of how an interior can be articulated with elements that had earlier been restricted to exterior walls which faced streets or courtyards. See quotation of J. Shearman, in Sinding-Larsen, *The Laurenziana...*, p. 215.

# REFERENCES

Ackermann, J.S.: *The Architecture of Michelangelo*, Middlesex 1970

Alberti, L.B.: *Ten Books on Architecture,* (Facsimile of J. Leoni's translation of 1755). London 1965

Alex, W.: *Japanese Architecture,* New York 1963

American School of Classical Studies at Athens: *The Stoa of Attalaos II in Athens*, New Jersey 1959

Amery C. (ed.): *Period Houses and their Details*, New York 1974

Argan, G.C.: *The Renaissance City*, New York 1969

Arnheim, R.: *Art and Visual Perception*, London 1954

Arnheim, R.: Inside and Outside in Architecture, *The Journal of Aesthetics and Art Criticism*, Vol. 25, Fall 1966

Arnheim, R.: *The Dynamics of Architectural Form*, Berkeley 1977

Artaud, C.: *Dream Palaces, Fantastic Houses and their Treasures*, London 1973

Astrup, B.: *Stortingsbygningen i Christiania. Dens förhistoria och tilblivelse samt analys av dess arkitektur*, Oslo 1972

*Av Henrik Sørensens Skissböcker*, Göteborg 1955


Bachelard G.: *La poétique de l'espace*, Paris 1958

Bacon E.N.: *Design of Cities*, London 1967

Baldwin Smith, E.: *The Dome. A Study in the History of Ideas*, New Jersey 1971

Basquin, R.: *Eveux*, Lyon 1971

Battersby, R.: *Art Nouveau*, Middlesex 1972

Benevolo, L.: *L'arte e la cittá antica*, Roma 1974

Benevolo, L.: *Storia della cittá*, Roma 1976

Berg, A.: Trefoldighetskirken, *Trefoldighetskirken 1858–1958. Festeskrift utgitt i anledning kirkens og menighetens 100 års jubileum*, Oslo 1958

Berg K.: Malmanger, M. & Skedsmo, T. (eds.): *Norske mesterverker i Nasjonalgalleriet*, Oslo 1981

Bergsøe, W.: *Rom under Pius IX*, København 1877

Berndt, H, Lorenzer, A. & Horn, K.: *Architektur als Ideologie*, Frankfurt am Main 1969

Berve, H. et al: *Greek Temples, Theatres and Shrines*. (Transl. by R. Waterhouse). London 1963

Bieber, M.: *The History of the Greek and Roman Theatre*, Princeton 1961

Bihalji-Merin, O. (ed.): *Brüchen der Welt*, Luzern 1971

Binswanger, L.: *Über Ideenflucht*, Zürich 1933

Binswanger, L.: Ausgewälte Vorträge und Aufsätze, Vol. II, Bern 1955

Birren, F.: *Color Psychology and Color Therapy*, New York 1950

Birren, F.: *Color & Human Response*, New York 1978

Bjerknes, K.: *Gamle borgerhus i Bergen*, Bergen 1978

Blake, M.E.: *Roman Construction in Italy from Tiberius through the Flavians*, Washington 1959

Blake, P.: *Mies van der Rohe*, New York 1966

Bloomer, K. & Moore, Chr. W.: *Body Memory and Architecture*, London 1977

Boëthius, A.: *The Golden House of Nero, Some Aspects of Roman Architecture*, Michigan 1960

Boëthius, A. & Ward Perkins, J.B.: *Etruscan and Roman Architecture*, London 1970

Bolle-Reddat, R.: *Notre Dame du Haut, Ronchamp*, Lyon 1969

Bollnow, O.F.: *Mensch und Raum*, Stuttgart 1963

Bollnow, O.F.: *Das Wesen der Stimmungen*, Frankfurt am Main 1968

Boyd, A.: *Chinese Architecture and Town Planning*, London 1962

Branner, R.: *Gothic Architecture*, New York 1961

Breasted, J.H.: *Geschichte Ægyptens*, Innsbruck 1936

Brochmann, J.: Fasade. In Dahl, H.F. et al (eds.) *Pax Leksikon*, Vol. II. Oslo 1979

Brochmann, O.: *Bygget i Norge, Vol. I, Oslo 1979*

Brown, C. (ed.): *Dictionary of New Testament Theology*, Vol. I, Exeter 1975

Buck, C.D.: *A Dictionary of Selected Synonyms in the Principal Indo-European Languages. A Contribution to the History of Ideas*, Chicago 1971

Bugge, G. & Norberg-Schulz, Chr.: *Stav og laft*, Oslo 1969

Bull, E.: Grünerløkka. Beste østkant, *St. Hallvard*, Oslo 1961

Burrell, J.: *Therapeutic Architecture and the 19th Century*, Essex 1972

Caboga, H.: *Die mittelalterliche Burg*, Rapperswil 1951

Camesasca, E. (ed.): *History of the House*. (Trans. by I. Quigly). London 1971

Casari, M. & Pavan, V., (eds.): *New Chicago Architecture*, Chicago 1981

Ceves, R, (ed.): *Palladio. Catalogo della Mostra*, Italy 1973

Charbonneaux, J, et. al.: *Das klassisches Griechenland*, Berlin 1966

Charbonneaux, J., et. al.: *Das archaische Griechenland*, Berlin 1969

Christ, Y. & Schein, J.: *L'Oeuvre et les rêves de Ledoux*, Chêne 1971

Collett, A.: *Gamle Christiania Billeder*, Christiania 1893

Collins, P.: *Changing Ideals in Modern Architecture 1750–1950*, London 1971

Corfiato, H.O.: *Piranesi Compositions*, London 1951

Cornell, E.: *Om rummet och arkitekturens väsen*, Göteborg 1966

Cornell, E.: *Bygnadstekniken. Metode och idéer genom tiderna*, Stockholm 1970

Coulton, J.J.: *Greek Architects at Work*, London 1977

Cowburn, W.: Popular Housing. *Arena: Journal of the Architectural Association*, London September/October 1960

Cramer, R.D.: Images of Home, *AIA Journal*, Washington September 1960

Cullen G.: *Townscape*, London 1971

Curtius, I.: *Die Wandmalerei Pompeijs*, Leipzig 1929


Dal Maso, L.B.: *Rome of the Caesars*, Roma 1977

Danbolt, G.: Das Taufbecken im Kloster San Nilo in Grottaferrata. Studie zu der Beziehung von Liturgie zu Kunst. *Institutum Romanum Norwegiae, Acta*, Vol. VIII, Roma 1978

Delevoy, R.L.: *Journal du Symbolisme*, Genève 1977

Demus, O.: *Byzantine Mosaic Decoration: Aspects of Monumental Art in Byzantium*, London 1953

de Vries, L.: *Victorian Invention*, London 1973

de Tolnay, Ch.: *Michelangelo, III, The Medici Chapel*, Princeton 1948

de Tolnay, Ch.: *Michelangelo. Sculptor, Painter, Architect*. (Tranl. by G. Woodhouse). Princeton 1975

*Die Erzählungen aus den Tausend und ein Nächten*, Vol. III (Transl. by E. Littmann). Leipzig 1924

*Dominikus Böhn*, München 1962

*Domus* 610, 1980

D'Onofrio, C.: *Le Fontane di Roma*, Roma 1957

Doré, G.: *Bibelen i Billeder*, København 1878

Downing, A.J.: *The Architecture of Country Houses*, (Facsimile of first edition (1850).) New York 1969

Doxiadis, K.A.: *Raumordnung im griechischen Städtebau*, Heidelberg 1937

Drerup, H.: Bildraum und Realraum in der römischen Architektur, *Mitteilungen des deutschen Archaeologischen Instituts*, Vol. 66, Heidelberg 1959

Drerup, H.: Architektur als Symbol, *Gymnasiumm* Vol. 73, Heidelberg 1966

Drexler, A. (ed.): *The Architecture of the École des Beaux-Arts*, London 1977

Drange, T, Aanensen, H.O. & Brænne, J.: *Gamle trehus. Reparasjon og vedlikehold*, Oslo 1980

Dronning Wilhelmina: *Ensom men ikke alene*. (Translator, Unknown). Oslo 1959

Dyggve, E.: Funktionalismen i amfiteatret, *Studier i Sprog. og Oldtidsforsk-*

*ning*, Vol. 213, København 1950

Eaton, L.K.: *American Architecture Comes of Age*, Massachusetts 1972
Eliade, M.: *Det hellige og det profane*, (Tranl. by Trond Berg Eriksen) Oslo 1969
Ellis, W.D.: *A Source Book of Gestalt Psychology*, London 1950
*Die Erzählungen aus den Tausend und ein Nächten*, Vol. III, /Tranl. by E. Littleman). Leipzig 1924
Evans, B. (ed.): *Dictionary of Quotations*, New York 1968

Fast, J.: *Kroppsspråket*, (Tranl. by H. Simonsen). Oslo 1973
Favole, P.: *Piazze d'Italia*, Milano 1972
Finelli, L.: Finestra. In Portoghesi, P. (ed.), *Dizionario Enciclopedico di Architettura e Urbanistica*, Vol. II, Roma 1969
Fletcher, B.: *A History of Architecture*, London 1956
Forssman, E.: *Dorisch, jonisch, korintisch*, Stockholm 1961
Forssman, E.: *Karl F. Schinkel. Bauwerke und Baugedanken*, München 1981
Frankl, P.: *Gothic Architecture*. (Transl. by D. Pevsner). London 1962
Frankl, P.: *Principles of Architectural History. The Four Phases of Architectural Style, 1420–1900*. (Transl. by J.F.O'Gorman) London 1968
Fraser, D.: *Village Planning in the Primitive World*, London 1962
Frey, D.: *Grundlegung zu einer vergleichenden Kunstwissenschaft*, Innsbruck 1949
Friedländer, M.F.: *Von Kunst und Kennerschaft*, Zürich 1946
Fry, N.: *Treasures of World Art*, London 1975
Furneaux Jordan, R.: *A Concise History of Western Architecture*, London 1969
Futagawa, Y. (ed.): MLTW/Moore, Lyndon, Turnbull, Whitaker, *GA*, Vol. 3, Tokyo 1976

Gangneux, M.-Ch. et al: Moore is More, *L'architecture d'aujourd hui*, 184, Paris 1976
Gehl, J.: *Livet mellem husene*, København 1971
Gibson, E.J. & Walk, R.D.: The Visual Cliff, *Scientific American*, 202, New York 1960
Giedion, S.: *Mechanization takes Command*, New York 1948
Giedion, S.: *Space, Time and Architecture*, Cambridge 1967
Giedion, S.: *Architektur und das Phänomen des Wandels. Die drei Raumkonzeptionen in der Architektur*, Tübingen 1969
Giurgola, R. & Metha J.: *Louis I. Kahn*, Zürich 1975
Gjesdal Christiensen, A.L.: Småhusmiljøet og trivsel. In Thiis-Evensen, Th. (ed.) *Byfornyelse i Miljøvernperspektiv*, Oslo 1975

Goldman, B.: *The Sacred Portal*, Detroit 1966

Goldstein, K.: Some Experimental Observations concerning the Influence of Colors on the Function of the Organism, *Occupational Therapy and Rehabilitation*, Vol. 21, Baltimore 1942

Goldwater, R. & Treves, M. (eds.): *Artists on Art*, London 1976

Gombrich, E.H.: *Meditation on a Hobby Horse, and other Essays on the Theory of Art*, London 1978

Gottlieb, C.: *The Window in Art. From the Window of God to the Vanity of Man*, New York 1981

Graves, M.: Sunar Showroom, *Architectural Design*, Vol. 5/6, London 1980

Grumach, E.: *Goethe und die Antike*, Vol. I, Berlin 1949

Gutheim, F.: *Alvar Aalto*, New York 1960


Hager, W.: *Barock Architektur*, Baden-Baden 1969

Hall, E.T.: *The Hidden Dimension. Man's Use of Space in Public and Private*, London 1966

Hals, H.: *Fra Christiania til Stor-Oslo. Et forslag til generalplan for Oslo*, Oslo 1929

Hansmann, W.: *Baukunst des Barock*, Köln 1978

Hauglid, R.: *Norske Stavkirker. Dekor og utstyr*, Oslo 1973

Hauglid, R.: *Norske stavkirker. Bygningshistorisk bakgrunn og utvikling*, Oslo 1976

Hauser, A.: *The Social History of Art*, Vol 1–4, London 1962–1968

Heidegger, M.: *Vorträge und Aufsätze*, Vol. II, Pfullingen 1967

Hersey, G.L.: *High Victorian Gothic. A Study in Associationism*, London 1972

Hesselgren, S.: *Arkitekturens utrycksmedel*, Stockholm 1954

Hilberseimer, L.: *Mies van der Rohe*, Chicago 1956

Hitchcock, H.R. (ed.): *World Architecture*, London 1963

Hitzer, H.: *Die Strasse*, München 1971

Hudspeth, H.: The Cult of the Door amongst the Miao in South-West China, *Folklore*, Vol. 33, London 1922

Huebner, V.: Fiktiva ingångar, *Magasin Tessin*, Vol. I, Lund 1980

Huyghe, R. (ed.): Art and Mankind. *Larousse Encyclopedia of Renaissance and Baroque Art*, (Translated by E. Evershed et al.). Middlesex 1967


Itten, I.: *Kunst der Farbe. Subjektives Erleben und objektives Erkennen als Wege zur Kunst*, Ravensburg 1961

Iwamiya, T. & Itoh, T.: *Imperial Gardens of Japan*, New York 1970


Jager, B: Horizontality and Verticality. A Phenomenological Exploration into Lived Space; *Duquesne Studies in Phenomenological Psychology.* Vol. I, Pittsburgh 1971

Jan & Jon, *Byggekunst*, Vol. 4, Oslo 1973

Jan & Jon, Wenches hus. *Byggekunst*, Vol. 6, Oslo 1973

Janson, H.W. & Janson D.J.: *Maleriets historie*, (Tranl. by P. Anker). Oslo 1958

Jencks, Ch.: *Le Corbusier and the Tragic View of Architecture*, London 1973

Jencks, Ch.: *The Language of Post-Modern Architecture*, London 1977

Jencks, Ch. (ed.): Post-Modern-Classism, *AD*, Vol. 5/6, London 1980

Jencks, Ch.: Toward a Radical Eclecticism, *The Presence of the Past. First International Exhibition of Architecture*, Venezia 1980

Joedicke, J.: *Geschichte der modernen Architektur*, Teufen (n.d.)

Johnson, Ph.C.: *Mies van der Rohe*, New York 1947

Johnston, N.: *The Human Cage*, New York 1973

Josephson, R.: *Barocken*, Stockholm 1948


Kähler, H.: *Hadrian und seine Villa bei Tivoli*, Berlin 1964

Kähler, H.: *Der griechische Tempel. Wesen und Gestalt*, Berlin 1964

Kähler, H.: *Rom und sein Imperium*, Baden-Baden 1964

Kähler, H.: *Die Hagia Sophia*, Berlin 1967

Kähler, H.: *Der römische Tempel*, Berlin 1970

Kähler, H.: *Die frühe Kirche. Kult und Kultraum*, Berlin 1972

Kafka, F.: *Der Bau. Die Erzählungen*, Frankfurt am Main 1961

Kandinsky, W.: *Uber das Geistige in der Kunst*, Bern-Bümpliz 1959

Kandinsky, W.: *Om det andliga i konsten*. (Transl. by U. Linde / S. Martinson). Stockholm 1969

Kandinsky, W.: *Punkt und Linie zu Fläche*. (Facsimile of first edition (1926).) Bern-Bümpliz 1973

Katz, D.: Der Aufbau der Tastwelt, *Zeitschrift für Psychologie und Physiologie des Sinnesorganen*, Vol. XI, Leipzig 1925

Kaufmann, E.: *Von Ledoux bis Le Corbusier*, Wien 1933

Kaufmann, E. & Raeburn, B (eds.): *Frank Lloyd Wright. Writings and Buildings*, New York 1970

Keswick, M.: *The Chinese Gardens*, New York 1978

Klages, L.: *Die Sprache als Quell der Seelenkunde*, Stuttgart 1959

Klopfer, P.: *Von Palladio bis Schinkel*, Eszlingen 1911

Klotz, H.: *Die Früwerke Brunelleschis und die mittelalterliche Tradition*, Berlin 1970

Koepf, H.: *Baukunst in fünf Jahrtausenden*, Stuttgart 1963

Kouwenhoven, J.A.: *The Columbia Historical Portrait of New York*, New York 1972

424

Krautheimer, R.: *Early Christian and Byzantine Architecture*, Harmonsworth 1965

Kruse, L.: *Räumliche Umwelt*, Berlin 1974

Lang, J., Burnette, Chr., Moleski W. & Vachon, D.: *Designing for Human Behaviour*, Strasbourg 1974

Laugier, M.-A.: *Essai sur l'architecture*, Paris 1753

Lautenbach, H. & Joedicke, J.: *H. Häring, Schriften, Entwürfe, Bauten*, Stuttgart 1965

Le Corbusier: *Le Modulor 1948*, Paris 1950

Le Corbusier: *Le Modulor II*, Paris 1955

Le Corbusier: *Vår bostad*. (Transl. by L. Holm). Stockholm 1962

Le Corbusier: *Oeuvre complète 1910–65*, Zürich 1964

Le Corbusier: *Towards a New Architecture*. (Transl. by F. Etchells). London 1970

Lee, V. Empathy. In Weitz, M, (ed.), *Problems in Aesthetics*, New York 1967

Leichtentritt, H.: *Music History and Ideas*, Cambridge 1958

Lethaby, W.R.: *Architecture, Mysticism and Myth*. (Facsimile of first edition (1891).) London 1974

Linn, B.: *Storgårdskvarteret. Ett bebyggelsesmønsters bakgrunn och karakter*, Stockholm 1974

Linschoten, J.: Die Strasse und die unendliche Ferne, *Situation*, Vol. I, Utrecht 1954

Lipps, Th.: Raumästhetik und geometrisch-optische Täuschungen, *Schriften der Gesellschaft für psychologische Forschung*, Vol. II, Leipzig 1897

Lipps, Th.: Aesthetische Einfühlung, *Zeitschrift für Psychologie und Physiologie des Sinnesorgane*, Vol. XXII, Leipzig 1900

Lloyd, S.: *Architettura mediterranea preromana*, Roma 1972

Lobell, J.: *Between Silence and Light. Spirit in the Architecture of Louis I. Kahn*, Boulder 1979

L'Orange, H.P. with von Gerkan, A.: *Der Spätantike Bildschmuck des Konstantinsbogens*, Berlin 1939

L'Orange, H.P.: *Keiseren på himmeltronen*, Oslo 1949

L'Orange, H.P.: *Rom efter forvandlingen*, Oslo 1949

L'Orange, H.P.: *Fra principat til dominat*, Oslo 1958

L'Orange, H.P. & Nordhagen, P.J.: *Mosaikk fra antikk til middelalder*, Oslo 1958

L'Orange, H.P.: *Mot middelalder*, Oslo 1963

L'Orange, H.P.: *Sentrum og periferi*, Oslo 1973

L'Orange, H.P., Lux aeterna: l'adorazione della luce nell arte tardo – antica ed alto – mediovale, *Rendiconti*, Vol. XLVII, Roma 1974–75

L'Orange, H.P. with Thiis-Evensen, Th.: *Oldtidens bygningsverden*, Oslo 1978

L'Orange, H.P.: Tempelet som kosmos. Summum templum architecturae; *Ord og bilde. En essaysamling. Festeskrift til Erik Egelands 60-årsdag 21. juli 1981*, Oslo 1981

Lowry, B.: *Renaissance Architecture*, New York 1962

Lund, K.: Svar til Thomas Thiis-Evensen; *Arkitektnytt*, Vol. 3, Oslo 1969

Lund, N.-O.: *Teoridannelser i arkitekturen. Arkitektur og idéer fra 40'rne til idag*, København 1970

Lyndon, D.: Stairs, *GA Houses*, Vol. 8, Tokyo 1981


Macaulay, D.: *Katedralen bygges*. (Transl. by J. Knap). Oslo 1977

MacDonald, W.: *Early Christian and Byzantine Architecture*, New York 1962

MacDonald, W.L.: *The Architecture of the Roman Empire*, New Haven 1965

Mack, E.: *Expedition*, Hamburg 1977

Malmanger, M.: Form as Iconology. The Spire of Sant'Ivo alla Sapienza; *Institutum Romanum Norvegiae Acta*, Vol. VIII, Roma 1978

Maslow, A.H. & Mintz, N.L.: Effects of Aesthetic Surroundings, *Journal of Psychology*, Vol. 41, Provincetown 1956

Meeks, L.V.: *The Railroad Station. An Architectural History*, New Haven 1964

Meischke, I.R.: *Het nedelandse woonhuis*, Haarlem 1969

Merleau-Ponty, M.: *Phénoménologie de la perception*, Paris 1945

Merleau-Ponty, M.: *Phänomenologie der Wahrnehmung*. (Transl. by R. Boehn). Berlin 1966

Milton, J.: Samsons Agonistes. *The Poems of John Milton*, London 1961

Moore, Ch.: Piazza d'Italia, *Architectural Design*, Vol. 5/6, London 1980

Moore, Ch., Allen, G. Lyndon, D.: *The Place of Houses*, New York 1974

Morris, D.: *Vår forunderlige adferd*. (Transl. by A.S. Seeberg). Oslo 1980

Morrison, H. *Louis Sullivan. Prophet of Modern Architecture*, New York 1963

Müller, W.: *Die heilige Stadt*, Stuttgart 1961

Mütsch-Engel, A.: *Wohnen unter schrägem Dach*, Stuttgart 1975

Muschenheim, W.: *Elements of the Art of Architecture*, London 1965


Naylor, G. et. al.: Hector Guimard. *Architectural Monographs*, Vol. 2, London 1978

Nervi, P.L.: *Aesthetics and Technology in Building*, Massachusetts 1965

Neufert, E.: *Bauentwurfslehre*, Berlin 1936

Neumann, R.: Gebäude für den Post-Telegraphen und Fernsprechdienst,

*Hantbuch der Architektur*, Vol. IV, 2 halvbind, 3 hefte, Darmstadt 1896

Noble, Ch.: *Philip Johnson*, London 1972

Norberg-Schulz, Chr.: *Intensjoner i arkitekturen*, Oslo 1967

Norberg-Schulz, Chr.: *Kilian Ignaz Dientzenhofer e il barocco boemo*, Roma 1968

Norberg-Schulz, Chr.: *Barock Architecture*, New York 1971

Norberg-Schulz, Chr.: *Existence, Space & Architecture*, New York 1971

Norberg-Schulz, Chr.: *Alla ricerca dell'architettura perduta*, Roma 1975

Norberg-Schulz, Chr.: *Meaning in Western Architecture*, New York 1975

Norberg-Schulz, Chr.: Sted og identitet. Thiis-Evensen, Th. (ed.), *Byfornyelse i miljøvernperspektiv*, Oslo 1975

Norberg-Schulz, Chr.: *Genius Loci*, London 1980

Norberg-Schulz, Chr. with Digerud, J.G.: *Louis I. Kahn. Idea e immagine*, Roma 1980

Nordin, E.: Träbyggande under 1800-talet, *Den nordiska trästaden*, Vol. 16, Stockholm 1972

Norwick, J.J. (ed.): *Verdensarkitekturen*, (Transl. by B. H. Jacobsen). København 1977


Oliver, P. (ed.): *Shelter, Sign and Symbol*, London 1975


Paavilainen, S.: Classicism of the 1920's and the Classical Tradition in Finland; *Abacus*, Museum of Finnish Architecture, Helsinki 1979

Palladio, A.: *The Four Books of Architecture*. (Facsimile of the edition of 1738, transl. by Isaac Ware). New York 1965

Papathanassopoulos, G.: *The Acropolis*. Athen 1977

Parsons, T.: *Societies. Evolutionary and Comparative Perspectives*, New Jersey 1966

Paulsson, G.: *Konstverkets byggnad*, Stockholm 1942

Pehnt, W.: *Expressionist Architecture*, London 1979

Petit, J.: *Un Couvent de Le Corbusier*, Paris 1961

Pevsner, N.: *An Outline of European Architecture*, Harmonsworth 1966

Pevsner, N.: *A History of Building Types*, London 1976

Pevsner, N. & Honour, J.F.H., (eds.): *Lexikon der Weltarchitektur*, Darmstadt 1971

Pfankuch, P.: *Hans Scharoun*, Berlin 1974

*Philharmonie Berlin*, Berlin 1963

Phleps, H.: *Der Blockbau*, Berlin 1926

Phleps, H.: *Vom Wesen der Architektur*, Karlsruhe 1950

Placzek, A. K., Ackermann, J.S. & Rosenfeld, M.N.: *Sebastian Serlio. On Domestic Architecture*, New York 1978

Plessner, H.: *Zwischen Philosophie und Gesellschaft*, Bern 1953

Portoghesi, P.: *Roma Barocca, Storia di una civiltà architettoria*, Roma 1967
Portoghesi, P. (ed.): *Dizionario Enciclopedico di Architettura e Urbanistica*, Vol. I, II og IV, Roma 1969
Portoghesi, P. & Zevi, B. (eds.): *Michelangelo Architetto*, Torino 1964
Post, K. & Dekkes, G.: *Oude Boerderijen*, Deventer 1976
Pothorn, H.: *Das grosse Buch der Baustile*, München 1979
Propertius, *Elegiae, IV* (Draft translation by J.W. Dietrichson).
Pugin, A.W.: *The True Principles of Pointed or Christian Architecture*. (Facsimile of first edition of 1861). London 1973

Raab, E.: *Bildkomplexität, Farbe und ästhetischer Eindruck*, Graz 1976
Rapoport, A.: *House, Form and Culture*, London 1969
Rappe, A.: *Domus Ecclesiae*, Stockholm 1963
Rasmussen, S.E.: *Om at opleve arkitektur*, København 1975
Rasmussen. S.E., Böggild, M. & Kock, M.: *Studiebog fra Holland*, København 1972
Rausch, A.: *Die Apokryphen und Pseudepigraphen des Alten Testaments*, Tübringen 1900
Reichlin, A.: Cupola. In Portoghesi, P., (ed.): *Dizionario Enciclopedico di Architettura e Urbanistica*, Vol. I, Roma 1968
Reinle, A.: *Zeichensprache der Architektur*, Zürich 1976
Révész-Alexander, M.: *Der Turm als Symbol und Erlebnis*, 1953
Richter, G.M.A.: *A Handbook of Greek Art*, London 1969
Robertson, D.: *Pre-Columbian Architecture*, New York 1963
Robertson, D.S.: *Greek and Roman Architecture*, Cambridge 1971
Rombold, G.: Asthetische und antropologische Raumqualitäten, *Kunst und Kirche*, Vol. I, Linz 1976
Rosenau, H.: *Boullée & Visionary Architecture*, London 1974
Rudofsky, B.: *Architecture without Architects*, New York 1964

# DIAGRAMS

The following diagrams show in essence the archetypes commented on in the book and are, in the same way, divided into themes and motives within the three determinations of space — the floor, the wall and the roof.

# THE FLOOR

Nature's floor: a) the surface  and b) the mass:

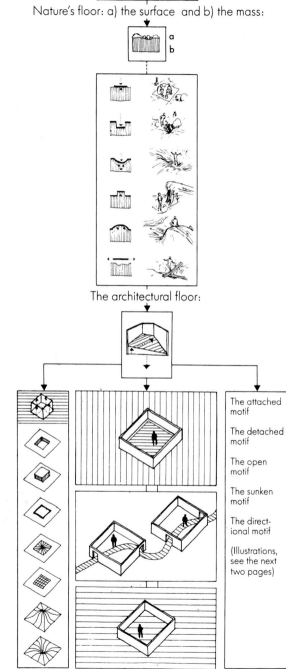

The architectural floor:

The delimit-
ing theme

The directional theme

The supporting
theme

The attached
motif

The detached
motif

The open
motif

The sunken
motif

The direct-
ional motif

(Illustrations,
see the next
two pages)

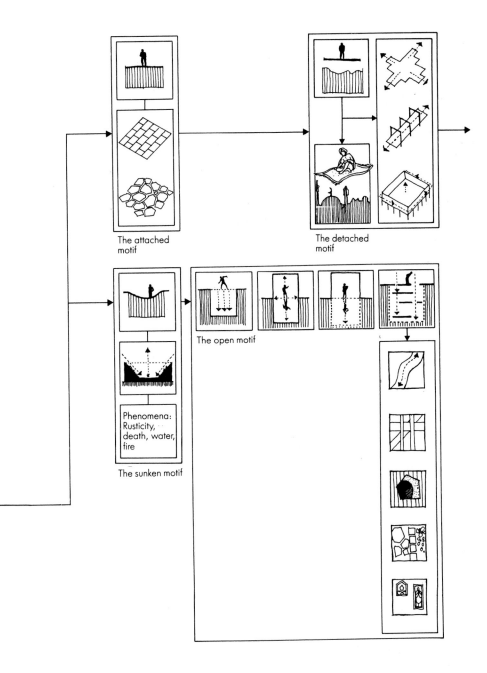

The attached
motif

The detached
motif

Phenomena:
Rusticity,
death, water,
fire

The open motif

The sunken motif

431

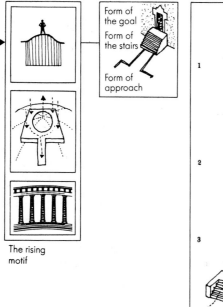

The rising
motif

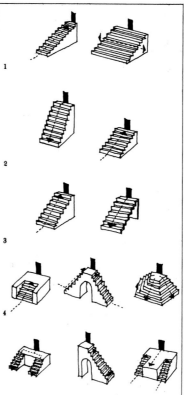

The directional motif: stairs
1) breadth: a) narrow, b) wide,
2) slope: a) steep, b) gentle,
3) attachment: a) attached, b) free,
4) form: a) plateau stair, b) frontal stair,
    c) fan stair, d) divided stair, e) side stair,
    f) overlapping stair

432

# THE WALL

Nature's and culture's wall:

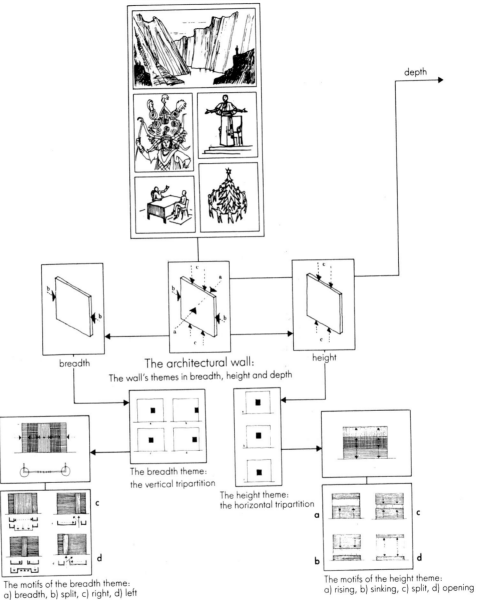

breadth

The architectural wall:
The wall's themes in breadth, height and depth

height

depth

The breadth theme:
the vertical tripartition

The height theme:
the horizontal tripartition

The motifs of the breadth theme:
a) breadth, b) split, c) right, d) left

The motifs of the height theme:
a) rising, b) sinking, c) split, d) opening

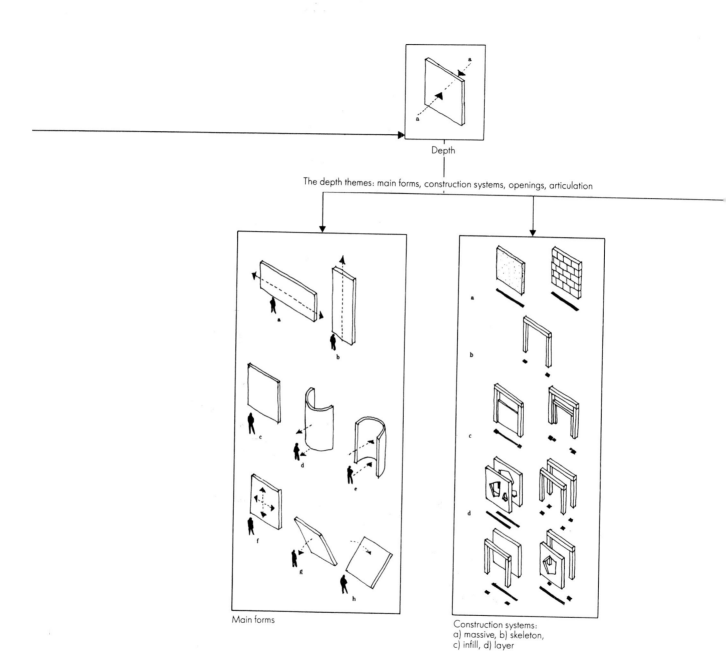

Depth

The depth themes: main forms, construction systems, openings, articulation

Main forms

Construction systems:
a) massive, b) skeleton,
c) infill, d) layer

434

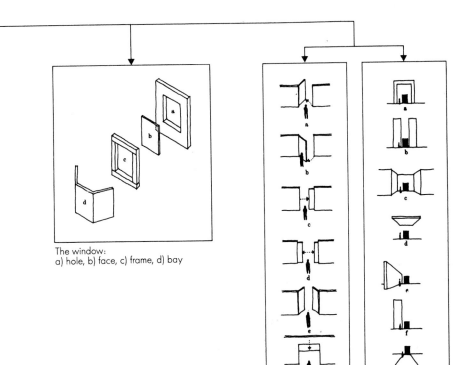

The window:
a) hole, b) face, c) frame, d) bay

The entrance: The door. The door-casing : (right).
a) frame, b) split, c) riche, d) shelter,
e) directional wall, f) side tower, g) path,
h) stair

435

The massive system:

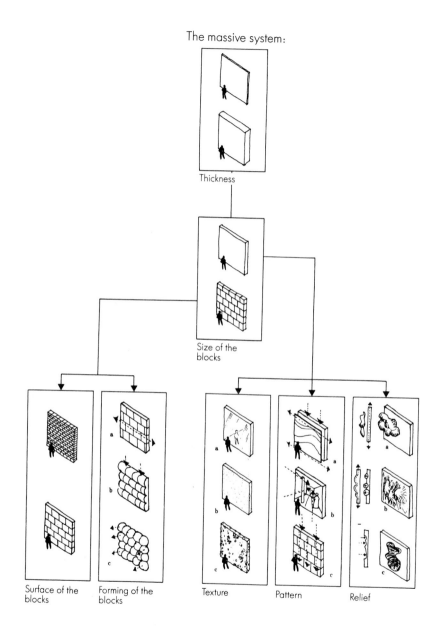

Thickness

Size of the
blocks

Surface of the
blocks

Forming of the
blocks

Texture

Pattern

Relief

The skeleton system:

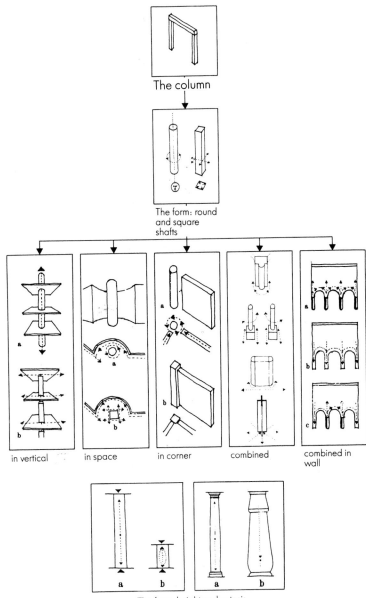

The column

The form: round
and square
shafts

in vertical      in space       in corner       combined        combined in
wall

The form: height and entasis

437

The orders

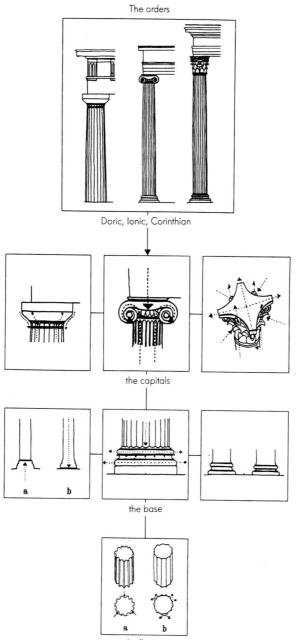

Doric, Ionic, Corinthian

the capitals

the base

the fluting

The frame:

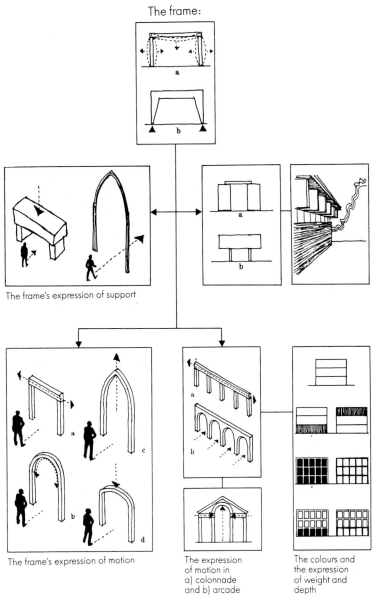

The frame's expression of support

The frame's expression of motion

The expression
of motion in
a) colonnade
and b) arcade

The colours and
the expression
of weight and
depth

439

The beam:

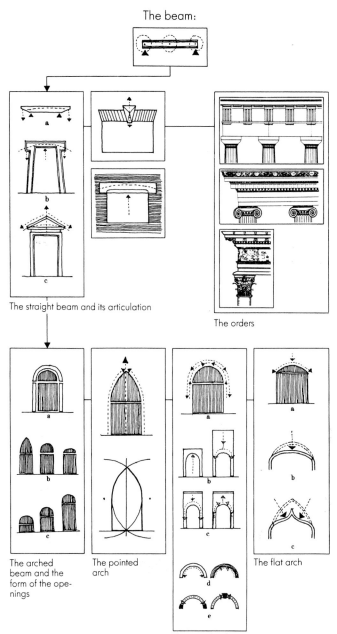

The straight beam and its articulation

The orders

The arched beam and the form of the openings

The pointed arch

The round arch

The flat arch

440

The window:

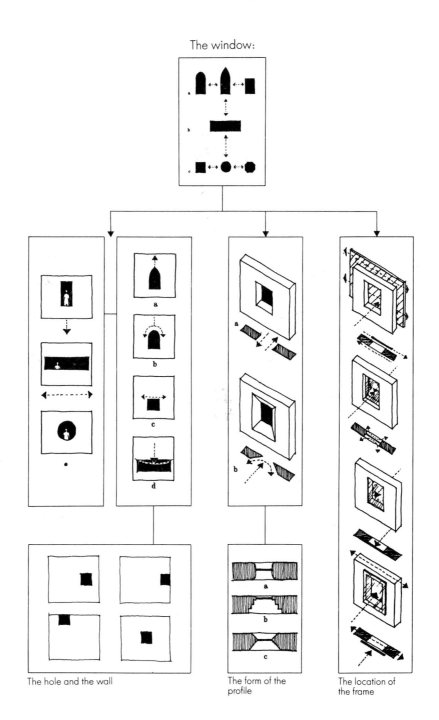

The hole and the wall

The form of the profile

The location of the frame

441

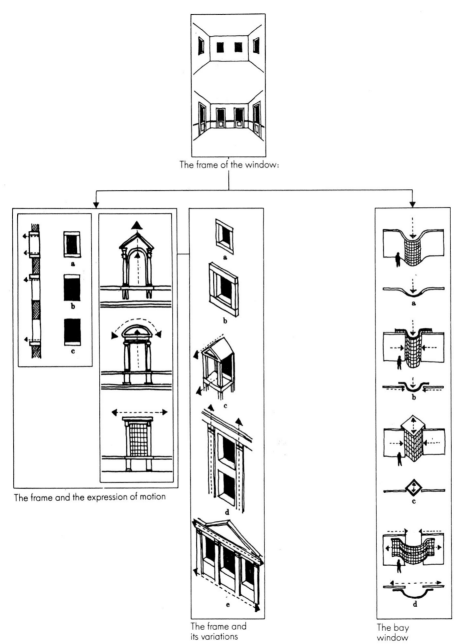

The frame of the window:

The frame and the expression of motion

The frame and
its variations

The bay
window

442

# THE ROOF

Nature's roof:

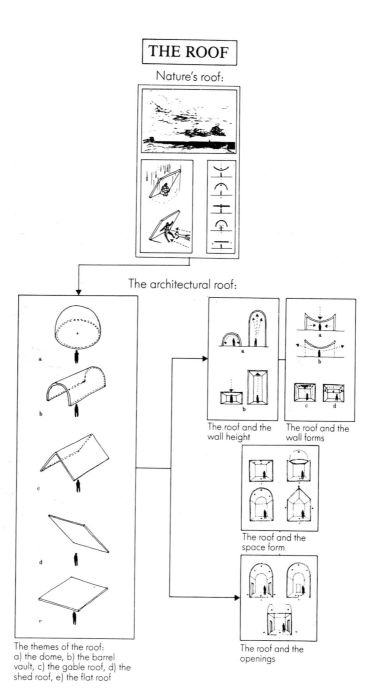

The architectural roof:

The themes of the roof:
a) the dome, b) the barrel vault, c) the gable roof, d) the shed roof, e) the flat roof

The roof and the wall height

The roof and the wall forms

The roof and the space form

The roof and the openings

The dome:

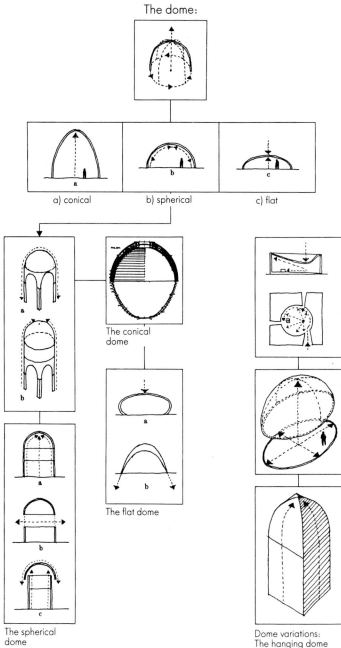

a) conical  b) spherical  c) flat

The conical
dome

The flat dome

The spherical
dome

Dome variations:
The hanging dome
The directionalized dome
The broken dome

The barrel vault:

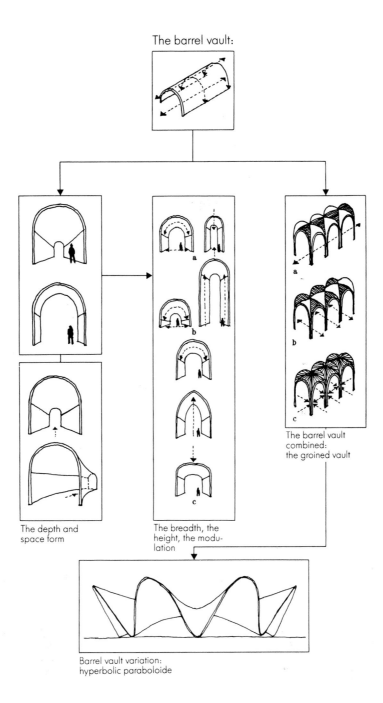

The depth and
space form

The breadth, the
height, the modu-
lation

The barrel vault
combined:
the groined vault

Barrel vault variation:
hyperbolic paraboloide

445

The gable roof:

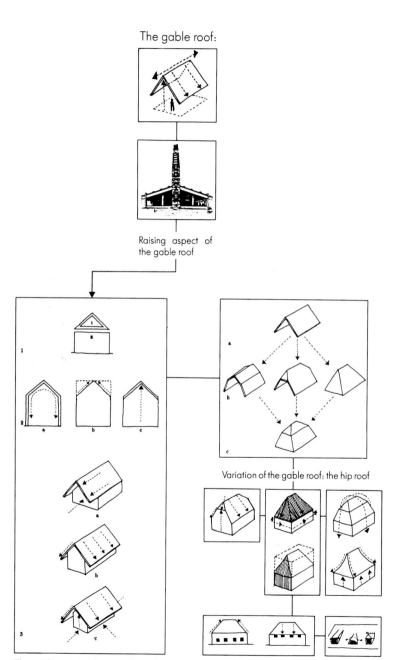

Raising aspect of
the gable roof

Variation of the gable roof: the hip roof

The gable and the relation to the walls
underneath

The articulation of the hip roof

446

The shed roof:

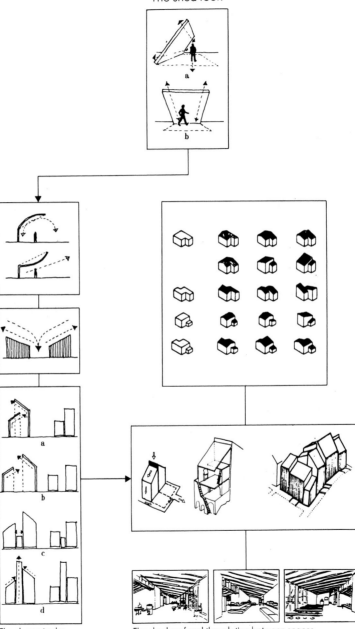

The dynamics be-
tween shed roofs

The shed roof and the relation between spaces

447

The flat roof:

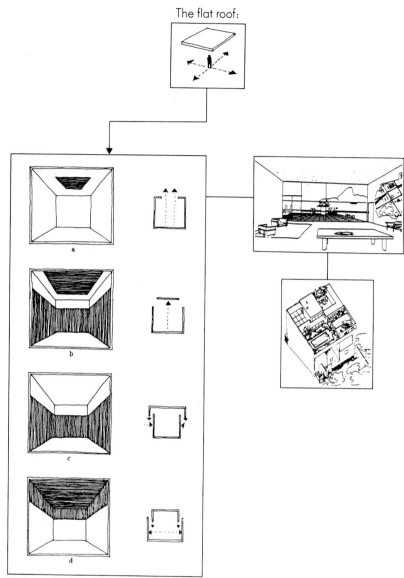

The flat roof and the articulated transition between ceiling and wall: a) opening articulation, b) uplifting articulation, c) expanding articulation, d) sinking articulation

# INDEX OF NAMES

# DETAILED TABLE OF CONTENTS